ZEW Economic Studies

D1342271

Publication Series of the Centre for
European Economic Research (ZEW),
Mannheim, Germany

ZEW Economic Studies

Vol. 1: O. Hohmeyer, K. Rennings (Eds.)
Man-Made Climate Change
Economic Aspects and Policy Options
1999. VIII, 401 pp. ISBN 3-7908-1146-7

Vol. 2: Th. Büttner
Agglomeration, Growth, and Adjustment
A Theoretical and Empirical Study
of Regional Labor Markets in Germany
1999. XI, 206 pp. ISBN 3-7908-1160-2

Vol. 3: P. Capros et al.
Climate Technology Strategies 1
Controlling Greenhouse Gases.
Policy and Technology Options
1999. XVIII, 365 pp. ISBN 3-7908-1229-3

Vol. 4: P. Capros et al.
Climate Technology Strategies 2
The Macro-Economic Cost and Benefit
of Reducing Greenhouse Gas Emissions
in the European Union
1999. XIII, 224 pp. ISBN 3-7908-1230-7

Vol. 5: P. A. Puhani
Evaluating Active Labour Market Policies
Empirical Evidence for Poland During Transition
1999. XVI, 239 pp. ISBN 3-7908-1234-X

Vol. 6: B. Fitzenberger
Wages and Employment Across Skill Groups
An Analysis for West Germany
1999. XII, 251 pp. ISBN 3-7908-1235-8

Vol. 7: K. Rennings et al. (Eds.)
Social Costs and Sustainable Mobility
Strategies and Experiences in Europe
and the United States
1999. VI, 212 pp. ISBN 3-7908-1260-9

Vol. 8: H. Legler et al.
Germany's Technological Performance
2000. X, 191 pp. ISBN 3-7908-1281-1

Vol. 9: O. Bürgel
The Internationalization of British Start-up Companies in High-Technology Industries
2000. XIV, 230 pp. ISBN 3-7908-1292-7

J. Hemmelskamp · K. Rennings · F. Leone (Eds.)

Innovation-Oriented Environmental Regulation

Theoretical Approaches and Empirical Analysis

With 37 Figures
and 28 Tables

Physica-Verlag
A Springer-Verlag Company

ZEW

Zentrum für Europäische
Wirtschaftsforschung GmbH

Centre for European
Economic Research

Series Editor
Prof. Dr. Wolfgang Franz

Editors
Dr. Jens Hemmelskamp
Dr. Fabio Leone
European Commission
Joint Research Centre
Institute for Prospective Technological Studies
W.T.C. Isla de la Cartuja
41092 Sevilla
Spain

Dr. Klaus Rennings
Centre for European Economic Research (ZEW)
L7, 1
68161 Mannheim
Germany

ISBN 3-7908-1313-3 Physica-Verlag Heidelberg New York

Cataloging-in-Publication Data applied for
Die Deutsche Bibliothek – CIP-Einheitsaufnahme
Innovation-oriented Environmental Regulation/Jens Hemmelskamp, Fabio Leone, Klaus Rennings (Eds.).
ZEW, Zentrum für Europäische Wirtschaftsforschung GmbH. – Heidelberg; New York: Physica-Verl., 2000
(ZEW economic studies; Vol. 10)
ISBN 3-7908-1313-3

Physica-Verlag .
a member of BertelsmannSpringer Science+Business Media GmbH

© Physica-Verlag Heidelberg 2000
Printed in Germany

Cover design: Erich Dichiser, ZEW, Mannheim

SPIN 10771491   88/2202-5 4 3 2 1 0 – Printed on acid-free paper

Contents

Part III: Econometric and Modelling Studies on the Impact of Regulation on Environmental Innovation

Introduction

Klaus Rennings

Centre for European Economic Research (ZEW)
P.O. Box 103443, D-68034 Mannheim
Germany

Jens Hemmelskamp and Fabio Leone

Institute for Prospective Technological Studies (IPTS)
W.T.C. Isla de la Cartuja, E-41092 Sevilla
Spain

It is often argued that environmental protection imposes additional costs on firms and thus has negative effects on growth and welfare. Therefore, it is not surprising that an innovation oriented environmental policy is extremely attractive for policy makers, since it is expected that innovations can cut costs of environmental measures and overcome existing trade-offs between economic and ecological goals. Consequently, one main policy strategy is to explore new ways and means to efficiently support the development, the market introduction and the diffusion of clean and sustainable technologies by designing and adopting environmental policies. For example, as the president of the European Commission Romano Prodi stated in his speech to the European Parliament: "We should now give substance to the sustainable development option, always doing more to ensure that the quality of the environment is a positive factor for innovation and thus for the competitiveness of our economy."

As a consequence, the Institute for Prospective Technological Studies (IPTS) of the European Commission's Joint Research Centre in Sevilla and the German Federal Ministry for Education and Research (BMBF) supported a joint international conference focusing on impacts of environmental policy on innovation activity, under the German Presidency of the European Union. The conference was organised by IPTS, the Centre for European Economic Research (ZEW) and the Maastricht Economic Research Institute on Innovation and Technology (MERIT). The conference was held in Potsdam in May 1999 and brought together 60 experts from Europe, USA and Japan.

The objectives of the conference were:

✓ to provide a forum for the dissemination and discussion of recent major studies on this topic,

✓ to enhance further research and interaction between researchers and decision-makers,

✓ to identify innovative approaches for innovation-friendly environmental regulation.

Specifically, results from two major research projects on this issue were presented and discussed:

• The German project "Innovation Impacts of Environmental Policy" (German Acronym: FIU) involved an interdisciplinary consortium of 10 institutes and 18 sub-projects. It was conducted from 1996 to 1998 and mainly included case studies, which were supplemented by model comparisons and a German industry survey.

• The IPTS framework project on "The Impact of Regulation on Innovation in European Industry", on behalf of the Directorate-General for Enterprise. The aim was to develop a new methodological approach encompassing the complex interdependencies between regulation and other factors influencing innovative behaviour by companies. The project has applied this approach in a number of studies addressing specific sectors such as the chemical and recycling industries.

Additionally, results from other major European and American research projects were presented.

This book contains the papers presented at the conference and thus provides a good overview of the state of research in the area of environmental policy and innovation. The book contains three main parts which are as follows:

1. Theoretical approaches towards a framework of environmental regulation and innovation

2. International case studies on environmental regulation and innovation

3. Econometric and modelling studies on the impact of regulation on environmental innovation.

1: Theoretical approaches towards a framework of environmental regulation and innovation

In his contribution Robert Ayres (European Institute of Business Administration, INSEAD, Fontainebleau) explains the nature of the relationship between environmental regulation and innovation. He describes the dilemma, that on the one hand modern society wants a clean natural environment because of the direct effects to health and living quality. But, on the other hand high economic growth is necessary to be able to finance social systems and to ensure the high living standard of the people. The resulting question is how to achieve maximum economic growth and simultaneously a minimal environmental pollution and resource use. Ayres concludes that the answer is the integration of sustainable development in technological, organisational and social innovations, which are the main driving forces for economic growth. Ayres gives the example of internet shopping which, in his view, decreases the need to construct new shopping centres and reduces individual traffic.

However, the internet as an information technology is only an example of technologies which may reduce environmental burdens. Candice Stevens (OECD, Paris) points out that solar technologies, biotechnology, sensors, new materials or renewable energies are also important in this respect. Stevens argues that an adequate market demand is an important precondition for the introduction and the wider application of clean products, processes and services. Studies show that the environmental awareness of the consumer is increasing, but that consumer behaviour only partly reflects this. Stevens concludes that in future, government-supported basic research in the area of environmentally friendly and resources-saving technologies is also needed. She criticises that only 2 per cent of the public R&D budget of the OECD countries is used for environmental related research.

René Kemp (University Maastricht, MERIT), Keith Smith (STEP Group, Oslo) and Gerhard Becher (Prognos, Basel) stress the complexity of the framework conditions for environmental innovations. They present a systems framework, which emphasises the collective and interactive character of innovation as an appropriate entry point for analysing the complex institutional, social and networking aspects of the impacts of regulation. With respect to regulation, they seek to challenge the neo-classical stimulus-response model of the impacts of regulation on innovation. Regulation is generally understood as "a modulator of technical change, changing directions and modes of innovation, rather than just stopping or starting it." In a systems approach, innovation decisions are influenced by different constraints such as company size, the geographical location of the market, the labour supply, or the financial framework. Impact of environmental regulation should not be investigated within individual firms, but rather along a production chain.

Nick Ashford (Massachusetts Institute of Technology, MIT) develops a technology-based approach for addressing and setting priorities for environmental problems. Based on a number of MIT studies which began in 1979 (i.e. more than ten years before the Porter hypothesis), Ashford argues that "regulation could stimulate significant fundamental changes in product and process technology which benefited the industrial innovator, provided the regulations were stringent and focused". This opposes the view of Kemp et al. since Ashford assumes that regulation can indeed create and not only support niche markets for environmental innovators.

Ulrike Lehr and Klaus Löbbe (Rhine Westphalia Institute for Economic Research, RWI, Essen) summarise the main goals and results of the German FIU-project. The aims of the research group were to identify characteristics, determinants and obstacles of environmental innovations with special reference to the role of environmental policy. Joint hypotheses were formulated and tested in sub-projects. The main results are the strong dependence of environmental innovation on state intervention, the need of a policy mix, the fact that environmental innovations can only be explained by a multitude of factors (so-called multi-impulse hypothesis) and the importance of policy styles as described in a sub-project of Jaenicke et al.

Martin Jaenicke (Free University Berlin, FFU), Jens Hemmelskamp (Institute for Prospective Studies, IPTS, Sevilla), Jürgen Blazejczak and Dietmar Edler (German Institute for Economic Research, DIW, Berlin) argue that the government is only a part of the innovation system and the effects of policy measures are highly uncertain. Thus, the simple view of traditional environmental policy, which is strongly focused on the use of specific instruments, is problematic. "Instrumentalism" in environmental policy is criticised, i.e. the assumption that the choice of a single policy instrument determines the success of a policy. According to the authors, specific instruments (taxes, permits) are overestimated in the discussion, while important elements of successful environmental policy are underestimated. Their thesis is that innovation effects can be achieved without overburdening a single instrument, but instead by using a broader policy approach with a mix of instruments, dialogue, close networks among participating actors, etc. Based on the criticism of "instrumentalism" and on seven international case studies, the authors have identified three essential success factors for innovation-oriented environmental policy: Instruments, policy styles and actor constellation. With regard to instruments, a "policy style"-approach postulates that important success factors are a mix of instruments, strong economic incentives, strategic planning and a consideration of the different phases of the innovation process. With regard to policy style, calculable goals (e.g. long-term national environmental policy plans) are an important element to stimulate innovation especially when they are combined with flexible means. Actor constellations should include inter- and intra-policy integration, co-ordination between regulators and target groups and between stakeholders along the production chain.

Sylvie Faucheux (University of Versailles-Saint Quentin, C3ED) in her paper proposes an approach of deliberative governance for inducing technological and social change toward sustainable development. The approach is based on negotiations between stakeholders to reach consensus and exploit win-win options. For a continuous process of consensus building, new institutions have to be developed. Following such a strategy means that satisfying technological choices have to be identified, since optimal choices (as assumed in neo-classical models) do not exist.

2: International case studies on environmental regulation and innovation

The contribution from Jürgen Blazejczak and Dietmar Edler (German Institute for Economic Research, DIW, Berlin), represents three out of the seven international case studies following the "policy style" approach as described above. The authors investigate environmental innovations in the paper sector in Sweden, Japan and the United States. They conclude that the policy scheme in Sweden conforms most closely to the requirements of the "ideal" policy pattern. Search for consensus between regulators and regulated firms is combined with long-term strategic planning. As the authors write: "The success observed in Sweden was made possible by an outstanding position of the pulp and paper industry on the Swedish R&D policy agenda combined with an attitude of innovation-oriented companies which understand the reduction of environmental impacts as a strategic aim."

Vicky Norberg Bohm (Harvard University, Cambridge) takes a historical look at the role of public policy in the development of wind and gas turbines for power generation in the United States, driven by the questions which lessons can be learned for current and future climate policy. Different kinds of market failures are identified requiring an active supply-push and demand-pull policy strategy. Similar to the "policy style" approach, policy design, implementation and co-ordination are identified as main success factors rather than the choice of a single policy instrument.

Ulrike Lehr (Rhine Westphalia Institute for Economic Research – RWI) investigates the impact of the German ordinance on "Thermal Insulation on innovations in the windows and panes industry". The analysis shows that regulation lags behind the technological development. While Lehr finds no effects of regulation on invention, substantial effects on the diffusion of energy saving panes (which are already available on the market) can be detected.

A further example of the interrelationship of environmentally related innovation processes is the end-of-life vehicle (ELV) recycling. About 8.8 million ELV have to be scrapped each year in the European Union. About 75 per cent of the volume are currently recycled but 1.8 million tons of residue from the shredding activity must be landfilled, annually. According to Roberto Zoboli (IDSE-CNR) the problem is the harmfulness of some of the substances. Since 1965 the weight of cars has clearly increased, but at the same time the share of easily recyclable materials has decreased. The increasing relevance of non-recyclable materials like plastic, rubber, glass and fibre is the main environmental problem of ELV recycling. Since the eighties, initiatives for the reduction of non-recyclable ELV residues have been stimulated by expectations of the adoption of an EU regulation on ELV recycling. Thus, European car manufacturers already consider recycling criteria in the R&D process, for example, by trying to use recyclable materials. Zoboli concludes that these efforts were considerably supported by policy initiatives of the Member States of the European Commission. Notwithstanding this, the volume of non-recyclable residues is increasing and there is no demand for some of the recycled materials. Thus, a switch from so-called "soft" instruments like voluntary agreements to tough requirements for the car industry to fulfil certain standards in a fixed time frame is needed.

3: Econometric and modelling studies on the impact of regulation on environmental innovation

In his literature review, Carlo Carraro (Fondazione Eni Enrico Mattei and University of Venice) analyses the incentives for firms to innovate. He highlights market imperfections leading to sub-optimal investments by firms in environmental R&D. Therefore, policy interventions can be legitimised. Carraro recommends a mix of policy instruments including carrots (subsidies for environmental R&D) and sticks (taxes, tradable permits). Moreover, Carraro describes the need of a fast and wide diffusion of new technological know-how and of contacts between universities and innovative companies. He also points out that the government should support radical innovations by creating new markets. In particular Carraro mentions international aspects of environmental innovations and the need for effective international technology transfer.

Faye Duchin (Rensselaer Polytechnic Institute Troy, New York) highlights the relevance of the consumer and the need for suitable governmental policy initiatives that could foster green consumer behaviour. She argues that households, like companies, are able to change their behaviour towards a sustainable lifestyle. This market push effect would then influence companies' innovation behaviour. Changes towards sustainable consumer behaviour in the industrialised countries would also have global effects since such "social innovations" would be adopted in poorer countries. Faye Duchin suggests modelling studies on the effects of changes of consumer behaviour, categorised in different types of households. Formal models should be expanded to explicitly include lifestyle decisions made by households. Environmental impacts of lifestyle decisions should also be investigated in demonstration projects.

Jens Hemmelskamp (European Commission, Joint Research Centre-IPTS, Sevilla) presents an analysis of German innovation survey data. He argues that it is necessary to examine in each case which instrument is superior regarding innovation impacts. He points out that his analysis shows a weaker impact of environmental policy instruments on innovation than commonly assumed in the scientific debate. In particular, it is possible that instruments can have positive impacts in one case and negative effects in another, because innovation behaviour of companies is influenced by a multitude of other factors, like the market structure, the location of a company, or the information flow. Thus environmental policies must be considered as a part of a complex framework of factors influencing companies innovation behaviour.

Thomas Cleff and Klaus Rennings (ZEW, Mannheim) investigate the determinants of innovative behaviour in companies with regard to various areas of end-of-pipe and integrated environmental protection, including integrated product innovation. They pay particular attention to the influence of environmental policy instruments on product and process innovation. The approach could be placed somewhere between environmental and industrial economics: in contrast to the current dominant approach of environmental economics, it integrates discoveries from the field of innovation research. The paper uses data of the Mannheim Innovation Panel, complemented by a subsequent telephone survey of environmental innovators. In a multivariate analysis, significant influence of strategic market goals on environment-related product innovation becomes evident. This differs from environment-related process innovation, which is mainly determined by regulation. With respect to individual environmental policy instruments, a significant influence of so-called "soft" regulation (e.g. eco-labels, eco-audits) on product integrated environmental innovation can be discerned.

Conclusions and perspectives

To sum up the overall results, this conference report cannot be read as a cookbook on how to design innovation oriented environmental regulation. A recipe for how to induce innovation in a particular case, if it exists at all, cannot easily be transferred from one context to another, but the studies show that research programs in Germany, Europe and the United States identified some common ingredients of successful, innovation-oriented environmental policy. The main results are :

- R&D policy is more relevant for invention, where as environmental policy is more relevant for the diffusion of environmental innovations,

- a mix of instruments is decisive, rather than the choice of a single policy instrument,

- economic incentives for innovators are nevertheless a crucial element in each policy mix,

- social and institutional innovations have to be considered in addition to technological solutions,

- the subject of analysis should be an environmental innovation system rather than a single company,

- strategic planning and long-term policy goals support innovation.

This may already outline some directions of future research needs. It seems obvious that environmental innovation systems (on the level of firms, regions, countries and unions of countries) will receive increasing attention. Nevertheless specific aspects of the innovation process (for example specific innovation phases - in climate policy the diffusion of existing technology is extremely important) have to be carefully investigated. The same is true for the interaction between the various policies (e.g. R&D and environmental policy), instruments and actors. While the focus of past research has been mainly on the determinants of environmental innovations, the innovation impacts (ecological, social and economic) have also to be assessed, for example the impacts of environmental innovations on employment and competitiveness. Moreover, little research is available on environmental innovation in the service sector. Last but not least, data bases on environmental goods and service markets still mainly include end-of-pipe technologies and neglect cleaner production technologies. In the context of innovations toward sustainable development, better indicators and data on cleaner or integrated technologies are inevitable.

Acknowledgements

We would like to thank several people for helping in assuring the success of the conference and publication of the papers. On behalf of the participants of the conference we would like to acknowledge their appreciation of the financial and organisational support of the German Federal Ministry of Education and Science (BMBF) and the European Commission's Joint Research Centre – IPTS. In particular, we would like to thank Per Sorup (IPTS) and Helmut Schulz (BMBF) for the goodwill necessary for our work. We also thank René Kemp and Alexander Grablowitz (BMBF)for his support in organising the conference, Gunter Grittmann (ZEW) for the public relations work, our research assistant Steffen Jörg who supported us in proof reading of papers and technical edition and Maria Arranz for administrative support. Last but not least, we would like to thank the participants of the conference for investing time in joining the conference, preparing presentations, and papers, and for the intensive and very fruitful discussion during the conference.

Part I

Theoretical Approaches towards a Framework of Environmental Regulation and Innovation

On Green Technology: A Framework for Evaluation

Robert U. Ayres

European Instiut of Business Administration (INSEAD)
Boulevard de Constance, 77305 Fontainebleau Cedex
France

Keywords. risk assessment, technical change, technology evaluation, green technology.

Abstract. There is a complex interrelationship between technological change, economic growth and environmental risk/protection. Since the 1950s, at least, it has been clear that factors other than capital and labor must be responsible for most economic growth. Historical and anecdotal evidence suggests that the substitution of machines powered by fossil energy for human and animal labor must play a significant role in driving growth. On the other hand, consumption of fossil fuels and other extractive resources certainly constitutes one of the major sources of environmental pollution and damage.

An influential school of thought, promoted especially by the World Bank, argues that economic growth is actually a prerequisite for environmental protection, both because the latter is a 'superior' good – i.e. a luxury – desired mainly by the rich, and because advanced technology and wealth are needed for purposes of both prevention and abatement of environmental damage.

On closer scrutiny it is clear that technologies vary widely in both growth-creation potential and environmental risk. The question then arises: to what extent can these different aspects be anticipated and evaluated *ex ante*? This paper proposes a simple framework for such an evaluation methodology.

1 Background

It is evident, and hardly controversial, that the natural environment is increasingly threatened by land-use changes and waste products associated with economic activity. Population is growing. People must be fed. Poverty is still widespread. Yet even the poorest and remotest in the "global village" now aspire to middle class lifestyles now enjoyed by Americans and Europeans. But those lifestyles involve massive consumption of natural resources, both renewable and non-renewable.

Materials and fuels that are extracted from the natural environment must be physically embodied in the 'anthroposphere' (as structures or durable goods) or they must be discarded again as wastes (Ayres and Kneese 1969). Wastes and pollutants far outweigh 'permanent' additions to the built environment. For instance, in the US in 1993 extraction and agricultural/forestry activities alone generated 7.1 billion metric tons of solid waste (mostly from mining) while yielding 5 billion metric tons of minerals, ores, and fossil fuels, plus 1.4 billion metric tons of harvested biomass. Energy conversion and manufacturing processes consumed an additional 11 billion tons of atmospheric oxygen for fuel combustion and generated nearly 15 billion metric tons of combustion and waste products, (dry weight) while producing 2.1 billion tons of construction materials, 82 million tons of other durable goods, and 300 million tons of other consumables, of which 205 million tons were food and food beverages. About 90 million tons were recycled, mostly metals.

It was thought a few years ago that the availability of "low entropy" exhaustible resources – such as minable ores and fossil fuels – would constitute near-term, as well as ultimate limits to economic growth. The economist Nicolas Georgescu-Roegen was the best-known advocate of this 'entropic' view (Georgescu-Roegen 1971). The combined impact of resource exhaustion and environmental pollution was emphasized in the famous Club of Rome Report (Forrester 1971, 1975; Meadows, et al. 1972). But mainstream economists took prompt exception to these pessimistic views, largely on the ground that the economic growth depends more on technological innovation and capital investment than on natural resources (e.g. Nordhaus 1973; Solow 1974; Stiglitz 1974). As regards the degree to which man-made capital and human technology can substitute for natural resources or natural capital, the debate continues to this day.

It is recognized that waste emissions and pollutants do constitute a problem because the use of the environment in this way is largely free to the polluter, although costly to society as a whole. Hence these social costs are externalities, not automatically built into the price of manufactured goods and services. Nevertheless, environmental problems and unpaid social costs associated with all materials/energy intensive activities have already created political pressures in some countries, at least, to 'internalize' such externalities.

The end result will be to make materials and fossil energy producers pay more to reduce pollution and thus more costly to users. This will encourage users to be more efficient and to seek alternatives where possible. Many of these gains in materials/energy productivity must be achieved – in effect – by substituting labor or capital for energy or materials.(Insulating houses to reduce the need for hydrocarbon fuels would be an example). Other gains will be achieved by extending the useful life of material products by increasing the level of re-use, repair, renovation, remanufacturing and recycling.

All of these examples are inherently more labor-intensive than original mass production. At first glance these changes appear to be very desirable from the standpoint of reducing unemployment. But they also reduce labor productivity, *ceteris paribus*. Increasing resource productivity has a downside in the form of reduced economies of scale for the raw materials processing industries and the mass producers of consumer products. This would be reflected in higher prices and reduced demand. Reduced demand is generally regarded as desirable by environmentalists – consider the current debate on "sufficiency" – but it has a negative impact on economic growth.

A few economists have questioned the desirability of perpetual economic growth, for just these reasons (e.g. Boulding 1966; Mishan 1967; Daly 1973). Herman Daly, in particular, has advocated a steady-state economy. On the other hand, continued economic growth itself continues to be an important political and social objective. Indeed, the needs of aging populations and increasing health-related entitlements, not to mention more investment in education and research, seem demand that economic growth should accelerate, if anything. Historically, economic growth has been closely correlated with materials and energy consumption. In fact, the first industrial revolution in the 18th century was unquestionably a direct consequence of the development of the steam engine and its early applications to coal mining,[1] iron smelting and transportation. The effect was to initiate a positive feedback loop such that declining energy – and power – costs led to declining manufacturing costs and prices, which in turn stimulated consumer demand and exports. This positive feedback loop constituted a sort of "growth engine" that is still in operation, although nowadays it depends more on prices of petroleum products and electricity. Indeed, so close is the correlation between economic growth and energy consumption that there is a plausible case for arguing causation, and a number of economists and others have argued that energy (more properly *exergy*) deserves to be identified as a "factor of production".[2]

So, a rather stark question now arises: how is future economic growth to be reconciled with declining energy/materials consumption? Is it possible? To be sure, Solow, Stiglitz and others cited above have made a theoretical argument to this effect (Solow 1974; Stiglitz 1974). But their theoretical case depends on very simplified models of the economy in which there are many crude assumptions, including the assumption that man-made capital can substitute without limit for natural capital. In a recent revisitation of this issue, both Solow and Stiglitz have argued that their ultrasimplified models were not, after all, intended to apply to the

---

[1]   Newcomen's first practical steam engines were designed to pump water from flooded coal mines, thus replacingexpensive horses (which had to be fed) and cutting the cost of coal.

[2]   The literature is too extensive to summarize here. For a review see (Ayres 1999).

indefinite future, but only to reflect conditions in an intermediate time-frame (*Ecological Economics* 1997). My own view has been consistent with that theirs, insofar as there is no evidence of an upper limit to the amount of service (GNP) that can be 'extracted' from a given material/energy input (Ayres and Kneese 1989).

More to the point, perhaps, is the related question: is economic growth itself "green"? If so, to what extent? There is an influential school that argues in the affirmative, based largely on the so-called Environmental Kuznets Curve (EKC). The argument is summarized briefly below, although I have a different view.

2 The E/GNP Ratio and the Kuznets "Inverted U"

One of the stylized facts of long term economic growth and development, that has attracted renewed attention recently, is the so-called Kuznets (inverted U) curve, as exemplified by the E/GDP ratio.[3] This pattern suggests that during the early stages of industrialization GNP tends to be increasingly dependent on commercial energy, whereas after some point in the developmental pattern commercial (and total) energy requirements per unit output begin to decline as services begin to dominate material production. This is an empirical observation that has been qualitatively repeated for a number of countries. The importance of non-commercial energy during the early stages of industrialization, especially for domestic heating and cooking, is clear. In most countries this domestic fuel consists of agricultural wastes or· wood harvested from public lands. It largely accounts for the deforestation that is now occurring in Asia and Africa and which took place in colonial America, largely to clear land for planting crops.

The natural interpretation of the E/GNP curve is that energy inputs are complementary to capital and labor at the early stages of industrial buildup. This is presumably because infrastructure creation requires earth moving machines that are powered by commercial energy as well as energy intensive materials such as steel, aluminum and cement. On the other hand, later in the process, the relationships change and capital increasingly becomes a partial substitute for energy by in-

---

[3]   For early work see (Kuznets 1930, 1963). The history energy consumption per unit of GNP for the U.S. was firstcalculated in detail by (Schurr and Netschert 1960), based on Kuznets' estimates of GNP for the years before 1910 and Kuznets-Kendrick's estimates of GNP in 1929 prices (Kendrick 1961), updated in terms of 1958 prices by the Bureauof Economic Analysis (BEA) for later years, based on *National Income and Products Accounts of the United States1929–1965*. For the more recent work involving the so-called Environmental Kuznets Curve (EKC), see (World Bank1992; Selden and Song 1994; Beckerman 1995; Grossman and Krüger 1995, 1996; Stern *et al.* 1996).

creasing the efficiency of energy use. For instance, the substitution of wood stoves for open fireplaces for domestic heating in the US in the early 19th century resulted in a fourfold reduction in fuel consumption per unit of heat output (Schurr and Netschert 1960, p. 49, footnote). The substitution of electric drive for steam power in factories early in this century also increased energy use efficiency (Devine 1982). Increasing compression ratios of automobile engines from 1920 to 1950 (which became possible thanks to higher octane fuels) resulted in dramatic increases in automobile fuel economy (Ayres and Ezekoye 1991). Turbo-diesel engines are more expensive but use less fuel than gasoline engines. More and better insulation reduces the need for space heating. Similarly heat exchangers and recuperators increase efficiency but cost more money. During the later stages of industrialization machines driven by commercial energy also substitute increasingly for human labor. Modern agriculture is a particularly good example of this substitution (Steinhart and Steinhart 1974).

In short, the *complementary* relationship between capital, labor and energy use dominates in the early stages of industrialization. The *substitution* relationship becomes increasingly important over time, however, as capital becomes less scarce and labor becomes more costly. Eventually, it would seem, the substitution relationship becomes dominant.

But the question remains: is the (empirically observed) EKC a valid justification for assuming – as some mainstream economists, especially at the World Bank have done – that economic growth is a sufficient condition for assuming that growth is inevitably "green", at least in the long run (e.g. Beckerman 1974, 1995; World Bank 1992; Grossman and Krüger 1995, 1996)? The theoretical argument in support of this proposition is based on the notion that environmental amenities are a 'superior good', which means that as incomes rise above the subsistence level people will allocate an increasing proportion of their disposable wealth to buying environmental protection. There is also some empirical support for this view, inasmuch as the rich countries (on average) devote more of their resources to environmental protection than the poor countries. The same tendency is observable at the individual level, at least with regard to investment in residential locations: uphill, upstream and upwind sites are generally preferred – and consequently more pricy – than downhill, downstream and downwind sites.

Yet there are also very serious objections to this rather simplistic argument. In the first place, some of the rich countries do not devote significant resources to environmental protection. (The lack of environmental investment in Italy is especially noteworthy.) At a more fundamental level, the 'superior good' argument applies, even in principle, only to environmental amenities that are clearly recognizable to the tax-paying voters. There will be much greater willingness to pay for sewage treatment, smoke control, refuse collection and even cleaning up old industrial waste accumulations, than for undertaking measures with immediate costs (in terms of jobs, if not taxes) and distant or intangible benefits. The lack of voter enthusiasm for preserving tropical rainforests for the sake of biodiversity, and the skepticism about the need for limiting greenhouse gases (GHGs) if this means higher energy prices, exemplify this point.

Finally, there is a strong argument that environmental services are, in themselves, an important constituent of 'real' wealth, as well as a necessary condition for the creation of economic wealth. The most obvious case in point is agriculture, which is extremely dependent on natural inputs, including sunlight, topsoil creation, rainfall, climatic stability, organic nutrient recycling by biological organisms,[4] pollination of crops, and so forth. Forestry and fisheries are also sectors directly dependent on the products of photosynthesis, while waste disposal (including the disposition of human remains) is equally dependent on natural decay processes. There are, of course, even subtler ways in which the industrial economy depends on the natural system in which it is embedded.

The UN Commission on Environment and Development and its famous report "Our Common Future" was the spearhead of a major effort to establish the case for this linkage (Brundtland 1987). Unfortunately, the phrase 'sustainable development', introduced by that Report, has become something of a cliché, used rather indiscriminately. For a few years after publication of the Report, there was a serious debate on the economic implications of ecological sustainability.

However, in recent years the debate has changed. The emphasis in some influential circles, at least, has shifted to whether measures needed to assure long-run sustainability should be taken now (for reasons of prudence) or delayed until they are more 'affordable'. The underlying assumption, of course, is that future generations will be richer than we are, and that science/technology will meanwhile have made progress in both ascertaining the true seriousness of the threats and improved the means of ameliorating them.

3 Long-term Technical Change

It is very attractive, at this point, to interpret technical change in terms of two measurable long-term trends in the economy. One is the increasing complexity of the economy, as new sectors are introduced between the primary raw materials extraction activities characteristic of a primitive economy, and the increasingly sophisticated products and services being produced today. The creation of an information processing sector, in the last half century, underlines this trend (Machlup 1962). Since Machlup's pioneering work most information-intensive activities have expanded dramatically.

---

4   The carbon cycle, the oxygen cycle, the nitrogen cycle and others. There is an
       extensive literature on these cyclicprocesses that cannot be summarized here.

The other measurable long-term change is the increasing efficiency of energy (exergy) conversion, especially at the production end. This trend has been acknowledged (but not explained) in a number of long-term models of economic growth, where it is called "autonomous energy efficiency increase", or AEEI. This is commonly introduced as a parameter reflecting exogenous annual improvement, consistent with the Solow growth model.

Yet there is nothing in the endogenous growth literature except spillovers to explain why energy efficiency, in particular, should improve autonomously in this way.

Introducing exergy (via consumable intermediates) as suggested in the previous section, goes part way to solving the problem. The need for an exogenous time-dependent multiplier can be eliminated, at least in the short run. This leaves us, however, with a theory of growth that explicitly depends on increasing resource/exergy consumption – at least in processed (intermediate) form – to drive most economic growth. Increasing exergy consumption, in turn, depends on decreasing resource prices over the long term.[5]

To be sure, this long-term price decline can probably be explained endogenously, as a spillover from investment in human capital, and/or as a direct consequence of R&D investment. But the underlying neoclassical assumption of growth-in-equilibrium makes such an explanation unsatisfying. It fails to answer the crucial question: why should any price-taking firm operating in a quasi-static equilibrium invest in either human capital or R&D at all? Absence of any convincing answer opens the door to the neo-Marxist implication that such investment must necessarily be the role of government.

Of course, Schumpeter provided a key insight nearly a century ago (Schumpeter 1912, 1934). He pointed out that progress is a process of "creative destruction" driven by innovation – in the broadest sense of the term – and driven by the straightforward incentive to gain monopoly profits through appropriation and protection of the resulting competitive advantage. However the Schumpeterian paradigm is inherently inconsistent with the equilibrium model of growth. In a Walrasian equilibrium, there is no incentive to innovate. Clearly, a satisfactory theory of growth should reflect the Schumpeterian incentive, which in turn depends on the existence of a persistent disequilibrium and information asymmetries.

The critical question arises, then: Is there a built-in source of disequilibrium that could explain continuing innovation, growth and structural change? The answer is, again, yes. In fact, there are at least three sources of quasi-perpetual disequilibrium. One is the fact that the real economy depends a lot (as noted) on extracting crude materials and fossil fuels from the environment, in order to replace human

---

5   This trend has been well documented. See (Barnett and Morse 1962; Smith 1979).

and animal labor. As the highest quality resources are used first, they will be exhausted first, whence ever-lower grade resources must be utilized (Herfindahl 1967). This creates an imperative for developing more efficient means of discovery, extraction and processing, as well as development of alternative substitutes, to maintain the downward trend in intermediate commodity (processed exergy) prices on which the historical "growth engine" depends. Responding to the Club of Rome's "limits to growth" thesis in the early 1970s, many economists were quick to emphasize this automatic market-driven response mechanism (e.g. Nordhaus 1973; Solow 1974; Stiglitz 1974).

A second source of perpetual disequilibrium is closely related to growth itself. It arises from the generation of wastes and environmental pollution, which is a direct consequence of extractive resource-driven economic activity and growth (Ayres and Kneese 1969). The capacity of the environment to absorb, detoxify and recycle industrial and consumption wastes is limited. In fact, these functions of the biosphere are themselves being degraded as humans destroy or degrade more and more natural systems in the ever-more intensive push for increasing agricultural and forestry production using "industrial" techniques. The consequence can be characterized as an increasingly strong imperative toward "dematerialization" of the economy.

The explicit and detailed mechanisms by which these overall imperatives are translated into R&D and technological innovations in the short and medium term cannot be thoroughly discussed in this paper. Suffice it to say that the existence of such mechanisms can be postulated without any theoretical inconsistency with neoclassical economic micro-foundations, at least in a multi-sectoral context. However, there are some straightforward implications for policy, especially with regard to long-term greenhouse gas (GHG) control, that deserve further discussion, subsequently.

A third long-term source of disequilibrium is technological progress. Not only is technological progress a consequence of disequilibrium, it is also a cause. While it is analytically convenient in some models to assume that new knowledge is disseminated instantaneously, the reality is that knowledge of commercial value is typically protected quite effectively for considerable periods, assisted of course, by patent and copyright laws. Moreover, knowledge embodied in organizations and institutions is extraordinarily difficult to transfer, even when both the would-be donors and beneficiaries are actively engaged in the transfer process. (The problems associated with economic development clearly illustrate this fact.) Innovators can often maintain an advantage for long after the initial knowledge monopoly has been broken.

In this context it is relevant to suggest that the foregoing arguments, taken together, suggests the possibility of developing a quantifiable indicator of technical progress, at the macro level, as a ratio between "raw" exergy inputs and finished service (information) outputs, with one or more intermediate steps, such as the efficiency of converting "raw" materials (as exergy) into "finished materials" (also as exergy). The results cannot be reproduced here, but a rough first approximation has been published recently (Ayres 1999-a).

4 Disequilibrium, Double Dividends, and "Crowding Out"

The conventional neoclassical model assumes that R&D investment is always optimal (even though it provides no real justification for doing R&D in the first place). If this simple picture were correct it would follow that any government policy that encouraged investment or R&D in a direction different than that chosen by the "free market" must *ipso facto* reduce economic growth. This assumption is built into most computable general equilibrium (CGE) long-run models. It underlies the conclusions of 'top-down' neoclassical modelers to the effect that CO_2 abatement policies would 'cost' a great deal of money in lost growth.[6]

The contrary suggestion has been made by a number of 'bottom up' analysts that there is a significant potential for negative costs, 'free lunches' and 'double dividends' (e.g. Krause *et al.* 1992, 1993; Lovins and Lovins 1981, 1997). Generally speaking, mainstream economists have not taken the 'free lunch' claims very seriously in the past, arguing that if such opportunities really existed on a large scale, entrepreneurs would soon exploit and thus eliminate them. The apparent failure of profit-seeking firms to do so is generally attributed to 'hidden costs', even though the latter are rarely identified or quantified (e.g. Jaffee *et al.*1995; Gabel and Sinclair-Desgagné 1998). In fact, the existence of possible negative costs or double dividends seems to have gained greater credibility over time, partly because a number of specific institutional barriers to adjustment are fairly easy to identify, and partly because the empirical evidence is increasingly hard to ignore.

As the first paragraph of this section suggests, the case for negative costs and free lunches is essentially the same as the case for assuming that firms rarely operate on or very near the production frontier, meaning that there are many opportunities to produce at lower cost while polluting less. (There is an impressive empirical evidence that significant energy conservation savings can often be achieved at zero or negligible cost). This situation is tantamount to economic disequilibrium

---

6   Examples of such long-run CGE models include the Dynamic General Equilibrium Model (DGEM) (Jorgenson and Wilcoxen 1993), the OECD's GREEN model (Burniaux *et al.* 1992), the Goulder model (Goulder 1992, 1995), thePacific Northwest Laboratories Second Generation Model (Edmonds *et al.* 1993), and Whalley and Wigle (Whalley and Wigle 1991, 1993). See also (Goulder and Schneider 1996).

(Ayres 1994). The double dividend argument is slightly subtler; it usually refers to the benefits of recycling revenues from an hypothetical carbon tax to reduce labor costs and thus encourage increased job creation. The benefit depends, ultimately, on the (well-founded) assumption that labor markets are not currently in equilibrium. (If they were, unemployment would not exist).

A further possibility in the double-dividend tradition would be that some kinds of environmental or other regulation can encourage profitable innovation. This is usually referred to as the 'Porter hypothesis' (Porter 1991; Porter and van der Linde 1995). The usual reaction of economists is dismissive. However several authors have recently acknowledged the possibility of induced technological change (ITC) (Grubb *et al.* 1995; Goulder and Schneider 1996). They point out that most policy evaluation tools (based on standard growth theory) have treated technological change as *autonomous*. This implied that productivity improvements would occur without investment or effort. To modify this assumption Goulder and Schneider introduced an explicit R&D investment loop in their CGE model. Under the conventional assumption of scarce knowledge-generating resources and optimal R&D resource allocation, they show that ITC increases the gross costs of CO_2 abatement policies(not counting environmental benefits). However, they also admit that, "if there are serious prior inefficiencies in R&D markets (whereby the marginal social product of R&D is much higher in alternative energy sectors than in carbon-based energy sectors) ITC can imply lower gross costs than would occur in its absence."[7]

There are no established inter-sectoral or time-series data on returns to R&D, whence this possibility may remain speculative for the present. However, it is easily verified that most of the energy-related R&D investment in the past half century – hundreds of billions of dollars – have gone into nuclear power. Yet, since the 1970s there has been no real cost reduction in the generation of nuclear power. (On the contrary, due to tighter safety-related and waste disposal requirements, nuclear fission power is now more costly than it was three decades ago.) Two major programs, breeder reactors and fusion power, have yielded no benefits at all, and may never do so. The second largest cumulative R&D investment, scores of billions of dollars, has gone into coal gasification and coal shale liquefaction. Again, there has been no economic return whatever on that investment. There are some intermediate cases. But the two alternative energy technologies with the highest returns, as demonstrated by rapidly falling costs, are wind power and photovoltaic power. Yet these two technologies have jointly received only a tiny fraction of the total available R&D funding, both public and private.

In fact, the global energy R&D market is almost ludicrously inefficient in economic terms. The amounts invested in various technologies have been almost

---

[7]   In addition, Goulder and Schneider note that ITC can also increase the net environmental benefits of a carbon tax.

inverse to the returns. Given comparably inefficient allocation of resources in other areas of investment, it is hard not to conclude that ITC might very well accelerate rather than retard economic growth. Such a possibility is entirely consistent with the history of technology, where many of the most important and fertile innovations have resulted from a scarcity. It is said that "necessity is the mother of invention". More generally, it is difficult to dispute that technological progress due to innovation is virtually inconceivable in the absence of incentives attributable to significant disequilibrium, and that both natural resource scarcity and environmental overload constitute likely sources of disequilibrium. The implications of this point are discussed in the next section.

5   Economic Growth in the Greenhouse

In recent years there has been growing concern about the problem of climate warming and sea-level rise, due to the buildup of so-called Greenhouse Gases or GHGs (mainly CO_2) attributable mostly to fossil fuel use. These gases trap heat in the stratosphere and reradiate it to earth. There is obviously a link between economic activity (and fuel use) and GHG emissions. On the other hand, the extraction, processing and distribution of fuels and electric power constitute a significant economic activity in themselves. Consequently the relationship between energy use and economic growth has become a hot topic among macro-economic modelers.

It has been widely accepted by most economists working in this field that the proper tool for assessing policies for controlling GHG emissions economic growth is an optimal growth computable general equilibrium (CGE) model (Edmonds and Reilly 1985; Edmonds et al. 1986; Nordhaus 1992, 1993, 1994; Manne and Richels 1992; Hourcade 1993; Grubb et al. 1993; Jorgenson and Wilcoxen 1993; Grubb et al. 1995; Goulder 1995; Goulder and Schneider 1996).The use of such models assumes (1) that the economy grows in equilibrium (2) that the 'engine' of growth is exogenous (i.e. increasing productivity) and (3) that any constraint on the model – such as a regulation – must *ipso facto* reduce growth below the optimal level (Ayres 1994).

One particularly contentious assumption built into the CGE framework is that growth along the 'business-as-usual' trajectory is not only optimal but also costless and automatic. If this were true it would also be true that any deliberate intervention by government to shift the trajectory (e.g. to develop non-polluting energy sources) must automatically reduce the rate of economic growth.

However, this implication is supported only by the standard neo-classical theory of growth-in-equilibrium, which assumes that technical progress is costless and automatic. It is certainly inconsistent with the Schumpeterian model of growth. It is also contradicted by the history of technology, which is replete with examples of shortage-induced innovations that subsequently stimulated a host of inventions and applications in completely new areas and left the innovator with a long-lived comparative (and competitive) advantage.

Contrary to the neo-classical view, there are rather strong arguments suggesting that the economic system, as a whole, is actually very far from equilibrium. This statement is not inconsistent with the possibility that some elements of the system – notably markets for labor and for capital, and for most commodities – are extremely competitive and may well be much closer to optimality. But the competition between factors of production is probably nowhere near equilibrium, and neither is the "market" for R&D resources, at least in the energy area.

In the context of greenhouse policy, what this means is that (1) there is still plenty of room for so-called 'double dividends' and even some 'free lunches' and (2) there is no reason, apart from tradition, to suppose that well-conceived government intervention should necessarily reduce economic growth. On the contrary, there is at least as much evidence to suggest that the opposite result might occur. Meanwhile, economists should refrain from offering strong policy advice based on theories with simplistic assumptions and a weak empirical base.

6   Towards a Taxonomy of Green Technologies

To summarize the foregoing in a few words: (i) the environment is increasingly at risk, due in large part to growing (and possibly already excessive) consumption of materials/energy and associated wastes and pollutant emissions; (ii) population growth and economic growth are the primary culprits, since economic growth has – up to now – been tightly linked to materials and energy consumption; (iii) but economic growth has a very high priority for governments – the world is not ready for a steady-state economy; (iv) and, despite some reason for skepticism, there is also a plausible theoretical argument that economic growth may also be a necessary condition for long-term sustainability.

A further point of some importance, that has not been made already, is that technologies are all different. While every new technology may be presumed to be profitable to some individuals and/or firms, they are not equally beneficial to society. Moreover, while some developments are highly probable, if not inevitable, others are not. Much depends on choices among alternatives, made by firms, government officials, and even by legislators. Policy-makers therefore face a problem comparable to threading a needle or "walking the razor's edge". The problem is essentially to "pick winners", although commercial or national competitiveness should not be the sole criterion for choice.

The selection criteria must not be too precise, of course. The implicit goal is to maximize economic growth while minimizing environmental damage. It is well-known that one cannot, in principle, maximize (or extremize) more than one objective function at the same time. So, a compromise is necessary. The usual approach is to combine the multiple objectives into a single objective, using judgmental weight-factors. (In reality, this procedure is rarely explicit, and is most commonly done inconsistently. But that does not matter for our purposes). The judgements, of course, will vary from one decision-maker to another and from situation to situation.

All technologies in general can be characterized roughly in terms of their impact on labor use, capital use, resource consumption, and demand. The ideal 'win-win' technology would be simultaneously labor-saving, capital-saving, resource-saving (i.e. pollution-reducing), and demand-increasing. However, the ideal is rarely achievable, in practice, because of tradeoffs between these characteristics. To save labor it is normally necessary to invest capital and/or consume more natural resources, if not both. To save capital it is normally necessary to increase labor inputs. To increase demand it is normally necessary to improve performance, which requires investment (capital). And so forth.

However, there are some win-win examples in the real world due to the fact that firms and/or governments have made sub-optimal choices in the past and have failed to search for, or implement, alternatives. There are both psychological and institutional reasons for such situations, although this is not the place to explore them. There are also occasional examples of true breakthroughs that save labor, capital and resources at the same time. As the table below suggests, internet commerce (shopping) may be an example of this, inasmuch as it has great potential for reducing the need for local retail distributors as well as consumer shopping trips by car.

However, having said all this, one can compare technologies, both existing and emerging, in relative terms. The approach is illustrated schematically in Table 1. The table can be filled in qualitatively for screening purposes without detailed analysis, as shown. A 'plus' (+) in columns 2-4 means that less labor, capital or resource inputs will be required for all purposes, including manufacturing and maintenance over the life of the product. Conversely for a minus (-).

A plus in the last column means that demand is likely to increase, either because of lower price or significantly better performance. Note that longer life for a durable good, *ceteris paribus*, corresponds to reduced inputs of all inputs, including labor, capital and resources, as well as reduced demand. However the *ceteris paribus* condition is difficult to meet, if demand is reduced, due to loss of economies of scale in mass production. In practice, the result depends on tradeoffs between the factors. Such evaluations are not always easy for an emerging technology, such as PV.

Clearly, a quantitative assessment is a non-trivial exercise, requiring engineering cost analysis, market analysis, I-O analysis to take into account intermediate and indirect effects, and environmental impact life cycle analysis. However, the methodology is relatively straightforward, at least in principle.

Table 1: Technology evaluation

Technology	Labor Saving	Capital Saving (a)	Resource Saving/ Pollution Reducing	Demand Increasing
Biofuels	-	-	+	-
GM crops	0	-	(b)	+
CF lighting	(c)	+	+	(d)
ATM	+	-	0	0
Robotics	+	-	0	0
CIM	+	-	+	0
Digital TV	0	-	0	+
Interactive TV	0	-	0	+
Internet shopping	+	+	+	+
Car sharing	+	+	(e)	(e)
Tire remanufacture	(c)	+	+	(d)
Car remanufacture	(c)	+	+	0
Paper recycling	-	-	+	0
CO$_2$ storage	-	-	(f)	-
PV for buildings	-	(g)	+	0
Electric cars	-	(h)	+	-
Fuel cell cars	-	-	+	-
PV hydrogen	-	-	+	-

(a) Regarding durable goods as capital; also "natural capital".
(b) If the modifications include N-fixation and/or pest resistance.
(c) Depends on scale vs lifetime tradeoff.
(d) Depends on consumer price, life capital cost and convenience.
(e) Depends on tradeoff between cost and convenience.
(f) Regarding climate as natural capital.
(g) In favorable circumstances; e.g. where peak demand occurs in mid-day, midsummer.
(h) Assuming longer life than conventional vehicles.

References

Ayres, R. U. and A. V. Kneese (1969), Production, Consumption & Externalities, *American Economic Review* June 1969. (AERE 'Publication of Enduring Quality' Award, 1990)

Ayres, R. U. and I. Ezekoye (1991), Competition & Complementarity in Diffusion: The Case of Octane, *Journal of Technological Forecasting & Social Change* 39 (1-2), 145-158.

Ayres, R. U. (1994), On Economic Disequilibrium & Free Lunch, *Environmental & Resource Economics* 4, 435-454. (Also INSEAD Working Paper 93/45/EPS)

Ayres, R. U. (1999), Technological Progress: A Proposed Measure, *Journal of Technological Forecasting & Social Change,* forthcoming. (also INSEAD working paper 97/101/EPS)

Ayres, R. U. (1999-a), The 2nd Law, the 4th Law, Recycling & Limits to Growth, *Ecological Economics* 29 (3), 473-384. (also INSEAD Working Paper 98/38/EPS)

Barnett, H. J. and C. Morse (1962), *Scarcity & Growth: The Economics of Resource Scarcity*, Baltimore.

Beckerman, W. (1974), *In Defense of Economic Growth*, London.

Beckerman, W. (1995), *Small is Stupid*, London.

Boulding, K. E. (1966), Environmental Quality in a Growing Economy, in: Garrett (ed.), *Essays from the Sixth RFF Forum*, Baltimore.

Brundtland, G. H. (ed.) (1987), *Our Common Future*, New York.(Report of the World Council For Economic Development)

Burniaux, J.- M., G. Nicoletti and J. Oliveira-Martins (1992), GREEN: A Global Model for Quantifying the Costs of Policies to Curb CO_2 Emissions, *OECD Economic Studies* 19, 16-47.

Daly, H. E. (1973), *Toward a Steady State Economy*, San Francisco.

Devine, W. D. Jr. (1982), *An Historical Perspective on the Value of Electricity in American Manufacturing*, Technical Report (ORAU/IEA-82-8(M)), Oak Ridge TN.

Edmonds, J. A., J. M. Reilly, R. H. Gardner and A. Brenkert (1986), *Uncertainty in Future Global Energy Use & Fossil Fuel CO2 Emissions, 1975 to 2075*, Technical Report (TRO36,DO3/NBB-0081), National Technical Information Service, United States Department of Commerce, Springfield VA.

Edmonds, J. A., H. Pitcher, D. Barns, R. Baron and M. Wise (1993), *Modeling Future Greenhouse Gas Emissions: The 2nd Generation Model Description*, Global Change & Modeling, United Nations University.

Edmonds, J. A. and J. M. Reilly (1985), *Global Energy- Assessing the Future*, New York.

Forrester, J. W. (1971), *World Dynamics*, Cambridge MA.

Forrester, J. W. (1975), *New Perspectives for Growth Over the Next Thirty Years*, Conference on Limits to Growth '75, Massachusetts Institute of Technology, Houston TX, October 20.

Gabel, H. L. and B. Sinclair-Desgagné (1998), The Firm, its Routines & the Environment, in: Tietenberg and Folmer (eds.), *The International Yearbook of Environmental & Resource Economics 1998/1999: A Survey of Current Issues*, Edward Elgar, Cheltenham UK & Lyme Ma.

Georgescu-Roegen, N. (1971), *The Entropy Law & the Economic Process*, Cambridge MA.

Goulder, L. H. (1992), *Do the Costs of A Carbon Tax Vanish When Interactions with Other Taxes are Accounted For?*, Working Paper (406), National Bureau for Economic Research, Washington DC.

Goulder, L. H. (1995), Effects of Carbon Taxes in an Economy with Prior Tax Distortions: An Intertemporal General Equilibrium Analysis, *Journal of Environmental Economics & Management* 29(3), 271-297.

Goulder, L. H. and S. H. Schneider (1996), *Induced Technological Change, Crowding Out, & the Attractiveness of CO_2 Emissions Abatement*, Draft, Institute for International Studies, Stanford University, Palo Alto CA.

Grossman, G. M. and A. B. Krüger (1995), Economic Growth & the Environment, *The Quarterly Journal of Economics* 60, 353-377.

Grossman, G. M. and A. B. Krüger (1996), The Inverted-U: What Does It Mean?, *Environment & Development Economics* 1, 119-122.

Grubb, M., J. Edmonds, P. Brink and M. Morrison (1993), The Cost of Limiting Fossil Fuel CO2 Emissions: A Survey & an Analysis, *Annual Review of Energy and the Environment* 18, 397-478.

Grubb, M., T. Chapuis and M. H. Duong (1995), The Economics of Changing Course: Implications of Adaptability & Inertia for Optimal Climate Policy, *Energy Policy* 23 (4/5), 417-432.

Herfindahl, O. (1967), Depletion & Economic Theory, in: Gaffney, M.(ed.), *Extractive Resources & Taxation*, Madison WI.

Hourcade, J.-C. (1993), Modeling Long-run Scenarios: Methodology Lessons from a Prospective Study on a Low CO2-intensive Country, *Energy Policy* 21, 309-326.

Jaffee, A., S. Peterson, P. Portney and R. Stevens (1995), Environmental Regulations & the Competitiveness of US Manufacturing, *Journal of Economic Literature* XXXIII(1), 132-163.

Jorgenson, D. W. and P. J. Wilcoxen (1993), Reducing US Carbon Emissions: An Econometric General Equilibrium Assessment, *Resource & Energy Economics* 15, 7-25.

Kendrick, J. W. (1961), *Productivity Trends in the United States*, NewYork. (National Bureau of Economic Research)

Krause, F., W. Bach and J. Kooney (1992), *Energy Policy in the Greenhouse* , London.

Krause, F., with E. Haites, R. Howarth and J. Koomey (1993), Cutting Carbon Emissions: Burden or Benefit? The Economics of Energy-Tax & Non-Price Policies, in *Energy Policy in the Greenhouse* 2; part 1, International Project for Sustainable Energy Paths, El Cerrito CA.

Kuznets, S. (1930), *Secular Movements in Production & Prices- Their Nature & Bearing on Cyclical Fluctuations*, Boston.

Kuznets, S. (1963), Quantitative Aspects of the Economic Growth of Nations, *Economic Development & Cultural Change* 11(2/II), 1-80.

Lovins, A. B. and L. H. Lovins (1981), *Energy/War: Breaking the Nuclear Link*, New York.

Lovins, A. B. and L. Hunter Lovins (1997), *Climate: Making Sense & Making Money*, Snowmass CO.

Machlup, F. (1962), *The Production & Distribution of Knowledge in the U. S.* , Princeton NJ.

Manne, A. S. and R. G. Richels (1992), *Buying Greenhouse Insurance*, Cambridge MA.

Meadows, D. H., D. L. Meadows, J. Randers and W. W. Behrens III (1972), *The Limits to Growth: A Report for the Club of Rome's Project on the Predicament of Mankind*, New York.

Mishan, E. J (1967), *The Costs of Economic Growth*, London.

Nordhaus, W. D. (1973), World Dynamics: Measurement without Data, *Economic Journal*, December, 1156-1183.

Nordhaus, W. D. (1992), *The "DICE" Model: Background & Structure of a Dynamic Integrated Climate Economy*, New Haven CT.

Nordhaus, W. D. (1993), Optimal Greenhouse-gas Reductions & Tax Policy in the DICE Model, *American Economic Review* 83, 313-317.

Nordhaus, W. D. (1994), *Managing the Global Commons: The Economics of Climate Change*, Cambridge MA.

Porter, M. (1991), America's Competitiveness Strategy, *Scientific American*.

Porter, M. E. and C. van der Linde (1995), Green and Competitive, *Harvard Business Review*, September-October, 120-134.

Schumpeter, J. A. (1912), *Theorie der Wirtschaftlichen Entwicklungen*, Leipzig.

Schumpeter, J. A. (1934), *Theory of Economic Development*, Cambridge MA.

Schurr, S. H. and B. C. Netschert (1960), *Energy in the American Economy, 1850-1975*, Baltimore.

Selden, T. and D. Song (1994), Environmental Quality & Development: Is There a Kuznets Curve for Air Pollution Emissions?, *Journal of Environmental Economics & Management* 27, 147-162.

Smith, H. (1969), The Cumulative Energy Requirements of Some Final Products of the Chemical Industry, *Transactions of the World Energy Conference* 18 (Section E).

Solow, R. M. (1974), The Economics of Resources or the Resources of Economics, *American Economic Review* 64.

Steinhart, C. E. and J. S. Steinhart (1974), Energy Use in the US Food System, *Science* 184, April 19, 312.

Stern, D. I. E., M. S. Common and E. B. Barbier (1996), Economic Growth & Environmental Degradation: The Environmental Kuznets Curve & Sustainable Development, *World Development* 24 (7), 1151-1160.

Stiglitz, J. (1974), Growth with Exhaustible Natural Resources. Efficient & Optimal Growth Paths, *Review of Economic Studies.*

Whalley, J. and R. Wigle (1991), The International Incidence of Carbon Taxes, in: Dornbush, R. and J. M. Poterba (eds.), *Global Warming: Economic Policy Responses,* 233-262.

Whalley, J. and R. Wigle (1993), Results of the OECD Comparative Modeling Project from the Whalley-Wigle Model, in: OECD, *The Costs of Cutting Carbon Emissions*, Paris.

World Bank (1992), *World Development Report*, New York.

OECD Programme on Technology and Sustainable Development

Candice Stevens

OECD, Working Group on Technology and Sustainable Development
2 rue André-Pascal, F-75775 Paris CEDEX 16
France

Keywords. *technology cooperation, innovation systems, technology policies, public/private partnerships.*

1 Introduction

Technology is one of the topics being treated in the OECD Horizontal Programme on Sustainable Development, which involves most Directorates of the OECD (e.g. Economics, Environment, Agriculture, Science and Technology), the International Energy Agency (IEA) and the Nuclear Energy Agency (NEA) in a three-year effort to develop policy recommendations for Member governments for achieving sustainable development goals. The underlying objective of the horizontal effort is to achieve policy coherence in addressing sustainable development issues. There will be a series of interdisciplinary workshops and conferences as well as analytical reports. A policy report will be delivered to the OECD Ministerial Council Meeting in 2001.

The following are among the technology areas to be studied as part of the OECD horizontal programme on sustainable development: 1) the concepts of eco-efficiency and resource efficiency and their relationship to sustainable development, including the development of indicators that can be applied to countries, sectors and technologies; 2) how innovation systems and the design of environmental policies and regulations can best provide the conditions and incentives needed to promote environment-related innovation; 3) specific technologies and their contributions to sustainable development, including nuclear power and biotechnology; 4) case studies of how enterprises incorporate environmental objectives into their management strategies, including investments in clean technologies; and 5) means for facilitating international collaboration in research and development on environmental problems and technologies. The following text reflects OECD views on the role of technology and innovation in sustainable development as contained in the 1999 Interim Report to OECD Ministers.

2 The Role of Technology

Technology is critical to securing sustainable development goals, in particular in de-linking economic growth, as measured by GDP, from environmental degradation and unsustainable resource use. Significant reductions in energy and materials intensity and polluting emissions will require technological advances in products and processes, as well as organisational and behavioural changes. These technologies can contribute to the improved performance and competitiveness of industry. Global environmental concerns – including loss of biodiversity, climate change, ozone layer depletion and desertification – will also require the best scientific and technical insights for assessment and solution.

But appropriate technological change is not automatic. In traditional growth theories, new technology is an *exogenous variable* appearing from outside at the right time and right price. In reality, market failures in terms of information deficiencies and inappropriate pricing risk suffocating rather than stimulating technologies capable of enhancing sustainable development. Producers and consumers may lack knowledge about the environmental impacts of different products and activities. The prices of many goods and services often do not reflect resource use or environmental externalities. As a result, new substitutes tend to be more expensive than conventional technologies. The costs of developing new, clean technologies and integrated approaches are often high and the timeframes long. Where the benefits are more public than private, the result is insufficient industrial investment and inadequate technological innovation. Providing proper price signals would increase investment in clean technologies.

Endogenous growth theories acknowledge that technological change occurs as a result of identifiable processes including corporate investment and public policies. Governments have an important role to play in getting the prices right and in providing a climate for environment-related innovation. The economic, legal and physical infrastructure is an important determinant of levels and patterns of research and development, institutional interactions, education and training, investment and finance, communications, etc. Market factors, such as consumption trends, and government regulation are important influences on the innovation climate. In general, the design of framework conditions for sustainable development should be set from the perspective of balancing increases in material welfare with long-term environmental and social challenges and the actions needed to address them.

Governments have a more direct role in developing and diffusing technology for sustainable development and in the financing of the basic research that underlies innovation. Technology development has become the focus of an increasing number of public research partnerships with the private sector. Governments may also act to ensure that existing valuable technologies are more widely used. For example, the technologies needed to meet the Kyoto targets for greenhouse gas reduction are mostly available today, but may require government action to see that they are much more widely deployed (Box 1). At the international level, governments need to work together to promote the use of clean technologies on a global scale as well as to address global-scale ecological issues.

3   Creating an Innovation Climate for Sustainable Development

3.1   Improving Framework Conditions

Technological breakthroughs for sustainable development can be promoted by incorporating environmental and social criteria into innovation systems. Enterprises are the motors of innovation and their performance depends on the incentives they receive from the economic and regulatory environment. For example, reforms may be needed in *intellectual property regimes* to stimulate innovation and technology diffusion; in *competition policies* to promote healthy rivalries and to facilitate collaborative research; in *education and training policies* to develop human capital on a continuing basis; in *financial and fiscal policies* to enhance the availability of capital to innovative firms; and in *communications policies* to increase the flow of information. Developing technology for sustainable development can be facilitated through an improved understanding of the innovation process.

New insights into the nature of the innovation process have changed perceptions about the appropriate role of governments. The specific instruments of science and technology policy are being adapted within a broader framework that stresses the importance of policy coherence and of inter-linkages within innovation systems. Policies to promote research collaboration, facilitate firm networking and clustering, encourage institutional ties, diffuse technology and increase personnel mobility are taking on new significance. However, the success of these approaches depends on the overall policy environment, encompassing both macroeconomic and structural conditions. Policy coherence also implies improved integration of environmental and technology policies and better co-ordination among environmental and technology agencies. Some recent approaches to environmental innovation have been based on the concept of *"environmental clusters"* (Box 2).

Box 1:   Energy technology and climate change

> The Kyoto Protocol has committed OECD governments that are Parties to Annex 1 to take actions to reduce greenhouse gas emissions. Technology will play an important role in achieving targeted emissions reductions and can facilitate reductions at lower cost. Important energy technologies include large-scale wind turbines, photovoltaics, nuclear power, natural-gas fired combined cycle turbines, and fuel cells for transportation and power generation.
>
> The adoption of these technologies has been slow. Long lead-times are needed for the refinement and commercialisation of new energy technologies. Investments in replacement stock with improved environmental performance are costly and only periodic for industry. Most energy technologies with superior environmental performance are more expensive than current techniques. Relatively low prices for fossil fuels make it difficult to justify replacing them from the cost perspective of an individual agent. Getting the prices right for energy inputs will help get the right technologies in place.
>
> The technologies needed to meet the Kyoto targets are mostly available "on the shelf" today, but governments may need to take action to ensure that they are broadly implemented. Demonstration and diffusion programmes can help make clean energy technologies more widely known and available. Verification and certification programmes can help more experimental energy technologies clear the last technical and regulatory hurdles. Research and development partnerships with industry can accelerate the emergence of new energy technologies. Government procurement programmes can steer technology development towards a sustainable path. Fiscal and financial incentives may speed-up the adoption of innovative energy techniques.
>
> Beyond Kyoto, ever more demanding targets for reduced emissions will be required. Current, even cutting-edge, technologies may not be able to meet such targets. In the longer-term, fundamental research on alternative energy technologies is needed to lower emissions. Changing practices of energy use and consumption will also help put the world on a lower-emissions path. Governments need to promote lifestyles and technologies that alter the relationship between the supply of energy services and environmental degradation. They need to work together to underwrite the research and development costs for technologies which are crucial for addressing global-scale ecological issues.
>
> *Source: Committee on Energy Research and Technology, International Energy Agency (IEA).*

3.2   Encouraging Market Pull

One of the most important conditions for innovation to support sustainable development is technology pull from consumers and markets. It is often not a lack of research, but a lack of demand that limits technological progress as well as a lack of correct pricing. Industry will not have an incentive to produce greener products or to invest in cleaner production processes in the absence of market rewards. Making the leap to less wasteful consumption in the longer-term will require changes in existing styles of working and living and from the highly-resource intensive habits that now predominate. Research indicates that awareness of environmental issues is on the increase among consumers, but this has not yet translated into far-reaching changes in everyday buying and living patterns. Although environmental investments are starting to be rewarded in the marketplace, public policies should seek to accelerate these trends and strengthen market pull.

Box 2:   Fostering environmental clusters

Innovation mostly occurs within clusters of inter-related firms. Firms generally do not innovate alone. Rather they interact with similar companies, specialised suppliers, service providers, firms in related industries, and associated institutions such as universities and research institutes. Such clusters revolve around knowledge spillovers, pooled labour markets and exchanges of products and technology. As seen in Silicon Valley, they are usually found at the juncture of an entrepreneurial business climate, readily available risk capital and a business-friendly academic infrastructure. Clusters might also be based on geographic or natural resource advantages. Innovative clusters are emerging as drivers of growth and employment and are determining the pace and direction of development for entire regions, industries and sometimes countries. Governments can influence the development of clusters. Regional and local policies and development programmes can play a nurturing role. National governments must establish the appropriate frameworks in terms of competition, education, and financial and other policies. Newer approaches to stimulating cluster creation are also being tried by OECD governments, ranging from focused R&D schemes and competitions for funding to public procurement and investment incentives.

Finland launched an *Environmental Cluster Research Programme* in 1997 to promote both environmental entrepreneurship and sustainable development. It targets the emerging environmental goods and services industry, one of the country's fastest growing sectors. The government provides seed funding for research on new environmental technologies to be carried out by consortia of producers and suppliers, universities and institutes. Collaborative projects enhance networking among researchers and users and facilitate innovation. Improving eco-efficiency through the application of life-cycle techniques in agriculture, forestry, basic metals and water management is the initial subject for research. The Ministry of the Environment coordinates the programme together with the Ministry of Trade and Industry, the Technology Development Centre (TEKES) and the Academy of Finland.

Source: OECD Committee for Scientific and Technological Policy, National Innovation Systems project.

Governments are taking initiatives to shift consumer behaviour towards modes that are more supportive of the environment. They can implement mandatory and voluntary product standards to promote energy and water efficiency. They can use taxes to influence consumption away from harmful goods, such as certain batteries or fuels, and encourage the development of substitutes. They can support ecolabelling schemes to inform consumers on the environmental characteristics of products and processes and broaden their choices. They can encourage reporting by enterprises on emissions and the environmental implications of their activities as well as increase public access to these registries. They can use green government procurement and encourage green investment instruments to further sustainability priorities. Mostly, governments can overcome information deficiencies by increasing consumer knowledge of the ecological impacts of their behaviour and product choices and of the potential benefits of alternative consumption patterns. However, resolving many of the environmental challenges posed by current market trends, such as growing demand for more mobility and transport, may require more far-reaching changes in consumption behaviour. It will also depend on broader societal participation and support, as well as on government cooperation with industry, the media, schools and other influential institutions and groups.

Public resistance to certain technologies can also be a barrier to use. New technologies can lead to pressures on natural resources and health and safety hazards and raise difficult ethical considerations for society. There are major trust implications for technology acceptance, which may result in certain technology options being rejected or inadequately developed. For example, both nuclear energy and biotechnology may offer valuable technical solutions to enhance sustainable development. A challenge is to increase our knowledge and public understanding of the social costs and benefits of alternative technologies, which involves agreeing on approaches for risk management. Public perceptions and understanding of different technologies can be enhanced by broader involvement of society in setting research agendas and standards of use and oversight. This will help stimulate technology development that responds to the broader needs and preferences of society.

3.3   Formulating Environmental Policies

Environmental innovation takes place mostly in industry, where environmental policies and regulations are an important influence. The need to comply with environmental regulations has led industry to develop and adopt various pollution control techniques and equipment. However, traditional forms of environmental regulation have not generally led to radical technological change, although they have contributed to significant pollution abatement over the years. In many cases, command and control approaches have been a predictable stimulus to small, incremental improvements along established pathways, often in the form of end-of-pipe technologies. More dynamic environmental policies that promote prevention rather than abatement, and the development of clean technologies and integrated approaches – including economic instruments – are needed.

Environmental policy instruments differ in their effects on innovation. *Product standards* tend to prompt incremental innovation or modifications at the margin. *Product bans* can stimulate radical innovation in the form of replacements but entail disruptions and costs. *Performance standards* are technically flexible while *technology specifications* tend to stifle innovation. *Economic instruments*, such as pollution charges and tradable permits, have more dynamic potential to stimulate innovation but have not always been set at sufficiently high levels in the case of the former or used extensively in the case of the latter. Nor have *voluntary agreements* brought much pressure for technological change thus far.

In general, economic instruments should be used more frequently as substitutes for and complements to traditional forms of regulation. Changes in implementation as well as new approaches could also substantially improve the regulatory framework for environmental innovation. The ways regulations are implemented and enforced have a strong influence on industry programmes to develop technologies to comply with new standards. Systems for early warning and timed introduction of new policies can help reduce regulatory uncertainty for industry. Expedited government review procedures and verification and certification schemes can speed market introduction of new technologies. Shifting away from technology specifications towards end results can increase the flexibility for industry in meeting compliance. Also valuable are new types of voluntary agreements and approaches such as extended producer responsibility, disclosure requirements and environmental management systems, which can encourage changes in resource inputs and the complete redesign of products and processes.

4 Developing and Diffusing Environmental Technologies

4.1 Conducting Research and Development

Shrinking research budgets and shorter research timeframes in industry and government raise concern about the long-term innovation needed for sustainable development. Governments must assure a continuing basic research and development (R&D) effort on broad enabling technologies to support sustainable development goals. However, R&D related to the environment is only a small share of public research portfolios in OECD countries: about 2 per cent of R&D budgets in the case of research directly on the environment, as narrowly defined, and an estimated 5 per cent when environment-related research on other objectives is added, such as that on energy, agriculture and the atmosphere. It is true that research in many technology fields – such as biotechnology and information technology – can lead to beneficial environmental spillovers. In the case of information technology, new developments can help organisations monitor different aspects of their environmental performance at reduced cost. But overall, given the pressing nature of many ecological concerns, government expenditures on research that could be environmentally beneficial seem to be very low by most measures and may thus warrant review.

From the perspective of concepts such as *eco-efficiency* and *resource efficiency*, environmental technologies are those which minimise the resource and energy intensity of goods and services and polluting emissions. They are technologies that enhance society's overall management of its resources. Technology foresight exercises have been one means of identifying useful technologies and important areas for research, including in the environmental realm. Although not intended to pick "winners", technology foresight helps enterprises and countries identify useful areas for research and development. And the foresight process is valuable in forging linkages between society and research and generating interactive processes to match technology development to social needs and market pull. Recent foresight studies have underscored the seriousness of ecological challenges and the importance of environment-related research. They have highlighted a number of key technologies for sustainable development, e.g. biotechnology, information technology and fuel cells, as well as specific applications, e.g. clean cars (Box 3).

4.2 Forming Public/Private Partnerships

While new technologies are primarily developed and brought into use as a result of business decisions, governments also play a role in developing technology and are increasingly conducting applied research in partnership with industry. Such public/private partnerships are a means for doing more with less, although there may be risks of misdirecting resources and capture by private interests. They can leverage private investments in innovation and direct it towards critical research needs. They can enhance linkages among enterprises, and between enterprises, universities and public research institutions, and foster interactions that are crucial to the innovation process. In the environmental realm, partnerships are valuable because they reduce obstacles to the development and diffusion of clean technologies. Many OECD governments are initiating partnerships to develop technologies that can contribute to both sustainable development and industrial competitiveness (Box 4). Further evaluation is needed on the cost-effectiveness of such partnerships and on their influence on longer-term technology development and research-related linkages.

Box 3:   Technologies for sustainable development

Clean car technologies. Future cars could feature alternative batteries, lightweight materials, direct injection engines, fuel cells and/or enhanced recyclability – all leading to lower fuel consumption and emissions.

Photovoltaics. Buildings, automobiles and decentralised power units using photovoltaics or light-based energy are envisioned .

Biotechnology. Biotechnology holds vast potential for sustainable development. Bioprocesses can reduce resource inputs, pollutants and wastes from manufacturing. Agro-genetics can limit adverse impacts from pesticides and other chemicals in agriculture as well as enhance food security.

Advanced sensors. Sensors will be used to monitor air and water quality as well as global changes in the climate, stratospheric ozone layer, marine environment and varied ecosystems. Global information systems can aid precision farming, saving resources while maximising output.

New materials. Advanced materials technologies will facilitate recycling of consumer goods and of manufacturing inputs and further the implementation of life-cycle concepts.

Smart water treatment. New membrane technologies and biological treatments will be able to purify wastewater by removing organic compounds and could lead to community or home-based water treatment units.

Smart waste treatment. Approaches to reducing municipal waste, cleaning-up hazardous waste and treating nuclear waste will be based on new enzymes, catalysts and other advanced techniques such as transmutation.

Renewable energy. Improved power storage technology and combined conversion systems will increase the use of electricity from renewable sources such as solar power, wind power and biomass.

Source: OECD Workshop on Technology Foresight for Sustainable Development, December 1998.

4.3   Diffusing Technology and Know-How

As already mentioned, cleaner technology exists that is not yet in widespread use because of its price, the lack of information on the part of firms or the need to adapt it to users. Diffusion of technology and know-how is essential to enhancing participation in the sustainable development process. To this end, OECD governments are implementing schemes to disseminate information about clean technologies and to promote enhanced use of these techniques (Box 5), although such programmes must be carefully designed and evaluated to ensure cost-effectiveness and avoid unfair subsidisation. Encouraging information flows is at the core of all diffusion programmes and this is increasingly being done through electronic networks such as the Internet. Also prominent are demonstration programmes that illustrate the technical feasibility and benefits of new environmental technologies, and benchmarking schemes that help firms compare their environmental performance to that of similar enterprises. Technical assistance programmes provide more hands-on advice in diagnosing environmental problems and recommending responses. Governments are also mounting "soft" diffusion activities focusing on workforce training and encouraging managerial and organisational changes within firms to improve their ability to assess and adapt clean technologies.

Box 4:   Examples of environmental technology partnerships

Canada — Technology Partnerships Canada. Environmental technology is one of the three categories supported by this programme which provides repayable contributions for research on technologies for air pollution control; water and wastewater treatment; clean cars/transportation systems; climate change; and recycling.

Germany — Research for the Environment. A research programme intended to "support scientific initiatives aimed at developing, together with partners from industry, new environmental technologies and/or new concepts of environmental engineering and use".

Japan — Research Institute of Innovative Technology for the Earth (RITE). RITE has created a partnership scheme to develop technologies for reducing greenhouse gas emissions, using biotechnology in production processes, developing substitutes to ozone-depleting substances, and monitoring techniques for air, water and soil pollution.

United Kingdom — Foresight Vehicle Programme. A LINK scheme aiming to develop a clean, efficient, lightweight, telematic, intelligent, lean vehicle which will satisfy stringent environmental requirements while meeting mass market expectations for safety, performance, cost and desirability.

United States — Industries of the Future Initiative. A collaborative effort between the Department of Energy and seven energy-intensive industries (steel, aluminium, metal-casting, glass, chemicals, petroleum refining and forest products) to develop competitive technologies which fully integrate energy and environmental considerations.

Source: OECD (1999). Technology Policies for the Environment.

Fiscal incentives may also be used for encouraging the take-up of environmental technologies. The scope for diffusing technology is often limited by low capital stock turnover rates, averaging 10 to 15 years for many manufacturing processes. Businesses generally bring new technologies into play only when the existing capital equipment is replaced. To speed up this cycle, some countries are giving accelerated depreciation allowances or investment tax credits targeted to environmental investments. For example, Finland offers accelerated depreciation for investments in air and water pollution control. Canada allows certain energy conservation and renewable energy equipment to be written off at a 30 per cent declining rate. The Netherlands offers accelerated depreciation on expenditures that improve energy efficiency and for pollution prevention equipment. Regional governments are also experimenting with environmental tax credits. For example, Quebec offers a 20 per cent tax credit on investments in clean technology. In the United States, pollution control technology gets tax relief in Illinois, recycling equipment investments are eligible for tax deductions in Virginia, and Oregon has tax credits directed at specific pollution prevention technologies. However, such programmes are still too limited and recent to evaluate their effectiveness in stimulating such investments and in determining their optimal design so that they have real value-added benefits.

Box 5:   Examples of environmental technology diffusion schemes

---

Australia — Cleaner Production Demonstration Project. This project aims to promote implementation of cleaner production technologies and processes through hands-on demonstration of innovative techniques.

France — Agence de l'Environnement et de la Maîtrise de l'Énergie (ADEME). A specialised agency which assists enterprises to reduce usage of energy and raw materials, to limit waste production and maximise recovery and re-use of waste, to reduce noise pollution and to prevent and/or treat soil pollution.

Ireland — Clean Technology Centre. An independent, non-profit corporation supported by a combination of public and private sources to advise and assist industry and public authorities on the adoption of waste minimisation techniques, clean technologies and cleaner production methods.

Netherlands — Cleaner Production Programme. A programme to disseminate information and stimulate the utilisation of clean technology in smaller firms, focusing on foods, wood and furniture, printing, chemicals, rubber and plastics, building materials, metal products and motor vehicle sectors.

Norway — GRIP Centre for Sustainable Production and Consumption. A GRIP (Green Management in Practice) centre to stimulate adoption of innovative environmental management practices in the public and private sectors, particularly smaller firms, through information dissemination and demonstration.

United Kingdom — Environmental Technology Best Practice Programme. A scheme focusing on waste minimisation and the use of cleaner technologies through the dissemination of "good practice" guides in the foundry, textiles, paper and board, volatile organic compounds, glass, food and drink, chemicals, printing, metals finishing, ceramics, and plastics and packaging industries.

Source: OECD (1999). Technology Policies for the Environment.

---

5   Addressing International Issues

5.1   Assisting Developing Countries

Sustainable development depends on the application of clean technologies on a broad scale by non-OECD as well as OECD countries. A special challenge is to enable developing countries to take full advantage of energy-efficient and cleaner production options and to adapt them to their needs. The main constraints in many of these countries relate to a lack of human, institutional, technical, managerial and financial capacities needed to manage technological change. Support for the dissemination of technological know-how, therefore, must concentrate first on capacity development to underpin the long-term application of new technologies. Since the private sector is the largest source of finance for cleaner production and a major actor in technology innovation, diffusion and application, policy efforts should also focus on providing the private sector with an open, competitive and sound policy environment.

In this context, development co-operation can act as a catalyst to foster public and private actions at the policy, sectoral and firm levels. While developing countries must take a leadership role, donors can assist in vital areas like capacity building and the formulation of policy frameworks conducive to increasing demand for cleaner technologies. This includes designing market incentives such as removal of inappropriate subsidies and the introduction of user fees and fiscal incentives and ensuring the necessary institutional mechanisms for their implementation. Official Development Assistance (ODA) in these areas aims to complement and leverage investments in cleaner technologies which depend primarily on domestic resource mobilisation and access to foreign direct investment. Special schemes have also been set up to assist developing countries in addressing specific environmental concerns, including the Global Environmental Facility (GEF), the Multilateral Fund for the Implementation of the Montreal Protocol, the Clean Development Mechanism established under the Kyoto Protocol, and the UNIDO/UNEP National Cleaner Production Centres Programme.

5.2   Enhancing International Technology Co-Operation

Some problems are so global in nature that only concerted international action can resolve them. Addressing issues such as climate change, ozone layer depletion, desertification and biodiversity will require joint action by countries to develop and disseminate innovative technology. Large-scale and long-term, these issues require the insights of many disciplines and the efforts of many countries to be understood and addressed. Individual researchers and countries cannot solve these problems on their own. The world's most advanced science and technology resources are concentrated in the OECD countries and much more co-operation could occur in a wide variety of areas of research and development. Research co-operation and technical collaboration is crucial for attaining the most critical sustainable development goals, such as addressing climate change (Box 6).

Box 6:   Climate Technology Initiative

Through the Climate Technology Initiative (CTI), countries are working together to support the objectives of the Framework Convention on Climate Change through joint science and technology programmes. The CTI provides a framework for countries to collaborate to accelerate the contribution of technology to addressing the problem of global climate change. The wider adoption of existing climate-friendly technologies and the development and deployment of new and innovative technologies are an important part of the climate response. The CTI was launched at the First Conference of the Parties (COP1) in Berlin, Germany in 1995 by 23 IEA/OECD countries and the European Commission. It has evolved to include regional workshops and country-specific consultations on the best climate-friendly technology options .

In addition to sharing the experience and benefits of national climate technology research and programmes, the CTI promotes and sponsors joint research and development on climate-friendly technologies. Four multilateral research projects were launched at COP3 to investigate ocean sequestration of carbon dioxide, geological sequestration of carbon dioxide from fossil fuels, combustion in recycled CO_2/O_2 mixtures, and very large-scale photovoltaic power generation systems utilising desert areas. Collaborative research proposals are also being developed on: hydrogen production from fossil fuels; biological hydrogen production; chemical CO_2 fixation and utilisation; different pathways for methanol production; transportation fuels from biomass; CO_2 as a chemicals industry feedstock; and integrated supply of heat and CO_2 to the horticultural industry.

Source: International Energy Agency

References

International Energy Agency (1998), *Electric Technologies: Bridge to the 21ˢᵗ Century and a Sustainable Future*.

Nuclear Energy Agency (1998), *Nuclear Power and Climate Change*.

OECD (1994), *IEA/OECD Scoping Study on Energy and Environmental Technologies to Respond to Global Climate Change Concerns*.

OECD (1997), *OECD Observer Special Edition on Sustainable Development*.

OECD (1998), *Biotechnology for Clean Industrial Products and Processes: Towards Industrial Sustainability*.

OECD (1998), *Eco-Efficiency*.

OECD (1999, forthcoming), *Interim Report on the Horizontal Programme on Sustainable Development*.

OECD (1999, forthcoming), *Technology Policies for the Environment*.

How Should We Study the Relationship between Environmental Regulation and Innovation?

René Kemp

Maastricht Research Institute on Innovation and Technology (MERIT) of Maastricht University
P.O. Box 616, NL-6200 MD Maastricht
Netherlands

Keith Smith

STEP Group (Group for studies in technology, innovation and economic policy)
Storgaten 1, N-0155 Oslo
Norway

Gerhard Becher

PROGNOS, Basel
Switzerland

Keywords. production chain, systems approach, filière, environmental innnovation.

1   Introduction

This paper offers a conceptual framework for understanding the relationship between environmental regulation and innovation. It seeks to widen the concepts of innovation which are used in environment-oriented studies, while at the same time challenging the idea that regulation is either a straightforward facilitator or inhibitor of innovation. With respect to innovation, we present a 'systems' framework, one which emphasises the collective and interactive character of innovation, as an appropriate entry point for analysing the complex institutional, social and networking aspects of the impacts of regulation. With respect to regulation, we seek to challenge the stimulus-response model of the impacts of regulation on innovation. We contest the view that regulation either stops or starts innovation in any simple way. Rather, we take the view that regulation shapes or modulates innovation across networks of firms, and across groups of related industries. A productive way to think about the shaping of innovation is that firms innovate as a method of removing constraints. These may be constraints on the size or geographical location of the market they face, or constraints in labour supply, or finance, and so on. A significant constraint is the regulatory environment, which does not necessarily hinder innovation, but rather says that if firms are to innovate then they must do so with respect to certain performance parameters.

2   Characteristics of Innovation

There is a huge literature on innovation. Within it there are two types of approaches: those which take as their starting point the individual innovator, and those which emphasize the economic, institutional and social system within which innovation occurs. In the first type of approach there is often a tacit assumption that firms innovate mainly on the basis of technological opportunity – that is, that the rate of innovation is governed by the scope of available technological opportunity, and that the direction of innovation is explained by whatever it is (often unexplained) which generates these opportunities. From this perspective, regulation is something which limits the ability to exploit the available technological opportunities, and is therefore something whose effects are mainly to slow down innovation. This of course leaves a major gap in our understanding, since from a regulatory point of view it is determinants rather than rates of innovation which are at stake.

'Systems' approaches to innovation are founded on one of the most persistent themes in modern innovation studies, namely the idea that innovation by firms cannot be understood purely in terms of independent decision-making at the level of the firm. Rather, innovation involves complex interactions between a firm and its environment, with the environment being seen on two different levels. On one level there are interactions between firms – between a firm and its network of customers and suppliers, particularly where this involves sustained interaction between users and producers of technology. Here the argument is that inter-firm linkages are far more than arms-length market relationships – rather, they often involve sustained quasi-cooperative relationships which shape learning and technology creation. The second level is wider, involving broader factors shaping the behaviour of firms: the social and perhaps cultural context, the institutional and organizational framework, infrastructures, the processes which create and distribute scientific knowledge, and so on. These environmental conditions are often seen as specific to regional or national contexts, but they are also dynamic: their forms of operation change with political conditions, changing technological opportunities, economic integration processes and so on. The basic argument of systems theories is that system conditions have a decisive impact on the extent to which firms can make innovation decisions, and on the modes of innovation which are undertaken: "The coordination of an innovative endeavour almost always requires a network of independent organizations with different competencies. The exception – internal networks of multi-unit diversified firms – confirms the rule. Networking not only has become but has always been a requirement for innovation."(DeBresson, 1999).

Within this systems framework, innovation is seen as a collective, explorative activity which is distributed across many agents. It requires specific competences (both technological and organisational, including the ability to foster linkages with external knowledge holders), and is guided by engineering and managerial notions (judgement) of what is worthwhile to do technologically and economically. Innovation is a variegated, multi-actor process which occurs in networks: in economic networks of suppliers and customers but also across knowledge networks and policy networks. It involves both competition and collaboration, and games (between companies in product markets and between companies and regulators in policy arenas and policy implementation networks). The economic and systems aspects of innovation furthermore mean that innovation is shaped by frame conditions.

This framework includes:

- the overall economic situation and development, such as the state of the economy, price stability, the development of exchange rates or the situation in the financial and labour markets,

- the availability of an efficient and complete tangible and intangible infrastructure,

- regulations contained in collective agreements and labour law,

- political determinants such as command and control policy, economic policy, financial policy or the vast sphere of regulations, for instance in the area of consumer protection, insurance, in banking and the transport sector, in the energy industry or in the field of social regulations,

- influences emanating from society and impacting the economic players, like social stability, a society's openness for technological innovations and for economic growth in general, the willingness to put up with negative environmental impacts, etc.

What the above suggests is that we are not simply concerned with individual firms, or individual isolated decision-making. Innovation is a multi-faceted phenomenon, characterised above all by complexity in interactions between people and institutions. On one level it involves new thinking, new ideas and solutions to problems, and so it can be seen in terms of creativity and intellectual effort. On another, it involves marshalling financial and material resources, often on a large scale, and in conditions on serious uncertainty. But neither of these dimensions of innovation can realistically be seen in terms of purely individual effort, either by people or by organizations. Rather, innovation is a *distributed* process – its inputs in terms of knowledge and resources are distributed among many participants and contributors, linked to each other in networks of relationships. Moreover it is a dynamic process, one which involves learning and change within the social and economic spheres.

3   The Production Chain (Filière)

Can we translate these insights into something which is more operational with respect to regulation? One approach might be as follows; it is represented schematically in the following diagram (see Figure 1). In thinking about the impact of regulation on a 'subject industry' (meaning an industry with which we are primarily concerned), attention in the past has focussed either on the production process of the industry, or on the technical characteristics of its end product. Clearly, either can be affected by some specific regulatory initiative. But we must bear in mind that there are also a range of inputs deriving from other firms across other industries; this input range may be very extensive. At the same time, the output of the subject industry may be sold to a wide range of other industries, and/or to final consumers; in this case, the subject industry must respond to demand conditions which affect product characteristics, social acceptability, cost limits, and so on. Most of these linkages are not 'arms-length' market relationships, but rather are persistent co-operative relationships. Either way, the knowledge required for producing the output of the subject industry is distributed across many input sectors, and may be shaped by many user sectors. This implies two things. Firstly, the impulses to innovation may stem from any point in this overall system of demand and supply. Second, the innovative response to regulatory change may be something which must or should occur in an industrial sector possibly far removed from the 'subject industry'.

From an empirical point of view the problem is to gain some descriptive overview of the overall process. From a conceptual point of view, Figure 1 corresponds to sectors of production and use in an input-output table, but it is unlikely that input-output data will be available at appropriate levels of aggregation for the study of environmental regulation impacts. So what is necessary is some more descriptive method of looking at the direct and indirect knowledge inputs to production, and the research activities and opportunities for achieving environmental improvements at different points of the production chain.

The approach outlined here is similar to that of Robert Boyer and his colleagues. This is a systems approach based on the concept of 'filière'. A filière is made up by a specific set of infrastructures, technologies, institutions, practices and actors.

Behind the notion of a filière is the idea that technologies are best understood not as individual techniques, but as integrated systems. This view of the technology of a firm implies strong interdependence, because relevant technological knowledges are located in different firms, with interactions between firms in terms of technological capability. That is, the capabilities of any individual firm are shaped in part by its historical experience and its dynamic development of competence, but also by accompanying developments in related firms. The development of specialisation, accompanied by inter- and intra-industry flows of technology, implies that we should think of the technological structure of an economy not as an agglomeration of independent micro-level decisions, but as an integrated system shaped partly by the input-output relations between firms, and partly by intra-firm specialisation of tasks.

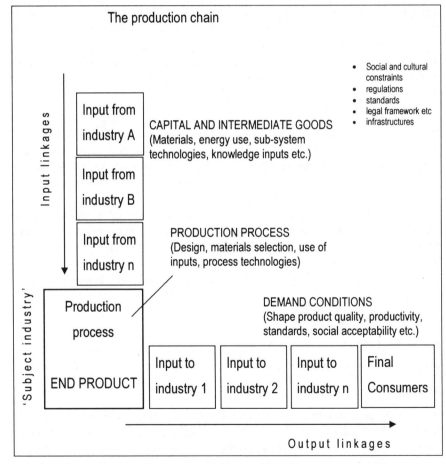

Figure 1:   The production chain

It is clear that a full description of these linkages would be a very major task. But it is important that, at least in general terms, it is important to describe the structure of the production and use links for the sector concerned. The production chain approach helps to see the inter-industry and wider systems aspects of achieving environmental benefits. Such aspects differ per type of environmental technology, for products and for integral process change. Pollution control technologies and clean-up technologies are usually provided by EGS firms who have specialised knowledge about pollution and how it may be handled. Relationships which such companies may exist, which may explain why a regulated company chooses for pollution control instead of prevention. Prevention requires environmental management and auditing systems that may or may not be absent, depending on whether the company or a sector attest a great importance to environmental issues. Waste management of course depends on the waste management infrastructure and frame conditions that influence the costs of waste: requirements to treat the waste before disposal, restriction on the transport of waste, availability of land fill locations, etc. Waste business involves a chain of its own consisting of such activities as the collection, transport, separation, treatment, recycling and controlled disposal. There is also the use of environment-friendly materials manufactured material suppliers that depends on waste policies and the regulations that govern it.

Much of the literature on environmental management emphasises the need for firms to adopt an environmental consciousness or 'ethos'. But environmental benefits may be achieved without the express aim of avoiding or reducing environmental harm. Environmental gains may be a side-effect of other goals such as the goal to reduce energy costs or the goal of enhanced product quality. An example is the use of light-weight materials in products and energy-efficient process technologies. In the organisational literature on environmental technology the focus is on innovations that are developed/adopted for environmental protection reasons. A taxonomy of environmental-relevant innovation which does not assume that the innovation is developed or adopted for environmental reasons per se is by Howes et al., 1997 in their book *Clean and Competitive?*, which draws a distinction between

- integral process change,

- product design,

- cost-saving investment,

- compliance technology.

The advantage of this distinction is that it makes the connection between environmental technologies and companies' decision-making structures. This is important because in a production organisation there is a technology-related hierarchy of decisions that has implications for the nature and timing of environmental technology choices. Although environmental improvements may be made across the entire product-production system of a company, the economic opportunities and responsibilities for changing technological parameters differ greatly. Integral process change and product design are typically the subject of strategic business considerations because they are of prime importance to the economic sustainability of the company. The window of opportunity for making integral process change is limited, it is very much restricted to those moments of new investment (the replacement of old plant or the investment in new production capacity), and even then it is difficult to factor in environmental considerations.

The same is true for product design where many of the design parameters are already been set, especially for standardised products; to change these creates considerable costs and potential risks to the company they would unkindly accept. Environmentally improved products must meet important user requirements. It is difficult to sell a product on the basis of environmental advantages alone. The success of the body shop is misleading because the products are bought for health reasons rather than environmental reasons. The market for cosmetics with natural ingredients in which the body shop is so successful is still a small one, as is the market for biological food products (1 per cent in the Netherlands). Environmental products often suffer from scale disadvantages and a poor distribution system. Again this shows the importance of the filière for innovation. Environmental innovation requires changes across the filière. Such changes are difficult to manage. They require adaptation at different levels. It is only the bigger companies such as the electronics company Philips and paints manufacturers who are active in environmental chain management by putting environmental demands on their suppliers and educating customers.

Innovation counts are not a good way of capturing the innovation effects of regulation. Innovation is not a homogenous thing. One should look at the characteristics of innovation output and the determinants of innovation, how these are affected in different ways by regulation. Regulations may have 'ripple' effects across an entire chain; important effects may be occurring at places outside the subject sector. Regulation may also lead to the adoption of solutions that are suboptimal from a wider systems perspective, such as the adoption of end-of-pipe solutions or favour incremental change at the expense of more radical change. This things are easily missed in a study which focuses on the firm as the unit of innovation, or when asking questions about the innovation effects of regulations in a non-qualified way.

To summarise, there are different options for achieving environmental benefits, each with their own costs and benefits for the adopting unit and society. Environmental innovation may be developed with or without the express aim of avoiding or reducing environmental harm. The incentive system for the options differs along the filière and between different types of environmental innovation. How regulations affect the incentive systems for different types of innovation will be discussed below.

Environmental innovation may be analysed at different levels:

1. the level of R&D, focussing on the design rules and projects being undertaking,

2. the level of invention, being proto-innovations,

3. the level of products, processes and systems,

4. the level of organisational arrangements and practices,

5. the level of innovation networks,

6. the level of a filière,

7. the level of technology systems like the energy system or chlorine-based chemistry.

Attention should be given at all levels, as there may be important linkages which are easily missed or under-appreciated in a study of the innovation effects of regulation. Asking companies about the effects of regulation or what regulation are most important for innovation is not a good way of analysing innovation effects. Important ripple effects of regulation may occur within a chain, both upstream and downstream a subject sector. A company may perceive their own waste management activities as voluntary or driven by normal economic motivations, and by doing so it may fail to see that the economics of waste management are heavily influenced by the regulations that govern the waste sector at the end of the production chain (emission norms of incinerators, economic regulations towards waste management). Innovation has many dimensions and aspects. One shouldn't be focussing too much on particular innovation outputs. It is the *determinants* of innovation rather than innovation outputs that should be analysed – how these are affected by regulation.

In innovation impact studies of environmental regulation the focus is on the regulated sector: how this sector has responded technologically to regulatory demand for reduced emissions from manufacturing processes and for environment-friendlier products.

Little attention has been paid to the range of innovation possibilities across the chain, the processes by which certain technology options became adopted at the expense of others (how regulation shaped those choices), and how the regulations were based on the technology options available and the strategic actions of technology holders and regulated industry. To know more about these issues attention should be given to the way in which the innovation and policy are linked. This requires a change in perspective and research method, one that puts a greater focus on innovation patterns (supplier-dependent, R&D-based) and the regulatory context with its institutions and specific ways of policy making and implementation.

Such a study would pay attention to:

1. The technological basis of the regulated sector: the process technologies in use, their age, possibilities for retrofitting, as an important contextual factor,

2. The solutions available for dealing with an environmental problems at different points of the production chain: the costs (and the distribution of these costs), environmental effects/benefits, impact on product quality,

3. The problem definitions and preferences of policy actors for particular solutions,

4. The research activities by the regulated sector and outside suppliers and the extent to which regulators rely on such research,

5. The implementation games (bargaining processes) over permit conditions that occur within a policy community. In particular, the influence of industry as an important information holder on the conditions of compliance.

4 Regulation as Modulator of Innovation

At a general level, environmental innovation is very much governed by the same factors as normal innovation. It requires in-house technological knowledge, an ability to absorb external knowledge on the part of an innovating company, and the willingness of key individuals within an organisation (or unit within the organisation) to embark on and manage a technological project.

For social innovation regulation is often regarded as the mother of invention (Ruttenberg, quoted in Ashford et al., 1985: 434). For normal innovation it is just the opposite. For normal innovation regulation is often viewed as an inhibitor, preventing companies to exploit technologically opportunities. Such views are too simple. What is controlled and stimulated inhibited are certain innovation features, not innovation as such. Innovation should not be viewed as something homogeneous. For example the overwhelming influence of regulation on information technology and biotechnology is not the inhibiting of certain innovations but the application of IT and biotechnology for environmental protection purposes, such as the use of environmental sensors in waste streams and waste-water treatment plants. Regulation acts as a filter and focussing device for technical change by setting certain performance standards and focussing the attention of companies on socially/environmentally desirable aspects. Environmental regulation is the institutionalised response to public demand for environmental protection. It translates the pressures into specific policies that lay down specific requirements that give guidance to polluters and suppliers of environmental technologies in terms of what is actually required. Regulations thus have an informative content, besides a normative content. Regulation acts as a *modulator* of technical change, changing directions and modes of innovation rather than just stopping or starting it. Of course, regulations may have a general inhibiting effect on innovation. Long and costly new substance approval procedures may have this effect, by changing the payoffs of innovation unfavourable.

The stimulus-response model is too simple. For one thing it assumes that social innovation starts with regulation which is most often not the case. Regulation is not the be-all and end-all of social innovation. The knowledge for such innovations is usually there, regulations may provide the leverage or extra stimulus for the exploitation. Regulation is but one of many stimuli. It may in fact not be needed for social innovation. In the case of an environmentally harmful product there will always will be pressures to reduce the harm. Apart from regulatory demands, social innovations must also meet other types of demand: they should be expendable, it should be possible to fit them into existing processes, and in the case of products, they should meet user requirements in terms of performance characteristics. Water saving shower heads should be comfortable and environmentally improved detergents should have good washing performance. User benefits and social performance benefits must be *co-optimised*. It is this co-optimisation that creates a problem for innovators and for environmental regulators. For example, it proved to be very difficult to develop phosphate free detergents with equal washing power as the phosphate-based. Global efforts to find a substitute for phosphates in detergents amounted to 500 million DM until 1973 (figure is by a representative of Henkel, reported in Hartje, 1994). What this shows is that innovations can not be elicited by legal fiat (Heaton), moulded in a pre-defined, socially desirable shape; there are technical, economic and organisational limits to what may be achieved. Regulations are not defined independently of what is technologically possible and economically affordable but based on techno-economic assessments; environmental permits often rely on the concept of Best Available Technology or Best Practicable Means that are specified in BAT lists or guidance notes. There is an interplay between innovation and regulation; the stimulus response model fails to appreciate this. (In fact, innovation, in the sense of a available technological solution to a problem, may pave the way and thus be the stimulus for regulation, which suggests that the causality goes either way.)

There exists a small literature on the impact of actual environmental regulations on compliance innovation and clean technology. This literature consists of the work of Ashford and Heaton in the 1980s in the US, Kemp, 1997 and a number of German studies (Hartje, 1985; Hemmelskamp, 1996 and 1997). The focus of these studies is on technical innovation. What these studies show is that the technology responses range from the diffusion of existing technology, incremental changes in processes, product reformulation to product substitution and the development of new processes. The most common responses to regulation are incremental innovations in processes and products and diffusion of existing technology (in the form of end-of-pipe solutions and non-innovative substitutions of existing substances).

Often the new technologies are developed by firms outside the regulated industry, which means that in the past industry was reliant upon suppliers, capital good suppliers and environmental technology suppliers. (This is changing with the growing attention in environmental policy and industry to prevention and product change). The studies also show, unsurprisingly, that the stringency of the regulation is an important determinant of the degree of innovation with stringent regulations such as product bans being necessary for radical technology responses. Technology-forcing standards appear to be a necessary condition for bringing about innovative compliance responses. The studies further show that long before the regulations are promulgated there is a search process for solutions to the problem, both by the regulated industry (mostly for defensive reasons), their suppliers and outsiders. This happened in the case of PCBs and CFCs where firms both in and outside the chemical industry were looking for substitutes 10 year before the use of PCBs and CFCs was banned (Ashford, et al., 1985). Of course, the certainty that their product or activity would be subject to regulations was an important factor.

As to the nature (incremental or radical, product or process related) and the source of technological solutions an internal OECD report found that:

- High volume, mature sectors were resistant to change, although very amenable to environmental monitoring and process controls that improved efficiency. This fits with the Abernathy-Utterback product life cycle model that during the life time of a product a sector becomes rigid, especially those sectors that are capital intensive. An alternative explanation is that such sectors are powerful and able to fight off regulations that require a major change in their process technologies.

- Significant process innovations occurred in response to stringent regulations that gave firms in the regulated industry enough time to develop comprehensive strategies. There is a trade-off between achieving quick results and radical change.

- Smaller firms and potential new entrants tended to develop more innovative responses. A possible explanation for this is that incumbent firms, especially the big ones, are vested in old technologies both economically and mentally.

- The environmental goods and services industry provided compliance strategies that were at best incrementally innovative, but which diffused fast, due to their lack of disruption and acceptability to regulators.

- Regulatory flexibility toward the means of compliance, variation in the requirements imposed on different sectors, and compliance time periods were aspects of performance standards that contributed to the development of superior technological responses.

In the impact studies the focus is on the technologies being developed and adopted. There is little attention to the innovation system and policy *context* from which the solutions emerged: the production chain (filière) with its innovation pattern (supplier-dependent, science-based, with customers as an important source of innovation) and the regulatory context with its institutions and specific ways of policy making and implementation.

In general, the studies tell us little about the policy process: who was involved in it, what kind of issues were discussed, the framing of issues, how the learning process was structured (about the problem to be controlled and the solutions available to it), and the strategies deployed by various actors (industrial companies, suppliers of environmental goods and services, environmentalists, environmental authorities, politicians) to obtain favourable outcomes for themselves.

They also tell us little about the influence of policy styles on technology responses. This is unfortunate because the policy interactions are likely to have an important impact on the technological outcomes and costs of regulation.[1]

In impact studies, more attention should be given to the policy interactions that preceded the choice and design of instruments and, especially, the ways in policy instruments are implemented: flexibly or rigorously, with or without consultation with operators, the use of guidance notes and BATNEEC lists by permit writers, and the dependence on information provided by companies about the environmental performance and the appropriateness of particular compliance solutions. This requires a change in perspective and research method, one that puts a greater focus on actors and systems of interaction. Policy network theory (described in Rhodes and Marsh, 1992, and applied to pollution control issues by Smith, 1997) may be used to analyse the links between policy and technology. This is done in the TEP project analysing the implementation of European environmental policies and their impact on technology.[2]

Such a study would then examine not only the impact of a particular policy on technology responses but also examine the policy interactions over the formulation of an environmental policy or Directive (who were involved in it, what solu-

---

[1]   There is small literature on the influence of policy styles on policy outcomes. According to Murphy and Gouldson, 1996 and Wallace, 1995 interactive and collaborative styles are likely to result in more efficient compliance responses; they furthermore induce regulated companies to search for preventive, innovative solutions to environmental problems (also in areas not subject to environmental regulations). There is a danger however that co-operative styles promote incremental rather than more radical solutions that yield greater environmental and economic benefits in the long term. One way to overcome this problem is through the use of long-term performance targets (as is done in the Netherlands). Targets give clarity to what is expected from industry in what time frame, it sets requirements for management at the highest level, and introduces an element of strategic foresight into innovative activity which facilitates and encourages radical innovation rather than incremental improvements (Murphy and Gouldson, 1996: 14).

[2]   TEP is a project for the Environment and Climate programme. It is co-ordinated by René Kemp of MERIT. Information about TEP can be found at http://meritbbs.unimaas.nl/tep/

tions were championed by various policy actors, the search directions being undertaken by regulated industry, EGS suppliers, universities and government laboratories as part of special research programmes) and the policy interactions in the implementation process: the deliberations of what is a Best Available Technology, the reliance on company data and company environmental protection programmes, on self regulation, the finding of a compromise, the enforcement practices.

5   Determinants of Environmental Innovation

The above sections show that the determinants of environmental innovation are varied. Regulation does not limit innovation is a simple way. And innovation is not a simple response to regulation. There are many other factors. To structure and simplify the discussion, we grouped the factors governing (environmental) innovation in three categories:

1. the incentives to innovate: which depend on the intensity of competition, the prevailing cost and demand conditions (for example the costs of waste disposal, energy prices, demand for environmentally improved products, lower insurance rates for companies that produce (environmentally) safe products) and appropriability conditions (the extent to which an innovation is able to capture the economic benefits from its innovation);

2. the ability to assimilate and combine knowledge from different sources (within and outside the company), which is necessary for producing a new process or product; this knowledge consists of both technological knowledge and knowledge about markets;

3. managerial capability to manage the process of innovation – which according to the Minnesota study of van de Ven requires a special type of management: the management of attention, of riding ideas into currency, of managing part-whole relationships (integrating functions, organisational units and resources) and the institutionalisation of leadership.

Regulations are part of the *institutional matrix* of a sector or filière. This matrix, together with the prevailing cost and demand conditions, provides the incentives that dictate the kinds of knowledge, skills and innovations to be developed and acquired (North, 1993). The incentives created by different type of regulations operate alongside with other incentives. In some case the incentives of regulation are very strong in other cases they are very weak. For waste management the incentives are varied and complex, working in different directions. For example, the recycling of packaging waste is positively affected by national and EU packaging policies setting standards for the amount of packaging material that must be recycled, and negatively by high costs of collecting, sorting, processing of packaging material, and the contracts of municipalities with incinerator companies.

The institutional matrix defines the incentives (pressures) and opportunity set for innovation. Innovation is thus rule-governed; it is governed in particular by the rules of the market but also by the rules contained in regulations, engineering practices, product standards and process technologies of a sector. A major element of the rule set or rules of the game is competition. Competition forces companies to be innovative, but not in an unqualified way: it forces them to be innovative in ways that are valued positively in the market. When analysing the impact of regulation one should look at competitive pressures that are operating on companies and competition between different environmental technology options. There exists a long literature on the influence of market structure on innovation. But this is a topic that is very complex, so this literature may not be very useful. It is often stated that there is too little competition in the waste market which is too much controlled, giving rise to high costs, which creates a disincentive for waste management activities. This is only partially true: it creates a disincentive for waste treatment in the waste sector but a positive incentive to prevent and re-use waste upstream in the chain, at the manufacturing level. The system of incentives created by regulations may thus be quite complex, having indirect and unintended outcomes.

We also like to reiterate the point that the incentives from regulations are not only normative and economic, but also informational. Regulations define desirable performance characteristics and things that are acceptable. Like prices they are an informational device, guiding investment decisions in research, products and processes.

According to North the institutional matrix defines the opportunity set. The opportunity set is thus not technologically defined. This is why it is important to pay attention to environmental innovation-relevant institutions and adopt a more systemic view.

Understanding the incentive/rule system for environmental innovation is needed to comprehend why certain innovations were developed and used (or not used) and should be the starting point of any impact study of regulation on innovation. A main task for researchers doing an analysis of the impact of regulation on innovation is thus to describe the incentive/rule systems as a precursor of an assessment of the impact of ESH regulations. When doing such an assessment it is important to pay attention not only to the short term effects of costs and investment but also to the long term effects. The *long term* effects consist of:

- the creation of first-mover advantages for pollution control technologies and environmentally improved products induced by environmental regulation;

- the restructuring of a sector through takeovers or the fossilisation of existing structures through the creation of entry barriers;

- the development of new competences and linkages with other actors that may constitute a source of competitive advantage and environmental protection in the future.

It is the long term effects that matter most. These long term effects are of course far more difficult to assess, involving a element of speculation.

Attention should further be given to the *ways* in which environmental policy exercises an influence on technical change and economic activity. The ways in which environmental policy exercises an influence on innovation and economic development are varied. What they do (or might do) is :

1. Change the cost and demand conditions in a sector.

2. Set limits to permissive practices and products.

3. Signal environmental needs and wants.

4. Define problems (for example, the packaging of goods as an environmental problem).

5. Communicate environmental (societal) values.

6. Lead to a diversion of management time and R&D resources.

7. Shape business expectations (about their place in the world, the way in which their sector will be going, emerging threats and specific business opportunities).

8. Change the terms of competition, by creating entry barriers for new companies or products or causing the restructuring of a sector.

Environmental policies give rise to direct and indirect effects. The direct effects consist of limits to what is permissive. The use of compliance technologies and environmental management systems is another direct effect. The diversion of R&D away from productive activities is an indirect effect. Another indirect effect as is the relocation of companies to countries with lax environmental laws. There is little evidence however that this is happening.

6   Some Final Guidelines

We will end this section by offering some general guidelines for studying the relationship between environmental regulation and innovation. They are:

1. Look at institutional matrix and incentive system for (different types of) innovation. This requires a major research effort because the incentive system is usually quite complex (involving regulations, pressures from public, willingness to pay from users for environmentally beneficial products or technolo-

gies, competition from alternatives, liability for environmental hazards, appropriability conditions). In addition, the regulations themselves often lay down a complex rule and incentives system in terms of the actual requirements (in terms of authorisation procedures, emission limit values, moment at which compliance is due), long term targets, enforcement practices, and son on. There is usually a difference between what is required by law and the real conditions of compliance.

2.   Describe the filière and markets within a production chain: the players, things that are exchanged (goods, knowledge), the competition process and the rules of the game (what it takes to be successful in the market). Attention should be paid to (impending) changes in the competitive, regulatory and sociotechnical landscape (due to globalisation, liberalisation, privatisation, advances in knowledge and technology, shifts in demand). (An example of a change in the sociotechnical landscape is the emergence of the electronic highway which allows customers to select producers, find information about products and product appraisals).

3.   Describe the existing innovation pattern and innovation network of an industry in terms of the actors, key technologies, knowledge bases. Important questions are: What are the main technical components of production activity within the sector concerned? What must a firm do to be a viable operator in the industry? What are the techniques which the firm must master in order to be able to undertake the activities described above? What are the codified knowledges with which the technical operations are designed, analysed, and produced? And who develops the relevant knowledge inputs, and on what resource basis?

4.   Describe the environmentally relevant research activities and responses undertaken by various actors (suppliers, regulated industry, university and research institutes. The research directions should be mapped. The innovations should be categorised in terms of type of innovation[3], significance and motivation (environmental or non-environmental). Their environmental and eco-

---

[3]   Environmental technologies may be grouped in: (i) Pollution control technologies that prevent the direct release of environmentally hazardous emissions into the air, surface waters or soil (classic end-of-pipe technologies like fluegas-desulphurization and biofilters).(ii) Waste management: handling, treatment, and disposal of waste both on-site by the producer of waste and off-site by waste management firms. (iii) Clean technology: process-integrated changes in production technology that reduce the amount of pollutants and waste material that is generated during production. (iv)Recycling: waste minimisation through the re-use of materials recovered from waste streams. (v) Clean products: products that give rise to low levels of environmental impact through the entire life cycle of design, production, use and disposal. Examples are low-solvent paints and bicycles. (vi) Clean-up technology: remediation technologies such as air purifiers and land farming.

nomic significance should be assessed. This may be done on the basis of costs, research money, environmental benefit and (expected) sales.

5. Look for examples of conflicting and suboptimal regulations and how they came to be formulated and implemented.

6. Look at the ways in which demand for environmental improvements is exercised: through regulation, customers, banks, the threat of product boycotts and other type of actions. Assess their relative influence.

7. When describing the regulatory system, also pay to the organisations responsible for the implementation of regulation and the relationship between government and industry.

8. When you look at the policy formulation process look at problem definitions, the openness of the policy process and the role that technological expectations play in it. Were the regulations based on specific technological solutions? Were the technology responses prescribed in some sort of way? How did particular solutions came to be favoured? What we are saying is that you should pay attention to the ways in which technology choices are embedded in the policy process. Don't only look at the actors, the coalitions and their problem definitions and positions with regard to policy proposals and technological solutions but also at the interactions and the outcomes of the interactions, how these shaped further interactions and outcomes by changing actors' expectations, orientation, strategies, mind sets, strategies, capabilities and the economic and political frame conditions. Policy network and implementation theory may be used to study policy interactions.

9. Look at the synergetic relationship between organisational (institutional) innovation and technical innovation. Attention should also be given to the ways in which innovations are linked: how product innovations are linked with process innovations, types of equipment, routines and practices within a filière or innovation chain.

10. Make sure that you measure innovation output and regulatory systems correctly. In doing statistical analyses you should use a set of different indicators and take into account the characteristics (value) of the innovation.

11. Pay attention to the competition between environmental technologies/clean solutions, and the influence of regulations on the terms of competition. Did the regulatory process favour certain options, such as end-of-pipe solutions? A related topic is the optimality of the technology responses, which may be assessed through life cycle analysis, bearing in mind that the outcomes of such studies tend to accord with the desires of the commissioning party.

12. Look at the interaction between different types of regulation (between national policies and EU regulations/directives, between environmental regulations controlling different pollutants and substances, and between economic

and ESH regulations), looking at how such interactions influence search directions and activities and innovation (identification of synergies and conflicts). Again one should draw a distinction between intended and non-intended effects. The interplay of regulations oriented to different goals is likely to produce perverse or suboptimal results.

13. Assess 1st and 2nd order effects. The latter include: creation of new competences and tools, new knowledge, intra- and intercompany linkages that facilitate further change, a greater focus on environmental issues and orientation towards environmental protection. See the report by Brousseau for possible measures.

14. Try to assess also the long-term effects of regulatory and technology developments. They may be more important than the short term immediate effects. For example, it takes time before an invention lead to a tradable product which produces a handsome profit. Of course, assessing the long-term effects involve an element of speculation. In the space of time a great deal may happen. Remember that answers with respect to regulatory issues can be sensitive and prone to strategic bias. This provides an additional reason for using different sources of expertise: industry operators, analysts, suppliers of EGS and policy makers at different levels. Interactive workshops may be used to deal with the problem of differing interests and perspectives.

Two methodological pointers:

1. Apply different research methods to assess the robustness of the findings and to benefit from complementarities. There may also be synergies between research methods. Case studies for example help to inform quantitative studies.

2. When doing comparative research, make sure that the research design allows for comparative research. Ways to do this is through the use of common definitions, indicators, research questions and uniform method.

References

Aichholzer, G., and G. Schienstock (eds.) (1994), *Technology Policy: Towards an Integration of Social and Ecological Concerns*, Berlin.

Ashford, N. A., G. R. Heaton Jr. and W. C. Priest (1979), Environmental, Health, and Safety Regulation and Technological Innovation, in: J.M. Utterback and C. Hill (eds.), *Technological Innovation for a Dynamic Economy*, 161-221.

Ashford, N. A. (1993), Understanding Technological Responses of Industrial Firms to Environmental Problems: Implications for Government Policy, in: K. Fischer and J. Schot (eds.), *Environmental Strategies for Industry: International Perspectives on Research Needs and Policy Implications*, Washington D.C.

Ashford, N. A., C. Ayers and R. F. Stone (1985), Using Regulation to Change the Market for Innovation, *Harvard Environmental Law Review* 9, 419-466.

Barbara, A. J. and V. D. McConnell (1990), The Impact of Environmental Regulations on Industry Productivity: Direct and Indirect Effects, *Journal of Environmental Economics and Management* 19(1), 50-65.

Becher, G. (1994), Regulation and Innovation – Some new Prospects of Science and Technology Policy in the Federal Republic of Germany, in: G. Becher and S. Kuhlmann (eds.), *Evaluation of Technology Policy Programmes in Germany*, Dordrecht, 331-357.

Bennett, G. (1991), *Air Pollution Control Policy in the European Community. Implementation of the EC Directives in the Twelve Member States*, London.

Boyer, R. (1988), Technical change and the theory of Regulation in: G. Dosi et al., *Technical Change and Economic Theory*, London: Pinter.

Brousseau (1998), *Conceptual and Methodological Approach for Investigating the Impact of Single Market Regulation on Innovation*, ATOM, Paris.

Carraro, C. (1994), Technical Innovation and Environment Protection, *European Economic Review* 38(3-4).

Crandall, R.W (1981), Pollution Controls and Productivity Growth in Basic Industries, in: T.G. Cowing and R.E. Stevenson (eds.), *Productivity Measurement in Regulated Industries*, New York, 347-368.

Cutler, L. N. and D. R. Johnson (1975), Regulation and the Political Process, *Yale Law Journal*, 84(7), 1395-1409.

Denzau, A., and D. North (1993), Shared Mental Models: Ideologies and Institutions, *Kyklos* 47(1), 3-31.

Downing, P. B. and L. J. White (1986), Innovation in Pollution Control, *Journal of Environmental Economics and Management* 13, 18-29.

Eads, G. C. (1980), Regulation and Technical Change: Some Largely Explored Influences, *American Economic Review* 70(2), 50-55.

Economist, (1996), Overregulating America. Tomorrow's Economic Argument, July 27, 1996.

Edquist, C. (ed.) (1997*), Systems of Innovation. Technologies, Institutions and Organizations*, London.

Francis, J. (1993), *The Politics of Regulation. A Comparative Perspective*. Oxford..

Gallop, F. M., and M. J. Roberts (1983), Environmental Regulations and Productivity Growth: The Case of Fossil-Fueled Electric Power Generation, *Journal of Political Economy* 91, 654-674.

Gibbons et al. (1994), *The New Production of Knowledge. The Dynamics of Science and Research in Comtemporary Societies*, London.

Gray, W. B., (1987), The Cost of Regulation: OSHA, EPA, and the Productivity Slowdown, *American Economic Review* 77(5). 998-1006.

Gray, W. B. and R. J. Shadbegian (1993), *Environmental Regulation and Manufacturing Productivity at the Plant Level*, NBER working paper 4321.

Gray, W. B., and R. J. Shadbegian, (1994), *Pollution Abatement Costs, Regulation and Plant-Level Productivity*, National Bureau of Economic Research, Cambridge MA.

Green, K., A. McMeekin (1995), *Excellent at What? Environmental Business and Technology Strategies*, Working paper 9505, CROMTECH, Manchester.

Groenewegen, P. and P. Vergragt (1991), Environmental Issues as Threats and Opportunities for Technological Innovation, *Technology Analysis and Strategic Management* 3(1), 43-55.

Ham, C. and M. Hill (1994), *The Policy Process in the Modern Capitalist State*, Hemel Hempstead.

Hart, S. L. and G. Ahuja (1996), Does it Pay to be Green? An Empirical Examination of the Relationship between Emission Reduction and Firm Performance, *Business Strategy and the Environment* 5, 30-37.

Hartje, V. J., R. L. Lurie (1985), *Research and Development Incentives for Pollution Control Technologies*, International Institute for Environment and Society (IIUG), Wissenschaftszentrum Berlin.

Hartje, V. J. (1984), *Environmental Product Regulation and Innovation: Limiting Phosphates in Detergents in Germany*, International Institute for Environment and Society (IIUG), Wissenschaftszentrum Berlin.

Haveman, R. H. and G. B. Christiansen (1981), Environmental Regulations and Productivity Growth, in: Peskin, H., P. Portnoy and A. V. Kneese (eds.), *Environmental Regulation and the U.S. Economy*, Washington D.C., Resources for the Future, 55-75.

Hemmelskamp, J. (1996), *Environmental Policy Instruments and their Effects on Innovation*, ZEW Discussion Paper 96-22, Mannheim.

Hemmelskamp, J. (1997), Environmental Policy Instruments and their Effects on Innovation, *European Planning Studies* 5(2),177-193.

Heaton Jr., G. R. (1990), *Regulation and Technological Change*, paper for the WRI/OECD-Symposium Toward 2000: Environment, Technology and the New Century, Annapolis, Maryland, June 13-15, 1990.

Hogwood, B.W. and L.A. Gunn (1984), *Policy Analysis for the Real World*, Oxford.

Howes, R., J. Skea and B. Whelan (1997), *Clean and Competitive? Motivating Environmental Performance in Industry*, London.

Hucke, J. (1982), Implementating Environmental Regulations in the Federal Republic of Germany, *Policy Studies Journal* 1, 130-40.

Irwin, A. and P. D. Hooper (1992), Clean Technology, Successful Innovation and the 'Greening of Industy', *Business Strategy and the Environment* 1(2), 1-12.

Jaffe, A., S. R. Peterson, P. R. Portney and R. Stavins (1995), Environmental Regulation and the Competitiveness of U.S. Manufacturing: What Does the Evidence Tell Us?, *Journal of Economic Literature* 33(1), 132-63.

Jaffe, A. B. and K. Palmer (1996), *Environmental Regulation and Innovation: A Panel Data Study*, Washington DC.

Johnson, B. (1992), Institutional learning, in: B.Å. Lundvall (ed.), *National Systems of Innovation. Towards a Theory of Innovation and Interactive Learning*, London.

Jorgenson, D. W. and P. J. Wilcoxen (1990), Environmental Regulation and U.S. Economic Growth, *Rand Journal of Economics* 21, 314-340.

Kemp, R. and L. Soete (1992), The Greening of Technological Progress: An Evolutionary Perspective, *Futures* 24(5), 437-457.

Kemp, R., X. Olsthoorn, F. Oosterhuis and H. Verbruggen (1992), Supply and Demand Factors of Cleaner Technologies: Some Empirical Evidence, *Environmental and Resource Economics* 2(6), 615-634.

Kemp, René, X. Olsthoorn, F. Oosterhuis and H. Verbruggen (1994a), Policy Instruments To Stimulate Clean Technology, in: J.B. Opschoor and R.K. Turner (eds.), *Economic Incentives and Environmental Policies*, Dordrecht, 275-300.

Kemp, R., I. Miles, K. Smith et al. (1994), *Technology and the Transition to Environmental Stability. Continuity and Change in Complex Technology Systems,* final report from project "Technological Paradigms and Energy Technologies" for SEER research programme of the CEC (DG XII).

Kemp, R. (1994), Technology and the Transition to Environmental Sustainability. The Problem of Technological Regime Shifts, *Futures* 26(10), 1023-46.

Kemp, R. (1996), The Transition from Hydrocarbons. The Issues for Policy, in: S. Faucheux, D. Pearce and J.L.R. Proops (eds.), *Models of Sustainable Development*, Aldershot, 151-175.

Kemp, R. (1997), *Environmental Policy and Technical Change. A Comparison of the Technological Impact of Policy Instruments*, Cheltenham.

Kemp, R., A. Rip and J. Schot (1997), *Constructing Transition Paths through the Management of Niches*, paper for workshop "Path Creation and Dependence", Copenhagen, Aug 19-22, 1997 (will be published in R. Garud and P. Karnoe (eds.), *Path Creation and Dependence*).

Kemp, R., J. Schot and R. Hoogma (1998), Regime Shifts to Sustainability through Processes of Niche Formation. The Approach of Strategic Niche Management, *Technology Analysis and Strategic Management* 10(2), 175-195.

Knoepfer, P. and H. Weidner (1982), Formulation and Implementation of Air Quality Control Programmes: Patterns of Interest Consideration, *Policy and Politics* 10(1), 85-109.

Lazonick, W. (1991), Business Organisation for Competitive Advantage: Capitalist Transformations in the Twentieth Century, in: G. Dosi, R. Giannetti, and P.A. Toinelli (eds.), *Technology and Enterprise in a Historical Perspective*, Oxford.

Lenox, M. and J. Ehrenfeld (1996), Organizing for Effective Environmental Design, *Business Strategy and the Environment* 6, 187-196.

Lévêque, F. (ed.) (1996), *Environmental Policy in Europe. Industry, Competitiveness and the Policy Process*, Cheltenham.

Lundvall, B.Å. (ed) (1992), *National Systems of Innovation. Towards a Theory of Innovtion and Interactive Learning*, London.

Magat, W. A. (1979), The Effects of Environmental Regulation on Innovation, *Law and Contemporary Problems* 43(1), 4-25.

Majone, G. (1976), Choice Among Policy Instruments for Pollution Control, *Policy Analysis*, 589-613.

Majone, G. (1989), *Evidence, Argument and Persuasion in the Policy Process*, New Haven.

Malaman, R. (1996), Technological Innovation for Sustainable Development: Generation and Diffusion of Industrial Cleaner Technologies, *Nota di Lavoro 66.96*, Fondazione Eni Enrico Mattei.

Maruo, K. (1992), The Three-Way "Catalysis": How the Three-Way Catalyst Became the Ruling Technical Solution to the Automobile Emission Problem, in M. Hart (ed.), *Automobile Engineering in a Dead End: Mainstream and laternative Developments in the 20th Century*, publications in Human Technology nr 5, Gothenburg University.

Mayntz, R. and J. Hucke (1978), Gesetzesvollzug im Umweltschutz, Wirksamkeit und Probleme, *Zeitschrift für Umweltpolitik*, 217-44.

Milbrath, L. W. and F. R. Inscho (ed.) (1975), *The Politics of Environmental Policy, Beverly Hills*, London.

Miles, I. and K. Green (1996), A Clean Break? From Corporate Research and Development to Sustainable Technological Regimes, in: R. Welford and R. Starkey (eds.), *The Earthscan Reader in Business and the Environment*, 120-44.

Milliman, S. R. and R. Prince (1989), Firm Incentives to Promote Technological Change in Pollution Control, *Journal of Environmental Economics and Management* 17, 247-265.

Norsworthy, J. R., M. J. Harper and K. Kunze (1979), The Slowdown in Productivity Growth: Analysis of Some Contributing Factors, *Brookings Papers on Economic Activity* 2, 387-421.

North, D. C., (1990), *Institutions, Institutional Change and Economic Performance*, Cambridge.

North, D. C. (1993), Institutions and Credible Commitment, *JITE*.

OECD (1985), *Environmental Policy and Technical Change*, Paris.

OECD (1989), *Economic Instruments for Environmental Protection*, Paris.

OECD (1997a), *The OECD Report on Regulatory Reform, Vol II: Thematic Studies*, Paris.

OECD (1997b), *Environmental Policies and Innovation: Analytical Framework, Draft report, Oct 1997*, Paris.

Peacock, A. (ed.) (1984), *The Regulation Game. How British and West German Companies Bargain with Government*, Oxford.

Pearce, D. and I. Brisson (1993), BATNEEC. The Economics of Technology-Based Environmental Standards, with a UK Illustration, *Oxford Review of Economic Policy* 9(4), 24-39.

Porter, M. E. and C. van der Linde (1995), Towards a new Conception of the Environment–Competitiveness Relationship, *Journal of Economic Perspectives* 9(4), 97-118.

Repetto, R., (1995), *Jobs, Competitiveness and Environmental Regulations: What are the issues?*, Washington DC.

Ringeling and Hanf (1998), *Internal document of INSTRUFECT project.*

Rip, A. and R. Kemp (1998), Technological Change, in S. Rayner and Liz Malone (eds.), *Human Choice and Climate Change*, Washington D.C.

Rothwell, R. (1992), Industrial Innovation and Government Environmental Regulation: Some Lessons from the Past, *Technovation* 12(7), 447-458.

Roome, N. (1994), Business Strategy, R&D Management and Environmental Imperatives', *R&D Management*, 24(1), 65-82.

Scharpf, F. W. (1993), *Games in Hierarchies and Networks. Analytical and Empirical Approaches to the Study of Governance Institutions*, Frankfurt a. M.

Schmidheiny, S. (1992), *Changing Course: A Global Business Perspective on Development and the Environment*, Cambridge (MA).

Schot, J. (1992), The Policy Relevance of the Quasi-Evolutionary Model: The Case of Stimulating Clean Technologies, in: R. Coombs, P. Saviotti and V. Walsh (eds.), *Technological Change and Company Strategies*, London, 185-200.

Shrivastava, Paul (1995), Environmental Technologies and Competitive Advantage, *Strategic Management Journal* 16, 183-200.

Skea, J. (1995), Environmental Technology, in: H. Folmer, H. L. Gabel, and H. Opschoor (eds), *Principles of Environmental and Resource Economics. A Guide for Students and Business Makers*, Aldershot, 389-412.

Smith, K. (1997), Economic infrastructures and innovation systems in: C. Edquist (ed.), *Innovation Systems: Institutions, Organisations and Dynamics,* London, 86-106.

Smith, K. (1999), Innovation as a systemic phenomenon: rethinking the role of policy, in: K. Bryant (ed.), *A New Economic Paradigm? Innovation-Based Evolutionary Systems*, Discussions of Science and Innovation 4, Department of Industry, Science and Technology, Canberrra.

Smith, A. (1997), *Integrated Pollution Control*, Aldershot.

Soete, L. and A. Arundel (eds.) (1993), *An Integrated Approach to European Innovation and Technology Diffusion Policy. A Maastricht Memorandum*, Brussels.

Stewart, R. (1981), Regulation, Innovation and Administrative Law: A Conceptual Framework, California Law Review, 69(5), 1256-1377.

Stewart, R. (1994), Environmental Regulation and International Competitiveness, *Yale Law Journal* 103, 2039-2122.

Teece, D. J., G. Pisano and A. Shuen, (1997), Dynamic Capabilities and Strategic Management, *Strategic Management Journal* 18(7), 509-34.

UNICE (1995), *Releasing Europe's Potential Through Targeted Regulatory Reform.*

Vogel, D. (1986), *National Styles of Regulation. Environmental Policy in Great Britain and the United States*, Ithaca.

Vollebergh, H. (ed.) (1989), *Milieu en innovatie*, Groningen.

Wallace, D. (1995), *Environmental Policy and Industrial Innovation: Strategies in Europe, the US and Japan*, RIIA, London.

Weale, A. (1992), *The New Politics of Pollution*, Manchester.

Wichers, T. F. (1996), *Green is the Colour of Money. Innovation Management in Environmental Technology*, Graduation Thesis, Faculty of Economics and Business Studies, Maastricht University.

Williams, H. E., J. Medhurst and K. Drew (1991), Corporate Strategies For A Sustainable Future, in: Fischer, K. and J. Schot (eds.), *Environmental Strategies for Industry: International Perspectives on Research Needs and Policy Implications*, Washington, D.C., 117-146.

An Innovation-Based Strategy for a Sustainable Environment[*]

Nicholas A. Ashford

Massachusetts Institute of Technology, MIT (E40-239)
77 Mass Ave., Cambridge, MA 02139
USA

Keywords. innovation policy, priority settings, technology-based approach.

1 Introduction

This article explores a role for government to provide a solution-focused, technology-based approach for addressing and setting priorities for environmental problems. It is argued that there is a need for a significant industrial transformation or displacement of those technologies and sectors that give rise to serious environmental problems, especially those that have remained stagnant for some period of time and that are ripe for change. Achieving sustainable production and consumption requires (1) a shift in policy focus from problems to solutions, (2) an appreciation of the differences between targeting technological innovation and diffusion as a policy goal, (3) the realization that the most desirable technological responses do not necessarily come from the regulated or polluting firms, (4) understanding that comprehensive technological changes are needed that co-optimize productivity, environmental quality, and worker health and safety, and (5) an appreciation of the fact that in order to change its technology, a firm must have the *willingness, opportunity,* and *capacity* to change.

Willingness, opportunity, and capacity are together the necessary and sufficient prerequisites for a firm undertaking technological change. The three affect each other, of course, but each is determined by more fundamental factors. Therefore, policy instruments need to be chosen and designed for their ability to change these more fundamental factors. *Willingness* is determined by both (1) *the firm's atti-*

---

[*]   Adapted with permission from "An Innovation-Based Strategy for the Environment" in Worst Things First? The Debate Over Risk-based National Environmental Priorities. A. M. Finkel and D. Golding (eds.), Resources for the Future, Washington, DC 1994.

tudes towards changes in production technology and products in general and by (2) *its knowledge about what changes are possible.* Improving the latter involves aspects of capacity building, while changing the former may be more idiosyncratic to a particular manager or alternatively a function of organizational structures and reward systems. The syndrome "not in my term of office" describes the lack of enthusiasm of a particular manager to make changes whose benefit may accrue long after he has retired or moved on, and which may require expenditures in the short or near term.

Opportunity involves both supply-side and demand-side factors. On the supply side, technological gaps can exist (1) between the technology used in a particular firm and the already-available technology that could be *adopted or adapted* (known as diffusion or incremental innovation, respectively), and (2) the technology used in a particular firm and technology that could be *developed* (i.e., major or radical innovation). On the demand side, four factors could push firms towards technological change – whether diffusion, incremental innovation, or major innovation – (1) regulatory requirements, (2) possible cost savings or additions to profits, (3) public demand for a less polluting and safer industry, and (4) worker demands and pressures arising from industrial relations concerns.

Capacity or capability can be enhanced by both (1) increases in knowledge or information about cleaner and inherently safer opportunities, partly through formal Technology Options Analyses (see later discussion), and partly through serendipitous transfer of knowledge from suppliers, customers, trade associations, unions, workers, and other firms, as well as reading about environmental and safety issues, and (2) improving the skill base of the firm through educating and training its operators, workers, and managers, on both a formal and informal basis. Capacity to change may also be influenced by the inherent innovativeness (or lack thereof) of the firm as determined by the maturity and technological rigidity of particular product or production lines. The heavy, basic industries, which are also sometimes the most polluting and unsafe industries, change with great difficulty, especially when it comes to core processes. Finally, it deserves emphasizing that it is not only technologies that are rigid and resistant to change. Personal and organizational flexibility is also important (Coriat 1995).

This article argues that government must provide the opportunity for technological transformation/sustainable development through the setting of clear standards and policy goals, while allowing flexible means for industry to achieve those goals. Care must be taken to avoid dominant technological regimes from capturing or unduly influencing government regulation. New entrants and new technology must also be given a chance to evolve to address environmental problems. Other demand-side policies (i.e., changes in public preferences for specific products, transportation systems, or services) are important in the long run for changing both government and private sector behavior. However, this article focuses on more direct intervention and competition for better environmental performance within the private sector.

Technological change is now generally regarded as essential in achieving the next major advances in sustainable development. The necessary technological changes include the substitution of materials used as inputs, process redesign, and final product reformulation. The substitution of products by services may also be needed. Initiatives focusing on technological change need to address multimedia pollution and to reflect fundamental shifts in the design of products and processes. Distinguished from end-of-pipe pollution control, those new initiatives are known as pollution prevention, source reduction, toxics use reduction, or cleaner technology (OECD 1987).[1]

Whichever term is used, this article argues that the key to success in achieving a sustainable environment is to influence managerial knowledge of and attitudes toward *both* technological change and environmental concerns. Encouraging technological changes for production purposes and for environmental compliance purposes must be seen as interrelated, rather than as separate, activities (Ashford, Heaton, and Priest 1979; Kurz 1987; Rip and van den Belt 1988; Schot 1992). In order to bring about this integration, managers must encourage their engineers, scientists, and technologists to work on environmental and safety concerns so that those concerns are reflected in both design and operational criteria of a firm's technology. This may require a fundamental cultural shift in the firm. A related cultural shift in the regulatory agencies that influence how firms respond to environmental demands is also essential.

The above discussion addresses managerial factors that influence technological change. The technology of the firm, however, also influences managerial style and may limit the kind and extent of technological changes that are likely or possible. Thus, the design of governmental or corporate policies for encouraging a fundamental shift in production technologies must rest on an appreciation of the different kinds of technological change, as well as the dynamics of achieving those changes under a regulatory stimulus.

Technological change can involve both innovation and diffusion. *Technological innovation*[2] is both a significant determinant of economic growth and important

---

[1]   In-process recycling and equipment modification are sometimes also included in the category of new initiatives. The term *waste reduction* is also used, but it appears to be less precise and may not include air or water emissions. Pollution prevention has also been discussed as a preferred way for achieving sustainable development, giving rise to the term *sustainable technology* (Heaton, Repetto, and Sobin 1991).

[2]   Technological innovation is the first commercially successful application of a new technical idea. By definition, it occurs in those institutions, primarily private profit-seeking firms, that compete in the marketplace. Innovation should be distinguished from *invention,* which is the development of a new technical idea, and from *diffusion,* which is the subsequent widespread adoption of an innovation by those who did not develop it. The distinction between innovation and diffusion is complicated by the fact that innovations can rarely be adopted by new users without modification. When modifications are extensive, the result may be a new innovation. Definitions used in

for reducing health, safety, and environmental hazards. It may be major, involving radical shifts in technology, or incremental, involving adaptation of prior technologies. *Technological diffusion,* which is the widespread adoption of technology already developed, is fundamentally different from innovation. The term *technology transfer* is somewhat imprecise, sometimes referring to the diffusion of technology from government to industry or from one industry or country to another. If that transfer involves significant modifications of the originating technology, the transfer can be said to result in incremental or minor innovation. Finally, the term *technology forcing* is used to describe regulation and is similarly imprecise, usually meaning forcing industry to innovate, but sometimes meaning forcing industry to adopt technology already developed and used elsewhere, i.e., technological diffusion.

2   The Evolution of Environmental Regulation

The discovery of harmful effects of chemical substances (including human-made chemicals, such as vinyl chloride; human-released chemicals, such as lead; and natural substances, such as radon) on human health and ecosystems has given rise to a variety of legislative responses. There have been several lines or waves of regulation addressing different problems (see Figure 1). Two early waves developed more or less concurrently. The first addressed media-specific emissions and effluents that were by-products of industrial production, energy use, and transportation activities. The end-products or uses neither depended nor focused on bioactivity or biologically active compounds. The emission by-products were mostly combustion products yielding carbon monoxide, sulfur dioxide, nitrogen oxides, particulates, ozone, and lead. The effluents of concern and components of hazardous waste were heavy metals and other oxygen-depleting materials or substances.

The second line of regulation focused on products and substances that were themselves intended to be bioactive and therefore were expected to have biological or ecological side effects. These included pharmaceuticals, such as thalidomide, and chemicals used in agriculture and food production, such as pesticides (DDT) and food additives (Red Dye No. 3).

Later, it was realized that many products not intended to be bioactive were in fact harmful to human health, as was the case with vinyl chloride and asbestos, and to ecosystems, as was the case with PCBs (polychlorinated biphenyls). A third resulting wave of regulation focused on processes while remaining substance-

---

this article draw on several years' work at the Center for Policy Alternatives at the Massachusetts Institute of Technology, beginning with a five-country study (CPA 1975).

specific. This wave included regulations on occupational exposure, chemical production and industrial use, and consumer products.

MEDIA   PRODUCTS
Air   Drugs
Water   Pesticides
Waste   Food additives
Clean-up liability

PRODUCT AND PROCESS
Consumer products
Worker health and safety
Toxic substances

DEVELOPING AND RECENT INITIATIVES
Biotechnology
Indoor air

Figure 1:   Four stages in the regulation of toxics

More recently, concerns have focused on emerging biotechnologies, spanning every conceivable area in which synthetic inorganic and organic chemicals have been used historically, from pesticides to the remediation of hazardous wastes. Endocrine disruption from certain organo-chlorines is also of increasing concern, where adverse biological effects can occur in the parts per billion or trillion range, 3-6 orders of magnitude lower than conventional pollution effects. There is now also a focus on the indoor air environment in both homes and non-industrial work places where consumer products and building materials and practices converge and result in unintended side effects, exacerbated in part from decreasing building ventilation in an effort to respond to energy concerns. These sources give rise to sick-building syndrome, building-related illness, and chemical sensitivity at levels of exposure much lower than illness associated with conventional toxic effects. Tight building structures have also exacerbated the problem of radon exposure. The current wave of regulation is confronting health and environmental effects that may require substance bans or very much more stringent levels of control than previously thought necessary. New technology may be needed.

Examining and understanding this legislative evolution in the context of industrial and commercial activities that have contributed to environmental, occupational, and consumer hazards are necessary if we are to devise a technology-based strategy for prioritizing our concerns.

A technology-based strategy, which includes an emphasis on pollution prevention and cleaner technology, should not be confused with technology-based standards, where technologies of control or production are specified. In contrast, a technology-based strategy is focused on expanding the technological options for reducing or eliminating the variety of risks associated with production technologies, industrial materials, and consumer technologies, rather than constraining industry to adopt a particular technological solution. Oddly enough, the practice of *technology assessment* – characterizing the consequences of using or deploying a specific technology – mostly is not an assessment of technical options for replacing a given technology, and for our purposes here it relates to the conduct of risk assessment. Later, I describe what I have termed Technology Options Analysis (TOA) as an essential basis for a technology-based, as opposed to a risk-based, approach to environmental problems.

Legislation in the United States (the Pollution Prevention Act) and in the European Union (the Integrated Pollution Prevention and Control Technology Directive) has been enacted to reflect the realization that a focus on pollution prevention and cleaner technology, rather than on the control of emissions and effluents and the treatment of waste, is required for achieving a sustainable environment.

In the remainder of this article, I discuss the limitations of the traditional practices of risk-based approaches, the usefulness of regulatory impact analysis to guide decision making, and current technology-based standards and pollution prevention approaches. Finally, I propose an innovation-driven technology-based strategy that argues that regulation can be used creatively to foster the needed technological changes.

3   Risk Assessment and Risk-Based Approaches to Priority Setting

Risk assessment was described in 1983 in the now near-legendary report by the National Academy of Sciences (NAS 1983) as comprising four steps: (1) hazard identification, (2) dose-response assessment, (3) exposure assessment, and (4) risk characterization. Risk assessment, of course, has been and continues to be an activity fraught with methodological difficulties and challenges. Its results reflect choices of data, models, and assumptions, and it is an activity where both values and science necessarily enter. This is especially the case where there is considerable uncertainty, notwithstanding assertions that risk assessment can be clearly separated from risk management. (See Ashford 1988 for a critique of this view; also see Hornstein 1992.)

3.1   Perceptual and Political Influences on Risk-Based Priority Setting

Different environmental and health and safety legislation incorporates concerns for risk, costs, technology, and equity in different ways. While it might be said that there are inconsistencies among regulatory areas or regimes because the cost-per-fatality reduced differs markedly (Sunstein 1990; Travis and others 1987), those differences could well be explained by differences in the risk posture (i.e., risk neutrality or risk aversion) of various regulatory authorities, the nature of the risk addressed (for instance, voluntary versus involuntary, chronic versus acute, mortality versus morbidity), the characteristics of the risk bearers (such as sensitive populations, children, workers), and different mandates in the legislation itself on balancing the costs and benefits of regulations. The regulatory systems are risk-driven; i.e., action is triggered by the discovery or assessment of risk. However, the differences among regulatory agencies are not, in fact, necessarily "irrational," unless rationality is tautologically defined as minimizing cost per unit of population risk as quantified via a "best estimate" (Shrader-Frechette 1991).

The exercise of priority setting becomes incredibly complicated depending on the context. It is one thing to prioritize options for controlling occupational carcinogens; it is another to prioritize efforts to reduce hazards with such diverse consequences as cancer, emphysema, acute poisoning and traumatic accidents, even within the same industry or context of exposure. Simply counting fatalities from each hazard does not fully capture the human impact of these hazards. While heroic assumptions have been made to value a life lost in economic terms, we scarcely know where to begin with the far more prevalent effects of morbidity, attended by great differences in pain and suffering, or with ecological effects resulting in the loss of a species. Even when we are comparing like hazards, such as fatal accidents, it is not clear that we should place equal emphasis on valuing opportunities for, say, reducing occupational risk versus highway deaths.

Even if we were to make no distinctions in the type of injury sustained, society has seen fit through legislation to regard, for example, exposure to carcinogens (and more recently to endocrine disrupters) through additives to the food supply as different from other consumer exposures. If the priority-setting discussion intends to revisit the wisdom of existing legislative directives, it will need to decide on the weighting criteria and principles involving issues of risk profiles, risk types, distribution of risks among risk-bearers and of costs among cost-bearers, the nature of the assumption of risk and many other factors. While the political agenda can be altered, it is not clear that a rational, inherently correct system based on risk can be identified. Moreover, even seemingly simpler challenges, such as that of prioritizing water effluents, also become unwieldy in the real world.

The problems are not simply political. Since regulation focuses on controlling or reducing particularized or specific hazards, political demands are translated into contests between affected publics and affected industries over a specific hazard and often within such specific regulatory regimes as food additives, occupational exposure, community contamination, or consumer products. The legislative structure and risk assessments on a specific hazard define the debate.

One cannot prioritize particularized political demands. Crisis driven demands (such as those arising from Love Canal or from Alar on apples) divert resources from a general plan in order to address them in a timely fashion. More general political demands (such as for worker safety and environmental protection) are juggled in the annual budgeting process. On the other hand, even where political demands did not drive or bombard an agency, attempts to act ahead of political demand – for instance, by prioritizing chemicals to be tested, ranking chemicals for riskiness, and finally regulating them – led to difficulties. During the first four years of the implementation in 1976 of the Toxic Substances Control Act (TSCA) under a willing administration, the U.S. Environmental Protection Agency (EPA) became hopelessly bogged down in its efforts to build a rational system. Prioritizing even the 100 chemicals in most common use was hardly begun after four years of effort. In order to understand this lack of success, it is necessary to examine priority setting in greater detail.

3.2   The Inherent Nonuniformity in Priority Setting

Priority setting for addressing and remedying environmental problems involves the articulation of an organizing principle for setting priorities and the establishment of a social/political/legal process for implementing the system. Even left to its own devices – and free from political pressures – responsible government faces challenges at several levels.

Given that different environmental problems are managed by different regulatory agencies or offices and fall under different legislative mandates, the first question of priority setting concerns the relative allocation of resources to different regulatory regimes; for example, controlling air emissions versus pesticide registration. In practice, this is influenced largely by the political process and is not based on some rational analytical scheme. However, even if this initial allocation does not seem to be rational, greater or fewer environmental benefits can be realized depending upon the extent to which each regulatory regime coordinates its activities with the others. For example, simultaneous, though separate, requirements for controlling cadmium in occupational environments, water effluents, and consumer products can be more cost-effective than uncoordinated efforts spread out in time. Part of this cost-effectiveness stems from the fact that those firms responsible for cadmium use and production have an opportunity to adopt a multimedia focus, where changes in the technology of production can have multiple payoffs for reducing risks. Being able to achieve multiple environmental payoffs through coordinating various regulatory efforts could alter an agency's internal priority scheme (discussed later) by placing a particular substance/problem higher on its list than the substance/problem would have been placed based on a single regulatory focus.

Even in the best of political times, such as when the U.S. Interagency Regulatory Liaison Group (IRLG) was formed to coordinate efforts, the attempt to coordinate regulatory efforts was not entirely successful. Within EPA, the more recent establishment of "multi-office clusters" to promote integrated cross-media problem solving on specific pollutants (such as lead) or on specific industries (such as petrochemicals) or efforts to address indoor air pollution may eventually be more successful, but fundamental problems remain. Later, this article explores an approach whereby the coordination of agency efforts focuses not on regulation of a single substance or class of substances, but on establishing a concerted effort to change an industrial process or production technology.

Given the political influence on the allocation of resources to different regulatory regimes, it is understandable that government would turn its attention to establishing priorities *within* each regime, rather than among them. The internal priority system for taking action could take on any of three forms:

- ranking problems by the number of persons at risk;

- ranking problems by expected (maximum individual) risk (for instance, a lifetime risk of cancer of one in 1,000 would rank higher than a risk of one in 10,000); and

- ranking regulatory interventions by their health-effectiveness, i.e., the amount of risk reduced per compliance dollar expended.

Generating these priority schemes would, of course, rely on risk assessments (and as mentioned earlier, a way of weighing different kinds of risks). The third option would need, additionally, estimates of compliance cost. All three options would also need to reflect a determination of how much residual risk would be "acceptable" or permissible under various legislative mandates. Finally, all three options would need to establish the means by which compliance would be achieved. Cost-effective means would be preferred, except where unjustifiable inequities exist as to either the beneficiaries of protection (citizens, workers, consumers) or those who bear the costs (small versus large firms, different industrial sectors, and so forth). For example, it has been suggested that the Occupational Safety and Health Administration (OSHA) abandon efforts to protect all workers from asbestos or noise exposure when it becomes too expensive. Equity concerns for differential treatment of workers in different plants prohibit this approach. On the other hand, the Clean Air Act permits differential treatment of new plants under its New Source Performance Standards.

All the complexities involved in priority setting within regulatory regimes reveal priority-setting schemes that take many factors into account: risk, efficiency of reducing risk, equity, technological and economic feasibility, and responsiveness to public demands and private concerns. All extant schemes are used to rank hazards, not industrial processes or industrial sectors, and only OSHA and the Consumer Product Safety Commission have promoted significant technological changes. [See Ashford and Heaton 1983 for examples, such as PVC (polyvinyl chloride) polymerization and substitutes for PCBs; see also OTA 1995]. While there have been constant calls for uniform approaches to risk assessment and uniform balancing of regulatory costs and benefits, the legal mandates and individual cultures of different regulatory regimes prevent the achievement of uniformity. Although uniformity might be a preferred goal of some analysts, differences between agency approaches should not be too quickly labeled as inconsistencies. The differences may be defensible. Demands for consistency that move all systems to a lower common denominator of environmental protection may simply be motivated by antiregulatory interests. Demands for tighter levels of protection to achieve consistency are made by different players from those who demand relaxing "overly restrictive" regulatory systems.

Given that priority setting for regulation involves an integration of benefits, cost, and equity concerns, the next section of this article delves into the possible decision rules for trade-offs that are made in deciding whether and how far to go in controlling a particular risk. Determining the appropriate level of control or regulation for a particular risk is a necessary first step in creating a priority-setting scheme for many risks. In other words, since priority setting depends on ranking the opportunities for risk reduction, a decision has to be made first as to how much of each risk type we would want to reduce. To facilitate this determination, an impact analysis of different amounts of regulation needs to be undertaken.

4   Impact Analysis of Proposed Regulations

Priority setting often begins by evaluating the impacts of a proposed regulation or regulatory options. These impacts include economic and health consequences for a variety of actors, as well as effects on the environment. Comparing these different kinds of impacts (i.e., incommensurables) and valuing their distributional consequences among actors and over time present special difficulties. These difficulties are beyond the familiar problems of discovering or observing a market-based value for reducing risk, or of discounting future streams of economic, health, and environmental effects. Consider the qualitatively different effects a regulation may have on a variety of actors.[3] Table 1 is an impact matrix that attempts to clarify the differences among the economic, health and safety, and environmental effects of regulations and to elucidate the relationships among actors. For each type of actor, this matrix illustrates the consequences of a particular decision, such as regulating

---

[3]   This discussion is taken in part from Ashford and Ayers 1985. See also Ashford, Ayers, and Stone 1985; Ashford and Caldart 1991.

a particular technology. The actors are divided into four groups: producers, workers, consumers, and "others," which might include residents of communities downwind from a polluter. The last group is distinguished from workers and consumers because its members are usually unconnected with producers, being in neither a contractual nor an employment relationship (as are workers), nor in a commercial relationship (as are consumers). Workers, consumers, and the others also have no relationship with each other, either contractual or commercial.

Table 1:   Impact matrix of environmental and safety regulation

Actors	Economic effect	Health and Safety effect	Environmental effect
Producers	$C_\$$	$B_{H/S}{}^{*}$	
Workers	$C_\$$	$B_{H/S}{}^{*}$	
Consumers	$C_\$$	$B_{H/S}{}^{*}$	
Others[**]	$C_\$$	$B_{H/S}{}^{*}$	$B_{Environment}$

* $B_{H/S}$ refers to benefits of reducing hazards that impair health or safety.
** Those with no employment or commercial relationship with producers.

Net costs, $C_\$$, include items that have been accepted, noncontroversial dollar values such as profits, wages, and medical costs, as well as the often-contested estimates of the costs of compliance. Risk assessment methodologies are used to provide estimates in the second and third columns of the matrix. Health and safety benefits, $B_{H/S}$, include items that can be quantified but that are difficult to monetize or to compare, such as incidence of disease and changes in longevity, morbidity, and probability of harm. Analytic efforts have traditionally concentrated on reduced fatalities. Far more important, in terms of total impact, may be reductions in nonfatal injuries and disease.

Environmental benefits, B_E, include nonmonetizable items, such as the benefits of preserving a species or the recreational value of fishing. The monetizable environmental costs, such as those reflected in loss of property value, are included in the net costs, $C_\$$.

In filling in the matrix (i.e., in undertaking an impact analysis), the net of inquiry must be cast broadly enough to capture all important effects – those important in magnitude and in distributional terms. As Shrader-Frechette (1991) points out, the risk of partial quantification in cost-benefit analysis is that the qualitative effects are recognized in principle but ignored in the calculations. For example, in the case of reducing the use of chlorofluorocarbons (CFCs), the costs and benefits conferred by possible substitutes must also be included. Economic costs (profits lost in CFC production) must be considered, but so must economic gains (profits increased in substitutes production). A similar duality is warranted in analyzing health effects, although while it is possible that unanticipated significant health, safety, and environmental consequences could arise from substitutes, it is becoming less likely given the close scrutiny received by new products or new uses of existing products before they enter the market.

4.1   The Costs of Compliance

It is especially important to look closely at economic effects associated with regulatory compliance. It is often assumed that, because the costs of complying with regulations can be easily monetized, they are reliable estimates of true costs. Unfortunately, there are many instances in which the costs are not only uncertain, but unreliable. Agencies depend to a large extent on industry data to derive estimates of compliance costs. The bias of those estimates has often been questioned. The regulatory agencies themselves often do not have access to the information that would enable them to develop the best estimates of the costs of compliance, i.e., information concerning alternative products and processes and resultant costs. In addition, compliance cost estimates often fail to take three crucial issues into account:

- Economies of scale inevitably arise in the demand-induced increase in the production of compliance technology or environmentally sounder technology.

- A regulated industrial segment is able to learn over time to comply in a more cost-effective manner – what management scientists call the "learning curve."

- Technological innovation yields benefits to both the regulated firm[4] and to the public intended to be protected.

Indeed, some environmental, health, and safety regulation has been recognized as "technology forcing" by the courts and by analysts. The costs of compliance should not be based on static assumptions about the firm and its technology (Porter and van den Linden 1995). Otherwise, a large overestimation of regulatory costs can result.[5] Further, in the case of a displacement of a product or technology

---

[4]   Ashford et al. (1979, 1983, and 1985) and Porter and van den Linden (1995) have independently argued that there are "ancillary benefits" or "innovation offsets" to compliance costs for the firm in terms of the benefits of correcting production inefficiencies resulting from pollution. These may be of great economic benefit to innovating firms by conferring first mover advantages. Also see remarks in the concluding section of this article.

[5]   The minimal effects of the OSHA vinyl chloride standard on the private sector is a striking example of how different the actual economic impacts can be, compared to some ominous preregulation predictions of the economic demise of the industry (Ashford, Hattis, et al. 1980). In 1995, the U.S. Office of Technology Assessment

by a new entrant (or a new response by the old firm), a total impact assessment must include the new profits, jobs, and opportunities created by that displacement or shift.

In the last analysis, the costs and benefits of a regulation must be compared against what might have happened in the absence of that regulation. For example, if we were to estimate the benefits and costs of adopting a safety standard for a consumer product, we must ask whether the producer industry might not have made the product somewhat safer in the absence of regulation by responding to increasing product liability suits in the courts (see Ashford and Stone 1991). In this example, it would not be correct to attribute to regulation either all of the costs expended or all of the benefits conferred. The alternative scenario chosen by the evaluator can make the actual regulation look better or worse. Unless we have an alternative universe that we can define with reasonable certainty for analytical purposes, evaluations of the effects of a regulation are on very shaky ground. Often we are certain that a regulation will be promulgated later, even if it may not be imminent. In this case, what promulgating the regulation promptly represents are the marginal costs and benefits compared to a later enactment.

4.2   Cost-Benefit and Trade-Off Analyses Distinguished

Having faithfully uncovered all the direct effects of a proposed regulation and expressed them relative to likely alternative scenarios, the analyst can take two very different courses of action: complete a traditional cost-benefit analysis or undertake a trade-off analysis (Ashford and Ayers 1985). A traditional cost-benefit analysis confers monetary values to all impacts, sums the costs, and compares those costs to the sum of benefits, irrespective of the parties to whom the costs or the benefits accrue. Regulations whose net benefits are positive are justified in economic terms. More correctly, regulations are permitted to the extent that the marginal benefits exceed marginal costs; i.e., risk reductions should only go as far as "appropriate levels." (See Figure 3, which graphs economic efficiency as a criterion for regulation, and its related discussion later in this article).

In other words, traditional cost-benefit analysis reduces all effects to a common metric and, aside from possibly valuing distributional effects in the utility functions of the actors themselves (see Keeney and Winkler 1985), is indifferent to distributional effects.[6] This indifference calls into question the usefulness of tradi-

---

published a review of many OSHA standards, with the general finding that post-compliance costs were actually one-third to one-fifth the costs of the pre-promulgation estimates as a result of unanticipated technological changes (OTA 1995).

[6]   Note here, especially, the application of the Kaldor-Hicks criterion for a *potential* Pareto improvement, whereby those made worse off by a regulation could be compensated by those made better off and a net positive benefit might still remain.

tional cost-benefit analysis and, further more, may make it the wrong paradigm entirely. For example, the net benefit calculations for regulations that have long-term, multigenerational consequences may be insensitive to the effects felt in future generations because future health or environmental benefits are discounted to small present values. What justification is there in essentially disregarding the distributional inequities among generations? Perhaps there is something wrong with the traditional cost-benefit paradigm or at least with its application to certain types of problems (Mishan 1982).

Instead, the decision maker could use a trade-off analysis, which does not cloud the differences between factors such as health, environment, and economic costs. This approach also does not cloud the distinction between those who benefit and those who suffer as a result of adopting a particular regulation. The analyst must utilize the impact matrix in Table 1 without collapsing (summing) the economic, health, and environmental effects into a single metric or summing the benefits or costs across different actors or generations.[7] The decision maker/analyst is forced to express any decision in terms of, for example, trading costs to consumers and producers now for a variety of benefits to citizens over the next three generations. (As has been discussed above, the possible benefits of substitute products and new firms entering the market in economic, health, and environmental terms must also be explicitly considered). This explicit trade-off reveals the preferences of the analyst, preferences in terms of both the magnitude of the effects and their distributional or equity consequences. Requiring the analyst to make these explicit trade-offs prevents what Tribe (1984) terms "the sin of abdicating responsibility for choice." In this sense, the monetization of benefits and costs does not ensure analyst accountability: it actually facilitates obfuscation of the trade-offs.

In traditional cost-benefit analysis, maldistributions are invisible and hence ignored. Moreover, trade-off analysis allows an explicit consideration of societal or individual risk averseness to worst-case probabilities, not "expected values." In contrast, in traditional cost-benefit analysis, while there is explicit valuation of health, safety, and environmental factors in monetary terms, what is missing is explicit valuation of what is traded off for what.

The actual transfer between winners and losers, which is a condition for a Pareto improvement, is not usually required by the regulatory agency or analyst (Mishan 1981).

[7] This does not mean that the analyst cannot collapse some elements of the trade-off matrix into a single metric. Frequently, such a procedure is desirable for both analytical and practical reasons. The difference is that this should not be required or automatically done. The assumptions underlying the procedure, which blur distributional or other effects when utilized, must be explicitly introduced, whereas in the case of cost-benefit analysis, summing *all* effects into a single monetary figure is imposed by the very nature of the cost-benefit paradigm. The construction of a benefit-to-cost ratio is only slightly more desirable than a net benefit calculation and suffers from most of the same deficiencies.

It is also useful to compare an economic efficiency or cost-benefit approach to yet other alternatives. Consider the simplified case where the trade-offs involved are risks (to human health from an environmental carcinogen) versus costs (to the producer). In this case, referring to the impact matrix in Table 1, only two matrix elements predominate: producer costs and health/safety benefits to others. For different levels of environmental control, different benefits accrue. Figure 2 depicts the costs of risk reduction facing the producer as a function of different levels of risk. The curves represent the costs to reduce risks for a variety of different technological approaches open to the firm. At any given risk level, the point on the solid curve represents the lowest cost approach using the best existing technology. This curve represents the *efficient frontier* for compliance with risk reduction regulation. As more and more risk reduction is required, the cost per unit of additional risk reduction increases to what economic analysts call "the point of diminishing returns," where enormous costs are incurred for small reductions in risk.

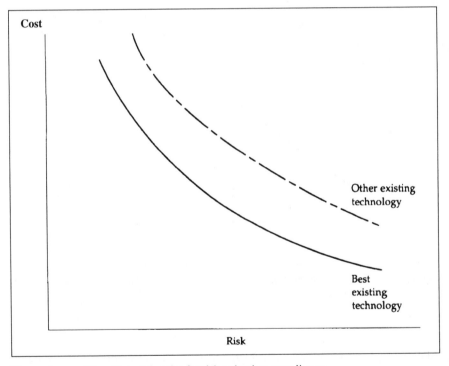

Figure 2:   The efficient frontier for risk reduction compliance

In Figure 3, we add to the curve representing the efficient frontier in Figure 2 a curve representing societal or worker demand for risk reduction as a function of risk. Where the two curves cross is the equilibrium point where the benefits of risk reduction equal the costs. [Note, strictly speaking, marginal cost and demand curves rather than total cost and demand curves should be used to determine the classical equilibrium point. However, the less stringent criterion that the benefits of regulations at least equal their costs is closer to political decision rules.] This is the "optimal" level of risk R_0 using economic efficiency criteria. Of course, public or worker demand must be expressed in monetary terms to use the efficiency criterion.

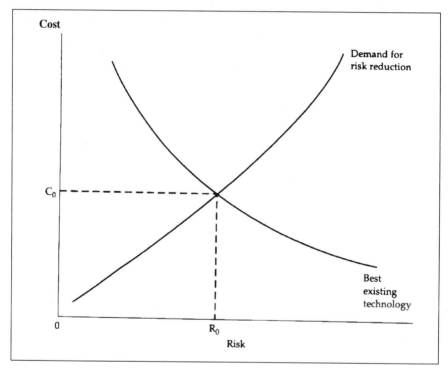

Figure 3:   Equilibrium level of environmental risk as determined by costs of controls and perceived benefits

Alternatives to cost-benefit or efficiency criteria for choosing the appropriate level of risk reduction include:

- Reducing risk by imposing control options at the *limits of economic or existing technological feasibility*, i.e., the limits determined by rising cost curves as discussed. Maximum achievable control technology (MACT) in the Clean Air Act and OSHA standards are examples of this.

- Specifying *existing, easily accessible technologies* of control or production, usually "best available technology"(BAT) in the U.S context.

- Establishing a *strict health or environment-based standard* for a maximum acceptable risk, such as a lifetime excess cancer risk of one in one million, independent of cost considerations.

Requiring levels of risk reduction that represent more risk reduction than allowed by economic efficiency criteria usually can be justified on grounds of social justice or equity. However, economists are quick to point out that this uses scarce monetary resources inefficiently and can even give rise to negative effects.[8] As has been discussed earlier, different regulatory agencies impose different criteria for achieving risk reduction.

Regulatory regimes that establish acceptable levels of risk (the third approach), if stringent enough, may impose on industry the need to develop new technology or technological approaches giving rise to the label "technology-forcing regulation." Note that this is not technology-based standard setting, as the term is usually understood, represented in the first two approaches above. These two options only require the diffusion or adoption of technology already developed. However, all three options have the potential to shift the debate from risk to technology; for instance, which specific technology satisfies BAT or MACT requirements or whether industry can meet a strict, risk-based standard without developing new technology.

All the above discussion assumes that industry is already on the efficient frontier and is providing some level of risk reduction. If a particular firm is above the efficient frontier in Figure 2 (i.e., the firm finds itself on the dashed line and is not using the most cost-effective technology to comply with regulations), a technology-based regulatory focus may encourage it to change the particular technology it is using. It is here that the oft-heralded pollution prevention approach is relevant. For those firms not already using the best available technologies, costs of achieving compliance could be greater than for firms on the efficient frontier. However, firms that declined to devote expenditures in the past could in principle use the monies not spent in order to leapfrog to more cost-effective means of compliance especially by using pollution prevention options.

4.3   Technology-Based Standards and Pollution Prevention Distinguished: Does Either Go Far Enough?

For the purposes of discussion here, technology-based standards can be standards that either specify a particular control technology or material use or those that di-

---

8   See the inappropriate proposals for the use of risk-risk analysis by Keeney (1990) and resulting criticism of that approach (U.S. GAO 1992).

rect that control technology used be the best available or that which achieves the
maximum pollution reduction achievable. (As discussed below, using these standards is to be distinguished from a technology-based *strategy* for addressing environmental problems.) The success of a governmental program predicated on technology-based standards can be evaluated by the extent to which individual firms
and sectors adopt the most efficient technology for the level of risk reduction they
each are obligated to achieve,[9] and the extent to which the collective effort
achieves the risk-reduction goal, reflecting both health and equity concerns.

In the last decade, we have witnessed four basic technological responses implemented by some firms: advances in control technology, input substitutes, changes
in final products, and process redesign. (These last three types of technological
response constitute the preferred hierarchy of what is called pollution prevention.
They were developed slowly as limits were reached on the ability to make significant advances by controlling pollution at the "end of the pipe.") In other words,
over time the efficient frontier depicted in Figure 2 has moved downward and to
the left toward greater efficiency and more risk reduction. Furthermore, the mix of
technologies becomes "richer" in pollution prevention options as traditional end-
of-pipe approaches reach their limits of effectiveness. However, in the United
States most firms over the period 1980-1992 did not move to the new frontier because enforcement of environmental laws had been lax. At the same time for those
firms whose environmental performance was advancing, its productivity gains
were also advancing due to technological changes. However, most firms were
slow to change their technologies. Gradually at first, faced with numerous constraints – increasing prohibition on landfills, off-site treatment costs, regulations
on publicly owned treatment works, growth restrictions in nonattainment areas for
air emissions, public scrutiny through community right-to-know laws, and environmental liability exposure – firms began to embrace pollution prevention.

It has been said that all industry needs to change its technology is a wake-up call.
But what changes can we expect? Here, the past predicts the future. Except for
product-based firms that focus continuously on new product development, what
has occurred largely is diffusion-driven pollution prevention – adaptation of technology that exists elsewhere and is only new *to the firm* (See U.S. EPA 1991;
INFORM 1985, 1992). A search by the regulated firm for better technologies to
reduce pollution, considering only existing off-the-shelf technological options,
does not require a cultural shift toward *developing* new technology – i.e., toward
innovation. The evidence shows that the bulk of pollution prevention efforts that
move firms to the new efficient frontier have involved "picking the low-hanging

---

9   Note that in some regulatory regimes, different firms may be required to
     respond differently. For example, under the Clean Air Act, new sources have
     more restrictions than existing sources, and states can impose different
     emission requirements on various existing sources, reflecting differences in
     their situations.

fruit" – i.e., using substitutes and technology already proven and used by a small number of firms, here or abroad. This tendency is useful in its own right, but eventually it is of limited benefit and unlikely to be long-lasting as more and more firms approach the efficient frontier. Of course, if some firms truly innovate, not all of them need to do so. The rest can simply adopt the new technologies developed by the technological leaders. What is important is to ensure that there is continuous leadership and innovation and that technology does not stagnate.

The much-heralded banning of CFCs, it should be remembered, did not bring about a new product. Rather, it allowed the substitution of an already-developed one with less ozone-depleting properties, but one that is an animal carcinogen (Zurer 1992). Had the Montreal Protocol been established with a longer time line for compliance, perhaps a different solution would have been developed by new entrants rather than one promoted by the dominant existing firms from old options. In other words, competition could have been created to develop a new and safer substitute for CFCs, had the dominant firms not been able to capture the international regulatory regime. Without sufficient advance notice requiring new substitutes and specifying the unacceptability of all current substitutes, no firm or entrepreneur would be likely to develop new substitute products. It should also be realized that pollution prevention options chosen from existing technologies are likely to be similar to the status quo – for example, the substitution of one organic solvent for another. Dramatic changes, such as the mechanical (pump) delivery system replacing CFC aerosol systems, are likely to require innovation.

5 Formulation of a "Win-Win" Technology-Based Strategy

The technology-forcing capability of regulation has been documented (Ashford and Heaton 1983), and theory has been developed on how to use regulation to encourage appropriate technological responses, be they new products, input substitution, or process re-design (Ashford, Ayers, and Stone 1985; Ashford et al. 1993). The challenge is how to use environmental regulation for win-win payoffs for *co-optimizing* growth, energy efficiency, environmental protection, worker safety, and consumer product safety. The idea is not fanciful, but it requires a shift from adopting technology new to the firm (diffusion) to developing new technology (innovation). Innovation can yield better performance for both environmental purposes and for productivity, but it is risky and requires that the firm be both capable and willing to innovate. Regulation, properly designed, can bring about a cultural shift in the firm or create opportunities for new entrants with better ideas.

5.1   Direct and Indirect Benefits of Regulation

It is significant that in its report *Preserving Our Future Today: Strategies and Framework* (U.S. EPA 1992), EPA moved from an approach that recommends choosing the options for risk reduction from existing technologies – the Science Advisory Board's (SAB) report *Reducing Risk (U.S. EPA 1990)* – to one recommending a greater reliance on economic incentives and innovation. In the later report, EPA states:

> Market forces are also part of a dynamic that produces innovations in technology and continued improvement in environmental protection will depend, in large part, on technological innovation. Economic incentives, for example, provide an important stimulus for creative pollution prevention and control. Innovative technologies include remedial methods, source reduction, treatment technologies, safer product substitutes, process controls and pollution controls. (U.S. EPA 1992)

What EPA as an agency has not addressed is *the strategic value of the combined interventions of regulation and economic incentives for directed innovation-driven pollution prevention.* However, the EPA National Advisory Council on Environmental Policy and Technology (NACEPT), in contrast to the SAB, has taken a technology-focused approach to environmental problems (NACEPT 1991, 1992, 1993). It is interesting to compare its work with that of the risk-focused SAB.

In devising a regulatory strategy, it must be realized that the benefits derived from direct regulation are only a part of the benefits that can be obtained from the regulatory process. Indirect, or leveraged, benefits are derived from the pressure of regulation to induce industry to deal preventively with unregulated hazards, to innovate, and to find ways to meet the public's need for a cleaner, healthier environment while maintaining industrial capacity. To put it another way, the positive side effects that accompany regulation need to be included in a complete assessment of the effectiveness of the agency's strategies. An example of leveraging is apparent in the observation that chemical companies are now routinely conducting short-term tests on new chemicals for possible carcinogenic activity, even though no general regulatory requirement exists. Specific regulations also induce leveraging. These indirect but by no means small effects are rarely included in any analysis.

Referring to the impact matrix in Table 1 discussed earlier, the leveraged effects rightly should be included in the assessment of the effects of regulation. They can be larger than direct effects. But further, an appreciation of the leveraging possibilities for regulation suggests an entirely new way to design strategies for approaching and prioritizing environmental problems. In developing this strategy, one must first understand how regulation can be used to influence the kinds of technological responses to meet environmental demands.

5.2   Regulation and Dynamic Efficiency

Several commentators and researchers have investigated the effects of regulation on technological change (Ashford 1993; Ashford, Ayers, and Stone 1985; Ashford and Heaton 1983; Hemmelskamp 1997; Irwin and Vergragt 1989; Kemp 1994 and 1997; Kurz 1987; Magat 1979; OECD 1985; Rothwell and Walsh 1979; Stewart 1981; Strasser 1997). Based on this work and experience gained from the history of industrial responses to regulation over the past twenty years, it is now possible to fashion regulatory strategies for eliciting the best possible technological response to achieve specific health, safety, or environmental goals. A regulatory strategy aimed at stimulating technology change to achieve a significant level of pollution prevention rejects the premise of balance: that regulation must achieve a *balance* or compromise between environmental integrity and industrial growth, or between job safety and competition in world markets.[10] Rather, such a strategy builds on the thesis that health, safety, and environmental goals can be co-optimized with economic growth through technological innovation (Ashford, Ayers, and Stone 1985).

The work of Burton Klein (1977) best describes the kind of industry and economic environment in which innovation flourishes. Klein's work concerns the concept of dynamic efficiency, as opposed to the static economic efficiency of the traditional economic theorists. In a state of *static efficiency,* resources are used most effectively within a fixed set of alternatives. *Dynamic efficiency,* in contrast, takes into account a constantly shifting set of alternatives, particularly in the technological realm. Thus, a dynamic economy, industry, or firm is flexible and can respond effectively to a constantly changing external environment.

Several conditions are critical to the achievement of dynamic efficiency. A dynamically efficient firm is open to technological development, has a relatively nonhierarchical structure, possesses a high level of internal and external communication, and shows a willingness to redefine organizational priorities as new opportunities emerge. Dynamically efficient industry groups are open to new entrants with superior technologies and encourage "rivalrous" behavior among industries already in the sector. In particular, dynamic efficiency flourishes in an environment that is conducive to entrepreneurial risk-taking and does not reward those who adhere to the technological status quo. Thus, Klein emphasizes structuring a macroeconomy that contains strong incentives for firms to change, adapt,

---

10   Environmental, health, and safety regulation, as seen by economists, should correct market imperfections by internalizing the social costs of industrial production. Regulation results in a redistribution of the costs and benefits of industrial activity among manufacturers, employers, workers, consumers, and other citizens. Within the traditional economic paradigm, economically efficient solutions reflecting the proper balance between costs and benefits of given activities are the major concern.

and redefine the alternatives facing them. Regulation is one of several stimuli that can promote such a restructuring of a firm's market strategy.

While a new technology may be a more costly method of attaining *current* environmental standards, it could achieve *stricter* standards at less cost than adoption of existing technology. Figure 4 illustrates the difference, as explained below.

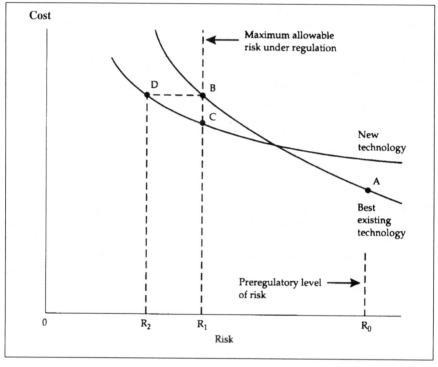

Figure 4:   An innovative response to regulation

Suppose that either market demand or regulatory fiat determines that a reduction in risk from R_0 to R_1 is desirable. Use of the most efficient existing technology would impose a cost represented by point B. Again, the "existing technology" curve represents the supply of lowest-cost technologies from among less-efficient existing technological options for achieving various levels of environmental risk. This curve is thus the present efficient frontier of existing pollution control and production technologies having different degrees of environmental risk. However, if it were possible to stimulate technological innovation, a new technology "supply curve" could arise, allowing the same degree of risk reduction at a lower cost represented by point C. Alternatively, a greater degree of health protection (R_2) could be offered if expenditures equal to costs represented by point B were applied instead to new technological solutions (point D). Note that co-optimization resulting in having your cake and eating it too can occur because a new *dynamic* efficiency is achieved.[11] Because end-of-pipe approaches have been used for a long time and improvements in pollution control have probably reached a plateau, it is argued that the new technology curve or frontier will be occupied predominantly by pollution prevention technologies (i.e., new products, inputs or production processes). Initiatives to bring firms into environmental compliance using new technologies are termed innovation-driven pollution prevention.

6   A Model for Regulation-Induced Technological Change

Prior work has developed models to explain the effects of regulation on technological change in the chemical, pharmaceutical, and automobile industries (Ashford and Heaton 1979, 1983; Ashford, Heaton, and Priest 1979; Kurz 1987; Rip and van den Belt 1988). Figure 5 presents a modified model to assist in designing regulations and strategies for encouraging pollution prevention rather than sharply to trace the effects of regulation on innovation. The particulars of this model – the nature of regulatory stimulus, the characteristics of the responding industrial sectors, and the resulting design of innovative technological and regulatory strategies – are discussed below.

---

[11]   The firm could improve its efficiency in risk management by using better end-of-pipe control technology or by engaging in pollution prevention, which could be accomplished if the firm changed its inputs, reformulated its final products, or altered its process technology by adopting technology new to the firm. This would be characterized as diffusion-driven pollution prevention, and the changes, while beneficial, would probably be suboptimal because the firm would achieve static, but not dynamic, efficiency. If one were to add to Figure 4 the societal demand for risk reduction, the equilibrium point would occur at lower cost and risk than that in Figure 3.

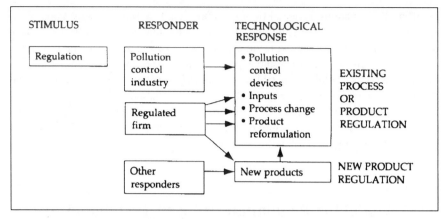

Figure 5:   A model for regulation-induces technological change

6.1   The Regulatory Stimulus

Environmental, health, and safety regulations affecting the industry that uses or produces the regulated chemical include controls on air quality, water quality, solid and hazardous waste, pesticides, food additives, pharmaceuticals, toxic substances, workplace health and safety, and consumer product safety.[12] These regulations control different aspects of development or production; they change over time; and they are "technology-forcing" to different degrees.[13] Thus, designers of

---

[12]   The statutes from which these regulatory systems derive their authority are as follows (listed as ordered in the text). Clean Air Act (CAA), 42 U.S.C. Sec. 7401-7642 (1990); Clean Water Act (CWA), 33 U.S.C. Sec. 1251-1376 (1982); Resource Conservation and Recovery Act (RCRA), 42 U.S.C. Sec. 6901-6987 (1982); Federal Insecticide, Fungicide, and Rodenticide Act (FIFRA), 7 U.S.C. 136 136y (1982); Federal Food, Drug, and Cosmetic Act (FDCA), 21 U.S.C. Sec. 301 392 (1982); Toxic Substances Control Act (TSCA), 15 U.S.C. Sec. 2601-2629 (1982); Occupational Safety and Health Act (OSHA), 29 U.S.C. Sec. 651-678 (1982); and Consumer Product Safety Act (CFSA), 15 U.S.C. Sec. 2051-2083 (1982).

[13]   Technology-forcing here refers to the tendency of a regulation to force industry to develop new technology. Regulations may force development of new technology by different types of restrictions. For example, air and water pollution regulation focuses on "end-of-pipe" effluents. See, for example, CAA, Sec. 111, 112, 202, 42 U.S.C. Sec. 7411, 7412, 7521; CWA, Sec. 301, 33 U.S.C. Sec. 1311. OSHA, in contrast, regulates chemical exposures incident to the production process. See OSHA, Sec. 6, 29 U.S.C. Sec. 655. The FDCA, FIFRA, and TSCA impose a premarket approval process on new chemicals. See FDCA, Sec. 409, 505, 21 U.S.C. Sec. 348, 355; FIFRA, Sec.

regulation should realize that the effects on technological innovation will differ among regulations that ensure the following conditions:

- Product safety must be demonstrated prior to marketing (pesticides, food additives, pharmaceuticals, and in some cases new chemicals).[14]

- The efficacy of products must be demonstrated prior to marketing (pharmaceuticals).[15]

- Product safety must be proved or product use must be controlled after marketing (for existing chemicals under the Toxic Substances Control Act, for worker protection, and for consumer products).[16]

- Production technology is controlled to reduce risks to workplace health and safety.

- Emissions, effluents, or wastes are controlled in accordance with air, water, and hazardous waste regulation.[17]

Furthermore, the internal structure of regulations may alter the general climate for innovation. Elements of that structure include the form of the regulation (product versus process regulation), the mode (performance versus specification standards), the time for compliance, the uncertainty, the stringency of the requirements, and the existence of other economic incentives that complement the regulatory signal. The importance of these elements is discussed below; historical evidence is found in Ashford and Heaton 1983 and in Ashford, Ayers, and Stone 1985.

The distinction between regulation of products and regulation of processes suggests yet a further distinction.[18] New products differ from existing products, and

---

3, 7 U.S.C. Sec. 136a; TSCA, Sec. 5, 15 U.S.C. Sec. 2604. The degree of technology-forcing ranges from pure "health based" mandates, such as those in the ambient air quality standards of the Clean Air Act, to a technology diffusion standard, such as "best available technology" under the Clean Water Act. CAA Sec. 109(b)(1), 42 U.S.C. Sec. 7409(b)(1); CWA, Sec. 301(b), 33 U.S.C. Sec. 1311(b). For a discussion of this issue and a comparison of statutes, see LaPierre 1977.

[14] See FIFRA, Sec. 3, 7 U.S.C. Sec. 136a; FDCA, Sec. 409, 505, 21 U.S.C. Sec. 348, 355; TSCA, Sec. 5, 15 U.S.C. Sec. 2604.

[15] See FDCA, Sec. 505, 21 U.S.C. Sec. 355.

[16] See TSCA, Sec. 6, 15 U.S.C. Sec. 2605; OSHA, Sec. 6, 29 U.S.C. Sec. 655; CPSA, Sec. 7,15 U.S.C. Sec. 2056.

[17] See generally CAA, 42 U.S.C. Sec. 7401-7642; CWA, 33 U.S.C. Sec. 1251 1376; RCRA, 42 U.S.C. Sec. 6901-6987.

[18] In practice, product and process regulations may be difficult to distinguish. If a process regulation is stringent enough, it effectively becomes a product ban. Product regulation generally gives rise to product substitution, and process regulation generally gives rise to process change (Ashford and Heaton 1979, 1983).

production process components differ from unwanted byproducts or pollutants.[19] Regulations relying on detailed specification standards or on "best available technology" may discourage innovation while prompting rapid diffusion of state-of-the-art technology. Though a phased-in compliance schedule allows a timely industry response, it may prompt only incremental improvements in technology.

An industry's perception of the need to alter its technological course often precedes promulgation of a regulation. Most environmental regulations arise only after extended scrutiny of a potential problem by government, citizens, workers, and industry. Prior scrutiny often has greater effects on industry than formal rule making, because anticipation of regulation stimulates innovation (Ashford, Hattis, et al. 1979). For example, formal regulation of PCBs occurred years after the government expressed initial concern. Aware of this concern, the original manufacturer and other chemical companies began to search for substitutes prior to regulation. Similarly, most firms in the asbestos products industry substantially complied with OSHA asbestos regulation years before it was promulgated. This preregulation period can allow industry time to develop compliance technologies, process changes, or product substitutes while allowing leeway for it to adjust to ensure continued production or future commercial innovation.

The government's initial show of concern is often, however, an unreliable stimulus to technological change. Both technical uncertain ties and application of political pressures may cause uncertainty regarding future regulatory requirements. Nevertheless, some regulatory uncertainty is frequently beneficial. Although excessive regulatory uncertainty may cause industry inaction, too much certainty will stimulate only minimum compliance technology. Similarly, excessively frequent changes to regulatory requirements may frustrate technological development.

Regulatory stringency is the most important factor influencing technological innovation. A regulation is stringent either because compliance requires a *significant reduction* in exposure to toxic substances, because compliance using existing technology is *costly,* or because compliance is not possible with existing technology and hence requires a *significant technological change.* Legislative policy considerations dictate different degrees of stringency as well, since some statutes require that standards be based predominantly on environmental, health, and safety concerns; some on existing technological capability; and others on the technology within reach of a vigorous research and development effort.

In the early 1970s, most environmental, health, and safety regulations set standards at a level attainable by existing technology (LaPierre 1977). The regulations reflected both perceived limits to legislative authority and substantial industry influence over the drafting of standards. More recent regulations have tended to-

---

19   Note, however, that component regulations normally specify elements of the production process designed to prevent undesirable by-products, while pollutant regulations specify unwanted by-products of production.

ward greater stringency, but they still rely on existing technologies (but often those in minority or rare use).[20] (Examples are the technology-based standards for hazardous substances under Section 112 of the 1990 Clean Air Act Amendments requiring the use of MACT or the lowest achievable emission rate [LAER] under the new source regulation of Section 111). The effect of the agency's strategy on innovation is not confined to standard setting. Innovation waivers, which stimulate innovation by allowing noncompliance with existing regulation while encouraging the development of a new technology, are affected by enforcement strategies as well (Ashford, Ayers, and Stone 1985).[21] The degree to which the requirements of a regulation are strictly enforced may influence the willingness of an industrial sector to attempt to innovate. The implementing agency ultimately may strictly enforce environmental regulations against those firms receiving waivers or, alternatively, it may adopt a "fail-soft" strategy where a firm has made an imperfect but good faith attempt to comply (Ashford, Ayers, and Stone 1985). The latter strategy is an important element of the regulatory stimulus to innovate, as it decreases an innovator's risk of severe agency action in the event of failure.

6.2   Characteristics of the Responding Industrial Sector

The industry responding to regulation may be the regulated industry (or its suppliers), the pollution control industry, or another industry (see Figure 5). Regulation of existing chemical products or processes might elicit installation of a pollution control device, input substitution, a manufacturing process change, or product reformulation. The regulated industry will likely develop new processes and change inputs, sometimes with the aid of its suppliers; the pollution control industry will develop new devices; and either the regulated industry or new entrants will develop reformulated or new products. Regulation of new chemicals (such as premarket screening) will, of course, affect the development of new products.

Past research on the innovation process in the absence of regulation has focused on the innovation dynamic in diverse industrial segments throughout the economy (see Abernathy and Utterback 1978; Ashford and Heaton 1983). The model of the innovation process on which that research focused refers to a "productive segment" (a single product line) in industry, defined by the nature of its technology. Automobile engine manufacture would be a "productive segment," as would vinyl

---

20   This statement is based mainly on a review of the literature on regulations under the CAA, CWA, OSHA, CPSA, RCRA, and TSCA promulgated in the period 1970-1985. For a more current commentary, see Strasser (1997).

21   EPA has also initiated a pollution prevention element in enforcement negotiations for firms in violation of standards (i.e., the agency is encouraging state officials to press for the adoption of pollution prevention approaches by polluters in reaching settlements for violations of environmental laws and regulations). See Becker and Ashford 1995.

chloride monomer production, but neither the automobile industry nor the vinyl chloride industry would be a "productive segment" since they both encompass too many diverse technologies. Over time, the nature and rate of innovation in the segment will change. Initially, the segment creates a market niche by selling a new product, superior in performance to the old technology it replaces. The new technology is typically unrefined, and product change occurs rapidly as technology improves.[22] Because of the rapid product change, the segment neglects process improvements in the early period. Later, however, as the product becomes better defined, more rapid process change occurs. In this middle period, the high rate of process change reflects the segment's need to compete on the basis of price rather than product performance. In the latter stages, both product and process change decline and the segment becomes static or rigid. At this point in its cycle, the segment may be vulnerable to invasion by new ideas or disruption by external forces that could cause a reversion to an earlier stage.

6.3   The Design of Strategies

Three implications of this innovation model relate directly to the design of strategies to promote innovation.

- First, the model suggests that innovation is predictable in a given industrial context.

- Second, it asserts that the characteristics of a particular technology determine the probable nature of future innovation within an industrial segment.

- Third, it describes a general process of industrial maturation that appears to be relatively uniform across different productive segments (see Ashford and Heaton 1983). This process is related to the eventual decrease in the ability of an industrial product line to innovate along either product or process-dimensions. This model does not, however, describe sources of innovation within the firm, nor does it elucidate the forces that may transform a mature segment into a more innovative one. See Rip and van den Belt (1988), Schot (1992), and Kemp (1997) for insights into these dynamics.

The value of this theory of innovation is that it provides a rationale upon which the regulatory agency may fashion a regulation aimed at the industry most likely to achieve a regulatory goal and by which the private sector can develop a more appropriate response to environmental problems. Consistently, the theory relies on the assumption that *the regulatory designer can determine the extent of an industry's innovative rigidity (or flexibility)* and its likely response to regulatory stimuli

---

[22]   It is typical for the old technology to improve as well, although incrementally, when a new approach challenges its dominance.

with reference to objectively determinable criteria. The regulatory designer must make the following three determinations:

- What technological response is desirable?[23]

- Which industrial sector is most likely to diffuse or to develop the desired technology?

- What kinds of regulation and incentives will most likely elicit the desired response?

The first determination requires a technology options analysis, the second a knowledge of a variety of industrial segments, and the third an application of the model presented above.[24]

In sum, regulations must be designed explicitly with technological considerations in mind – i.e., regulations should be fashioned to elicit the type of technological response desired. Again, both stringency and flexibility (through innovation waivers or enforcement practices) are important. Enforcement and permitting procedures must augment, not frustrate, the regulatory signals (see NACEPT 1991, 1992, 1993).

Regulatory design and implementation are largely in the hands of government, the exception being negotiated rule making or "voluntary" compliance efforts involving an industry-government effort.[25] Once the regulatory signals are crafted, the firm must be receptive to those signals that require change. As discussed at the beginning of this article, the key to successfully changing the firm is to influence both managerial *knowledge* and managerial *attitudes* affecting decision making that involves both technological change and environmental concerns.

Managerial knowledge, managerial attitudes, and the technological character of the firm are not actually independent factors, however, although policies can be devised to affect each directly. Managerial attitudes and responses obviously are influenced both by incentives and by the knowledge base and general practices and procedures (i.e., the culture) of the firm. Management's attitudes and responses to environmental problems may also be determined or constrained by the particular technology of the firm itself. There is a kind of "technological determinism" that influences not only what can be done, but also what will be done. For example, firms that have rigid production technologies (i.e., processes that are

---

[23]   For example, should a regulation force a product or a process change (see Rest and Ashford 1988) and, further, should it promote diffusion of existing technology, simple adaptation, accelerated development of radical innovation already in progress, or radical innovation?

[24]   Ashford and Stone (1985) review and develop methodologies for assessing past and future dynamic regulatory impacts involving technological change.

[25]   For a detailed examination of negotiated agreements in both the environmental and worker health and safety areas, see Caldart and Ashford (1999).

infrequently changed) are unlikely to have managers confident enough to embark on process changes. Certain technologies beget specific management styles – if not particular managers per se. There is probably also a managerial selection in and out of the technology-based firm. For example, if changing or reformulating the final product requires a process using a different scale of production, the firm may not have managers experienced at operating at smaller (or larger) scales.

Relevant to managerial attitudes and decision processes, Karmali (1990) reviewed three different theoretical approaches useful in understanding what influences managerial attitudes that affect the willingness (or even the ability) of the technology-based firm to undergo change.

Technological determinism is based on the principle that technological developments have their own dynamics and constraints that determine the direction of change even when stimulated by external forces.[26] Economic *determinism* considers the market and economic competition to be the main driving forces behind technological innovation. Essentially, this approach treats technology as a black box. Unlike the first two approaches, *social constructivism* attempts to move away from such unidirectional models and suggests that different social groups, such as the users of the technology and those potentially affected by it or its impacts, are able to exert influence on those who develop the technology. Any technological change is thus seen as the product of a dynamic interaction, rather than one deriving force from inside or outside the firm. Social constructivism can thus be viewed as a means of bridging the gap between the organizational internalists and externalists (Cramer et al. 1989; Cramer et al. 1990; Karmali 1990; Kemp 1994 and 1997; OECD 1989; Rip and van den Belt 1988; Rennings 1998; Schot 1992).

All these factors may well influence managerial attitudes and hence decision making toward environmental demands. But further, policy instruments that *per se* affect technology, economic incentives, and social relationships can be used to influence the firm toward a more socially optimal technological response to environmental problems.

Decisions, of course, are also affected by the knowledge base of the firm. This can be improved by requiring the firm to identify technological options for source reduction and to conduct through-put analysis, i.e., a materials accounting survey (Hearne and Aucott 1992; NAS 1990). The regulatory agency can also provide or promote technical assistance to firms, demonstration projects, continuing education of engineers and materials scientists, and the use of appropriate engineering consulting services (Ashford, Cozakos, et al. 1988).

---

[26]   While much has been written on the influence of the organization of the firm (Karmali 1990; Kurz 1987; U.S. OTA 1986; Schot 1992), it is the author's contention that the technology of the firm can determine corporate structure and attitudes as much as the other way around.

7 Priority Setting Using a Technology-Based Strategy

Described above is the design of technology-based strategies that promote technological changes, whether via diffusion or innovation. Next, one might ask how to devise a priority-setting scheme using a technology-based strategy for addressing the many environmental problems facing an agency. Such a scheme is outlined below. First, the issue of information needs to be addressed. In risk-based approaches, much effort might be devoted to performing animal studies (costing upwards from S2,000,000 each), exposure studies, epidemiological studies, and risk estimates. In a technology-based approach, what is required first is a technology options analysis.

The Technology Options Analysis

In order to facilitate pollution prevention or the shift to cleaner technologies, options for technological change must be articulated and evaluated according to multivariate criteria, including economic, environmental and health/safety factors. The matrix developed to facilitate trade-off analysis (see Table 1) can be used to document the aspects of the different technology options and, further, it can be used to compare improvements that each option might offer over existing technological solutions. The identification of these options and their comparison against the technology in use is what constitutes Technology Options Analysis (TOA). Hornstein (1992) points out, in contrast, that "it is against the range of possible solutions that the economist analyzes the efficiency of existing risk levels" and that "to fashion government programs based on a comparison of existing preferences can artificially dampen the decision makers' actual preference for changes were government only creative enough to develop alternative solutions to problems" (Hornstein 1992).

At first blush, it might appear that TOA is nothing more than a collection of multivariate impact assessments for existing industrial technology and alternative options. However, it is possible to bypass extensive cost, environmental, health and safety, and other analyses or modeling by performing *comparative analyses* of these factors (such as comparative technological performance and relative risk and ecological assessment). Comparative analyses are much easier to do than analyses requiring absolute quantification of variables, are likely to be less sensitive to initial assumptions than, for example, cost-benefit analysis, and will enable easier identification of win-win options. Thus, while encompassing a greater number of technological options than simple technology assessment (TA), the actual analysis would be easier and probably more believable.

TOAs can identify technologies used in a majority of firms that might be *diffused* into greater use, or technologies that might be *transferred* from one industrial sector to another. In addition, opportunities for technology development (i.e., innovation) can be identified. Government might merely require the firms or industries to undertake a TOA.[27] On the other hand, government might either "force" or assist in the adoption or development of new technologies. If government takes on the role of merely assessing (through TA) new technologies that industry itself decided to put forward, it may miss the opportunity to encourage superior technological options. Only by requiring or undertaking TOAs itself is government likely to facilitate major technological change. Both industry and government have to be sufficiently technologically literate to ensure that the TOAs are sophisticated and comprehensive.

Encouraging technological change may have payoffs, not only with regard to environmental goals, but also to energy, workplace safety, and other such goals. Because many different options might be under taken, the payoffs are somewhat open-ended. Hence, looking to prioritize different problem areas cannot be the same kind of exercise as a risk-assessment-based approach. A fraction of the amount of money devoted to a single animal study could instead yield some rather sophisticated knowledge concerning what kinds of technology options exist or are likely in the future. Expert technical talent in engineering design and product development can no doubt produce valuable information and identify fruitful areas for investment in technology development.

7.1   Innovation-Driven versus Diffusion-Driven Strategies

Problem areas for encouraging technological change, by their nature, turn out not to be substance-focused, but rather industrial-process focused, so that by a single technological change, one might address not only multimedia concerns for many chemicals associated with the process, but also consumer and worker safety. One kind of prioritization that can proceed is *the identification of areas in which innovation, as opposed to diffusion, might be preferred.* Table 2 lists some of the characteristics of the polluting technology, the replacing technology, and the hazards addressed that favor an innovation – or a diffusion-driven approach.

Knowing just how far firms/industries are from the efficient frontier could provide an organizing principle for diffusion-driven strategies. If risk can be reduced to a socially acceptable level using existing technologies, priorities can be established based on achieving maximum risk reduction per compliance dollar expended, but tempered by favoring regulations with multimedia payoffs (inducing worker and consumer safety), advancing opportunities for changing the culture of the firm, and encouraging other technological responses. Examples of areas where diffusion-driven, technology-based strategies might be considered are: encouraging substitutes for permanent-press resins containing formaldehyde, using nonchemi-

---

[27]   For development of the argument that government should require technology options analysis in the context of chemical process safety, see Ashford, Gobbell, et al. 1993 and Ashford 1997.

cal degreasing technologies in replacing chlorinated solvents, and phasing out fertilizers containing cadmium.

Table 2: Conditions favoring innovation-driven and diffusion-driven strategies

Innovation	Diffusion
Large residual risks even after diffusion and/or high costs of diffusion	Distance from the efficient frontier (opportunities for significant and adequate risk reduction)
Innovative history/innovative potential or opportunity for new entrant	Noninnovative history; "essential" industry/product line
Multimedia response desired	Single-medium response adequate
Multihazard industry	Single-hazard problem
Flexible management culture	Rigid management culture

Innovation-driven strategies are by their nature even more open-ended than diffusion-driven approaches, more commercially risky, and more capable of yielding greater and broader payoffs, such as multimedia control of many substances and productivity gains. The discussion above has attempted to persuade the less heroic that innovation is largely predictable and can be directed readily, even if the exact outcome is not known.

7.2 Setting Priorities

Since innovation-driven approaches are likely to produce win-win strategies, rather than win-lose outcomes, criteria for choosing "which problem to attack first" take on a different character. They might include the presence of large risks left unaddressed by existing approaches, high costs of achieving risk reduction using even the best existing technologies, a history of or potential for innovation in the industrial segment responsible for the risks, and the enthusiasm and capability of the industrial sector or firm most likely to undertake the technological change involving product or process innovation. *Risk based approaches, in contrast, would never consider the third and fourth of these criteria, and would tend to regard the second as indicating a low-priority risk (because of the expense of control using existing technology) rather than a high-priority innovative effort.*

Areas ripe for change stimulated by an innovation-driven technology-based approach include some pesticide uses, chlorinated hydrocarbon uses, formaldehyde-containing industrial and consumer products, and endocrine disrupting chemicals. Innovative technology need not depend on chemical approaches. For example, we might also place a high priority on ultrasonic cleaning technology or on the substitution of electric vehicles for cars powered by the internal combustion engine.

It may not be important to prioritize problems according to payoffs in the narrow sense, but rather to choose to attack problems with the broadest possible applicability (i.e., transfer potential or likely subsequent diffusion of the approach), leveraging potential, and demonstration potential to contribute to both industry and agency cultural shifts. An innovation-driven pollution prevention policy, unlike a diffusion-driven one, is likely to produce some specific successes and failures (with more of the former preferable). For that reason, a portfolio approach to evaluating the outcome of that strategy applied to many targets is the appropriate approach. In order to get significant technological changes, some failures in attempts have to be tolerated. For those, "fail-soft" strategies need to be devised.

7.3   Risks of Innovation

Innovation is risky, but large returns on investment can be realized only with some risk taking. For some regulated firms that have lost their innovative capabilities, these risks are too large to take. Encouraging new entrants and competitors will not be welcomed by firms whose technology or products are likely to be displaced or replaced. But *innovation is more predictable and capable of being directed than invention or serendipitous discovery.* Unfortunately, in the case of highly polluting technologies, the existing markets are dominated by powerful and mature firms that block changes necessary for advancement. The firms or divisions not yet established, which would come up with better ideas, have no political representation. (One possible exception may be biotechnology firms using approaches that offer dramatically different ways to increase agricultural yield, control pests, produce pharmaceuticals, and remediate waste, as these are new and flexible emerging technologies). It is an innovation-driven technology-based strategy, rather than a diffusion of existing technologies, that represents the future private and public interest.

8   Final Commentary

Two different approaches are evident in addressing environmental problems and in setting environmental priorities. The first asks the question: how do we identify and rank the risks or opportunities for reducing risks to health and environment? The second asks: how do we identify and exploit the opportunities for changing the basic technologies of production, agriculture, and transportation that cause damage to environment and health? But further, do we want to effectuate a transformation of the existing polluting or problem industrial sectors are do we want to stimulate more radical innovation that might result in technology displacement?

Considerations of risks, costs, and equity are relevant to all these questions. Historically, the U.S. EPA and most economists, scientists, and risk analysts have dedicated their efforts to exploring rational approaches to answering the first question. They also implicitly assume a static technological world in pleading for a rational use of scarce resources and in assuming that the conditions dictate a zero-sum game. On the other hand, activists and those interested in an industrial transformation focus on the second question and argue for application of political will and creative energy in changing the ways we do business in the industrial state. The first effort promotes rationalism within a static world; the second is arational – not irrational – and promotes transformation of the industrial state as an art form. Interestingly, it is the first approach that is criticized as being too technocratic, but it is the second that argues for technological change.

In my view, an industrial transformation is essential in which the affected publics have major voices and that approaches to cutting up what is viewed as a shrinking pie, using dubious tools of risk and cost analysis, are regressive and now out of date.

In a January 1994 report, EPA reveals a clear evolution of its thinking from a preoccupation with risk to a concern for fundamental technological change. In the introduction to the report, EPA states:

> Technology innovation is indispensable to achieving our national and international environmental goals. Available technologies are inadequate to solve many present and emerging environmental problems or, in some cases, too costly to bear widespread adoption. Innovative technologies offer the promise that the demand for continuing economic growth can be reconciled with the imperative of strong environmental protection. In launching this Technology Innovation Strategy, the Environmental Protection Agency aims to inaugurate an era of unprecedented technological ingenuity in the service of environmental protection and public health...This strategy signals EPA's commitment to making needed changes and reinventing the way it does its business so that the United States will have the best technological solutions needed to protect the environment. (U.S. EPA 1994)

Unfortunately, this article of faith has not been followed up with action, and neither the U.S. nor Europe has come to grips with just how radical technological innovation should be encouraged, especially if it means the displacement of dominant technologies and even firms.

The Dutch 'Polder Model' boasts of success in stimulating environmentally superior technological solutions by involving the polluting firms with other stakeholders in a "covenant" to engage in continuous improvement of environmental performance. (See Gouldson and Murphy 1998). The 'Dutch Covenant' can be much more than a voluntary agreement between industry and government. There is participation by environmentalists, as well, and milestones and oversight with legal power to back up the agreements. Some success at incremental or modest innovation is apparent. Still, if Factor 10 (or greater) is what is desired in pollution or material/energy use reduction, cooperation with existing firms could limit success – especially if the targets, as well as the means and schedule for reaching the targets, are negotiated between government and those firms.

This article has reviewed the U.S.-based research into the effects of government regulation in the United States. In a number of MIT studies beginning in 1979, it was found that regulation could stimulate significant *fundamental changes in product and process technology* which benefited the industrial innovator, provided the regulations were stringent and focused. This empirical work was conducted fifteen years earlier than the emergence of the much weaker Porter Hypothesis which argued that firms on the cutting edge of developing and implementing pollution reduction would benefit economically through "innovation offsets" by being first-movers to comply with regulation. Perhaps paradoxically, in Europe where regulation was arguably less stringent and fomulated with industry consensus, regulation was not found to stimulate much significant innovation (Kemp 1997). Analysis of the U.S. situation since the earlier MIT studies reinforces the strategic usefulness of properly designed and implemented regulation complemented by economic incentives (Strasser 1997).

An important Dutch researcher whose views are informed mainly by European environmental regulation (Kemp 1994 and 1997) fails to see that regulation can be an important tool – maybe the most important tool – both to stimulate radical and environmentally superior technology and to yield economic benefits to innovating firms. In contrast, a comparison of the Dutch and UK regulatory systems (Gouldson and Murphy 1998) concludes that stringent regulation, without yielding to the pressure of the regulated firms common in the UK system, is essential to bring about significant technological changes. Kemp argues that for a technology regime to shift – i.e., to transform – there has to be a unique/new niche which a firm can carve out for itself through the process of "strategic niche management" (Kemp 1994). What he apparently fails to see is that regulation can indeed create that niche – and possibly not for the regulated firm alone. New entrants can be the responders, and it may be that technological innovation by new entrants is what is needed for sustainable development.

References

Abernathy, W. and J. Utterback (1978), Patterns of Industrial Innovation, *Technology Review* (June-July), 41.

Ashford, N. (1988), Science and Values in the Regulatory Process, *Statistical Science* 3 (3), 377-383.

Ashford, N. A. (1993) Understanding Technological Responses of Industrial Firms to Environmental Problems: Implications for Government Policy, in: K. Fischer and J. Schot (eds.), *Environmental Strategies for Industry: International Perspectives on Research Needs and Policy Implications*, Washington DC, 277-307.

Ashford, N. A. (1997), Industrial Safety: The Neglected Issue in Industrial Ecology, in: Ashford, N. A. and Côté, R. P. (eds.): The Special Issue on Industrial Ecology, *Journal of Cleaner Production*, 5(1/2), 115-121.

Ashford, N. and C. Ayers (1985), Policy Issues for Consideration in Transferring Technology to Developing Countries, *Ecology Law Review* 12 (4), 871-905.

Ashford, N., C. Ayers and R. Stone (1985), Using Regulation to Change the Market for Innovation. *Harvard Environmental Law Review* 9 (2), 419-466.

Ashford, N. and C. Caldart (1996), *Technology, Law and the Working Environment*. Second Edition, Washington, D.C.

Ashford, N., A. Cozakos, R.F. Stone and K. Wessel (1988), *The Design of Programs to Encourage Hazardous Waste Reduction: An Incentives Analysis*. Trenton.

Ashford, N., J. Gobbell, J. Lachman, M. Matthiesen, A. Minzner and R. Stone (1993), *The Encouragement of Technological Change for Preventing Chemical Accidents: Moving Firms from Secondary Prevention and Mitigation to Primary Prevention*. Cambridge, Mass.

Ashford, N., D. Hattis, G. Heaton, A. Jaffe, S. Owen and W. Priest (1979), *Environmental/Safety Regulation and Technological Change in the U.S. Chemical Industry*, Report to the National Science Foundation, CPA No. 79-6. Cambridge, Mass.

Ashford, N., D. Hattis, G.R. Heaton, J.I. Katz, W.C. Priest and E.M. Zolt (1980), *Evaluating Chemical Regulations: Trade-Off Analysis and Impact Assessment for Environmental Decision Making*. NTIS # PB81-195067-1980. Washington, D.C.

Ashford, N. and G. Heaton (1979), The Effects of Health and Environmental Regulation on Technological Change in the Chemical Industry: Theory and Evidence, in: C. Hill (ed.), *Federal Regulation and Chemical Innovation*, Washington D.C.

Ashford, N. and G. Heaton (1983), Regulation and Technological Innovation in the Chemical Industry, *Law and Contemporary Problems* 46 (3), 109-157.

Ashford, N., G. Heaton and W.C. Priest (1979) Environmental, Health and Safety Regulation and Technological Innovation, in: C.T. Hill and J.M. Utterback (ed.) *Technological Innovation for a Dynamic Economy,* New York.

Ashford, N. and R. Stone, (1985), *Evaluating the Economic Impact of Chemical Regulation: Methodological Issues,* CPA No. 85-01, February. Cambridge, Mass.

Ashford, N. and R. Stone (1991), Liability, Innovation and Safety in the Chemical Industry, in: Litan, R. and P. Huber (eds.),*The Liability Maze: The Impact of Liability Law on Safety and Innovation,* Washington, D.C.

Becker, M. and Ashford, N. (1995), Exploiting Opportunities for Pollution Prevention in EPA Enforcement Agreements, *Environmental Science & Technology* 29(5), 220A-226A.

Caldart, C. and Ashford, N. (1999) Negotiation as a Means of Developing and Implementing Environmental and Occupational Health and Safety Policy, *Harvard Environmental Law Review* 23(1),141-202.

Coriat, B. (1995) Organisational Innovations: The Missing Link in European Competitiveness, in: Andreasen, L. E. et al. (eds.) *Europe's Next Step: Organisational Innovation, Competition and Employment,* London, 3-32.

CPA (Center for Policy Alternatives) (1975). *National Support for Science and Technology: An Explanation of the Foreign Experience.* CPA No. 75-121. Cambridge, Mass.: Center for Policy Alternatives, Massachusetts Institute of Technology.

Cramer, J., J. Schot, F. van den Akker and G. Geesteranus (1989), *The Need for a Broader Technology Perspective Towards Cleaner Technologies,* Discussion paper for the ECE Seminar on Economic Implications of Low-Waste Technology, The Hague, The Netherlands, October 16-19.

Cramer, J., J. Schot, F. van den Akker and G. Geesteranus (1990), Stimulating Cleaner Technologies through Economic Instruments: Possibilities and Constraints, *UNEP Industry and Environment* (May-June), 46-53.

Gouldson, A. and J. Murphy (1998), *Regulatory Realities: The Implementation and Impact of Industrial Environmental Regulation,* London.

Hearne, S. and M. Aucott (1992), Source Reduction versus Release Reduction: Why the TRI Cannot Measure Prevention, *Pollution Prevention* 2 (1), 3-17.

Heaton, G., R. Repetto and R. Sobin (1991) *Transforming Technology: An Agenda for Environmentally Sustainable Growth in the 21st Century,* Washington, D.C.

Hemmelskamp, J (1997), Environmental Policy Instruments and their Effects on Innovation, *European Planning Studies* 5(2), 177 et seq.

Hornstein, D. T. (1992), Reclaiming Environmental Law: A Normative Critique of Comparative Analysis, *Columbia Law Review* 92 (3), 562-633.

INFORM (1985), *Cutting Chemical Wastes: What 29 Organic Chemical Plants Are Doing to Reduce Hazardous Waste.* New York.

INFORM (1992) *Environmental Dividends: Cutting More Chemical Wastes.* New York.

Irwin, A. and P. Vergragt (1989), Re-thinking the Relationship between Environmental Regulation and Industrial Innovation: The Social Negotiation of Technical Change, *Technology Analysis and Strategic Management* 1 (1), 57-70.

Karmali, A. (1990), *Stimulating Cleaner Technologies through the Design of Pollution Prevention Policies: An Analysis of Impediments and Incentives*, Manuscript submitted in partial fulfillment of degree in Master of Science in Technology and Policy, Massachusetts Institute of Technology, Cambridge, Mass.: MIT.

Keeney, R. L. (1990), Mortality Risks Induced by Economic Expenditures, *Risk Analysis* 10(1), 147-158.

Keeney, R. L. and R. L. Winkler (1985), Evaluating Decision Strategies for Equity of Public Risks, *Operations Research* 33, 955.

Kemp, R. (1994), Technology and Environmental Sustainability: The Problem of Technological Regime Shifts, *Futures* 26(10), 1023-1046.

Kemp, R. (1997), *Environmental Policy and Technical Change: A Comparison of the Technological Impact of Policy Instruments*, Cheltenham.

Klein, B. (1977), *Dynamic Economies*. Cambridge, Mass.

Kurz, R. (1987), *The Impact of Regulation on Innovation. Theoretical Foundation*, IAW Discussion Paper. Tuebingen.

LaPierre, B. (1977), Technology-Forcing and Federal Environmental Protection Statues, *Iowa Law Review* 62, 771.

Magat, W. (1979), The Effects of Environmental Regulation on Innovation, *Law and Contemporary Problems* 43, 4-25.

Mishan, E.J. (1981), *Introduction to Normative Economics*. Oxford.

Mishan, E.J. (1982), *Cost-Benefit Analysis*. London.

NACEPT (National Advisory Council for Environmental Policy and Technology) (1991), *Permitting and Compliance Policy: Barriers to U.S. Environmental Technology Innovation*, Report and Recommendations of the Technology Innovation and Economics Committee of the National Advisory Council for Environmental Policy and Technology. Washington, D.C.

NACEPT (1992), *Improving Technology Diffusion for Environmental Protection*, Report and Recommendations of the Technology Innovation and Economics Committee of the National Advisory Council for Environmental Policy and Technology. Washington, D.C.

NACEPT (1993), *Transforming Environmental Permitting and Compliance Policies to Promote Pollution Prevention*, Report and Recommendations of the Technology Innovation and Economics Committee of the National Advisory Council for Environmental Policy and Technology. Washington, D.C.

NAS (National Academy of Sciences), (1983), *Risk Assessment in the Federal Government: Managing the Process*. Washington D.C.

NAS (1990), *Tracking Toxic Substance at Industrial Facilities: Engineering Mass Balance versus Materials Accounting*, Report of the National Academy of Sciences Committee to Evaluate Mass Balance Information for Facilities Handling Toxic Substances. Washington, D.C.

OECD (Organization for Economic Co-operation and Development) (1985), *Environmental Policy and Technical Change*. Paris.

OECD (1987), *The Promotion and Diffusion of Clean Technologies in Industry*. Paris.

OECD (1989), *Economic Instruments for Environmental Protection*. Paris.

OTA (See U.S. OTA)

Porter, M. E. and C. van den Linden (1995) Green and Competitive: Ending the Stalemate *Harvard Business Review* September/October, 120-134. See also Porter and van den Linden, Towards a New Conceptualization of the Environment-Competitiveness Relationship, *J. Economic Perspectives* 9(4), 97-118.

Rennings, K. (1998), *Towards a Theory and Policy of Eco-Innovation: Neoclassical and (Co-) Evolutionary Perspectives*, ZEW Discussion Paper 98-24, Mannheim.

Rest, K. and N. Ashford (1988), Regulation and Technological Options: The Case of Occupational Exposure to Formaldehyde, *Harvard Journal of Law and Technology* 1, 63-96.

Rip, A. and H. van den Belt (1988), *Constructive Technology Assessment: Toward a Theory*, Zoetermeer.

Rothwell, R. and V. Walsh (1979), *Regulation and Innovation in the Chemical Industry*, Paper prepared for an OECD workshop, Paris, France, September 20-21.

Schot, J. (1992), Constructive Technology Assessment and Technology Dynamics: Opportunities for the Control of Technology, *Science, Technology, and Human Values* 17 (1), 36-56.

Shrader-Frechette, K. S. (1991), *Risk and Rationality*. Berkeley.

Stewart, R. (1981), Regulation, Innovation, and Administrative Law: A Conceptual Framework., *California Law Review* 69 (September), 1256-1377.

Strasser, K. (1997), Cleaner Technology, Pollution Prevention, and Environmental Regulation, *Fordham Environmental Law Journal* 9(1).

Sunstein, C. (1990), *After the Rights Revolution: Reconceiving the Regulatory State*. Cambridge, Mass.

Travis, C., S. Richter, E. Crouch, R. Wilson and E. Klema (1987), Cancer Risk Management, *Environmental Science and Technology* 21 (5), 415-420.

Tribe, Lawrence (1984), Seven Deadly Sins of Straining the Constitution through a Pseudo-Scientific Sieve, *Hastings Law Journal* 36, 155-172.

U.S. EPA (Environmental Protection Agency) Science Advisory Board (1990), *Reducing Risk: Setting Priority and Strategies for Environmental Protection*, Washington D.C.

U.S. EPA (Environmental Protection Agency) Science Advisory Board (1991), *Pollution Prevention: Progress in Reducing Industrial Pollutants*, EPA 21P-3003, Washington, D.C.

U.S. EPA (Environmental Protection Agency) Science Advisory Board, Office of Policy, Planning, and Evaluation (1992), *Preserving Our Future Today: Strategies and Framework*, Washington, D.C.

U.S. EPA (Environmental Protection Agency) Science Advisory Board (1994), *Technology Innovation Strategy*, EPA 543-K-93 002, Washington, D.C.

U.S. GAO (General Accounting Office) (1992), *Risk-Risk Analysis: OMB's Review of a Proposed OSHA Rule*, GAO/PEMD-92-33, Washington, D.C.

U.S. OTA (Office of Technology Assessment) (1986), *Serious Reduction of Hazardous Wastes*, Washington, D.C.

U.S. OTA (Office of Technology Assessment) (1995), *Gauging Control Technology and Regulatory Impacts in Occupational Safety and Health: An Appraisal of OSHA's Analytic Approach*, Washington, DC.

Zurer, P. (1992), CFC Substitute Cause Benign Tumors in Rats, *Chemical and Engineering News* 21 (September), 6.

The Joint Project "Innovation Impacts of Environmental Policy"

Ulrike Lehr, Klaus Löbbe

Rhine Westphalia Institute for Economic Research (RWI)
Hohenzollernstr. 1-3, 45128 Essen
Germany

Keywords. determinants, obstacles, peculiarities, state intervention.

Abstract. The paper summarizes the results of a German research project, which dealt with the impacts of environmental regulation on innovation. It outlines the main theoretical approaches and definitions. The paper provides the backbone of several case studies introduced in this volume by condensing the results into a table of hypotheses that have been rejected or accepted in the course of the research efforts.

1 Introduction

Innovation is a strategically important element in domestic and international competitiveness. Due to increasing globalization, international differences in pricing are becoming more and more apparent, so that quality issues are gaining in importance. Against this backdrop, innovation is regarded as one of the fundamental preconditions for survival in the context of the international competition, as well as the crucial engine promoting faster growth in the economy as a whole and in the number of well-qualified jobs.

The various fields of policy – not least environmental policy – may promote or restrict innovation. Thus an analysis of the effects on innovation of environmental policy instruments, or combinations of instruments which explicitly influence the behavior of economic actors, is of especial value, although there is still great uncertainty as to the actual effects themselves.

Moreover, above all regarding the demand for technology policy to be neutral in its structure and allocating funds, a certain change is becoming apparent in research and environmental policy, which also requires research. Under the heading "Making the Future Possible" – as the current German government R&D report is titled – supporting innovation is seen to contain opportunities for better environmental protection and more sustainability, and more support is recommended for so-called environmental innovation. The focus is above all on innovation that can make a contribution to the environment or sustainability.

In this context, the Federal Ministry for Education, Science, Research and Technology (BMBF), under the project funding number 07 OWI 50, set up the Research Group on Innovation and Environmental Policy (Forschungsverbund Innovation und Umweltpolitik, FIU), to examine the aforementioned questions with an interdisciplinary approach. The FIU attempted both to deal with the key issues of the problems sketched out above, and to exploit the interdisciplinary team structure to strike out in new directions[1].

The research project started from the question how far invention and diffusion of innovations are affected by the currently observable environmental policies. This question focused during discussions on so-called environmental innovations, i.e. the part of all possible innovations which are useful to fulfil certain ecological aims or the promise of more sustainability. Therefore, the research was narrowed and widened at the same time. A definition of environmental innovations became necessary to be able to concentrate on the issue subsequently. Defining environmental innovations, however, set the project at the intersection of several theoretical approaches focusing on either environmental or innovation issues. Mathematically speaking, if this intersection turns out being empty, one or more dimensions have to be added to the respective approach. This proved to be the case. Environmental economics, be it based on neo-classical theory or on the more recent approach of institutional economics, did not contribute much to the understanding of innovations. Traditional innovation research, on the other hand, was very little concerned with environmental regulation as of yet. Finally, New Growth Theory helped understanding the importance of innovations for economic growth, but not the innovation by itself - even less with the restrictions of environmental innovation.

2   Environmental Innovation

Environmental innovation here includes all *technological, economic, social and institutional innovation which contributes to a reduction in anthropogenic overuse*

---

[1]   For a summary of results cf. Klemmer, Paul, Lehr, Ulrike, Löbbe, Klaus, Environmental Innovation, *Impacts of environmental policies on innovation*, Vol. 2, Analytica, forthcoming (Summer 1999), for summaries of the case studies cf. Klemmer, Paul, (ed.), Innovation and the Environment - Case Studies on Adjustments in the Economy and Society, *Impacts of environmental policies on innovation*, Vol. 3 Analytica, forthcoming (Fall 1999).

of the environment, regardless of whether the innovation offers other – namely economic – benefits. Most of the studies certainly assume, explicitly of implicitly, that environmental innovation will support economic development at least in the *long term*, as it delays the exhaustion of certain resources or avoids exceeding the environment's assimilation capacity, thereby contributing to sustainable economic development.

However, this does not rule out many environmental innovations being associated with a "double externality" problem in the *short to medium term*: since neither the innovators nor those investing in environmental protection can automatically secure returns on their actions, there is a danger that the actual level of environmental innovation will lag behind that which is economically desirable. Where this is the case, environmental and research policy has the task of creating appropriate framework conditions and incentive mechanisms, to encourage economic actors in developing, applying and spreading environmentally sound innovations. In practice, the policy in all western industrialized countries fulfils this function with a highly refined system of general and specific rules. The task of the FIU research group is therefore to examine the research and environmental policy measures taken in individual cases against the backdrop of a broad political approach.

The key aim of the FIU research group was to develop fertile, practical approaches and conclusions on the innovation effects of environmental policy instruments. Using a selection of problem areas and case studies, the goal was to identify safe conclusions as to the characteristics of environmental innovation and the mechanisms by which it is encouraged and influenced. The aim was to demonstrate:

- whether and to what extent environmental innovation has special characteristics different from those of other innovation,

- the motives driving economic actors, when they develop or introduce environmental innovations, and the incentives which could reinforce this motivation,

- the obstacles standing in the way of developing and broadly applying environmental innovation, and how these might be overcome,

- the role which environmental policy plays or could play in this respect.

3　Hypotheses

A list of hypotheses can be derived from these considerations. Table 1 gives the joint set of hypothesis shared by the 18 case studies carried out by 10 research institutes. Eleven assumptions were confirmed by all projects and there have been only very few assumptions found with contradictory results. However, as a glance at Table 1 will show, some of the hypotheses are held rather generally reflecting the effort to get meaningful results for a majority of different studies.

Table 1:   Joint hypotheses of the FIU-Project

1.	The special nature of environmental innovation.	
1.1.	Environmental innovation is a subset of innovation. It shares the fundamental characteristics of all innovation, but differs in their relative weightings (e.g. forms, incentives, obstacles).	++ [a]
1.2.	As a rule, environmental innovation is the result of a variety of motives and incentives. Alongside the strategic goals of companies (first movers, marketing) and the preferences of single households, the environmental regulatory framework and social conditions also play a role. The environmental "pull" function of the market must be complemented by incentives from the state.	++
1.3.	Environmentally, it is particularly useful to distinguish between basic and incremental innovation. Basic environmental innovation is dependent to a special extent on accompanying organizational, institutional and social innovation. In this respect, technological change is an essential element of social change.	+
1.4.	Basic innovation is better suited to implementing environmentally desirable integrated solutions, incremental innovation tends to result in additive solutions.	+
1.5.	It is specially important to distinguish between the phases of environmental innovation (invention, adaptation, diffusion), as each phase involves a different package of motivations, which must be taken into account.	+
1.6.	Environmental innovation is particularly characterized by information deficits.	++
1.7.	Exchanging experience and cooperation between companies along the value chain is especially important for environmental innovation. This applies above all to integrated technologies, as these make demands on both suppliers and customers.	+
1.8.	Environmental innovation affects the competitive positions of both large and small to medium-sized companies to a particular extent. The former have better access to knowledge production, they can act strategically and prefer process innovation. The latter tend to produce product innovation, and have frequent problems in adapting.	+
1.9.	To the extent that large companies actually influence available knowledge, there is a danger of dead-ends developing in the technological paradigm. This danger is increased by certain environmental policy instruments.	0
1.10.	Environmental innovation is frequently bound up with building complex production plants. In this case, realizing environmental policy goals can be helped by fast, transparent licensing procedures and by making the same demands on all.	+

Table 1:   continued

1.11.	A company which uses a new technology for the first time is confronted with a series of innovations following on from this use, e.g. re-organizing workflows, changing the incentive structures and behavioral patterns of employees, or introducing environmental monitoring. These subsequent innovations may be especially significant in environmental innovation, where production may shift to manufacturing environmentally friendly products in environmentally sound processes.	+

2.   Incentives for and obstacles to invention

2.1.   Incentives for invention

2.1.1.	Innovation is not subject to a single determinant, but is initiated by interaction between individual and collective incentive mechanisms (goals of the company or decision-makers, regulations, patterns of household behavior).	++
2.1.2.	It is not single environmental policy instruments which are decisive in the incentive and compensation for innovation, but their role within complex regulatory frameworks, where interaction with economics conditions also plays a role.	++
2.1.3.	Substantial potential for substituting in integrated solutions can be discovered when the (usual) technological perspective is replaced by one oriented around function or benefit.	+
2.1.4.	The adoption of integrated solutions is determined crucially by demand, which depends firstly on the environmental awareness of customers, but is also influenced by state regulations or public purchasing policy.	+
2.1.5.	Environmental innovation cycles are, like others, tending to shorten, making it harder to recoup R&D expenditure and making time a strategic success factor. First users, through rapid product development, can gain a favorable position for future related innovations.	+
2.1.6.	Broad protection of intellectual property (through patenting) encourages large companies in particular to generate knowledge.	+
2.1.7.	Innovation support programs set priorities for the direction of research.	+
2.1.8.	Regulators gain expertise through research funding, and the state's negotiating position is strengthened.	+
2.1.9.	The effects of civil law make themselves felt to a considerable extent when measures are announced.	++
2.1.10.	Legal regulations bring about a great deal of innovation in the environmental protection industry, as the regulations guarantee markets for the products.	-
2.1.11.	Legal instruments generally provide little incentive to develop technologies which go beyond legal standards. However, incentives can arise from the expectation of tougher standards in future (e.g. with a flexible definition of Best Available Technology or continued pressure for political action).	+-
2.1.12.	Compared with civil law, economic instruments (charges, licences, liability) are flexible, efficient and innovation-friendly. However, they can only stimulate knowledge generation substantially, when they imply continually rising costs for environmentally harmful activities in the long term as well.	+-

Table 1:   continued

2.1.13.	The costs of waste emissions are a dynamic incentive to progress in environmental technology.	0
2.1.14.	Because of the possibility of market failure or subsidisees taking the money and running, subsidies are second best solutions.	++
2.1.15.	Criminal liability, like regulations, produces only static incentives to innovate, while civil liability has a dynamic effect on innovation (residual risks of damage which arise in spite of compliance with state regulations).	0
2.1.16.	The innovative potential in soft instruments is heavily dependent on company profitability and the availability of potential no-regret solutions.	++
2.1.17.	The use of soft instruments to promote environmental innovation is currently faced with limitations in constitutional and competitive law in Germany.	+

2.2.   Obstacles to invention

2.2.1.	Environmental innovation whose technology breaks new ground is tied to special risks (long-term unreliability, unintended effects on the environment), providing an apparent advantage for imitative strategies.	+
2.2.2.	Inertial dependency on incremental improvements and end-of-pipe solutions has given them a strong position relative to basic innovation and integrated solutions.	+
2.2.3.	The development of environmentally friendly products (consumer or investment goods) is neglected for as long as there is demand for established products.	+
2.2.4.	The window of opportunity for introducing integrated environmental technologies is brief: including the environment among R&D goals, and thereby implementing preventive measures, is almost only possible where fundamentally new products or processes are being developed.	+
2.2.5.	The majority of existing funding programs and the goals they embody favor additive or remedial environmental technologies in practice, part of their function is to assist in implementing regulations, and they therefore only contribute to reducing the implementation deficit in environmental policy.	+
2.2.6.	The effects of civil law on innovation are restricted by political inertia (in toughening up standards) and insufficient coordination of licensing procedures.	++
2.2.7.	Existing civil law effectively favors additive technologies.	+
2.2.8.	Economic incentives are often associated with greater financial burdens on the affected companies than civil law or voluntary commitments. The resulting political resistance tends to soften regulations (e.g. the extent of liability or the level of charges) and thereby the incentive to innovate.	0

3.   Incentives for and obstacles to adaptation and diffusion

3.1.   Incentives for adaptation and diffusion

3.1.1.	Adaptation of new technologies and innovations takes place faster where the company's experience is greater. Competence in acquiring expertise and "institutional learning" thus become central components of any innovative capability.	+

Table 1:   continued

3.1.2.	Diffusion of environmental innovation is particularly encouraged by information and communication.	++
3.1.3.	Civil law encourages the rapid diffusion of innovation, but is frequently associated with implementation deficits.	++
3.1.4.	Diffusion of new technologies can be achieved at minimum political cost if state goal-setting is followed by step-wise, flexible use of instruments, progressively and predictably raising the need for adaptation, and therefore providing for binding regulations as a last resort ("threat and control").	+
3.2.	**Obstacles to adaptation and diffusion**	
3.2.1.	Adaptation and diffusion of environmental innovation are obstructed by information deficits and restricted access to technical knowledge (patent protection), lack of market incentives and insufficient or unclear regulations.	+
3.2.2.	Introducing integrated environmental technologies generally requires comprehensive reorganization of a company's production flows, and is therefore dependent on internal and external changes in production activity, the company's innovation cycle and the rate of depreciation usual for the relevant sector.	0
3.2.3.	Programs to promote innovation are generally insufficiently well and/or imprecisely co-ordinated with adaptation and diffusion programs.	+
3.2.4.	Households are confronted with specific obstacles (legal, allocative, etc.), which restrict the selection of technologies.	++
3.2.5.	The variety of existing funding programs makes access especially hard for small and medium-sized companies, private organizations and households (poor program co-ordination).	+

++ majority agrees, + agree, 0 not relevant/ applicable, - no agreement, -- not true,
+- controversial.

4   Policy Recommendations

Seen as a whole, the studies bring together an impressive range of results as to the relationship between environmental innovation and environmental policy. Many of the hypothesis formulated initially have been confirmed, some modified, others rejected. Firstly, in answer to the question of whether and how far environmental innovation has special qualities: it does indeed appear to be generally characterized by a very long-term, often supranational or global perspective, as in the case of climate policy. Special risks can be made out, for example in the lengthy planning and maturation terms, or in the way demand for environmentally friendly technologies depends on state intervention; moreover, environmental innovation contrasts with other innovation in the specific problems with its adaptation and diffusion. In many cases, the success of realizing technological innovations commercially depends upon accompanying organizational, institutional or social innovation.

Virtually all the studies come to the conclusion that environmental innovation is the result of a complex, rather than one-dimensional, pattern of influences, shaped both by intrinsic motivation and by state incentives, characterized by many feedback loops and dependent to a great extent on the broad social environment: using various sectors or actor groups and different environmental policy problems, it has been proven that there is no instrument which should be favored or rejected a priori, and that it is the interaction between personal motivation, political activity and social environment which leads to environmental innovation (the multi-impulse theory). The factors which generally interact in the actual behavior of actors are as follows:

- The individual abilities and motives of the actors. Companies and households are taking increasing account of the needs of the environment, and searching – within their capabilities, alone or in co-operation – solutions to environmental problems. Here virtually all studies stress the importance of first mover advantages and image benefits for companies, as well as the influence of a persistently high level of environmental awareness in households. An obstacle remains the uncertainty of expected market development (under the influence of environmental regulation) and rising costs or higher prices for environmentally friendly products and processes, as well as limited opportunities for funding.

- The environmental regulatory framework. Individuals feel themselves confronted with a varied, sophisticated body of regulations to protect the environment, which they (must) include in their cost-benefit analyses and actions.

- Trends in social framework conditions (global development, changes in values, economic health and income growth, capital market yields, intensity of competition, broad legal framework, e.g. liability).

4.1 Environmental Policy

There is also a broad consensus that it is not – or not always – the consistent application of single instruments, but their selection and use within a specific regulatory framework which is decisive. The regulatory framework is defined (after JÄNICKE 1997) as the "sum of all calculable rules, procedures and contexts for action within one area directed by the state", and consists of the political and institutional context, the range of instruments and the accustomed policy style ("Politikstil"). Thus a successful, innovation oriented environmental policy is characterized by the following:

- Inclusion of different actor groups, even when formulating goals, and taking into account that changing constellations of actors may sometimes demand different measures to those planned.

- Selecting appropriate timescales and using the planned range of instruments flexibly.

- Showing a degree of consistency and predictability (but cf. the following discussion of the effects of notification).

Environmental policy successes must be conceived, as K. W. Zimmermann, with reference to Jänicke, also confirms, as a "multivariate function of (political, economic and other) factors" (K. W. ZIMMERMANN, 1998). The findings of the studies and the present summary report provide some preliminary suggestions as to the future shape of environmental policy and environmentally relevant research and technology policies.

Apart from the generally accepted basic belief that environmental innovation is the result of a multidimensional package of factors, there are clear differences between the studies in their assessments of individual policy instruments, such as in the question of the innovative effects of regulations or the advantages of an environmental tax reform. In the light of this, it is not surprising that no generally accepted ranking of the instruments to be used could be found, nor an optimal mix of instruments. The same applies to other questions:

- Would a different weighting of the instrument mix, in the sense of shifting (still) more from regulatory instruments to economic or informational incentives, be practical in every case, and should voluntary commitments be used more frequently than at present[2]?

- To what extent does it appear necessary to complement the given instrument mix with "new" instruments, such as by developing further the ideas of joint implementation, licenses, auditing and emissions trading (particularly with regard to coming climate conferences)?

On the other hand, there was broad agreement on the fact that there is still considerable room for maneuver for further development of environmental policy instruments in terms of their implementation. This applies firstly to consistent application of long-announced measures which are still required, breaking down implementation deficits and other obstacles, also to more dynamic regulations (for example the limits of pollutant emissions) or correcting rates of charges (such as the waste water charge) which have been set too low.

---

2   Even the question of whether voluntary commitments should be considered an instrument or regulatory framework within environmental policy proved a matter of controversy.

A surprising result from some of the studies, one which provoked lively debate within the research group, is the theory that inconsistency and imperfections in political implementation are not always counterproductive, but that even the announcement of possible measures can bring about efforts to innovate (announcement effects). In many cases, it is precisely the uncertainty as to the actual shape of future environmental regulation which causes the actors to research and develop or conduct pilot projects. This was generally associated with the expectation of finding environmentally effective and economically efficient solutions which policy could take up as a standard solution, or at any rate which would not be blocked. Nonetheless, it emerged that the policy must always be credible: the actors must be persuaded that the announcements will sooner or later be followed by the decree of a regulation or the conclusion of a "voluntary" commitment. In this respect - where other initial conditions remain the same – a predictable sequence of regulatory steps is of great importance to the success of a policy.

As the statistical analysis also shows, taking environmental policy goals into account is for companies no longer an isolated problem of meeting specific regulatory demands, but a problem of harmonizing the requirements with its own innovative strategies. In this respect the regulations on closed substance flows realized or foreseen up to now have had completely different and more far-reaching effects on innovative behavior than banning substances, for example. This has been announced in the past, and while it may have initiated a search for substitute products and techniques, it has had only marginal influence on long-term company strategies.

The goal of an innovation oriented environmental policy should be to promote both the environmental effectiveness and the economic efficiency of the measures it induces – not least through stronger incentives for a continued shift from additive to integrated solutions. Ideally, this could realize win-win situations, with both environmental and economic advantages; however, all too frequently it will be a matter of increasing the proportion of no regret plus strategies, i.e. inducing behavior from individuals that they would not choose for economic reasons alone.

An environmental policy is best suited to realizing this goal if it is long-term oriented and systematic, thus demonstrating its competence in governance and setting goals – especially where it provides for appropriate actor participation in the process of formulating goals. On the other hand, it should demonstrate variety and flexibility in the application of its instruments, to avoid detracting from personal motivation and environmentally aware behavior. This also covers the inclusion of environmental policy in the investment and innovation cycles of the economy and co-ordination with other policy areas (especially research and technology, but also fiscal and social policy).

Otherwise, it is unsurprising that there are still numerous unanswered questions. Much is still unconnected, many pieces of the puzzle remain to be added, which indicates the need for further research. Proposals for more detailed research on the relationship between environmental policy and innovation can be found in the recent literature, for example in the most recent research programs of the EU[3]. The following offers a few suggestions for further development of the environmental and research program, based on the experience and discoveries made by the FIU, from the general theoretical basis for a coherent theory of environmental innovation to support for specific environmental technologies or fields of application (sectors and media): if environmental innovation is characterized by certain special qualities, this implies not only the need for action in a specific policy for environmental innovation, but also the need for research into the basis for an independent theory of environmental innovation.

The present project focused on the emergence and spread of environmental innovation; the issue of its effects was restricted mainly to environmental aspects. There is therefore a need for research above all in estimating the economic and social effects of environmental innovation. Only extending the scope of research and correspondingly detailed analysis of its effects can indicate how far environmental innovation contributes to sustainable development. In this respect, it should be remembered that the environmental policy debate in recent years has in any case been shaped by an unmistakable shift towards long-term global issues and the realization of sustainable economic and social development; this is also reflected in the Federal Ministry for Education, Science, Research and technology's environmental research program mentioned earlier. However, more research is required to add detail to the idea of sustainable development; in this context, the possible technological, economic, organizational, institutional and social contributions of innovation require attention.

There are also open questions as to the actual implementation of regulations and making an innovation oriented policy style work. For example, how, under today's conditions, can the goal of inclusion be achieved, where the addressees of policy are even more involved in the process of formulating political goals and intent – small and medium-sized companies alongside employers' associations and large companies, environmental groups and non-profit organizations alongside employees' and consumer associations? How does the historical relationship between participation and subordination – in different countries, for example – affect the likelihood of success for a specific policy framework, what role does the size or industrial structure, or the relative scarcity of certain resources in a country play? What are the consequences of the (real or assumed) growth in global institutional and economic competition? All are questions which require attention in further international comparative studies.

---

[3]   cf. DG JRC, Institute for Prospective Technological Studies (IPTS), "Impact of EU Regulation on Innovation of European Industry". The project is currently focusing on environmental regulation.

Finally, it should not be forgotten that different environmental policy instruments
and patterns of implementation will promise success in different problem areas and
situations. It is therefore advisable for environmental and research policy to seek
confirmation of the theories formulated here, especially the multi-impulse theory,
in other protected areas (rivers, countryside, bio-diversity), for other (groups of)
actors and in other framework conditions.

4.2 Research and Technology Policy

The studies also provide numerous results of importance to research and technology policies. Questions addressed include:

- Does environmental innovation tend to be incremental, and under what organizational, institutional or social conditions is basic innovation successful?

- What conditions are required for abandoning certain paths of technological
  development and initiating paradigmatic change?

- To what extent certain economies of scale and synergy are associated with
  gaining and applying environmental and technical knowledge, owing to
  asymmetric information and learning effects?

- Are current regulations and practices adequate for protecting intellectual
  property on the one hand and promoting diffusion on the other?

Some of these results are taken up again in the following, where they appear to
have broad relevance.

From an epistemological perspective, it is interesting to note how recent research
approaches, such as New Institutionalism and evolutionary economics, have
proven helpful in explaining and assessing (environmental) innovation; the former,
by emphasizing the influence of institutions and the importance of transaction
costs, the latter, by enabling the emergence and spread of innovation to be described in terms of an open-ended process. The empirical application of these
ideas is admittedly still in its early stages (GAWEL 1995, 1996a, 1996b), nor the
present studies attempt much more than a qualitative description of the mechanisms at work. More detailed analysis and further case studies would appear useful
here.

The motivation of actors has been identified as an additional impact for environmental innovation. Households and public budgets may be guided to a certain
extent in their purchasing decisions by what is essentially a high level of environmental awareness, companies perceive environmental issues more than ever as an
element of their philosophy, and non-market organizations pursue environmental
goals even when this is not actually a part of their job. In this context there is a
danger that environmentally motivated incentives (regulations, taxation, charges)

may be politically counterproductive, as they encourage evasive attitudes and thereby destroy intrinsic motivation.

One way out of this dilemma might be a further increase in the environmental content of training and education in schools and universities. Curricula in the relevant natural and social sciences in schools should be extended, the examination requirements in colleges and universities should be revised, not only for technical professions, but also in business and management studies. The goal must be to raise the level of information about current and future problems, and to recognize and deal with the opportunities (and limitations) for environmental policy. In this way, environmental awareness and intrinsic motivation could be reinforced in all areas of social and economic life.

In addition, closer co-operation between universities and companies or the state (as regulator) appears desirable. The flow of information from potential adopters of new technologies – the companies, in particular small to medium-sized ones – to the "producers" in institutes and universities should be improved; existing obstacles to exploiting new knowledge (such as the difficulty in patenting innovations described in recent scientific publications) should be removed.

In this context, the current regulations and practices for protecting intellectual property (patent and design protection) should also be examined, particularly the costs and length of procedures. Although the majority opinion is currently that German patent law strikes a practicable balance between the extensive, and therefore innovation friendly protection in the USA on the one hand, and the restrictive, and therefore adaptation friendly patent law in Japan, an thorough examination of German regulations and practices would appear sensible.

In the interests of accelerating the transfer of environmental technologies, co-operation between actors all along the value chain and technology pipeline should be made easier, within existing competitive restrictions. Co-operation and early agreement between regulator (the state) and regulated (companies) also appear desirable in this context. The extent to which the state can influence the emergence of co-operation between actors – for example in reinforcing networks or supporting the development of data bases – is still unclear, and should be investigated.

Although research policy has in the past initiated numerous projects on material flows and product management – not least for electrical appliances – there is still a considerable need for research, for example with regard to the appropriate instruments for informing consumers about the possibilities for repairing and returning products, suitable strategies for dovetailing material flow and innovation management (especially in small and medium-sized companies), and with regard to new methods for product life cycle analysis (LCA) in technology assessments of various disposal paths (reuse or resale versus recycling complete appliances versus dismantling, separation and fractional recycling).

There is further need for research on the development of environmentally sound manufacturing and recycling processes for long-life goods (and not only the motor vehicles and electrical appliances which have been the focus of environmental policy to date). This issue requires integrated environmental innovation in assessing the environmental impact of recycling processes (cost-benefit analysis), developing integrated systems for recycling batteries, methods, instruments and the technology for estimating the remaining life of products and components, and in the design of pilot projects on workflow organization in (partially) automated dismantling plants.

The research project has also thrown up a number of questions affecting other policy areas, especially economic policy, above all with respect to small firms. The task for competition policy is to create space for adventurous innovation; this requires a certain amount of (indirect) protection for small and medium-sized companies, through an effective policy on cartels, strict monitoring of mergers and efficient supervision against market abuse by dominant companies. The example of waste disposal, where large companies (and former monopolies) have conquered significant market share in a very short space of time, proves that this could become a key issue for environmental policy also: existing solutions become set in stone, alternatives to the present disposal monopolists (the DSD and its recycling companies) are not subject to market tests. On the other hand, competition policy will also need to deal sensitively with temporary monopolies (by innovators) and the similarity to cartels of co-operation within R&D networks. There are certainly no universal rules for weighing up the issues involved here.

References

Gawel, E. (1995), Institutionelle Fragen der Umweltpolitik, in: Junkernheinrich, M., P. Klemmer and G.R. Wagner (eds.), *Handbuch zur Umweltökonomie. (Handbücher zur angewandten Umweltforschung, Bd. 2.)*, Berlin.

Gawel, E. (1996a), Institutionenökonomie und Umweltökonomik – Forschungsstand und Perspektiven, in: Gawel, E. (ed.), *Institutionelle Probleme der Umweltpolitik. "Zeitschrift für angewandte Umweltforschung"*, Sonderheft 8/1996, Berlin.

Gawel, E. and F. Schneider (1996b), *Umsetzungsprobleme ökologisch orientierter Steuerpolitik: eine polit-ökonomische Analyse*, Arbeitspapiere der Johannes-Kepler-Universität Linz, Sozial- und Wirtschaftswissenschaftliche Fakultät, Nr. 9621., Linz.

Jänicke, M. (1997), *Umweltinnovationen aus der Sicht der Policy Analyse*, FFU-Report 1997-3, Berlin.

Klemmer, P. (ed.) (1999), *Innovation and the environment. Case studies on the adaptive behavior in society and the economy*, Impacts of environmental policies on innovation, Vol. 3, Berlin.

Klemmer, P., U. Lehr, K. Löbbe, (1999), *Environmental innovations*, Impacts of environmental policies on innovation, Vol. 2, Berlin.

Zimmermann, K. W. (1997), Umweltpolitik, Effektivität und Effizienz, in: L. Mez and H. Weidner (eds.), *Umweltpolitik und Staatsversagen. Perspektiven und Grenzen der Umweltpolitikanalyse – Festschrift für Martin Jänicke zum 60. Geburtstag*, Berlin, 425-436.

Environmental Policy and Innovation: an International Comparison of Policy Frameworks and Innovation Effects[1]

Martin Jänicke

Environmental Policy Research Institut, Free University Berlin (FFU)
Ihnestraße 22, 14195 Berlin
Germany

Jürgen Blazejczak and Dietmar Edler

German Institut for Economic Research
Königin-Luise-Straße 5, 14195 Berlin
Germany

Jens Hemmelskamp

European Commission, Joint Research Centre,
Institute for Prospective Technological Studies (IPTS)
W.T.C. Isla de la Cartuja, E-41092 Sevilla
Spain

Keywords. policy style, instrumentalism, actor constellation, policy framework.

---

[1] Report on the research project "International Case Studies of the Innovation Effects of Environmental Regulatory Policy" a study by the German Institute for Economic Research (DIW), the Environmental Policy Research Centre at the Free University of Berlin (FFU) and the Centre for European Economic Research (ZEW) for the FIU.

1   Background and Common Aims

Lasting environmental quality and availability of natural resources within a sustainable development would appear to require fundamental changes in existing modes of production and lifestyles. Strategies for achieving sustainability goals can be divided into two categories: sufficiency strategies and efficiency strategies. The former are aimed at changing behaviour, while the latter emphasise the necessity of comprehensive technological change. Environmental innovation is meant to reduce consumption of resources, limit pollution of the environment and – taking note of a crisis in available resources – substitute environmental capital with produced capital.

Polity is then faced with the question of which environmental policy measures can bring about a shift in the innovation engaged in by companies towards more environmental innovation. In the Research Group on Innovation Effects of Environmental Policy Instruments (FIU), funded by the Federal Ministry of Education, Science, Research and Technology, this question has been investigated in a series of research projects.

The three projects presented here, conducted in a joint research effort by the DIW, the FFU and the ZEW, make an international comparison of the innovation and diffusion effects of environmental policy measures in specific target areas (paper production, domestic appliances such as refrigerators and wind energy[2]. These are case studies, inasmuch as they relate overall or predominantly to cases of success. The success of innovation is measured either in terms of the rate of diffusion (for electrical appliances and wind energy) or of environmental benefit through a series of more incremental technical innovations (paper production). No attempt is made to isolate the innovation effects of single environmental policy instruments. It is assumed rather that, due to the complex dynamic operating between the factors which typically influence innovation (DODGSON AND ROTHWELL 1994, KEMP et al. 1994, HEMMELSKAMP 1997a), it can only be explained as the combined effect of several factors.

The following section details the development of a common analytical framework used in the three studies presented here. Firstly, the term "environmental innovation" is defined, and then various theoretical and analytical approaches concerning the relationship between policy-making and innovation are described, from which elements of an innovation-friendly policy framework are derived in the third section. In the fourth section, this is used to assess the policy frameworks affecting the target areas of paper production, electrical appliances and wind energy in the corresponding countries. The fifth section concludes with a comparative interpretation of all seven policy frameworks.

---

[2]   cf. Blazejczak and Edler, Jänicke et al., Hemmelskamp, 1998.

2   Common Analytical Framework

2.1   Defining Environmental Innovation

The FIU agreed upon a working definition of environmental innovation: "Environmental innovation will be considered as all action taken by the relevant actors ... with which

- new ideas and behaviour, products and production processes are developed, applied or introduced

- benefit the environment or contribute to environmental sustainability." (FIU 1997).

There is still the question of whether this definition is sufficient and whether reducing use of the environment can be an adequate criterion for distinguishing environmental innovation. Such a reduction is always possible – at a cost (e.g. by restricting economic activity). The criterion must therefore be that innovation makes possible the same benefit to the environment at a lower cost than had previously been the case, or that greater environmental relief can be achieved at the same cost.[3,4]

Innovation can now be understood as environmental innovation if it is expected to lead to a better cost-benefit ratio than before in reducing the costs of environmental damage. This would include not only innovation which reduces the costs of damage prevention where the costs of damage are expected to fall or remain the same, but also those which, under the same conditions, reduce other costs (for materials or energy) or lead to improved returns.[5,6]

In principle this also takes into account shifting the environmental burden between media or to other times and places. However, the empirical analysis in the FIU project looks only at the reduction of single environmental burdens, ignoring the problems of drawing up a comprehensive environmental balance sheet.

The special nature of environmental innovation as compared to other forms of innovation comes from the component of public good, not in environmental inno-

---

3   In the case of other innovation, a definition by positive benefit does not mean the same thing. In this case, the economic use of an innovation "proves" its positive net benefit.

4   It is possible for the (net) marginal costs of damage prevention after innovation to be lower than previous marginal costs in one area and higher in another.

5   Net costs of preventing damage = damage prevented – costs of prevention + other cost savings or improved returns.

6   The definition can be modified without harming its general applicability to include also the clean-up of (reversible) damage and the diagnosis of environmental damage.

vation but in environmental goods. As soon as, and inasmuch as environmental goods are priced through regulation, environmental innovation becomes no different from any other. However, this brings with it the task of regulating the use of environmental goods in such a way that environmental innovation is not hindered but promoted[7].

The long-term nature of its benefits and the associated uncertainty are also occasionally cited as a peculiarity of environmental innovation. The definition proposed here can take uncertainty into account by formulating it in terms of expectation values. It still fails to take account of a comprehensive notion of caution. Innovation which is directed at unknown, merely possible, environmental problems (for example a general reduction of material flows) or which provides a store of solutions for them should, however, also be included.

The relationship between invention, innovation and diffusion is no different for environmental innovation than elsewhere. The view, occasionally put, that organisational[8] innovation carries more weight than technological innovation when dealing with the environment than in innovation with other goals also appears without foundation[9]. Changes in behaviour can immediately be subsumed under the demand pull factors which determine the direction of technological and the associated organisational innovation. The use of the terms innovation for changes in behaviour can be misleading, because these cannot be managed in the same way as technological or organisational innovation[10].

Alongside that between technological and organisational innovation, another important distinction (and not just for environmental innovation) is between incremental, one-off and radical innovation (cf. ROSSI 1998 and the literature cited). Radical innovation renders a considerable part of a company's investment in knowledge and expertise, processes and plant obsolete. Incremental innovation increases the efficiency and broadens the scope for using existing products and plant. One-off innovation alters individual products and stages in a process, without, however, large parts of a company's investment becoming obsolete. Equating innovation through add-on environmental technology with incremental innovation and innovation through integrated environmental technology at the process level with one-off or even radical (environmental) innovation seems somewhat glib. On

---

7   This can be more generally formulated: peculiarities emerge in environmental innovation inasmuch as interdependencies exist between the types of externality which characterise it.

8   Social or institutional innovation is often mentioned in this context, without there always being quite such a clear distinction between these terms.

9   By no means is this to say that a distinction between technological and organisational innovation might not be meaningful in terms of certain questions. But this is equally the case for all innovation.

10 Nevertheless, changes in behaviour can certainly be made easier by technical and/or organisational innovation.

the other hand, the hypothesis could be made that the transition from end-of-pipe to integrated environmental technology[11] regularly meets the criterion of an improved cost-benefit ratio in solving a particular environmental problem. Nor does the hypothesis that radical (environmental) innovation only meets this criteria when it is introduced as existing capital stock naturally becomes obsolete or when very great expected damage is to be prevented appear too far-fetched.

2.2 Approaches to Explaining Environmental Innovation

2.2.1 Environmental Economics

The innovation effects of environmental policy instruments are currently studied somewhat mechanistically by environmental economics, based on neo-classical theory (HEMMELSKAMP 1997b). The effects of individual policy instruments are analysed according to the criterion of dynamic efficiency, which determines "whether the use of this instrument provides incentives for a company to innovate in environmental technology and also to implement the innovations rapidly" (BALKS 1995, p. 57). As a result of neo-classical environmental economic research the use predominantly of so-called market solutions such as charges or certification is recommended to environmental regulators, as these instruments provide "a permanent incentive to seek new opportunities for reducing emissions" (MICHAELIS 1996, p. 48; cf. among others also MILLIMAN AND PRINCE 1989; DOWNING AND WHITE 1986).

However, the traditional neo-classical economic debate on environmental policy instruments has weaknesses in terms of its significance in practice. Its ideal conditions (competitive economic interaction, infinitely fast adaptation and low transaction costs) are not present in reality. Moreover, the models often only take into account the effects of an instrument on reducing one specific pollutant. The necessary framework conditions with respect to pollutants and technology for realistic modelling, such as the available end-of-pipe and integrated prevention technologies or the existing structure of emitters, are given scant consideration (cf. HOHMEYER AND KOSCHEL 1995, p. 14; MICHAELIS 1992, p. 12).

Another weak point in environmental economic studies is the broad neglect of supply and demand side factors influencing innovation, as well as of their effect on the use of environmental policy instruments. Nor is a distinction generally drawn between providers and developers of environmental technology. This excludes significant innovation on the part of providers, which is not directly induced by environmental policy measures. The benefit for the provider is not lower pollution costs but increased turnover, and thus the specific factors influencing environ-

---

[11]   Or more precisely pollution control or prevention.

mental innovation by providers ought to be analysed separately from those influencing regulated companies.

And finally, policy evaluators criticise the environmental economic approach not only for its fixation with single instruments, but also for its restricted "legislator perspective", with its one-sided, top-down view of matters. Instead, the case is being made for an analytical approach where the bottom-up perspective is included (SABATIER 1986), or even given priority (JÄNICKE AND WEIDNER 1995), as only this approach is sufficiently open to the complex dynamic of the potential factors.

2.2.2   Innovation Economics[12] and Innovation Research

Neo-classical theory deals with the question of the determinants of innovation by modelling the decisions of companies to invest in research and development. Environmental innovation – for the neo-classical model R&D expenditure on reducing the costs of measures to reduce environmental stress – are viewed in these terms as alternatives to the use of available technologies or to paying charges or other transfers. This approach succeeds in demonstrating the central importance of economic incentives for environmental innovation as well, even if it remains in the dark as to the factors behind the economic incentives. This formal approach necessitates radical simplifications. For example, it is frequently only the costs of environmental protection measures which are considered, ignoring savings in energy and material costs or greater returns due to improved product quality. In addition, the conditions under which R&D expenditure is successful are not included, nor is the existence of uncertainty adequately represented. Neither is there generally a sufficient distinction drawn between decision-making by developers and by users of the new technologies.

Further developments of the basic neo-classical model have analysed the importance of various framework conditions as determinants of innovation. Particular attention has been paid to the significance of differing market structures and the influence of patenting, while distinctions have been drawn according to the life-cycle phases of the sector and various types of innovation. The differentiation between generation and diffusion of new technologies has highlighted the importance of the demand side. Because of the complex interaction between a variety of parameters, the answers to the question of which market structure is most innovation-friendly are varied. In the case of spill-over, cooperation has the effect of promoting innovation. The effect of patenting is viewed as positive for the incidence of innovation, but as an obstacle to the diffusion of innovations and even, under certain circumstances, as ineffective in many sectors.

---

[12]   A more extensive description of economic approaches to explaining innovative behaviour can be found in Blazejczak and Edler 1998 and Hemmelskamp 1999.

Extended neo-classical models provide an opportunity for including the influence of (environmental) innovation on costs and product quality for users in judgements of profitability, and thereby for analysing the importance of these determinants for diffusion. The use of decision-making and game theory models can also take account of the risks and uncertainties associated with the introduction of (environmental) innovations.

In keeping with the evolutionary approach in innovation economics, economic development is full of analogies to biological evolution. Innovation is seen as an essential engine of economic development. They arise in a process of variation and selection, during which the discovery of technological or economic opportunities through entrepreneurial activity or within existing technological paradigms is of decisive importance. Changing the technological paradigm succeeds only when windows of opportunity opened by basic innovation are exploited, and the success of basic innovations is dependent on learning effects and on complementary technological and institutional innovation of an incremental nature. Characterising variation as problem-solving underlines the importance of combining the internal and external knowledge which can be exploited from within an innovation network. Noting the importance of the selective environment provides starting-points for policy as regards influencing the actors who determine this environment. The term "technology nexus" is used to describe the relationship between variation and selection and, in the case of environmental innovation this covers the dialogue between environmental requirements and technological possibilities, conducted by a great many actors within and outside the companies themselves. The technology nexus provides starting-points in subsidising environmental innovation.

The economic debate on the factors influencing innovation has thus far been very much dominated by the question of whether available technical expertise – the "technology push" hypothesis – or existing market opportunities – the "demand pull" hypothesis – exert a greater influence on the innovative behaviour of companies. There is however now a consensus in innovation research that both demand-side and supply-side determinants influence technical innovation (cf. PAVITT 1984, p. 271 or BECHER et al. 1993, p. 34). Technology push factors appear to have a greater effect at the start of the product cycle, while the influence of demand pull factors is seen above all in later stages of the cycle (cf. COOMBS et al. 1987, p. 103).

The increasing importance of environmental innovation has brought new life into the debate. The aforementioned special features of environmental innovation mean that returns on innovation are often uncertain, are garnered only in the long-term and/or by third parties, and the demand-side or supply-side impetus depends therefore to a large extent on the use of environmental policy instruments. However, innovation models to date have scarcely considered the use of environmental policy instruments as a factor, and they must now be included as additional technology push or demand pull factors.

Thus the use of environmental policy instruments is merely an additional factor in innovative behaviour within a package of supply-side and demand-side influences. These include (cf. HEMMELSKAMP 1997a):

- market demand (e.g. market size and customer needs)

- technological conditions (available expertise)

- company size and market structure (e.g. level of competition)

- the protection afforded to returns on innovation (e.g. opportunities for patenting)

- joining forces (e.g. cooperation with suppliers)

- internal company factors (e.g. position on risk).

The special influence of policy on environmental innovation has been ignored in the approaches mentioned above. Policy analysis from an economic perspective belongs to New Political Economics. New Political Economics provides, for example, the basis for explaining difficulties in the introduction of environmental policy instruments which offer dynamic incentives and points towards their solution. New Institutional Economics is above all a reaction to neo-classicism's blindness to institutions, and it considers the institutional functionality of economic coordination. By emphasising the importance of transaction costs for innovation, the importance of complementary institutional innovations to technical innovation is underlined. With the concept of transaction costs, New Institutional Economics points to the importance of information for innovation and, above all, diffusion. For this school, incentives to environmental innovation come from establishing and securing disposal rights for environmental resources, e.g. through liability law.

2.2.3   Policy Analysis[13]

What can already be seen in the extended neo-classical model and in more recent economic theory is clearly evident also in policy evaluation (cf. e.g. WALLACE 1995, JÄNICKE AND WEIDNER 1995): it is the entire process whereby demands and objectives are formulated which is important for the influence of the state on innovation, and not only the action finally decided upon. This is a question not only of individual instruments but of the entire range of instruments as a whole and, moreover, of the policy style which shapes the way objectives are formulated and the constellation of actors, in particular the relationship between regulator and regulated (JÄNICKE 1997). "In a complex world, no single response option is uniquely viable. Because of widely varying effects of given policy instruments in different national circumstances, it is difficult to define in general terms a mix of policies and measures which would be universally applicable. This suggests that

---

[13]   For a comprehensive description see Jänicke 1997.

policies should be part of a learning process, whereby the implementation of responses provides information about their effectiveness and enables improved development of a flexible and adaptable policy framework over time" (SOLSBERG 1997, p. 95).

With reference to the OECD's broad definition of regulation (OECD 1997), the term "regulatory framework" could be used for the totality of calculable regulations, procedures and contexts for action in any one area subject to state regulation[14]. However, this term is easily brought into association with the negative effects of regulation focused on in the debate on deregulation. To avoid misunderstanding, and to make clear that the range of instruments which work through incentives is also to be included, we use the term "policy framework" in the following.

Environmental policy research is also increasingly coming to recognise that the intended policy effects are achieved not by a single best instrument but by a mix of various instruments (OECD 1997, EEA 1996, JÄNICKE AND WEIDNER 1995). The fact that policy style, or the way in which an instrument is applied, can exert considerable influence on the result was emphasised for the first time by Richardson (1982). Formulation of goals, flexibility, timing, consultation are of great importance when taking action, especially in the case of innovation strategies. Empirical studies have shown that environmental innovation springs not only from targeted state action, but also from the dynamic interaction between state and private sector actors within a complex network of actions (JÄNICKE AND WEIDNER 1995, CONRAD 1996, BRESSERS AND KLOK 1991). The key aspects here are the institutional context, the actor constellation and policy learning in networks and negotiation systems (JÄNICKE 1996). Mayntz pointed out as early as in 1983 that the success of a regulation depends, apart from the problem itself, upon the "programme" formulated and the interaction between regulator and regulated (the "field of intervention"), and that the importance of the instruments used falls as actors reach consensus on their goals (MAYNTZ 1983).

In policy analysis case studies, the policy framework should thus first be related to the framework of action for the target group (top-down), and then this framework of action related back to the regulatory plan (bottom-up). Any factors which still remain unexplained will then be those which only indirectly affect state actions, if at all.

---

[14]   For the differing understanding of the term "regulation" in different countries, see Kemp 1998.

2.3   Methodology

The above overview of the various frameworks for explaining environmental innovation makes clear that simple analytical frameworks cannot do justice to the complex and interdependent influences of environmental policy on innovation.

While innovation research has, as yet, paid no specific attention to the special
characteristics of environmental innovation, traditional neo-classical environmental economic research has broadly ignored discoveries about the supply-side
and demand-side factors which influence innovative behaviour.

Correspondingly, the research in the present study is distinguished by a synthesis
of approaches from environmental economics, innovation economics and policy
analysis (cf. Figure 1). However, there are problems in the practical application of
such an approach. Rothwell is correct to point out that "...one consequence of the
multifactored nature of success and failure in innovation, of course, is that sepa-
rating the impact of government regulation from that of a myriad other factors is
generally extremely difficult" (ROTHWELL 1992, p. 454). The question of which
factors actually have an effect must therefore be examined on a case-by-case basis.
In order to isolate the effects of different factors, comparative analysis is also required. For this reason, what follows is an analysis of the influence of environmental policy on innovation, using seven examples from the chosen areas of paper
production, electrical appliances and wind energy in a number of countries (Sections 4 and 5). The development of the analytical framework used is described
below.

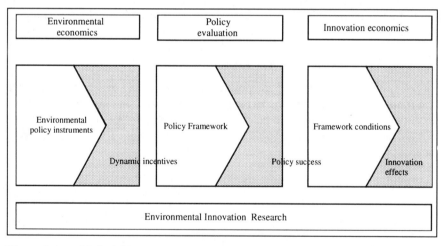

Figure 1:   Methodology

3   Elements of an Innovation-friendly Policy Framework[15]

To summarise what has gone before, there are three central dimensions to a policy framework, which should be tested to see whether they promote or hinder environmental innovation (see Figure 2):

1. the instrumentation, which, above and beyond individual instruments themselves, covers their formulation and combination

2. policy style, which describes the way in which goals are formulated and environmental regulations are implemented

3. the configuration of actors, which refers to the institutional framework conditions and the network of actors

---

Instruments are innovation-friendly if they...

⇒ provide economic incentives

⇒ act in combination

⇒ are based on strategic planning and formulation of goals

⇒ support innovation as a process and take account of the different phases of innovation

A policy style is innovation-friendly if it...

⇒ is based on dialogue and consensus

⇒ is calculable, reliable and has continuity

⇒ is decisive, proactive and ambitious

⇒ is open and flexible with respect to individual cases

⇒ is management and knowledge oriented

A configuration of actors is innovation-friendly if...

⇒ it favours horizontal and vertical policy integration and when the various regulatory authorities are closely networked

⇒ the various objects of regulation are networked with one another

⇒ the network between regulator and regulated is a tight one

⇒ through the inclusion of stakeholders in actor networks, it promotes the availability of existing knowledge and motivation

---

Figure 2:   Elements of an innovation-friendly policy framework

---

[15]   For a comprehensive treatment see Blazejczak and Edler 1998.

3.1   Instrumentation

Common to all the approaches discussed above is that they posit the creation of economic incentives as a criterion for innovation-friendly policy frameworks. However, this does not mean that exclusive use of economic instruments is recommended. What is shown to be decisive is rather the combination of various instruments. For example, it is recommended to associate flexible regulations with economic incentives in order to even up information asymmetry and make possible regulations adapted to the companies' prevention costs structure. Moreover, measures to complement environmental regulations, such as strengthening demand pressure through targeted information, are recommended.

The development and spread of new technologies is only likely where medium to long-term increases in profit can be achieved. Orienting instruments towards clear, binding goals, developed jointly in strategic environmental planning by all groups in society, can remove uncertainty, provide impetus to innovation and steer research activities towards socially desirable goals. These incentives are especially effective if strategic environmental planning signals regular fine-tuning of instruments which can be anticipated by companies. Environmental policy research is increasingly pressing for a flexible, strategic approach in principle and a consideration of factors beyond the influence of decision-makers in practice. More attention paid to the procedural nature of innovation is also seen as important for successful policy-making. The various phases of innovation – invention, innovation and diffusion – require a choice and combination of instruments which supports this process and does justice to the special features in each of the phases.

3.2   Policy Style

The term "policy style" belongs to policy analysis, and was first coined by Richardson (1982). Economic analyses also emphasise – noting the difficulties in implementing innovation-friendly environmental regulation and the role played by the spread of information in the success of innovation – the importance of close cooperation between the various actors participating in the political process. A pre-condition for this cooperation is a policy style with dialogue. Promoting cooperation in research by setting common goals through political, business and research channels is also conceivable. In such an alliance, state institutions could function as managers or "game makers"[16], bringing together the various actors and coordinating their research activities. In addition, without the breaking down of information asymmetries, the flexible shaping and application of instruments becomes more difficult.

---

[16]   cf. Schot: The government as game regulator. 1992, p. 50f.

Broader support for innovation-friendly forms of environmental regulation could be achieved by involving the relevant interest groups more closely in the political process. This would certainly require more intensive information dispersal. Continuity in environmental policy should nonetheless not be forgotten.

In order to reduce uncertainty as to companies' opportunities for profit, avoid bad investments and support the transition from end-of-pipe technologies to integrated environmental protection, attention should be paid to the calculability, reliability and continuity of environmental regulations.

Decisiveness from the regulator in formulating and implementing (ambitious) environmental policy goals increases the signalling effect of environmental policy and contributes thereby to its calculability and reliability. In particular, where the regulating authority makes clear its commitment to achieve a goal "by hook or by crook", this serves to reduce the investment risk for innovators. This in no way contradicts the idea that environmental policy must be open to new discoveries and each individual case in order to guarantee sufficient flexibility in the regulatory framework. A co-operative, flexible policy style only makes sense when conducted decisively. The political willingness to learn which is important for innovation affects primarily the operative side of policy.

In guiding management, it is a question of policy which does not direct through general regulations – as is traditionally the case – but implements concrete aims through organisation according to a plan (NASCHOLD AND BOGUMIL 1998, p. 79). Thus the bureaucrat assumes certain entrepreneurial qualities.

3.3 Configuration of Actors

The discovery of new, inexpensive possibilities for reducing environmental stress and their implementation require cooperation from various political arenas and administrative levels (European Union, National, Regional, Local). Alongside this (intrasectoral) policy integration, the (intersectoral) integration and networking of various policy fields is of great importance for the coordination and enhancement of stimuli to innovation. A common path for environmental, energy and technology policy, for example, can reinforce the orientation and motivation towards innovation in the field of energy. An absence of intersectoral policies is an obstacle above all when administrations pursue opposing policies (e.g. energy supply vs. energy conservation).

Innovation springs from specific knowledge and learning effects, and companies can therefore gain mutual benefit from well-targeted cooperation, in particular along the value creation chain. Impetus towards environmental innovation can also be expected from information exchange between basic and applied research and between companies and external research establishments, as specific knowledge frequently comes to light independently in more than one research area. The state can contribute to this exchange by setting up or supporting innovation networks, which can extend beyond the aforementioned research establishments and R&D departments to include regulatory authorities as well, thus bringing about not only the exchange of information, but also greater motivation in the participants.

Including the various important stakeholders is generally an appropriate way of expanding the basis for formulating political goals and extending the spectrum of options. If a goal is accepted by a broad base, its implementation becomes considerably easier. This is particularly the case where the target group belongs to a network, and the base therefore includes both regulator and regulated. In this case, not only the implementation of measures is potentially made easier. If the target group participates in formulating the goals, innovators within the group can adjust early on to the measures and at the same time seek to have the measure applied in a way which suits them.

4   The Studies

4.1   Innovation Effects of Sector-Specific Regulatory Frameworks in the Paper Industry[17]

Paper manufacture is characterised by a variety of complex interrelated environmental problems. The paper sector is, through its product, tied into a chain of economic activities with great importance to the environment: from forestry, engineering and chemicals through paper processing to printing and recycling and waste disposal. A decisive framework condition for innovation in the paper industry is the extraordinarily high capital intensity associated with the long active life of much plant in this sector. Paper manufacture is based on an "old", mature technological paradigm within which innovation has only an incremental character.

Against this backdrop, the study looks at what incentives there are for generating new knowledge about innovative production processes, for the first use of such technologies and for their diffusion. Clean technologies for energy transformation and consumption, as well as associated technologies for recycling waste paper and avoiding sewage are the most important. Incentive structures both for providers and for the users of these technologies are analysed.

International comparison of the paper industry shows, among other things:

- the development of important factors influencing environmental innovation in the paper industry in the countries compared

---

[17]   see for more details Blazejczak and Edler in this volume.

- examples of innovative approaches to promoting environmental innovation in the countries compared

(1) There has been a great number of incremental improvements in wood pulp and paper manufacture, leading in all to considerable reductions in environmental stress in the countries studied. Basic innovation has not taken place in this "mature technology". The decisive innovations for reducing environmental stress have involved both additive measures and integrated technologies at the process level. The dominant pattern in environmental innovation has been one of closing material flow systems (raw materials, pollutants). Product innovation (for wood pulp and paper) has played only a subordinate role. The most favourable conditions for implementing innovative process technologies (windows of opportunity) come at times when new production capacity is being built.

The crucial factors influencing the creation and diffusion of environmental innovation were, in order of importance:

- company efforts to reduce costs,

- the formulation of environmental policy, in combination or interaction with

- the level of public environmental awareness, especially where changes in behaviour triggered demand-side push.

High energy prices in Japan have lead to energy conservation measures (e.g. the use of heat and power co-generation) which go considerably further than in the USA or Sweden. In densely populated countries such as Japan (and Germany), additive technologies were developed and applied earlier to reduce emissions presenting an immediate danger to public health. The effectiveness of demand-side market push is demonstrated in the example of the first rapid (and then stagnating) diffusion of innovations in cellulose bleach (TCF cellulose) in Sweden, especially when the temporary added costs to frontrunners are (for a time) more than compensated for by increased returns. There are also indications of increased returns for plant manufacturers through gaining the lead in environmentally significant technologies; Scandinavian manufacturers, for example, are having success in the American market with chlorine-free bleaching technologies.

Clear differences can be found in the regulatory frameworks and policy styles in each country (cf. Figures 3, 4 and 5[18]):

- Environmental policy in the USA was for a long time hostile to innovation. However, since around 1990, a correspondingly radical shift in orientation has become evident, although it has failed to alter the – traditionally confrontational – policy style there.

---

[18]   The policy styles represented below relate to the innovation effects of environmental policy **up to now** in the paper industries of the three countries.

- Policy style in Japan is traditionally flexible and cooperative. There is no recognisable orientation specifically towards innovation to be found in the environmental policy relating to paper manufacture. Promoting innovation is the traditional task of the MITI's industrial policy in Japan, although the paper industry and licensed production of plant for cellulose and paper manufacture, as non-strategic sectors, do not benefit.

- In Sweden, a fundamentally consensual environmental policy with nonetheless demanding goals, working together with innovation-oriented companies who view the environmental soundness of their production as a strategic task, have lead to considerable progress in environmental innovation in the paper industry. This was achieved despite the fact that environmental policy is not explicitly oriented towards innovation. The long-term goals formulated by environmental policy and the high status accorded to research and development policy within the sector do, however, have a favourable effect.

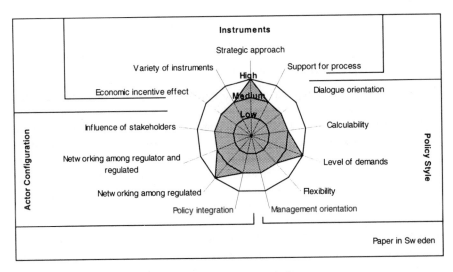

Figure 3:   Policy framework in the Swedish paper industry

(2) More recently, there has been increasing awareness of the inadequate atmosphere for innovation offered by a traditional environmental regulatory framework, based primarily on technical standards. Of the countries studied, this can be seen especially in the USA, to a lesser extent in Sweden but scarcely at all in Japan, as yet. The new approaches are – not least under the influence of the environmental regulatory framework which has dominated up to now – still tentative, but can be highlighted in some examples from the paper industry.

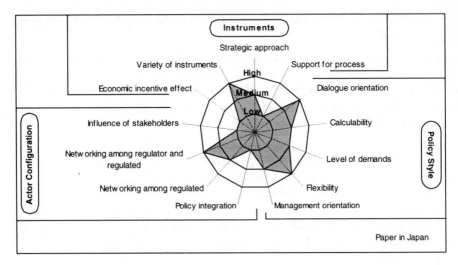

Figure 4:   Policy framework in the Japanese paper industry

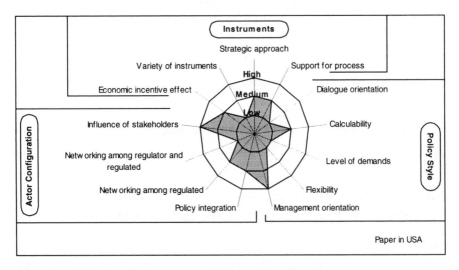

Figure 5:   Policy framework in the US American paper industry

In the USA, regulation of the cellulose and paper industry, which has been passed only recently after a lengthy political process, contains the so-called Cluster Rules, with new innovation-oriented elements:

• integrated limits for water and air pollution

• associated incentives for environmental relief beyond the legally required standards

In the face of the fundamental hostility to regulations in the USA, a series of "soft" instruments has been developed and successfully implemented, based on voluntary commitment and mutuality (the Green Lights and Energy Star programmes). The start of a long-term strategic orientation can be found in research and development policy (Vision 2020 for the paper industry).

Sweden's pro-active environmental policy, oriented towards the long-term goal of sustainability, sends out clear and effective signals. The important guidelines for the paper industry, Sweden 2021 and Ecocyclic Pulp Mill not only define environmental policy goals, but also send out the corresponding signals for knowledge generation through their research policy. It is also clear that, in Sweden, impetus towards environmental innovation is provided by embedding environmental goals in company strategies (and organisation) and by introducing environmental management systems.

Overall, the international comparison of regulatory frameworks in the paper industry makes it possible to identify a series of approaches which – with varying weightings according to the national framework conditions and policy styles – can make a particular contribution as elements of a policy framework to promoting the generation and diffusion of environmental innovation:

• strategic planning

• creation of (economic) incentives

• product chain management

• policy integration over various environmental media

• voluntary, mutual measures.

4.2   Innovation Effects of Sector-Specific Regulatory Frameworks for Energy-Saving Refrigerators in Denmark[19]

The study examines firstly the retail success of Class A, B and C energy-saving refrigerators between 1994 and 1997, where their market share rose from 42 per cent to 90 per cent. Secondly, it looks at the corresponding innovation by the leading Danish refrigerator manufacturer Gram, who have developed, among other things, a compressor which consumes another 40 per cent less electricity. To date (as of mid-1997), energy consumption by refrigerators has been reduced by a factor of two or three against ten-year-old appliances. The innovation described here

---

[19]   see Jänicke et al. 1998.

can improve on this by a factor of ten for refrigerators without a freezer compartment.

At first, the hypothesis presented itself that both processes – diffusion and innovation – can be traced back to the noticeable rise in energy taxation which took place under the comprehensive environmental tax reform in 1994 and continued gradually until 1998. However, the results showed that a broader approach is necessary to explain the success story.

At the very least, the explanation must consider a mix of different instruments: the energy tax – which is linked to a CO_2 charge – was certainly the necessary condition for the retail success of the top models. However, without the further instrument of labelling the consumption of appliances (1989, also adopted as an EU guideline in 1994, coming into force for refrigerators in 1995) the actual effect could scarcely have been expected. In addition, a section of retail staff was offered training as to the labelling scheme by the energy authority. The instrument which offers an additional explanation of retail success was national and regional energy-saving campaigns, in which energy supplier took part (1994 and 1995). In fact, one of these campaigns involved a part exchange scheme worth DKK 200 for old refrigerators replaced with the top models (1994). The broad awareness of environmental and climate issues within the Danish population must also be counted as a background variable.

In innovation by the Danish manufacturer Gram, state support for R&D played an essential role, implying the formation of innovation networks. The energy/CO_2 tax is also an important background factor here, although it was not classed as decisive by the companies themselves. They view the EU maximum consumption guideline, which will come into force in Denmark in 1999, and which will make existing top models the norm, as especially important. In this context, new markets were only to be opened up through further improvements. (At the same time, retailers had to make efforts to remove inefficient appliances quickly from their product ranges and warehouses).

The project has also borne methodological fruit. Looking at the breadth of the range of instruments which were effective, the importance and configuration of the participating actors and the cooperative, forward-looking policy style of regulating authorities, the broader concept of "policy style" has proven its problem-solving capabilities.

Figure 6 summarises the relative importance of factors influencing the policy framework in the Danish case. In this case study innovation follows diffusion, or more precisely: improved market conditions for top models promote further technological development. Both were brought about by an essentially strategic approach to environmental and climate protection policy, characterised by decisive, but negotiated formulation of goals (CO_2 reduction, energy conservation), a good technological infrastructure policy and tight networks between state and private sector actors. Special emphasis should be given to the breadth and flexibility of the application of instruments, ranging from indicative long-term planning, energy taxation, subsidies and information to efficiency standards.

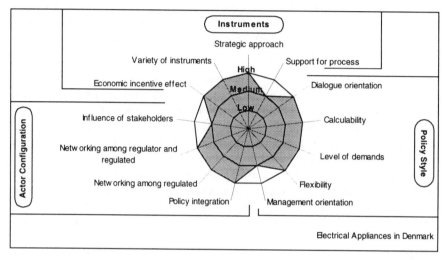

Figure 6:   Policy framework in the electrical appliances market (refrigerators) in Denmark

4.3   Wind Energy[20]

In the wake of the oil crises in 1973/74, an approach towards developing and introducing environmentally friendly wind energy technologies has been successfully followed in Denmark since the 1970s. Supported by a combination of various environmental policy instruments, especially subsidies, a technological niche, and subsequently a market niche for wind technology in Denmark was created, one which has now developed into a functioning market. The characteristics of Danish policy towards wind energy are:

• drawing up long-term energy plans

• supporting R&D to build up basic knowledge

• shifting investment subsidies early on towards support based on returns to promote diffusion

• financial stakeholding by wide sections of the population

---

[20]   see Hemmelskamp 1998.

- inducing involvement by energy suppliers in the expansion of wind energy

- linking wind energy policy to other policy areas, such as environmental policy and energy policy.

In Germany too, environmental and technology policy instruments promoted the emergence of a market niche for wind energy use, where technologically reliable and profitable wind farms were developed and institutional innovation made possible, such as forming associations and company networks or the development of investor models. The structure of state support policy in Germany is in this respect fundamentally similar to that in Denmark (cf. Figure 8).

In Germany, a support policy which took account of the nature of each phase in innovation when applying instruments was also decisive. However, this did not take place in the context of a strategic subsidies plan, but developed gradually and was therefore able to learn from experience. This could be criticised as short-termism, however this modus operandi proved itself to have been successful in practice, as the flexible use of instruments was thereby made possible (cf. Figures 7, 9 and 10).

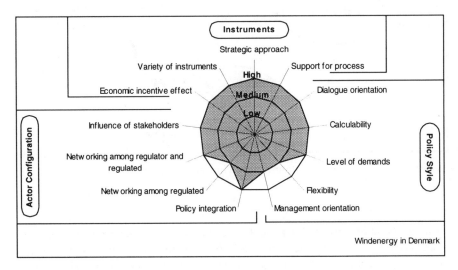

Figure 7:   Policy framework in wind energy in Denmark

With respect to subsidies policy, support for R&D projects in small companies proved, as in Denmark, to be successful. However, this process began later on in Germany than in Denmark. German companies were therefore able to build on experience in developing small wind farms and then continually accumulate further expertise in developing more powerful and efficient equipment. After technologically reliable wind energy equipment became available at the end of the 1980s, subsidies policy underwent a shift. Just as in Denmark, the dominant support for manufacturers was significantly reduced in favour of a returns-dependent, operator-oriented funding strategy. This provided the operators of wind farms with a sound basis for calculation and limited considerable the risk in investment decisions. At the same time, demand which was elastic in terms of price was induced and the equipment manufacturers were given incentives towards continually reducing costs. However, the development in wind energy use cannot be explained solely through the use of subsidy-based instruments, but also through further complementary regulation in taxation, planning and environmental law.

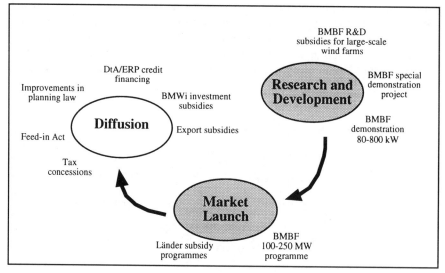

Figure 8:   State support instruments used in wind energy in Germany

From the point of view of allocation theory, state subsidies may well be considered relatively inefficient (cf. ERDMANN 1992, p. 183), but this temporary support has proved itself highly effective in overcoming existing market barriers. However, if they are to be efficient, it is crucial that these state subsidies are only provided for a limited period and that a maximum term is laid down. In Denmark and Germany this was the case, and the level of subsidies was tailored flexibly to the changing framework conditions as technology and the market develop, as well as being significantly reduced over time.

Increasing pressure on costs, both through the type of instruments used and reductions in the scale of support, has led to continuous competition in both countries. It is becoming ever more important for manufacturers to reduce the specific costs of equipment by exploiting the learning curve, in order to increase their own room for manoeuvre in pricing. This is done through R&D to innovate in products and processes and through attempting to secure the returns on their innovation through gaining a headstart in launching a product on the market and thereby achieving a high market share as fast as possible. As a consequence of this market pressure, the specific costs for generating wind energy have fallen significantly in past years. At the same time, market concentration among manufacturers in Germany and Denmark has risen sharply.

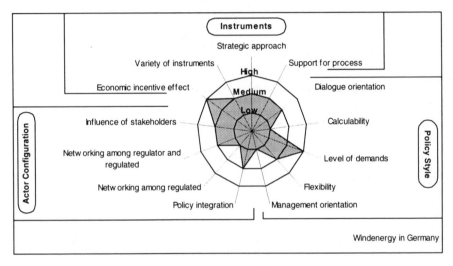

Figure 9:   Policy framework in wind energy in Germany

Since the Electricity Act in 1989, Great Britain has been trying a different way of supporting regenerative energy. The Electricity Act is complemented by the Non-Fossil Fuel Obligation (NFFO) and "renewable orders", where the regional electricity companies are obligated to accept regenerative and nuclear electricity. The higher purchasing costs for regenerative electricity are returned to the electricity companies by way of a fossil fuel levy. The regional electricity companies conclude contracts with private investors for constructing wind farms through competitive tendering However, only a quarter of the wind farms foreseen have as yet come on-stream, as there are problems with public acceptance, among other things, in realising the projects. In contrast to Germany and Denmark, a competitive wind energy industry has not developed in Great Britain, as support for market introduction through the NFFO began before the corresponding expertise had been built up in British companies (cf. STEVENSON 1996, p. 74). The overwhelming majority of wind farms in Great Britain is therefore supplied by more competitive Danish firms.

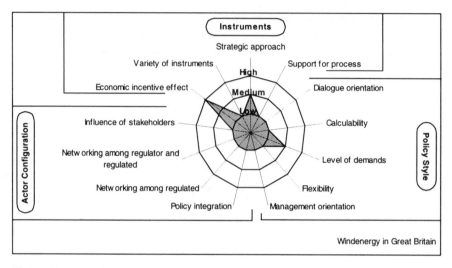

Figure 10:   Policy framework in wind energy in Great Britain

The future development of wind energy use in Germany is considerably less certain than in Denmark or Great Britain. In contrast to Germany, Great Britain's Electricity Act lays the legal groundwork for further expansion in wind energy, albeit at a fairly low level. In Denmark, a broad consensus on the further expansion of wind energy has been reached between the participating actors, i.e. energy suppliers, wind farm operators, the state and the general public. The existence of a market niche in Germany has up to now been based primarily on technology policy goals. This shows the disadvantages in the lack of a long-term perspective in planning subsidies. There is no agreement on the use of the existing supply of technological solutions in the implementation of environmental and energy policy goals. On the contrary, there is considerable resistance to the use of wind energy among energy suppliers, who wish to secure their existing monopoly and specialisation rents and protect their own overcapacity. This is expressed in capacity planning by suppliers which takes no account of expanding wind energy use. In consequence, fuel is saved through the wind energy capacity installed to date, but this has no further effects on the structure of generating capacity as a whole. Because of this situation, there is considerable uncertainty both for operators and manufacturers of wind power equipment as to the future development of the domestic market in Germany. In Great Britain and Denmark, on the other hand, energy suppliers were forced to participate through legal measures and steps were taken to decentralise energy supply further. In addition, acceptance by local populations is falling in Germany, as in Great Britain, with the increasing penetration of wind energy use. The response in Germany has included possibilities for financial participation by residents in the operating companies, learning from the experience of the Danish wind cooperatives in which the majority of Danes are stakeholders. This would appear hard to implement in Great Britain, due to the principle of competitive tendering. Finally, the dominant set of civil law instruments in Germany is obstructing the use of regenerative energy, favouring rather the use of end-of-pipe technologies to upgrade existing fossil-fuel power stations.

5   Common Features and Differences: a Comparative Interpretation of Seven Policy Frameworks

In interpreting the seven policy frameworks outlined here, certain restrictions arising from the methods used should be made: firstly, broad conclusions cannot be drawn because – quite apart from the small number of cases – specific innovations effects (to be explained) could not be ascribed to an equally specific policy framework (as explanation) in every case. This is the case for the three examples from the paper industry, where the policy framework is associated with several improvements, including incremental ones. Secondly, it is not possible to rank the level of innovation in the seven cases clearly. Whatever the case, the two Danish examples can be seen as examples of relatively far-reaching – and also specific – innovation, in the sense of being international pioneers. The innovation in the Swedish paper industry can also be understood as a first mover activity.

These three most advanced cases of innovation are at any rate also characterised by the most well-rounded policy frameworks: broad sets of factors promoting innovation. To this extent the cases studied tend to support the hypothesis that political action is best suited to the complex dynamics or factors influencing innovation when it follows a broad, non-restrictive approach to instruments. The policy frameworks in these three cases have in particular a strategic approach in common, along with strict commitment to goals and the high significance of networks.

The policy framework in the case of German wind energy, which may not have achieved the success of the Danish case, but has come close, is considerably different and less inclusive than the Danish framework. The policy framework is "tighter", with economic incentive mechanisms being more effective. This poses the question of whether better-targeted frameworks with a more focused use of instruments might not have a higher success rate in terms of their innovation effects. In this case, the effects of economic incentives were so massive that they may well have replaced a broad spectrum of further factors. On the other hand, a range of influences also comes into play here, going considerably beyond the effects of a single economic instrument, and thereby justifying the use of the term "policy framework". Moreover, there is certainly a difference between being able to claim success in achieving innovation effects after the fact and being able to predict it beforehand. As a rule, there is great uncertainty as to the innovation effects of a measure ex ante, which in itself speaks for a more inclusive approach.

The thesis can be made that, although it might well be shown ex post that a less broad approach to political intervention was highly effective for innovation in a single case, it must be seen that, before the fact, political strategies, especially those in support of innovation, are characterised by uncertainty as to the effects of factors specific to each case. The advantage of a broader approach in this situation – with a mix of instruments, dialogue, close networks among participating actors, etc. – is similar to the effect of a scatter gun. However, another advantage is shown to be that innovation effects can also be achieved without overburdening a single instrument (especially charges).

Taken as a whole, the seven cases treated here confirm the hypothesis that the innovation effects of political measures are, in practice, neither to be explained nor to be realised with a simple top-down approach. Innovation-oriented environmental policy demands comprehensive efforts, which can be conceived of rather in terms of strategic public management than of traditional administration, fixated on instruments and directed towards formal regulation. The new approaches in the paper industries in the USA, Japan and Sweden referred to here are already recognising this fact.

References

Balks, M. (1995), *Umweltpolitik aus der Sicht der neuen Institutionenökonomik*, Wiesbaden.

Becher, G., J. Hemmelskamp, W. Weibert and H. Wolff. (1993), *Ansatzpunkte für eine Verbesserung der Standortbedingungen für Forschung, Entwicklung und Technologie in der Bundesrepublik*, Studie der Prognos AG im Auftrag des Bundesministers für Forschung und Technologie, Basel.

Blazejczak, J. and D. Edler (1998), *Elemente innovationsfreundlicher Politikmuster – ein internationaler Vergleich am Beispiel der Papierindustrie*, Studie des DIW im Rahmen des Forschungsverbundes „Innovative Wirkungen umweltpolitischer Instrumente" im Auftrag des Bundesministeriums für Bildung, Forschung und Technologie, Berlin (vervielfältigtes Manuskript).

Bressers, H. and P.J. Klok (1991), *The Explanation of Policy Effectiveness*, Centre for Clean Technology and Environmental Policy, University of Twente.

Conrad, J. (1996), *Successful Environmental Manangement in European Companies*, Forschungsstelle für Umweltpolitik (FFU), Freie Universität Berlin, FFU-report 96-3.

Coombs, R., P. Saviotti and V. Walsh (1987), *Economics and Technological Change*, Houndsmill.

Dodgson, M. and R. Rothwell (eds.) (1994), *The Handbook of Industrial Innovation*, Aldershot.

Downing, P. and L.J White (1986), Innovation in Pollution Control, *Journal of Environmental Economics and Management* 13, 18-29.

European Environment Agency (EEA) (1996), *Environmental Taxes. Implementation and Environmental Effectiveness*, Copenhagen.

Erdmann, G. (1992), *Energieökonomik. Theorie und Anwendungen*, Zürich.

Ewers, H.-J. and A. Brenck (1992), Innovationsorientierte Regionalpolitik, in: Birg, H. and H.J. Schalck (eds.), *Regionale und sektorale Strukturpolitik*, Münster, 309-341.

FIU – Forschungsverbund Innovative Wirkungen umweltpolitischer Instrumente (1997), *Rundbrief September 1997*, Essen (vervielfältigtes Manuskript).

Hemmelskamp, J. (1997a), Umweltpolitik und Innovation – Grundlegende Begriffe und Zusammenhänge, *Zeitschrift für Umweltpolitik und Umweltrecht* 4, 481-511.

Hemmelskamp, J. (1997b), Environmental Policy Instruments and their Effects on Innovation, *European Planning Studies* 2, 177-194.

Hemmelskamp, J. (1998), *Innovationswirkungen der Umwelt- und Technologiepolitik im Windenergiebereich – ein internationaler Vergleich*, Studie des ZEW im Rahmen des Forschungsverbunds „Innovative Wirkungen umweltpolitischer Instrumente" (FIU) des Bundesministeriums für Bildung, Forschung und Technologie, Mannheim (vervielfältigtes Manuskript).

Hemmelskamp, J. (1999), *Umweltpolitik und technischer Fortschritt*, Heidelberg.

Jänicke, M. (1997), *Umweltinnovationen aus der Sicht der Policy-Analyse: vom instrumentellen zum strategischen Ansatz der Umweltpolitik*, Forschungsstelle für Umweltpolitik (FFU), Freie Universität Berlin, FFU-report 97-3.

Jänicke, M. (ed.) (1996), *Umweltpolitik der Industrieländer*, Berlin.

Jänicke, M., L. Mez, P. Bechsgaard and B. Klemmensen (1998), *Innovationswirkungen branchenbezogener Regulierungsmuster am Beispiel energiesparender Kühlschränke in Dänemark* Studie der FFU im Rahmen des Forschungsverbundes „Innovative Wirkungen umweltpolitischer Instrumente" im Auftrag des Bundesministeriums für Bildung, Forschung und Technologie, Berlin, Roskilde (vervielfältigtes Manuskript).

Jänicke, M. and H. Weidner (eds.) (1995), *Successful Environmental Policy. A Critical Evaluation of 24 Cases*, Berlin.

Kemp et al. (1994), Policy Instruments to Stimulate Cleaner Technologies, in: Opschoor, H. and K. Turner (eds.), *Economic Incentives and Environmental Policies*, Dordrecht, 275-300.

Kemp, R. (1995), *Environmental Policy and Technical Change: A Comparison of the Technological Impact of Policy Instruments*, Maastricht.

Kemp, R. (1998), *Environmental Regulation and Innovation. Key Issues and Questions for Research*, Maastricht (mimeo.).

Mayntz, R. (1983), Zur Einleitung: Probleme der Theoriebildung in der Implementationsforschung, in: Mayntz, R. (ed.), *Implementation politischer Programme*, Opladen.

Michaelis, P. (1996), *Ökonomische Instrumente in der Umweltpolitik: Eine anwendungsorientierte Einführung*, Heidelberg.

Milliman, S.R. and R. Prince (1989), Firm Incentives to Promote Technological Change in Pollution Control, *Journal of Environmental Economics and Management* 17, 247-265.

OECD (1997), *Environmental Taxes and Green Tax Reform*, Paris.

Pavitt, K. (1984), Sectoral Patterns of Technical Change: Towards a Taxonomy and a Theory, *Research Policy* 13, 343-373.

Richardson, J.J. (ed.) (1982), *Policy Styles in Western Europe*, London.

Rossi, M. (1998), *Environmental Technology Innovation in the U.S. Pulp and Paper Industry: The Role of Public Policy*, Cambridge, Mass. (mimeo.).

Rothwell, R. (1992), Industrial innovation and government environmental regulation: Some lessons from the past *Technovation* 7, 447-458.

Sabatier, P.A. (1986), Top-Down and Bottom-Up Approaches to Implementation Research: A Critical Analysis and Suggested Synthesis, *Journal of Public Policy* 6(1), 21-48.

Schot, J.W. (1992), Constructive Technology Assessment and Technology Dynamics: the Case of Clean Technologies, *Science, Technology & Human Values* 17(1), 36-56.

Solsberg, L. (1997), Energy Challenges and Opportunities for Action, in, OECD (ed.): *Sustainable Development: OECD Policy Approaches for the 21st Century*, Paris.

Stevenson, R. (1996), *Wind Energy Success Stories Wales Regional Report. Final Report for National Wind Power*, Machynlleth.

Wallace, D. (1995), *Environmental Policy and Industrial Innovation. Strategies in Europe, the USA and Japan*, London.

Environmental Policy and Technological Change: Towards Deliberative Governance

Sylvie Faucheux

Centre d'Economie et d'Ethique pour l'Environnement et le Développement
Université de Versailles-Saint Quentin en Yvelines
47 bd Vauban, 78047 Guyancourt CEDEX
France

Keywords. multi stakeholder approach, post-normal science, procedural rationality, win-win strategies.

1 Introduction

The future studies have made a remarkable comeback under the label of foresight (Martin and Irvine, 1989). The aera where these future studies have gained a new ground are foresight processes at the intersection of environmental policy and technology policy to initiate technological innovations that contribute to the fulfilment of environmental objectives, like reducing emissions, prevent pollution and cleaning industrial processes. The two linked and ambiguous questions at the heart of these foresights are the following one:

1. Which new environmental problems could stimulate technological innovation?

2. Which new technologies might contribute significantly to the solution of environmental problems?

However, at the difference of the traditional technological future studies, foresights do not provide forecasting. They can be defined as a "process by which one comes to a fuller understanding of the forces shaping the long term future which should be taken into account in policy formulation, planning and decision making" (Coates, 1985: 30). They widely recognise limitations of the traditional linear model of innovation where the emphasis for technological innovation is just on the constituent actors within that system-firms, universities, government research laboratories and so on, but more importantly on the relationships and linkages between them. "In short, foresight opens up the possibility of negotiating a new and more fruitful relationship or 'social contract' between science and technology, on the one hand, and society on the other" (Martin and Johnston, 1999).

The implementation of environmental policies, particularly through the sustainable development objective, involves also to reform the government methods of decision making. Indeed, with the emergence of this concept, a wide variety of participatory procedures are growing everywhere, in Europe and elsewhere in the world. These procedures place emphasis on conflict resolution and on the search for a widely acceptable course of action taking account of the diversity of interests, ethical positions and scientific views (Faucheux and O'Connor eds., 1998).

Therefore, this paper analyses how environmental problems and policy responses, particularly technological ones, are linked to the questions of a new deliberative governance. The problem of governance indeed arises as a matter of public concern whenever the members of a social group find that they are interdependent, but potentially in conflict. The actions of each individual member impinge on the welfare of the others and the efforts of individual actors to achieve their goals interfere with or thwart the efforts of others to pursue their own ends. Governance does not presuppose the need to create material entities or organisations of the sort one normally might think of as governments to administer the social practices that arise to handle the function of governance (Ellickson, 1991), but more particularly to develop sets of rules, decision-making procedures, and programmatic activities that serve to define social practices and to guide the interactions of those participating in these practices (North, 1990). Approached in this way, the initially counterintuitive distinction between governance and government, as well as the growing interest in the idea of "governance without government" become clear (Rosenau and Czempiel 1992; Young, 1997).

In this paper, the following definition of governance will be retained:

"Governance is the sum of the many ways individuals and institutions, public and private, manage their common affairs. It is a continuing process through which conflicting or diverse interests may be accommodated and a co-operative action may be taken. It includes formal institutions and regimes empowered to enforce compliance, as well as informal arrangements that people and institutions either have agreed to or perceive to be in their interest" (European Commission, 1995: 2).

The paper is organised as follows. In the first section, it is explained that many debates about the compatibility between sustainable development and competitiveness hinge on views about the extent to which technological change, pushed by environmental regulation, is thought to have the potential to reduce pollutant emissions and to improve efficiency of natural resource, land and water use.

The second section shows how encouraging technology development is no guarantee of environmental improvement. On the one hand, technological innovation implies dangers as well as opportunities. On the other hand, major business corporations and alliances are in position to influence the direction taken by environmental technological innovations and to impose "regulatory capture".

The third section explains how technology policy from the viewpoint of sustainable development should serve to strengthen the opportunities where possible and mitigate any dangers in good time. For that it looks necessary to introduce, as complements to competitiveness, other notions such as the public interest and collective responsibility for the future in the choice of environmental technological innovations. This means changing previous exclusive governance to reach an inclusive governance building a partnership to choose technological change in conformity with environmental concerns between all the stakeholders.

2 The New Ideology of "Virtuous Circle": Environmental Regulation, Technological Innovation and Sustainable Development

2.1 The "Win-Win" Strategy or the Environmental Regulation as a Motor of Competitiveness

Sustainable development aims at reconciling the pursuit of goals traditionally associated with economic growth (such as material wealth and consumer satisfaction), with ecological constraints on economic activity. A related evolution has taken place in the private sector and in regulatory theory and practice. On the one hand, firms have come increasingly to consider the necessity of "taking the environment into account" not just as an exogeneously imposed cost or constraint, but as a strategic opportunity. Necessity is thus converted into virtue.

These inter-related developments tend some prima facie support to Porter and van der Linde's suggestion (1995), that the growth of environmental controls (laws, policies, standards and public expectations) is compatible with continued economic competitiveness. Indeed their concept of "win-win" strategy, indicates a firm's strategy that allows to maintain or even to increase its level of competitiveness, while at the same time, the concerns for environmental quality is respected. What acted only in the form of an exogeneous necessity in the 1970s and 1980s, is being turned into a competitive advantage terrain in the 1990s.

Indeed, since the 1980s, the world has witnessed the development of what Porter (1990) refers to as the new competitiveness paradigm based on dynamic vision. According to this view, competitiveness at the industry level may well be achieved through higher productivity or lower prices, but also by the ability to provide different and better quality products thanks to the technological innovation. So, the technological innovation is the motor of the competiveness.

Therefore, environmental technological change plays a key role in this new dynamics of international competitiveness.

On the one hand, in the course of the last 10-15 years, a certain number of sectors have been placed under increased pressure for technological competition, due (in a large part) to the detection of new environmental problems and regulations. Concerned in particular by this development were the chemical industry (e.g CFC and its effects on the ozone layer, phosphates in detergents) as well as the automobile industry (e.g. catalytic converters vs. "clean motors" and acid rain).

On the other hand, according to studies done by Japanese government agencies, 40 per cent of the world's production of goods and services over the first half of the twenty-first century may be from environment or energy-linked products and technologies (MITI, 1988; Miller and Moore, 1994). In this perspective, the respect of environmental regulation (or the anticipation of regulation through proactive strategies of firms) becomes most important for the choice and diffusion of technologies in the framework of competitiveness (Faucheux and Nicolaï, 1998). Most of the future studies on technological innovation confirms that after 2010, there will an explosion of radical innovations to reduce and/or avoid environmental impacts and to offer renewable energies (NISTEP, 1997; Grupp and Reiss, 1997).

2.2   An Apparent Symbiosis of Technological Innovations and Sustainable Development Policy

In the two most widely debated conceptions of sustainable development, the role of technological change is determinant to improve the environment and more largely to allow a sustainable development path (Faucheux and O'Connor eds, 1998).

The so-called "strong sustainability" perspective as enunciated by Daly (1991) emphasises a strong degree of complementarity between technical (produced), human and natural capitals. The latter, natural capital, is viewed as sharply constrained (carrying capacity, rates of renewable resources, assimilation capacity by ecosystems of wastes), hence a long-run sustainability requires limiting the volume of economic activity to what is compatible with these ecological constraints. This can lead to the old propositions for zero-growth of economic activity, based on the structures of complementarity, alternatively to propositions to implement policies for increased "eco-efficiency through the dematerialisation of economic activity. This means reducing throughputs of the material and energy "services" of natural capital for a given level of economic goods and services production (Hinterberger, Luks and Schmidt-Bleek, 1997)

The so-called "weak sustainability" approaches, draw their inspiration from neo-classical capital theory extended to include natural capital (Faucheux, Pearce, Proops, 1995). It is presumed that technological change/progress can, automatically through market mechanisms, offer some relief from environmental constraints, through some combination of substitution (from natural capital towards human and produced capital) and secular increases in factor productivity. In this vision, competitive forces will push the economy progressively towards the application of "backstop technologies" involving high marginal productivity of scarce natural capital (such as nuclear fusion or high tech solar energy or technological capture emissions, etc...) (Faucheux, Muir & O'Connor, 1997).

In both approaches, the view of technological change potentialities determines the vision of sustainability and how to attain it. Correspondingly, both schools propose that measures of technical changes and of production levels can be key indicators of success or not in the implementation of environmental and more largely sustainability policies.

3   The "Dark Side" of the "Force"

3.1   Technological Innovation and Sustainability: Some Ambiguous Relations

In the spirit of these two visions, it can readily be agreed that advances in science are opening up new domains of potential technological innovation with potentialy vast consequences for interventions in human health, energy supply, food production and environmental engineering.These fields of advancing knowledge carry many hopes for humanity (Leisinger, 1998). However they also bring new risks to society and can lead to new forms of pollution. The new technologies such as genetic engineering that show potential for relieving some environmental constraints, also entail a deepening of environmental, health and technological risks. A feature of these (and other) domains of science-based innovation is their intervention – by accident or design- in complex biological and ecosystem processes where quality assurance in terms of outcomes is almost impossible to conduct (Funtowicz, Ravetz & O'Connor, 1998).

A lesson that may be drawn from many historical examples (CFCs, nuclear sector, catalytic converters, etc...) is that the relationships between advances in science and in science-based technologies on the one hand, and sustainable development on the other hand, is multifaceted and ambiguous. Just as the recognition of ecological constraints on the scale and forms of sustainable economic production and consumption means that "more output" is not the same as "good input", so it has be noted that more scientific knowledge put to work in innovations does not necessarily lead to more environmental quality and to a more sustainable economic process.

Moreover, when a technology is abandoned for a new one (for example, nuclear energy in Germany or the exploitation of coal mines in the past in France), its environmental impacts are not immediately solved. For example, in France, now, because of the flooding of the old mines, water and soil pollution arise. In Germany, several future generations will have to live with the potential risks of nuclear wastes. With the life cycle of technological innovations coming shorter and shorter, a new challenge of vigilance arises vis à vis the old or abandoned technologies. The necessity of maintaining a technological knowledge for technologies of the past will arise more and more in the future as a part of the effort to avoid negative environmental impacts. How to deal with the necessity of more and more technological innovation to improve the quality of environment with the necessity to manage the environmental impacts of more and more old technologies ?

The promotion of science and innovation for sustainable development requires procedures for evaluating science and technology contributions against criteria for environmental quality, particularly in the point of view of intergenerational equity which are not offered by any of the two conventional economic perspectives on sustainability explained in the previous section.

The reason for this common blindness vis à vis the ambiguous character of technological innovation on environment can be seen in the similarity of the conception of economic production and of technological change in the two approaches of "weak" and "strong" sustainability. Indeed, the question of production is reduced, at the aggregate level, to a problem of growth (or non growth); and technology change is correspondingly reduced to a single dimension, a rate, whose maximum is presumed to be exogenously determined.

This unidimensional conception means that neither party is able to incorporate the multidimensional nature of technological changes, bearing in qualitatively different ways on (inter alia) prospects for economic production, natural resource availability, waste production, mitigation or argumentation of the adverse environmental impacts of pollution, species viability, ecosystem conservation and biosphere life support functions. Moreover, even if the rate of technical change is considered, in some sense, as an economic variable, not much insight is given into the institutional, political or other determinants of the actual changes that do or might take place. The abstract parametric formulations also do not help to understand the roles of stakeholders (firms, citizens, governments, etc...) in the dynamics of technological change.

3.2   The Fundamental Roles that Firm's Strategies Play Vis-à-Vis the Direction of Environmental Technological Change

Some strategies of firms, mainly belonging to the win-win type, seem to be economically and environmentally advantageous in the short run, whereas they might encourage firms and the whole economy to develop technological pathways that turn out to be unsustainable and suboptimal in the long run. We can mention here the well-publicised replacement by McDonald's of a white polyethylene packaging sheet with polystyrene foam, which makes marginal difference from an environmental point of view – it is a matter of air pollution versus water pollution (Duchin, Lange and Kell, 1995). A comparable situation has been developed in the detergents industry, resulting from the polemics on phosphate-free detergents: Henkel has created a technological "lock-in" concerning phosphate-free washing powders. This "lock-in", based on a technological monopoly, originates in the existence of increasing returns to scale for manufacturing process adoption. Indeed, manufacturers came out with phosphate-free laundry detergents not because it had been ascertained that they were safer than traditional products, but because every time one company brought out a phosphate-free detergent, the probability rose that another company would do likewise. The debate on the ecological advantages of phosphate-free detergents is thus not closed (Faucheux and Nicolaï, 1998).

In the case of catalytic converters, the "lock-in" is of a more institutional nature. The European Commission, acting under the influence of certain pressure groups, did not allow the time to develop commercially some technological alternatives which, in the medium term, might have been ecologically more reasonable than the choices made. Since the implementation of the law concerning catalytic converters, these devices have been shown to decrease energetic efficiency and have also retarded the elimination of some lead additives in motor fuels. Moreover, recently, the potential risks of platinium emission from this new technology has been raised.

These examples show that choices initially made – reinforced by the opportunism of certain industrial actors – can have irreversible effects that are opposed to the objectives linked to sustainability, even if the outcome is economically advantageous for the firm, satisfying for the consumer in the short run, and responsive to certain environmental concerns.

3.3   The Tendency of Public Delegation for Environmental Regulation: The Risks for Governance

Under current globalisation and deregulation trends, the influence in environmental protection on a national or international level might no longer be in the hands of political institutions but more and more in those of private professional institutions and of large corporations. This would lead to a system of industrial "auto-regulation", in other words unilateral actions. The following examples underline this point: the 1990 agreement of the French chemical industry; the agreement of the German industrial sector on the reduction of CO_2 emissions in 1995; and the code of conduct developed by the International Council for Metals and Environment, an agreement signed by 27 multinational mining corporations. This type of unilateral industry agreement which is signed by no public authority, is a liberal variant of what are now widely called voluntary agreements (Borkey and Glachand, 1998).

The environmental performance impact of such agreements is however questionable. The key role of firms, in particularly TNCs, in the development of these instruments of environmental regulation can lead to a distortion of the decision, at the expense of public interest (the phenomenon of "regulatory capture"). Such a case of "regulatory capture" is illustrated by the strategies of Arco, the world's eighth-ranking oil company. Having developed a major R&D programme starting in 1988, it voluntarily put out a clean automobile fuel at the end of 1990. This company's proactive environmental strategy led to the development and implementation of an environmental technology innovation that ended up influencing and anticipating environmental regulations (including some 1990 amendments to the Clean Air Act). The company goal to obtain a competitive edge in the highly competitive oil industry was achieved, while a positive environmental impact is not yet definitely proved (Piasecki 1995).

Finally, we should mention the risk of "free rider" behaviour of certain firms when engaging in collective agreements. While hiding their actual environmental performance, they can benefit from the public relations advantages of such an agreement without having to bear the costs of depollution.

The state as the fundamental organ of governance at a national level, has been mandated (by elections in most of the cases) protector of sustainable development by the community which it represents. With the growth in importance of unilateral voluntary agreements, it is as if the government, and more largely public institutions, acted, not really to delegate, but to abandon the responsibility for environmental regulation onto private firms.

This progressive substitution of unilateral agreements for regulative and economic instruments can in fact be analysed as a Principal-Agent relationship, this is to say in the framework of the theory of contracts. Given the complexity and radical uncertainty of contemporary global ecological problems, phenomena as informational asymmetry (which are at the heart of economic analyses of Principal-Agent relations) are intensified. These informal problems have several consequences. Firstly the contract that links the different actors (state and firms) is incomplete. Secondly, the principal (state) does not have the technical, organisational and financial capacities to control perfectly and at zero costs the performance of the agent (firms) (problems of moral hazard and adverse selection).

These points help to explain why leaving environmental strategy up to firms and more generally to private policy networks, through delegation contracts, might be un-sustainable. The question for the governance able to implement a sustainable development policy are more complex that just correcting a problem of agent failure. The relation of Principal-Agent proposed by the theory of contracts is based on a methodological individualism, whereby every economic relation is seen as an aggregate of inter-individual relations mostly of bilateral nature in situations characterised by a hierarchy between the agents. But in the framework of sustainable development, the relations between actors cannot be seen as such a bilateral contracts for at least three reasons:

1. we are in a more complex situations than a simple relationship between two agents; we have a multitude of stakeholders;

2. the agents/stakeholders are not in equal positions, simply because the mutual acceptance to a same foot between non core stakeholders, such as developing countries, future generations or non-human nature or even SME is not established;

3. in an intergenerational equity perspective of sustainability, there are no contracts because there is no way to negotiate a contract with future persons or even non-humans what straises again the question of adequate decision-making procedures.

Therefore, the perspective of governance offered by the formalism of theory of contracts, as proposed by standard economics, offers a "weak deliberative governance" where only the participation of strong stakeholders is possible (Aggeri and Hatchuel, 1996).

4   How to Square the Circle with a Deliberative Governance ?

4.1   Towards an Evolutionary Perspective of Technological Change

The evolutionary perspective of technological change gives a central place to processes of disequilibrium in which the concept of transition and properties of non linearity have important roles to play (Beckenbach, 1998; Kemp, 1997). It concentrates on observing economic, institutional and ecological realities without trying to find a normative reference situation such as an equilibrium. The presumption is that an understanding of the functioning of technological path selection and the nature of technological societal economic interrelations can be gleaned only when technological elements are represented as a complex dynamic system (Saviotti, 1986). This has the advantage of allowing the representation of the essential role that technological change choices unfolding over time will have in possible "transition paths" for sustainable development (Norgaard, 1994). It further suggests the importance of economic policy for "steering" the economic system in the cumulative process of change. The approach looks more at conflicting relations and their development over time (the role of strategy in different forms), whereas most of the other analyses (even the more recent endogeneous growth theory) nullified conflicts by using optimisation (Faucheux, 1997). The focus is placed on strategy as a response to uncertain and changeable circumstances, on the degrees of freedom that actors possess on the constraints that they face, but also the freedom of movement that they may have and the range of opportunities that they may identify, and create over time. In this perspective, the analysis of the environmental firms strategy is central in the way that firms are interested players in the "endogenisation" of technological change. Moreover, the technological development is considered as inextricably linked, not only with economic and social dynamics, but also with institutional processes of change. In this way, this perspective of technological change is in conformity with the Brundland's report's one :

"In essence, sustainable development is a process of change in which the exploitation of resources, the direction of investment, the orientation of technological development, and institutional change are all in harmony and enhance both current and future potential human needs and aspirations" (WCED, 1987, p 46).

4.2   From Exclusive to Inclusive Governance

It is more and more recognised by European institutions that integrating in real time the divergent interests of the various stakeholders in a sort of multi-stakeholder and multidisciplinary dialogue, can provide a basis to help in the evaluation of risks on the long term, in the setting of priorities, and in the assessment of actions for the choice of environmental technological innovation. By this, decision makers are acknowledging that the choice and fulfilment of the objectives of an environmental, and more largely, a sustainable development policy, are mainly dependent on the ways in which the various stakeholders are associated with the preparation and the implementation of policies. At the heart of the concept of the "national innovation system", first described by Freeman (1987) and that can be easily generalised to a regional or global level, we also find this belief that a better understanding of the linkages between the component actors in the system is the key to improved technological performance.

"The national innovation systems approach stresses that the flows of technology and information among people, enterprises and institutions are key to the innovative process. Innovation and technology development are the result of a complex set of relationships among actors in the system (…) For policy makers, an understanding of the national innovation system can help identify leverage points for enhancing innovative performance and overall competitiveness (…) Policies which seek to improve networking among actors and institutions in the system…are most valuable in this context (original emphasis)" (OECD, 1997, p 7).

In the same way, European institutions are understanding that scientific practice is not fundamentally "value free" but that it has to find its justifications by reference to prevaling social concerns. The object of the scientific endeavour in this new context may well be to enhance the process of the social resolution of the problem, including the participation and mutual learning among stakeholders, rather than a definitive "solution" or technological implementation. This is an important change in the relation between the problem identification and the prospects of science-based solutions (Funtowicz, Ravetz and O'Connor, 1998), which has clearly been asked as a "new social contract by science" by Jane Lubchenco (1998) in her presidential address to the AAAS on 15 February 1997.

For example, future technology studies no longer claim to predict the future, but are seen as a strategic tool for improving strategic interaction between key actors and for anticipatory policy making, particularly in the field of environment. Up to now, the notions of foresight have been applied to technology (especially concerning environmental questions), and to the importance of based on scientific and technical expertise from research and industry. The well-known DELPHI surveys have for example considerably contributed to the principal orientations of science and technology in various industrialised countries for the last thirty years. The countries today disposing of the most elaborate foresight instruments for technological innovation, seem to agree on a new tendency with the success of the concept of sustainable development. The focal point has moved from merely scientific and industrial insights to social demand (hence equalising the importance of both production and demand) and thus to the emanating "weak signals", in order to influence the broad technological orientations of the coming century. In other words, the objective is to favour the expression of citizens. Some thus speak no more of "technological foresight" but of "social foresight" and the DELPHI surveys are, when still used, under complete reconstruction or used in complementary with consultative committee in order to integrate this new orientation (van der Meulen, 1999; Grupp, 1999). The British government, for example, recently announced the initiation of a new foresight programme from October 1999, focused on "social demand" (Masood, 1998; OST, 1999). Two recent French studies underline the idea that a social dialogue necessitates a complementarity between the anticipation of experts on the one hand, and of societal representatives, on the other hand, in order to create a system of foresight of environmental problems that contributes to the programmation of R&D (MENRT et MATE, 1997; BIPE et alii, 1997). One of the main results of these studies is the request to "practise science differently". In other words, the old conception of a largely one way traffic of information from the experts to the public should have to be replaced by a perspective of a mutual learning between those involved in the process.

This evolution shows, we have to go beyond the classical limits of the liberal and the welfare State by instituting new practices based on broader consultations, negotiated and other new forms of regulation extended power delegation to undependent authorities, judicial control of technology and administrative action, and extended use of evaluation and auditing tools.

This new mode of governance implies neither a change in the location of ultimate responsibility for decision making nor a diminution of the responsibility of public actors. Decisions, and particularly for technological innovations, should have to be taken on the basis of processes which are open, inclusive and contextualised. Public actors have an increased responsibility to ensure the adequacy of the procedures by which collective learning and co-ordinated action can be achieved. In other words, this implies to move from the "strategic" models of democracy where deliberation, learning, morality might figure to help individuals to determine their own interest toward a deliberative and co-operative conception of democracy where citizens engage in deliberation not so that each can determine or refine his or her own interests, but so that together they can discover a result which is not simply a function of their individual utilities (Estlund, 1993; Sagoff, 1998).

4.3 Towards a State Delegation on Public Policy Networks: A New Constitutive Role for Public Institutions and Regulations

Recently, a literature has developed which gives a typology of alternative governance arrangements. In this discussion, networks as a mode of governance have been given an important status (Williamson, 1975, Nohria, 1992). Governance by public policy networks differs from state-led industrial policy, in the sense that the principal mode of coordinating is not based on command or direction but rather on negotiation and bargaining. It also differs from market-led industrial restructuring in that every individual firm is not merely pursuing its own private interests. Normative mechanisms, negotiations, and socialisation within the group coordinates relationships and discourages opportunism over relatively long time periods. As such, a governance mode is given in which medium- and long-term policies are formulated and implemented to cope with the structural difficulties (Marin, 1990).

The problem is that in parallel with these multi-stakeholder public policy networks, other forms of policy networks can also be expected (particularly in the deregulation and globalisation context) to develop which consist of clubs of private actors, particularly TNC like we have explained before. These kinds of networks already are organising, by their own initiatives, in order to influence the choice of putative sustainable development policies, but partly (by design or by neglect) by excluding most of stakeholders. We can give the example of the worldwide private policy networks led by BP which have developed its own system of emission tradable permits since two years and which will probably be able to impose it in the framework of climate policy so to realise a phenomenon of "regulatory capture" (O'Connor, Faucheux et van den Hove, 1998). However, a good example illustrating the danger (even for the competitiveness of firms) of not establishing a "strong cooperation" between all stakeholders in sustainable development decision-making, is the scandal that the Shell Corporation caused in June 1995 with its plans for sinking an offshore oil platform (Brent Spar) in the North Sea after the oil well had been totally (optimally?) exploited (Faucheux, Nicolaï, O'Connor, 1997).

A more adequate mode of governance in the field of sustainable development, particularly for the choice of technological innovations, would thus be a re-orientation of public policy through the delegation by the State of responsibility to public policy networks. These arrangements would enable the design and implementation of medium or long-term policies for greater competitiveness, as well as facilating collective decisions on long run ecological risks. They help to discuss the need for, and distribution of, mutual burdens and benefits of restructuring plans between the "strong" and the "weak" stakeholders; and they can diffuse know-how and environmental technological innovations among them.

Within governance institutions in which public policy networks play a role, the structure of the state (or more largely of the public institutions) is characterised not only by decentralisation and delegation, but also by deliberation and cooperation. This cooperation results from a social fact – namely that in many concerns relative to sustainable development policies, public goals are increasingly more difficult to obtain without the cooperation of private collectivities. This might be taken as an argument in favour of a state that is simply less involved in substantive regulation; but the state we envisage here nevertheless tries to provide "rules of the game" for societal problem-solving processes. Consequently a "strong" de-centralized and cooperative state seems to be fruitful ground for the development of public policy networks adapted to the decision-making on sustainable development policies.

There exist, already in Europe, an evolution of the environmental regulation in this way. For example, some social-partner voluntary agreements seeking to implement sustainable development policies that are based on this kind of public policy network concept. Among them, within certain limits, we can cite the Dutch "covenants" between government and industry for target setting, whose formulation and implementation depend on the participation of thirds parties (NGOs, green action groups, local initiatives, etc...) through consultations and deliberations, even if these latter categories of stakeholders are not implicated in the contract by their signature (European Environmental Agency, 1997).

The importance of non-private sector actors – above all, environmental protection associations, citizens movements and trade unions – in the decision process in matter of sustainable development policies is also reflected in the German approach to implementation of the auditing procedure of the European Eco-Audit scheme (the Environmental Management and Audit Scheme, or EMAS). Similarly procedures for eco-labelling also with usually involve a range of interest groups in the elaboration of requirements and criteria for the programme, and for individual applications. These generally comprise consumers, producers, traders, the state and environmental organisations and other organisations such as trade unions may also have a part (Ootserhuis, Rubik and Scholl, 1996).

So, in drawing a clear distinction between governance and government, we need not, however, abandon the idea that organised authorities can and often do play important roles in coming to terms with governance arising in sustainable development challenges (Young, 1994). In particularly, governments and public institutions have to favour the emergence of public policy networks founded on new social institutions (and not necessarily organisations) based on wide societal and ethical reflections to perform the quality assurance function of technological innovation, notably in the point of view of their environmental impacts.

5   Conclusion

The challenge for environmental, and more generally sustainable development policies, entails a pursuit of strategies of solidarity, through a real governance with the participation of the main stakeholders in the technological path decision-making in the way of "post-normal science" as defined by Funtowicz and Ravetz (1994). Such a vision of a *"process of debate and dialogue operating continuously over all phases of a policy process"* (Funtowicz & Ravetz, 1991, p. 22) underscores the limits of classical libertarian and welfare-state political systems. What we advocate, is to initiate processes of extended consultations, of negotiated regulation, including methods of delegation to independent authorities that combine bottom-up stakeholder participation with top-down coordination, in order to implement systems of technology evaluation, communication and control. This can include the use of technology performance norms (such as best available technology principles) and firm eco-audit schemes, with the understanding that the guiding principles are not the monopoly of one interest group or sector but have to be permanently negotiated in a deliberative way between social partners. In this way, the choice and the implementation of sustainable development policies will rely less on the judgements and decisions of regulatory institutions alone, and more on the way in which the different social actors are brought together in the preparation and application of policies.

However, in telling that, the task is only starting because, we have to find now the adequate deliberative procedures (indirect methods such as focus groups, citizen's panels, citizens' juries, consensus conferences; or direct methods such as mediation) between government agencies and regulatory bodies, concerned citizens and the wider public, the scientific community, industrial and commercial interests, NGOs and "public interest" activist groups (O'Connor, 1998; O'Connor and Spash, 1999). Even if the decision-maker has always the right and the duty to decide, it is necessary to develop new methods to define the acceptable domain of decision-making by the different stakeholders. The objective generally speaking is to look for a consensus, and to avoid unilateral decision that is imposed whether the parties concerned agree or not. This is a "participatory" ideal, one that can be given only incomplete effect in different levels of environmental decision-making. Sometimes different groups of people simply cannot or do not want to agree. Nonetheless, the shared or "public" character of many environmental benefits and harms justifies the view that decisions ought best to be made through ongoing public debate on the public good. The premise is that something more than a straight compromise between fixed positions is possible (Stewart, 1996). By exposing participants' initial views to one another and to reasoned debate, they may change, and this may be brought together.

Because, it does not exist an "optimal technological choice" for everyone, we have to define a "satisfying technological choice". It implies to work with the procedural rational hypothesis and not with the substantive one (Faucheux, and Froger, 1995). When working with procedural rationality we are concerned that making choices and decisions, is inevitably a process of a construction of choice. As a result, all decisions must be understood to be inherently contingent and unstable. In this way, what is universal is less the content of models of decision than the procedures which develop this understanding of contingency and the need for a collective learning (Faucheux, O'Connor and van der Straaten, eds., 1998).

Acknowledgements

The research work lying behind this paper was made possible by the support of three research projects in course in France and led by C3ED:

1. For the French Ministry of Education, Research and Technology : "Analyse et prise en compte de la mondialisation des ressources et de la globalisation des rejets dans une stratégie de recherche technologique"

2. For the CEA: "Complémentarité des acteurs dans les processus décisionnels liés à des risques et des irréversibilités dans les choix technologiques. Quelques enseignements pour les politiques d'entreposage des déchets radioactifs" .

3. For the French Ministry of the Territory Planning and the Environment and the CEA : "Conception et réalisation d'un système de veille-prospective pour la programmation de la R&D publique en matière d'environnement"

References

Aggieri, F. and A. Hatchuel (1996), A Dynamic Model of Environmental Policies. The Case of Innovation Oriented Voluntary Agreements, in: *Conference The Economics and Law of Voluntary Approaches in Environmental Policies*. 18-19 November 1996, Venice.

Beckenbach, F. (1998), Socio-Technological Innovation and Sustainability, in: S. Faucheux, J. Gowdy and I. Nicolaï (eds), *Sustainability and Firms: Technological Change and the Changing Regulatory Environment*, Cheltenham.

BIPE, *Etude prospective de la demande environnement et sa traduction en termes scientifiques et techniques à des fins de programmation de R&D*, Etude pour le Ministère de l'Aménagement du Territoire et de l'Environnement et le CEA, Paris.

Borkey, P. and M. Glachant (1998), Les firmes face au développement soutenable : changement technologique et gouvernance au sein de la dynamique industrielle, *Revue d'Economie Industrielle* 83 (1), 213-225.

Coates, J.F, (1985), Foresight in Federal Government policymaking, *Futures research Quartely* 3, 29-53.

Daly, H. (1991), *Steady State Economics*, Washington D.C.

Duchin, F., G.M. Lange and G. Kell (1995), Technological Change. Trade, and the Environment, *Ecological Economics*, 14, 185-193.

Ellickson, R. (1991), *Order without law: How neighbors settle disputes*, Cambridge, Mass.

Estlund, D. (1993), Who's afraid of deliberative democracy, *Tex. Law. Rev* 71, 1437-1477.

European Commission, (1995), *Report of the Commission on Global Governance: Our Global Neighbourhood*, Oxford.

European Environmental Agency (1997), Environmental Agreements, *Environmental Issues Series* 1(3).

Faucheux, S. (1997), Technological Change, Ecological Sustainability and Industrial Competitiveness, in: Dragun, A.K. and K.M. Jacobsson (eds.), *Sustainability and Global Environmental Policy: New Perspectives*, Cheltenham, 131-148.

Faucheux, S. and G. Froger (1995), Decision-making under environmental uncertainty, *Ecological Economics* 15, 29-42.

Faucheux, S., E. Muir and M. O'Connor (1997), Neo-classical Natural Capital Theory and 'Weak' Indicators for Sustainability, *Land Economics* 73.

Faucheux, S., J. Gowdy J. and I. Nicolaï (1998), *Sustainability and firms: Technological change and the changing regulatory environment*, Cheltenham.

Faucheux, S. and I. Nicolaï (1998), Environmental technological change and governance in sustainable development policy, *Ecological Economics* 27, 243-256.

Faucheux, S., I. Nicolaï and M. O'Connor (1997) Economic globalisation, competitiveness, and environment, in: OECD, *Globalisation and Environment: preliminary perspectives*, Paris, 101-41.

Faucheux, S. and M. O'Connor (eds.) (1998), *Valuation for sustainable development: methods and policy indicators*, Cheltenham.

Faucheux, S., M. O'Connor and J. van der Straaten (1998), *Sustainable Development : Concepts, Rationalities and Strategies*, Dordrecht.

Freeman, C. (1987), *Technology and Economic Performance: Lessons from Japan*, London.

Freeman, C. (1992), *The Economics of Hope*, London.

Funtowicz, S.O. and J.R. Ravetz (1991), A new scientific methodology for global environmental issues, in: Costanza, R. (ed.), *Ecological Economics: The Science and Management of Sustainability*, New York.

Funtowicz, S.O and J. Ravetz (1994), The Worth of a Songbird: Ecological Economics as Post-Normal Science, *Ecological Economics* 10, 197-207.

Funtowicz, S., J.R. Ravetz and M. O'Connor (1998), *Challenges in the Utilisation of science for sustainaible development*, Background note for the panel discussion "Science and sustainable development", Sixth Session of the Commission on Sustainable Development, New York, 20April-1 May.

Grupp, H. (ed.) (1999), National Foresight Projects (special issue), *Technological Forecasting and Social Change* 60 (1).

Grupp, H. and T. Reiss (1997), Foresight in German Science and technology, in: Anderson, J., R. Fears and B. Taylor (eds.), *Managing Technology for Competitive Advantage*, London.

Hinterberger, F., F. Luks and F. Schmidt-Bleek (1997), Material flows vs. "natural capital". What makes an economy sustainable?, *Ecological Economics* 23, 1-14.

Kemp, R. (1997), *Environmental Policy and Technical change. A comparison of the technological impact of policy instruments*, Cheltenham.

Leisinger, K.M. (1998), Sustainable development at the turn of the century: perceptions and outlook, *International Journal of Sustainable Development* 1(1), 45-78.

Lubchenco, J., (1998), Entering the century of the environment a new social contract for science, *Science* 279(January), 491-497.

Martin, B. and R. Johnston (1999), Technology foresight for wiring up the national innovation system. Experiences in Britain, Australia, and New Zealand, *Technological Forecasting and Social Change* 60 (1), 37-51.

Marin, B. (ed.) (1990), *Governance and Generalized Exchange. Self-Organizing Policy Networks in Action*, Frankfurt a.M.

Meulen van der, B., (1999), The impact of foresight on environmental science and technology policy in the Netherlands, *Futures* 31, 7-23.

Miller, A. and C. Moore (1994), Strengths and Limitation of Governmental Support for Environmental Technology in Japan. *Industrial and Environmental Crisis Quarterly* 8(2), 155-170.

Ministère de l'Education Nationale et de la Recherche (MENRT) et Ministère de l'Aménagement du Territoire et de l'Environnement (1997), *Recherche et Environnement. Thèmes prioritaires et thèmes émergents, Enquête internationale auprès de la communauté scientifique*, Paris.

Ministry of International Trade and Industry (MITI) (1988), *White Paper on Industrial Technology: Trends and Future Tasks in Japanese Industrial Technology*. MITI, Tokyo.

National Institute of Science and Technology Policy (NISTEP) (1997), *The sixth Technology Forecast Survey. Future technology in Japan toward the Year 2025*, Report n° 52. June, Japan.

North, D. (1990), *Institutions, Institutional Change, and Economic Performance*, Cambridge.

Nohria, N. (1992), Is a Network Perspective a Useful Way of Studying Organizations, in: Nohria, N. and R. Eccles (eds.), *Networks and Organizations: Structure, Form and Action*, Boston/Mass.

Norgaard, R.B. (1994), *Development betrayed: the end of progress and a coevolutionary revisioning of the future*, London.

Norton, B., R. Costanza and R.C. Bishop (1998), The evolution of preferences: Why 'sovereign' preferences may not lead to sustainable development policies and what to do about it, *Ecological Economics* 24(2-3), 183-193.

O'Connor, M. (1998), *Walking in the Garden(s) of Babylon,: An Overview of the VALSE Project*, C3ED research project.

O'Connor, M. and C. Spash (eds.) (1998), *Valuation and the environment: Theory, Method and Pratice*, Cheltenham.

OECD (1997), *Science, Technology, Industry: National Innovation System*, Paris.

Oosterhuis, F., F. Rubik and G. Scholl (1996), *Product Policy in Europe: New Environmental Perspectives*, London.

Piasecki, B.W., (1995), *Corporate Environmental Strategy – The Avalanche of Change since Bhopal*, New York.

Porter, M.E. and C. van der Linde (1995), Toward a New Conception of the Environment-Competitiveness Relationship, *Journal of Economic Perpectives* 9 (4), 97-118.

Porter, M.E. (1990), *The Competitive Advantage of Nations*. New York.

Rosenau, J. and E.O.Czempiel (eds.) (1992), *Governance without Government: order and change in world politics*, Cambridge.

Sagoff, M. (1998), Aggregation and deliberation in valuing environmental goods: a look beyond contingent pricing, *Ecological Economics* 24(2-3), 193-213.

Saviotti, P. (1986), Systems Theory and Technological Change, *Futures* 18, 773-86.

Shrivastava, P. (1995), Democratic Control of Technological Risks in Developing Countries, *Ecological Economics* 14, 195-208.

Skea, J. (1994), Environmental Issues and Innovation, in: Dodgson M. and R. Rothwell (eds.), *Handbook of Industrial Innovation*, Cheltenham, 421-431.

Sunstein, C. (1988), Beyond the republican revival, *Yale Law J.* (97), 1539-1570.

Weterings R., J. Kuijper and E. Smeets (1997), *81 options. Technology for sustainable development*, Report for the Ministry of Housing, Physical Planning and the Environment. NL.

Williamson, O. (1975), *Markets and Hierarchies*, New York.

Young, R.A. (1997), *Global Governance. Drawing insights from the environmental experience*, Cambridge/Mass.

PART II
INTERNATIONAL CASE STUDIES ON ENVIRONMENTAL REGULATIONS AND INNOVATIONS

Elements of Innovation-Friendly Policy Regimes – An International Comparative Study for the Paper Industry

Jürgen Blazejczak and Dietmar Edler

German Institute for Economic Research
Königin-Luise-Straße 5, 14195 Berlin
Germany

Keywords. policy style, instrumentation, actor configuration, pulp and paper.

1 Research Objective and Approach

Environmental innovation allows to achieve reductions of pressure on the environment at lower cost and thus facilitates a transition towards sustainability. The present paper addresses the question of how to design environmental regulation in order to create incentives for generating and adopting environmental innovation[1].

Traditionally, environmental economics has studied the effects of environmental policy on innovation based on the concept of dynamic efficiency. This approach disregards however the complexities of the innovation as well as the policy process. Therefore, in the study presented in this paper an analytical framework has been applied which integrates concepts of environmental economics with results of innovation research such as the importance of the different phases of the innovation process and with insights from policy analysis for example into the process of formulating and implementing policies.

---

[1]   This paper is based on a study which was funded as a part of a larger research by the German Federal Ministry of Education, Research and Technology. An English summary of the results of this research project is in preparation. See KLEMMER, P. (ED.) 1999. Our special thanks go to our international cooperation partners Prof. Fumikazu Yoshida (Japan), Fernando Alvarado and Lennart Eriksson (Sweden) and Mark Rossi (USA). Without their help the case studies would not have been possible in such a productive way. We also enjoyed the discussions and exchange of ideas with Prof. Martin Jänicke and Jens Hemmelskamp.

The analysis is based on case studies of pulp and paper manufacturing in four countries: Germany, Japan, Sweden and the US. Although the industry in each of these countries has considerably lowered its use of the environment, different patterns of environmental innovation have emerged which can be linked to differences of policy regimes.

The core element of the analytical framework applied in this study is a set of requirements for an "ideal" innovation-friendly policy pattern, derived in an interdisciplinary effort of economists, innovation researchers, and policy analysts (BLAZEJCZAK, J. ET AL. 1999). The "ideal" innovation-friendly policy pattern plays a dual role in the present study. On the one hand, it is applied to interpret the cases underlying our research. On the other hand, it is tested and refined with information resulting from the case studies.

The paper proceeds as follows: In the following part we briefly sketch environmental problems of paper production and use, illustrate the role of innovation for reducing environmental pressure, and characterize the specific nature of environmental innovation in the paper industry. The third section discusses the motives of enterprises for developing and adopting environmental innovation and links public policy to these motives. In the fourth part we discuss public policy more closely. Firstly, we show how the requirements of an "ideal" innovation-friendly policy pattern we have developed elsewhere (BLAZEJCZAK, J. ET AL. 1999), are linked to the motives of enterprises to innovate elaborated before. Secondly, we show that the policy patterns that prevailed in the past in the countries investigated accounted for these requirements only selectively. We observe that countries the policy pattern of which corresponded more closely to the "ideal" policy pattern had a lead in environmental innovation. Finally we report some more recent attempts to promote environmental innovation by approaches which correspond more closely to these requirements.

2   Environmental Innovation in the Paper Industry

2.1   Environmental Pressures

The production and use of paper contributes to a wide variety of environmental problems. They include global warming, human toxicity, eco-toxicity, photochemical oxidation, acidification, nutrification, and solid wastes. According to the – unavoidably subjective – weighting of one study the most serious contribution of paper production is to photochemical oxidation followed by solid waste problems, whereas paper production does not aggravate global warming and acidification (WEAVER ET AL. 1997).

Environmental pressures originating from paper production and use are intensely interrelated (Fig. 1). The origin of the paper chain is marked by problems of nature conservation and sustainable forestry[2]. During the production process environmental problems are caused mainly through the consumption of energy and water as well as the use of a great number of chemicals. This results in atmospheric emissions, aqueous emissions, and the generation of numerous wastes. In densely populated areas odors and noise constitute major environmental problems. The specific profile of environmental pressures varies between different production processes. Modifications of specific processes usually affect other processes as well. In particular, there are wide margins for shifting emissions between different steps of the production process and between environmental media. Paper production and use also create a considerable volume of transports associated with severe emissions of various kinds. Last but not least, waste paper collection and treatment, besides being re-linked to forestry aspects, pose an array of environmental problems of their own[3]. Again, environmental problems arising at any particular step of the paper chain crucially depend on choices taken with respect to other steps.

2.2   An Illustration of the Role of Innovation for Reducing Environmental Pressure

The role of environmental innovation in the pulp and paper industry can be illustrated using the examples of energy consumption and of waste paper recycling.

The production of pulp and paper is an energy intensive production process which consumes heat and electricity in large amounts. The level of energy consumption as well as the relation between heat and electricity differ widely between different production processes. The production of kraft pulp requires large quantities of heat (in the form of steam) but only smaller amounts of electricity; under favorable conditions the kraft process produces an energy surplus because roughly 50 per cent of the raw material input end up in the production of energy namely steam. The production of thermomechanical pulp (TMP) and chemo-thermomechanical pulp (CTMP) uses large amounts of electricity (2000 to 3000 kWh/t) but results in a fiber yield of over 95 per cent. The production of secondary fiber from waste paper is more energy efficient than the pulping processes for primary fiber. Paper production requires large amounts of electricity (mostly for the drives of the paper-machine and for pumping) as well as large amounts of steam (for the drying sec-

---

2   These problems have been excluded from the scope of the investigation presented here.

3   This sketchy presentation disregards many environmental pressures such as problems associated with paper processing or problems of ecological ‚rucksacks‘ for the production of machinery.

tions of paper-machine). As a long-term trend the electricity consumption of paper making increases while the steam consumption decreases.

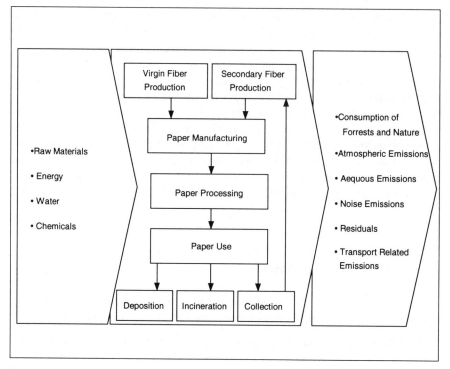

Figure 1:   Environmental problems of pulp and paper manufacturing and use

Since the seventies the energy consumption in absolute terms (measured in million tonnes of oil-equivalent) has increased in Germany, Japan and Sweden [4]. The biggest increase did occur in Japan, where the energy consumption more than doubled (Fig. 2). This is a result of the increase in production, while at the same time the energy efficiency remained more or less stable in Japan, although at the lowest level of the three countries. In Germany the specific energy consumption decreased steadily, but only moderately over the last period. Sweden displays a remarkable reduction of the specific energy consumption since 1980 following a sharp increase in the seventies.

---

[4]   Data for the US are not available from the sources used for this comparison.

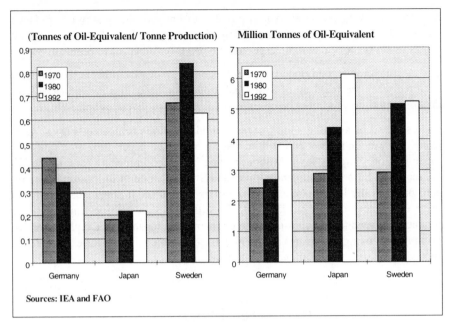

Figure 2: Energy consumption of the paper, cardboard and printing industry

Looking in detail at the production processes of pulp and paper manufacturing a lot of incremental innovations can be identified which contribute to the increase in energy efficiency. As examples the following innovations may be listed

- heat recovery in cooking and in bleaching processes,

- reduction of water consumption for pulp cleaning,

- use of mechanical pressing (instead of steam) in the drying section of the paper machine,

- reduction of waste paper in paper production.

Break-through innovations with high-potential for energy saving are in the process of development or in the early phase of diffusion. In pulp production black liquor gasification has a significant energy saving potential as it would allow to apply the efficiency of the co-generation of heat and power to the kraft pulping process. But diffusion is likely to be slow as big investments and process changes for existing plants are required[5]. In paper manufacturing the principle of impulse drying has a

---

5   The profitability is also depending on the price of electricity from external power plants which might be lower in the future due to market liberalization.

high energy saving potential. If it is possible to improve the quality of produced paper at the same time, a diffusion of this technology is likely. Up to now not all problems for the application in large-volume paper-machines have been solved.

The most favorable conditions for the diffusion of innovative process technologies occurred when the build-up of additional production capacities constituted a window of opportunity as could be observed in Japan in the seventies and eighties.

The use of recovered fibers has increased in all countries compared (Fig. 3). Germany displays the highest and still increasing recovered paper utilization ratios; in Japan it is only slightly lower without having increased in recent years. In the US the recycling ratio is significantly lower and Sweden's rate of utilization of recovered paper is the lowest among the countries compared. It should be noted that these differences cannot be explained by differences in the spectrum of paper products between these countries; both Germany and Japan have a higher share of printing (excluding newsprint) and writing paper – which has the lowest content of secondary fibers – than both the US and Sweden.

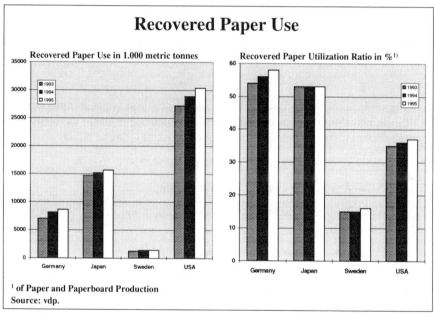

Figure 3:   Recovered paper use

Differences in recovered paper utilization ratios can be explained by two broad categories of determinants: the profitability of the reuse of waste paper relative to the use of virgin fibers and possible uses of secondary fiber products. The role of innovations is obvious. Improved processes mitigate the trade-off between fiber losses and brightness of secondary pulp, for example, as does the development of adhesives and printing colors which can be easier removed without negatively impacting on their function and applicability. Significant savings of inputs such as chemicals, water, and energy can also be achieved if the waste paper is appropriately separated in advance of conditioning. The same reasoning applies to improved collecting systems resulting in a higher quality of the waste paper supplied. This requires innovations which are less of a technical but rather of an organizational nature.

Innovations also help to overcome the restrictions of the demand for secondary fiber products. Technological innovations such as multi-layer papers allow to maintain certain functional properties of paper products thus permitting to enter 'higher' market segments with recycled paper products.

2.3   Characterization of Environmental Innovation in the Paper Industry

Environmental innovation in the paper industry can be characterized by its reach and by its degree of integration. The reach of an innovation indicates to what extent it changes existing procedures of production and consumption. Frequently it is argued that in a growing economy only *radical* innovations – which render a large part of tangible and intangible investments obsolete – are capable of reducing environmental pressure in absolute terms. *Break-through* innovations change individual processes or products; if focused on the 'hot spots' of environmental pressure they do not overstress the capacity of the economy to adjust. But even *incremental* innovations which improve the environmental efficiency of existing processes and products can contribute to sustainability by 'buying time', thus making break-through and eventually radical innovations less expensive.

Radical innovations did not happen in the paper industry as pulp and paper production relies on a mature technology cluster. Break-through innovations were very rare in the past, examples of such innovations in the stage of early diffusion might be black liquor gasification or impulse drying. Rather, in the past a variety of incremental technological improvements was introduced, which summed up to a notable reduction of environmental pressure in each of the countries investigated – although with different focus and to a different degree in each one of them.

We do not want to discuss the question whether in order to achieve sustainability radical innovations are necessary. We want to point out, however, that the great number of incremental innovations which prevailed in the paper industry along with a few break-through innovations went a long way to reduce environmental pressure originating from paper production and consumption.

One reason explaining this result is the relatively high degree of integration of environmental innovations in the paper industry. By the notion of integration we denote the extent to which synergies are exploited between different environmental and economic objectives. Such synergies can be found in sectoral, spatial, time, and many other dimensions. End-of-pipe technologies, modifications of production processes, product innovations, organizational changes, and source reductions each represent a higher degree of integration. Integration over as many dimensions as possible not only helps to reduce costs, it also avoids shifting pollution across media of phases of the life cycle. Additional synergies arise if these are combined with each other.

Although in the paper industry there was no contribution to lower environmental pressure from source reductions – which can be viewed as representing the highest degree of integration – overall integration was still high. Innovations leading to a reduction of environmental impact of paper production included end-of-pipe solutions as well as process integrated technologies. The dominant pattern of environmental innovation was the closing of cycles with respect to raw materials as well as pollutants through process modifications. Product innovation though not immediately visible also played a role, an example being the significant reduction of the area weight of paper. It should be noted that a prerequisite were improvements on the part of the suppliers of machinery for paper production. Successful integration also was achieved of organizational with corresponding technological innovations such as the establishment of waste paper collection systems. The most significant dimension of integration was between different industries along the paper chain ranging from manufacturers of adhesives, printing colors, and various kinds of equipment, to the printing and packaging industry.

Table 1 shows an informal assessment of the reach and integration of environmental innovation relevant for the paper industry in the countries investigated. Sweden pioneered the introduction of TCF pulp and thus ranks high with respect to the reach of environmental innovation. An example of the high degree of integration in Germany is waste paper recycling which was developed early and effectively. Japan held an intermediate course while paper companies in the US with some exemptions were reluctant to develop and apply far reaching or highly integrated environmental innovations.

Table 1:   Reach and integration of environmental innovation

	Japan	Sweden	USA	Germany
Reach	2	3	1	2
Degree of Integration	2	2	1	3

1 = Low   2 = Medium   3 = High

After a discussion of the motives of enterprises for developing and adopting environmental innovation in general and the role of public policy in particular, we will argue, that the reach and integration of environmental innovation in the different countries is related to the extent to which their policy regimes correspond to the requirements of an "ideal" policy pattern.

3 Incentives for Developing and Adopting Environmental Innovation

3.1 Long-Term Profits and Public Pressure

The incentives which have determined the development and adoption of environmental innovation in the paper industry were first, and most importantly, expected long-term profits (or lower losses for that matter), and second public pressure. Indeed, the role of public pressure can be explained by its impact on expected long-term profits. Public policy was effective through its impact on these motives.

Higher profits result from reductions of compliance costs, reductions of production costs, increases of revenues, and improved competitiveness of suppliers. The single most important factor explaining the generation and diffusion of environmental innovation in the paper industry is the endeavor of companies to reduce costs. A substantial part of environmental innovation in the pulp and paper industry is directed to a reduction of compliance costs. Normally, existing regulation limits the search of enterprises to ways to comply with existing regulation more cost-efficiently. The research activities in the US pulp industry for example do not focus on a transition to totally chlorine free (TCF)-processes but on the optimization of elemental chlorine free (ECF)-processes, which satisfy existing regulation. The priority of cost-reducing optimization is often the mitigation of trade-offs between conflicting goals, e.g. flotation processes in secondary pulp production have to be optimized with respect to the removal of much adhesives and printing color as possible and the prevention of as little fiber losses as possible at the same time.

In many cases environmental innovations are the by-product of innovations which are primarily motivated by the goal to reduce production costs. Examples are the related product, process, and intra-firm organizational innovations which have reduced the number of sheet breaks specially in Japan[6]. As a result the resource

---

6   According to Japanese sources the number of sheet breaks in printing newspapers is two third lower with Japanese paper than with foreign papers.

efficiency – as well as the capital and labor efficiency – has been significantly improved.

An indicator of the importance of costs as a motive for environmental innovation is the close correspondence between differences in energy prices and in the diffusion of energy-efficient technologies in different countries: Higher energy prices in Japan and Germany have induced a much broader diffusion of e.g. technologies of co-generation of power and heat in these countries compared to Sweden and the US, where energy prices are lower.

The increase in revenue accruing to first movers is a strong incentive for environmental innovation as well. This is illustrated by the diffusion of advanced bleaching technologies (TCF-pulp) in Sweden which at first accelerated but only as long as higher sales prices more than offset extra costs.

This case simultaneously demonstrates the importance of public pressure and its interaction with the profit motive. Swedish paper companies providing TCF-pulp were able to take advantage of public pressure that arose in Germany, one of its most important export destinations, partly as a consequence of activities of environmental groups and decisions of large paper consumers such as publishing houses.

In Japan, claims of victims of environmental pollution together with media attention have originally triggered strict environmental regulation. But traditions reduce the role of public pressure. Environmental organizations have scarce resources, a limited access to information, and a week legal standing. An auditing of environmental standards of suppliers through large customers is uncommon in Japan. Limited influence is exerted by labor unions at the plant level.

The role of public pressure is most pronounced in the US. It arises in particular from a large number of influential green organizations. However, the relation between the industry – and even more so industry associations – and environmental groups is marked by confrontation. Public pressure is reinforced by far reaching liability rules and nearly unconstrained freedom of information. In one case a paper manufacturer was forced to introduce chlorine free bleaching as a consequence of litigation of surfriders. Auditing of suppliers is common. Publishing houses such as Time Inc. evaluate paper suppliers. These in turn require certificates from pulp manufacturers.

3.2   The Role of Public Policy

The role of public policy for environmental innovation arises from its impact on the direct and indirect determinants of expected long-term profits. The immediate and probably most important requirement is that economic incentives for the generation and adoption of innovations are set up and maintained. This lesson has been largely ignored, however. Environmental policy has largely relied on technology-based standards which promote the diffusion of a particular technology but simultaneously lock in this technology. An incentive to reduce compliance costs is usually maintained even with technology-based standards. However, environmental policy often narrowly restricts the search for cheaper solutions by strict requirements or inflexible rules. Often environmental policy also has created rather than reduced uncertainties for innovators and investors whose expected revenues depend on a sustained high level of environmental goals.

Thus, there are many ways in which environmental policy may hinder – and actually has hindered – environmental innovation. Partly this has been counteracted by policies which actively sought to promote environmental innovation. These turned out to be most successful if they helped to create and maintain cooperation. An example are voluntary agreements on waste paper recycling ratios.

In addition, innovation policy can more easily target innovations in sectors 'further away' from the direct influence of environmental policy. In the case of the paper industry this relates to the chemical and packaging industry, for example. Targeting the many actors along the paper chain may contribute to lowering the relative costs of secondary fibers and to extending the uses of secondary fiber products. Simultaneously, this approach has a higher potential to coordinate the generation and implementation of complementary process, product, and organizational innovations.

The motive for environmental innovation most independent of public policy is the reduction of production costs. Consequently, the majority of environmental innovations observed in the paper industry were related to this objective.

4 Policy Patterns

In the preceding section we have argued that public policy has an important – though limited – effect on environmental innovation through its impact on the direct and indirect determinants of expected long-term profits. It has been shown that in the cases investigated in the present study costs and public pressure were of particular importance among these determinants. Public policy may either reinforce or weaken the motives for environmental innovation or – most importantly – restrict or direct the search for solutions. In order to demonstrate to which extent this happened in the cases of the present study, an 'optimal' policy has first to be defined. This can then be used to judge on actual policy patterns in the countries investigated.

4.1   Requirements for an Innovation-Friendly Policy Pattern

Synthesizing approaches from environmental economics, innovation research, and policy analysis three central dimensions of a policy framework can be identified, which determine whether it promotes or hinders environmental innovation (see Table 2):

1.   the instrumentation, which, above and beyond the selection of individual instruments, includes the way these are formulated and combined;

2.   the policy style, which denotes the way in which goals are formulated and environmental regulations are implemented;

3.   the configuration of actors, which refers to the institutional framework conditions and the network of actors.

Instrumentation

As has become evident from our discussion of the motives of enterprises for environmental innovation, the creation of economic incentives is an important requirement for innovation-friendly policy frameworks. This does not mean an exclusive use of economic instruments, however. Rather a combination of various instruments is appropriate to the complex nature of environmental innovation. That attention be paid to the procedural nature of innovation is also seen as important for successful policy-making. The various phases of the innovation process – invention, innovation and diffusion – each requires an appropriate choice and combination of instruments.

Policy style

Economic theory as well as policy analysis emphasize the importance of close coordination between the various actors participating in the political process. A precondition is a policy style promoting dialogue; in this framework government institutions can function as managers or 'game makers'. In order to reduce the uncertainty of companies environmental policy has to be calculable and reliability. Decisiveness in formulating and implementing ambitious environmental goals also reduces uncertainties with respect to opportunities for profits and investment needs. Nevertheless, environmental policy must be open to new discoveries and provide sufficient flexibility to be adapted to individual cases. A policy style that is management oriented provides organizational services in a joint process of defining implementing environmental goals. Central among these services are those that help to mobilise and link individual knowledge.

Configuration of actors

The discovery and implementation of new, inexpensive opportunities for reducing environmental pressure require the co-operation of various political and administrative levels. In addition, a common orientation of various policy fields can reinforce the orientation and motivation towards innovation. Innovation springs from the combination of specific knowledge and from learning effects. Companies can therefore mutually benefit from co-operation, in particular along the value creation chain. Impetus towards environmental innovation can also be expected from the exchange of information between basic and applied research and between companies and external research establishments, as specific knowledge frequently originates independently in more than one research area. The government can contribute to this exchange by supporting innovation networks including also regulatory authorities.

Table 2:   Central requirements for an innovation-friendly policy framework

Instruments are innovation-friendly if they
⇒ provide economic incentives
⇒ are applied in combination
⇒ are based on strategic planning and explicitly formulated goals
⇒ support innovation as a process and take account of its different phases
A policy style is innovation-friendly if it
⇒ is based on dialogue and consensus
⇒ is calculable, reliable and has continuity
⇒ is decisive, proactive and ambitious
⇒ is open and flexible with respect to individual cases
⇒ is management oriented and knowledge based
A configuration of actors is innovation-friendly if
⇒ it favors horizontal and vertical policy integration and a close networking of various regulatory authorities
⇒ the addressees of regulation are well connected with each other
⇒ the network between regulators and regulated is tight
⇒ it promotes knowledge and motivation through the inclusion of stakeholders

Involving all important stakeholders in the policy process not only facilitates implementation. If target groups participate in formulating the goals, innovators within the group can adjust early. At the same time they can propose ways of achieving these goals which are well adapted to their needs and possibilities.

4.2   Policy Patterns of the Past and their Effect on Environmental Innovation

Table 3 represents an informal assessment of the central elements of the policy regimes relevant for the paper industry in the three countries discussed; Table 4 summarizes the main characteristics in each of the countries compared. In Japan, the instrumentation is characterized by the great number of diverse instruments which are applied simultaneously. In Sweden, the strategic and cooperative orientation are the most pronounced features of the instrumentation. In the US, technology based standards are the dominant instrument of environmental regulation relevant for the paper industry. That the support of the process of innovation is regarded as weak in Japan is explained by the fact that the paper industry is not regarded a strategic sector in this country. Instruments which promote co-operation such as innovation networks or alliances along the paper chain are most intensively used in Sweden.

Table 3:   Central elements of the policy patterns relevant for the paper industry

Country	Japan	Sweden	USA
Instrumentation			
Economic Incentives	1	2	2
Variety of Instruments	3	2	1
Strategic Orientation	2	3	2
Support of Innovation Processes	1	2	2
Orientation on Co-Operation	2	3	1
Policy Style			
Orientation on Dialogue	3	2	1
Predictability	2	2	2
High Level of Aspiration	2	3	1
Flexibility	3	2	1
Management Orientation	2	2	3
Policy Integration	1	2	2
Configuration of Actors			
Networking of Regulators	2	2	2
- of Addressees	2	3	2
- of Regulators and Addressees	3	2	1
Influence of Stakeholders	1	2	3

The policy styles in the three countries compared are marked by even larger differences. In Japan, an intensive dialogue takes place in advance of introducing new regulation which explicitly is meant to build confidence. In the US, a fundamental antagonism is traditionally assumed to exist between regulators and addressees; only recently approaches have been tested which are based on the idea of mutual advantages (cf. section 4.3). This is the point of departure of environmental policy with respect to pulp and paper production in Sweden. This basic philosophy explains the high continuously level of requirements of environmental policy in Sweden which is – differently from the US – independent of short-term pressures. Thanks to the large number of only weakly hierarchical instruments, the policy style in Japan is extremely flexible. The contrary is true for the US; the legal system, and in particular its litigation and liability rules, rule out any flexibility. The same features are responsible for the eminent importance of scientific investigations as a basis for regulation. Management orientation, i.e. steering through organizational services, is not yet a prominent feature in any of the countries compared. With respect to policy integration deficits can be identified in each of the countries; in Japan the competitive attitude of different administrations turns out to be an obstacle to horizontal integration.

Table 4:   Characterization of policy patterns

Japan	Sweden	USA
Instrument Setting	**Instrument Setting**	**Instrument Setting**
• Variety of Instruments	• Strategic Orientation	
	• Cooperation	
Policy Style	**Policy Style**	**Policy Style**
• Dialogue	• High Aspirations	• Managementmindedness
• Flexibility		
Setting of Actors	**Setting of Actors**	**Setting of Actors**
• Networks between	• Networks between	• Influence of Stakeholders
Regulating Bodies and Regulated Companies	Regulating Bodies	

Apart from this feature there are little differences among the three countries with respect to the functioning of networks between different administrations. The cooperation in innovation networks seems to be more intense in Sweden than elsewhere. More marked differences can be observed with respect to the networks between regulators and addressees: it is particularly close in Japan, while in the US enterprises have an adverse attitude towards the administration. A feature favorable to environmental innovation of the configuration of actors in the US are far-reaching rights to proceed against environmental damages; in this respect deficits still exist in Japan.

In summary it can be stated for each of the countries compared, that

- in the US the pattern of environmental policy has been generally adverse to innovation. Technology based standards have promoted the diffusion of certain technologies but have failed to sustain incentives for continuous improvements. Because of the far-reaching rights of individuals to proceed against environmental damages, break-through environmental innovations have been implemented at some locations. It has to be noted, that since around 1990 a re-orientation has started; so far, however, the traditional policy style marked by confrontation still dominates.

- In Japan the policy style is traditionally co-operative and flexible. Despite the fact that a particular orientation on innovation of environmental policy as far as it relates to the paper industry has not existed, a continuous diffusion of incremental and partly even break-through environmental innovations took place. The promotion of innovation is traditionally the responsibility of the industrial policy of the MITI; the paper industry as well as the license based production of pulp and paper machinery are not regarded as strategically important and thus are no focus of MITI policy. Therefore break-through innovations reducing environmental pressure of pulp and paper production were not developed in Japan.

- Break-through environmental innovations have been developed in Sweden, favored by a policy pattern that is characterized by the search for consensus but still pursues challenging objectives. Even though Swedish environmental policy is not explicitly innovation oriented, it is characterized by long-term goals. The success observed in Sweden was made possible by an outstanding position of the pulp and paper industry on the Swedish R&D policy agenda combined with an attitude of innovation-oriented companies which understand the reduction of environmental impact as a strategic aim.

A very informal and exploratory judgement of the policy patterns in the three countries investigated suggests the hypothesis that the policy scheme in Sweden conforms most closely to the requirements of the "ideal" policy pattern. Policies in Japan rank second in this respect while the policy pattern in the US shows the least resemblance to the "ideal" one. It should be noted that this ranking resembles the one we proposed with respect to the reach and degree of integration of environmental innovation in the three counties.

4.3 Innovative Approaches

Recently some of the requirements for innovation friendly environmental policy stated above have been more widely recognized. This has resulted in innovative approaches to environmental policy. Innovative approaches can be characterized as measures which feature

- the creation of economic incentives,

- the creation of flexibility through a variety of instruments,

- the strategic orientation of environmental and technological policies,

- the setting-up of cooperative arrangements and the promotion of networking,

in order to increase the reach and degree of integration of environmental innovation.

Table 5 lists some examples of initiatives which seek to implement some of these requirements. Interestingly, such initiatives can be observed especially in the US, where the traditional style of regulation has been most unfavorable to innovation, to a lesser extent in Sweden, but not yet in Japan. Germany also seems to lag behind. It should be noted, however, that in all countries the traditional environmental regulatory system based primarily on technology standards still dominates.

Table 5:   Examples of innovative approaches in Sweden and USA

	Sweden	USA
Creating Economic Incentives	Environmental Management Systems, Eco-Taxes	Cluster Rules
Flexibility Through Variety of Instruments	Licensing Procedure	ReFIT
Strategic Orientation of Policy	Sweden 2021, Ecocyclic Paper Mill	Vision 2020
Cooperative Arrangments and Networking		Green Lights, Energy Star

After almost 10 years of research, lobbying and bargaining, the US Environmental Protection Agency (EPA) has released in September 1997 a new basic regulation for the paper industry, known as cluster rules. The regulation

- integrates – for the first time in the US – emission standards for water and air (hence 'cluster rules') and, even more importantly,

- includes specific incentives – such as longer adjustment periods, favorable conditions for obtaining permits, and easier monitoring requirements – for those companies which oblige themselves to implement innovative technologies with lesser environmental impacts.

Both features correspond to central requirements of a more innovation-oriented environmental policy pattern identified above.

Reacting to the anti-regulatory mood prevailing in the US, EPA has also started using 'soft' instruments, which are based on voluntary participation and the principle of mutual advantage. Examples are the *Green Lights* and *Energy Star* Programs.

Elements of a long-term-oriented research- and technology policy for the paper industry have been implemented by establishing the *Vision 2020* initiative. In this program the paper industry develops its own view of its future on which is government R&D-policy is then based.

The defining of environmental goals as elements of strategic orientation in Swedish companies – supported by the implementation of environmental management systems – create important incentives for the generation and diffusion of environmental innovations.

The orientation of environmental policy in Sweden towards the long-term goal of sustainable development is clearly signaled to the industry by defining research programs. One such program, *Sweden 2021*, is funded by the Swedish Environmental Protection Agency, another one, *Ecocyclic Pulp Mill*, is sponsored by public research funds. These initiatives define objectives for environmental policy and provide an orientation for research policy in order to promote the generation of appropriate knowledge.

References

Blazejczak, J., D. Edler, J. Hemmelskamp and M. Jänicke (1999), Environmental Policy and Innovation: an International Comparison of Policy Frameworks and Innovation Effects, in: Klemmer, P. (ed.), *Innovation Effects of Environmental Policy Instruments*, Berlin.

Klemmer, P. (ed.) (1999), *Innovation Effects of Environmental Policy Instruments*, Berlin.

Weaver et al. (1997), Optimizing Environmental Product Life Cycles, in: *Environmental And Resource Economics* 9, 199-224.

Technology Commercialization and Environmental Regulation: Lessons from the U.S. Energy Sector

Vicki Norberg-Bohm

Director, Energy Technology Innovation Project, Belfer Center for Science and International Affairs, John F. Kennedy School Government, Harvard University
79 JFK Street, Cambridge, MA 02138
USA

Keywords. energy sector, wind turbines, gas turbines, market failures.

1 Introduction

The development of new "green" technologies is a key component of strategies for the transition toward an environmentally sustainable industrial society. In some instances, private firms or NGOs have taken the lead in bringing greener technologies to market. However, more often, government must play a fundamental role in this process. Unlike some industrial sectors, in which government has historically had a minimal and only indirect role in the path of technological innovation, the energy sector has always been marked by strong governmental involvement. Current efforts to manage climate change join long-standing programs to manage the local and regional environmental impacts of energy production and consumption. Furthermore, energy production and consumption are tied to national security and economic well-being together, these concerns on the environment, development, and security make the energy sector a prime target for thinking about how to effectively use the forces of government to bring about technological innovation.

This paper takes a historical look at the role of public policy in the development of wind turbines and gas turbines for power generation, drawing lessons from this history for current efforts to bring a new generation of non-carbon and low-carbon technologies into the power sector. These cases suggest that a variety of policy mechanisms, with government supporting supply-push and demand-pull, will be needed to bring new energy technologies through the commercialization stage. This will be particularly true for technologies based in firms without strong financial capabilities and complementary technological assets, and when the attractiveness of the new technology is dependent solely on its public benefits (e.g. environmental protection) rather than private benefits (e.g. modularity, dispatchability and low capital cost.) This analysis also suggests that success is not dependent on the specific policy instruments, but whether the instruments are designed, implemented, and coordinated in a manner that overcomes key dilemmas in using policy to promote technological change. These dilemmas include: establishing niche markets, preferences for incremental rather than radical change, technological knowledge located largely in the private sector, and differing timeframes for public policy and technology development.

This paper is organized as follows. The next section examines the role of government in technology commercialization, focusing on the rationale for government involvement, the ways that government can influence private sector investment in environmentally-enhancing technology, and the dilemmas that arise when government chooses technology innovation as a policy goal. The following two sections describe the role government has played in the development and diffusion of wind turbines and gas turbines. The final section analyzes and compares these cases, drawing lessons for future energy and environmental policy. The research described in this paper is largely an examination of policy and technological developments in the US. Recognizing that firms and markets in the energy sector are increasingly global, we will be taking an international perspective in the next stage of this research.

2 The Role of Government in Technology Commercialization

Technological change is a complex, non-linear process, involving invention, innovation and diffusion. The pipeline model, which suggests that government support for scientific research will result in new commercial products, has proven inadequate. It is now clear that interactions between the phases are critical and that new inventions face considerable obstacles on their path to commercialization. Nonetheless, the distinctions in these phases remain useful for discussing technological change.

There are market failures in all these phases of technological change, as outlined in Figure 1, creating a role for public intervention throughout the process. Designing public policy to effectively address the market failures throughout this complex process remains a challenge. In the US, there is a consensus that the government should play of role in basic science and technology research (Branscomb and Keller 1998). This is based on the understanding that knowledge is a public good, and thus an individual researcher or firm cannot retain all the benefits from investment in basic scientific and technological R&D, and will thus under-invest. Moving to the other end of the process, the market failures related to diffusion are also fairly well understood, and include high transaction costs and the divergence of private and public discount rates. There are many examples of government efforts to reduce transaction costs or to stimulate private investment at socially desirable levels, including such diverse programs as appliance standards, voluntary programs such as Green Lights (EPA 1996, Eisele 1996), and information generation such as resource maps (Loiter and Norberg-Bohm). Compounding these types of market failures, that are relevant to many sectors of the economy, are the environmental and security externalities associated with energy production and use. These externalities operate to create under-investment throughout the process of technological change. While there is deep historical precedent for government programs on both ends of the process of technological change (i.e. invention and diffusion), we have less experience and it is a greater challenge to develop appropriate policy for the innovation or commercialization phase (PCAST 1999). The research presented in this paper is aimed at shedding light on this particular dilemma.

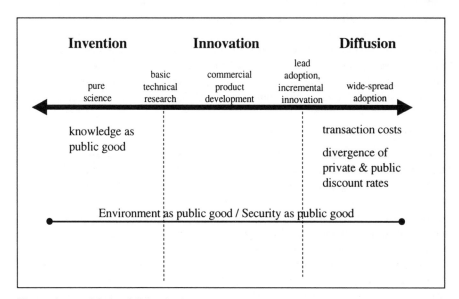

Figure 1:   Market failures in energy sector

It is much easier to argue why the government should be involved than it is to design effective government programs. The areas in which the government has been most effective in technology development are military and space technology, both non-commercial technologies (Dalpe 1994, Mowery and Rosenberg 1982 and

1979). The unique situation, which led to success in these cases, is that the government acted as a key player for both the supply and the demand of the technology. In other words, government was the main funder of R&D, as well as the first, and often only major procurer of the technology. This situation provided continuous feedback between the innovator (manufacturers) and the consumer (government). For civilian technology, such as power generation technology, the government will also need to play a role in both supply-push and demand-pull in order to overcome the market failures throughout the process of technological change. However, the government role on both sides will be diminished and less direct, focused on creating incentives for private sector investment and procurement.

Several factors influence the private sector decision to invest in bringing new technologies through the commercialization stage, as shown in the inner circle of Figure 2. The three variables in the upper half of this circle – the state of the technology, factor prices, and market demand – are critical to decisions about whether a new technology can be brought to market in a timely fashion and at a cost that is profitable. Decisions to invest in commercialization depend on assessments of the future states of these variables, assessments that are made under considerable uncertainty. Moving to the bottom half of this circle, industry structure is significant in understanding private sector decisions, as some industries are more innovative than others (Abernathy and Utterback 1978, Tushman, Anderson et al 1997, Pavitt 1984, Nelson 1982). The innovativeness of a particular industry sector depends on factors such as the maturity of the dominant technology, scale, capital intensity, R&D intensity of the industry, and competitiveness. Finally, within any industry, some firms are more innovative and more focused on environmental improvement than others, making firm characteristics another important factor (Gladwin 1993, Hart 1997, Maxwell et al. 1997).

The outer circle of Figure 2 outlines the types of policy mechanisms that can influence each of these factors. The goal here is to expand our vision of how government action can influence private sector investments in "green" innovation, recognizing a landscape more complex than the debate over single tools, such as market-based mechanisms vs. standards. Turning first to market demand for new environmentally-enhancing technologies, standards have been the tool most often used to create demand. The more stringent the standards, the more likely they are to stimulate investments in technology innovation, with product or chemical bans being the most extreme case (Ashford, Ayers et al 1985, Ashford and Heaton 1983, Porter and Van der Linde 1995). In practice, given the political negotiation and scientific uncertainty surrounding standard-setting, standards more often have led to the adoption of existing technologies and end-of-pipe solutions.

In the last decade, governments have experimented with an expanded set of tools for creating market demand for environmentally enhancing technologies, including market-based mechanisms such as taxes or tradable permits, voluntary programs, and public disclosure of facility level environmental performance data. Government-sponsored scientific and technological assessments may also influence private sector assessments of future market demand. Given the newness of these mechanisms, and in the case of assessments an increased use and complexity, while much advocacy exists, little research has been undertaken to empirically explore the conditions under which these mechanisms can influence the path and timing of technological change.[1]

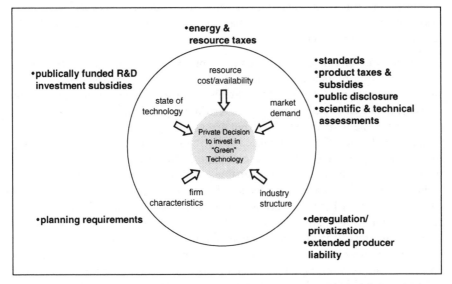

Figure 2:   Influence of public policy on private sector decision to invest in green technology

Turning next to the state of technology, public funding of R&D creates new inventions and can also be critical to bringing technology close enough to commercialization to stimulate the interest of private firms. This has been particularly true in the energy sector. The US government has invested in R&D for both new energy supply and end-use efficiency (PCAST 1997, Holdren 1997). The R&D has taken place at national labs as well as through government sponsorship of university and industry-based research. Although the budget for energy R&D is far below that necessary for meeting future environmental challenges (PCAST 1997, Margolis and Keyman 1999), in terms of public funds the energy sector has fared better than most. It has been extremely difficult to win congressional approval for

---

[1]   See Norberg-Bohm (1999) for a critical look at several of these mechanisms. See Ashford (1999) for examination of several approaches to negotiated rulemaking and collaboration. See Stavins and Jaffee (1995) on market mechanisms. See Levy and Rothenberg (1999) on assessments. See Stoughton (1995) on voluntary programs.

presidential initiatives for a broad-based R&D program for environmental technology.[2]

The third lever is a set of policies used to influence resource cost or availability, i.e. to change factor prices, and includes taxes, subsidies, price controls, and quantity controls. All of these have been used in the energy sector, as will be clear from the wind turbine and gas turbine cases that follow, and have significantly influenced the course of technology development. Equally important have been market fluctuations in the cost of oil and gas, which have been outside of the direct control of energy policy.

The fourth variable, industry structure, can be influenced directly by regulation and deregulation of industry sectors. New approaches to environmental policy, such as extended producer liability may also lead to changes in the structure of industry, in this case relationships in the vertical supply chain (Lifset 1994). In the power sector, the issue of regulation and deregulation is particularly salient, as the sector has until recently been regulated as a natural monopoly. This created biases toward supply expansion, and the use of large-scale generating technologies. Deregulation, or more correctly re-regulation, of this industry is occurring worldwide, and is creating an opening for a different set of technologies. As the wind case will show, in both the regulated monopoly of the past and the emerging regulated competition, government programs have been necessary to bring renewables into the mix. It is important to note that in a less direct way, the four levers mentioned above can create an impetus for change within an industry sector. In energy, we are now seeing the entrance of large oil and gas firms into the renewables market, something that also occurred briefly during the 1970s. In both cases, the perception of strong future market demand, at least in part created by environmental concerns and government policies, led to this outcome.

The final variable, firm characteristics, can be influenced both directly and indirectly by government action. Policies that provide a more direct influence are those that require planning, the adoption of environmental management systems, and the requirement for information generation (INFORM 1995, Gottlieb 1995, Massachusetts Toxics Use Reduction Program 1997, Ortz 1995). All of these are aimed at creating new flows of information within a firm, and some require new institutional structures as well.

To this point, this essay has set out a clear rationale for government involvement and presented a variety of policy tools that can be used to influence private sector

---

2   In 1994 the Clinton Administration launched the Environmental Technology Initiative (ETI), a 10-year multi-billion dollar program to fund R&D for technologies that improve environmental performance. The Congress funded this at the level of $32 million in 1994 and $72 million in 1995. By 1997, the only remaining part of ETI is the Environmental Technology Verification Program, which verifies the performance of new environmental technologies and had a budget of $10 million in 1997 (EPA 1997b).

investment in environmentally enhancing technology. Our concerns do not end here, as there are difficulties in using these tools effectively. Leaving the not insignificant issue of political support aside, there are incompatibilities between the policy process and the technology innovation process that must be addressed for policy to be effective. As outlined in Figure 3, these include establishing niche markets, dynamics of change, technological knowledge, and time frames. Figure 4 describes policy advice and possible policy designs for addressing the dilemmas created by these incompatibilities.

establishing niche markets:	private valuation of public goods
	limited coordination of supply-push
	& demand-pull
dynamics of change:	public & private preference for incremental change
technological knowledge:	largely in private sector
time frames:	technology cycles vs. policy cycles

Figure 3:   Dilemmas in policy for technological change

The first challenge to using policy to stimulate technological innovation is the issue of establishing niche markets (Kemp, Schot et al. 1998, Rip and Kemp 1998). In the commercialization process for private goods, firms are able to charge more to lead adopters, the group of consumers willing to pay a premium for qualities that the new good provides. Over time, the cost of successful products comes down, due to ongoing innovation and economies of scale, thereby allowing the markets to expand. New products whose value over existing goods is based solely on public good qualities are unable to charge a premium in the marketplace, making it more difficult for successful commercialization. Although there is a group of green consumers in the US, it is not large enough or willing to pay a high enough premium to bring many green technologies, including renewable energy technologies, through commercialization (Wiser and Pickle 1997, Law Fund and CORE 1997).

Dilemma	Policy Advice	Policy Mechanisms
niche markets private / public supply/demand	• public support for generic, pre-competitive technology R & D • demonstration • "buy down" for lead adopters	• public/private R & D • procurement • subsidies
dynamics of change radical / incremental	• stringency	• standards and bans • eco-taxes
tech knowledge	• flexibility • private sector participation/ leadership	• administrative discretion • tradable permits
		• challenge regulations • voluntary programs • public/private partnerships for R & D
time frame	• reduce uncertainty	• ratcheting standards • voluntary agreements • scientific assessments • reward beyond compliance behavior

Figure 4:   Policy response to dilemmas

The second issue is the fact that technological capability lies largely in the private sector. This creates the oft-cited problem of governments' poor ability to direct technology development for civilian applications. The antidote for this is twofold. First, government regulations aimed at creating market demand should allow firms to respond flexibly, making their own choices about what technology is most appropriate. Some specific mechanisms that addressed these concerns are: administrative discretion in implementation and enforcement of regulations (Freeman 1997, Susskind et al. 1989), market-based mechanisms such as tradable permits (Stavins 1997, Burtraw 1996), challenge (Ausubel 1989), and voluntary programs (EPA 1996). Second, government-sponsored R&D programs should be designed to allow private sector participation and leadership, guarding, of course, against private sector captures (Noll and Cohen 1998, Borrus and Stowsky 1998). This can be addressed through the development of scientific advisory bodies and public-private partnerships for R&D.

The third key challenge relates to the dynamics of change. Both governments and firms most often exhibit a preference for incremental change. Each must face a severe threat to consider more radical changes; both need to envision an opportunity to push for more radical change (Abernathy and Clark 1985, Kingdon 1984). Given the uncertainties accompanying threats to public health or valued ecosystems, technological solutions often must exist before governments enact environmental regulation that requires changes in production or consumption patterns. This suggests the need for both push and pull. In other words, as the cases presented below demonstrate, to create green technologies, government must invest in R&D as well as create market demand.

The fourth concern is that there is often a mismatch in the timeframe of technology cycles and policy cycles. In the case of energy supply technologies, the timeframe for bringing a new power source from invention through commercialization is in the order of decades. In contrast, in the policy world long-term is often only as long as the time until the next election, a two-year to four-year cycle. The basic prescription for addressing this issue is to design policies that reduce long-term uncertainties about the demand for increasingly stringent environmental performance (Ashford 1994, Porter and van de Linde 1995, Norberg-Bohm 1999). Policy mechanisms to address this include ratcheting standards, long-term voluntary agreements, rewards for beyond compliance behavior, and on-going scientific and technological assessments.

In summation, this section has reviewed the rationales for government involvement in the development of environmentally enhancing technology, the range of policy mechanisms that can be used to influence the private sector's decision to invest in environmentally enhancing technology, and the incompatibilities between the process of technological change and policy change that often lead to failed governmental programs. In the next section, we discuss the development of gas turbines and wind turbines. In each of these, multiple policy instruments influenced the case and direction of technology development. The dilemmas described above provide a heuristic for understanding the success and failure of these government efforts.

3   Wind Turbines

Wind turbines are one of the oldest technologies for harnessing energy. Reliable wind generated electricity became available in the early 1920s (Shephard 1994). From the 1920s through the 1940s, wind turbines were used in the Midwestern United States for rural electrification (Righter 1996). With the passage of the Rural Electrification Act, grids were extended throughout this region, bringing an end to this niche for wind turbines. Interest in wind turbines surged again in the early 1970s, as one solution to the oil crises and growing environmental pressures. In the US, governments at the national and state levels responded by supporting technology deployment of wind turbines (Gipe 1995, Righter 1996), as well as other renewable energy technologies. In contrast to their earlier use for rural electrification, in the 1980s wind turbines were being connected to the electricity grid, creating demand for larger turbines and wind farms. Currently, wind power accounts for about 1/2 per cent of the grid-connected electricity in the US, with over

90 per cent of this capacity located in California (EIA 1997b). Most of the turbines were installed during a relatively short boom period in the mid-1980s.[3]

Technological innovation during this recent round of wind turbine diffusion has
been impressive. As shown in Figure 5, the cost of wind-generated electricity
dropped substantially, from 25 cents per kilowatt-hour in 1980 to about 5 to 7
cents per kilowatt-hour in 1995. Nonetheless, the competing technology of gas
turbines has also shown impressive gains in efficiency, with associated decreases
in cost, as will be discussed in the next section. The result is that wind turbines are
not yet cost-competitive in the private market. The analysis that follows is presented in greater detail in Loiter and Norberg-Bohm 1997 and 1999.

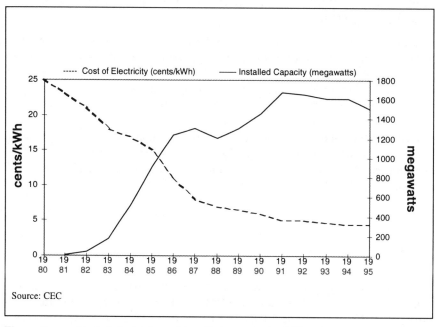

Source: CEC

Figure 5:   Cost of electricity and installed capacity in California

Figure 6 provides an overview of the government programs that contributed to the
development and diffusion of wind turbines from 1970 through 1995. Government
played a critical role in the state of the technology, the market demand, and the
industrial structure. Market forces, such as the sharp rises in oil prices during the

---

[3]   This picture is changing. More recent government efforts have led to the development
of wind farms in other parts of the country (Parsons 1998, Guey-Lee 1998,
Giovado 1998).

1970s, and then the equally sharp fall in the 1980s also played a critical role in the perception of future market demand.

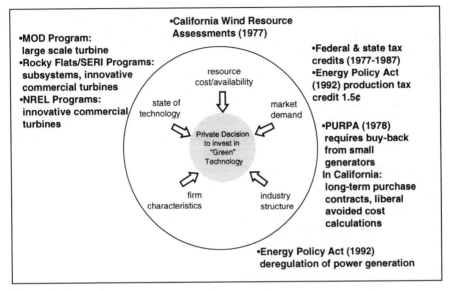

Figure 6:   Public policy for wind turbines

The US took two different approaches to wind turbine R&D. The first, a "big science" approach, called the Mod Program, was administered jointly by the National Aeronautics and Space Administration (NASA) and the Department of Energy. The concept behind this program was to a apply U.S. expertise in high-technology R&D to the challenge of building a reliable, cost competitive wind turbine for grid-connected electricity generation. Nearly half of federal wind spending during the 1970s was spent on this program, totaling $200 to $300 million. (Davidson 1991; Spera 1994; Brooks and Freedman 1996; Righter 1996). The program involved construction of several large turbines, with the goal of producing a 3 to 5 MW machine. The size was considerably larger than commercial wind turbines of that era, which were in a range of 100 kW, and of today's largest commercial turbines that are in the 1 to 1.5 MW range. This decision reflected the institutional culture of the utility industry and the agencies administering the program. The program managers believed that large turbines were necessary to interest the presumed manufacturers (existing heavy industrial suppliers of power technology) and the presumed adopters (utilities) who were accustomed to large base-load plants. They also believed large turbines could provide a technological umbrella for smaller sizes. Furthermore, NASA's aerospace culture led to an emphasis on lightweight designs (Spera 1994).

In hindsight, the reasons for pursuing a large turbine were incorrect and the design focus was ineffective. No commercial turbines of the 3 to 5 MW size have been built. There were some useful, albeit expensive, achievements through the Mod Program. It was instrumental in demonstrating that medium scale wind turbines could successfully deliver high-quality electricity to the utility power grid. It also demonstrated the ability to operate at variable speed while connected to a utility grid and gathered much experimental data.

The second approach was practice-driven and focused on component innovation as well as advanced wind turbine designs featuring multiple component innovations. These programs were led by the Department of Energy, and administered first by the Solar Energy Research Institute and then by its successor, the National Renewable Energy Laboratory. These programs looked at the challenges faced by wind turbines in operation, and in this way identified areas where component innovation was both necessary and promising. NREL is continuing this approach, both by sponsoring advanced wind turbine designs and innovation for specific components (DOE 1995). NREL is now also providing funds for demonstrations to utilities that install small test plants using the latest technology. With the falling off of the utility market for wind turbines in the early 1990s, as will be described below, this was the only way to get the new technologies tested under actual operating conditions.

The component innovation research was much more effective than the Mod program, contributing substantially to the improvements in wind turbine efficiency during the 1980s. Of the 12 key innovations in wind turbine components that we identified in our research, seven relied on partial or total public funding, and three were developed in the private sector for other industries and transferred for use in wind turbines. We were unable to identify the funding source for the remaining two (Loiter and Norberg-Bohm 1999).

As these statistics indicate, the federally funded supply-push efforts were supplemented by innovation in the private sector. During the early and mid-1980s, when incentives to invest in wind energy were highest, a large amount of innovative activity occurred and a great many companies began producing wind turbines (Karnøe 1993; Spera 1994; Gipe 1995; Chapman 1997). By 1985, 28 manufactures had installed turbines in California, half of them foreign firms (CEC 1985-1994). Without the incentives of the market there would have been only laboratory invention and no technological change in commercially available wind turbines (Tangler and Somers 1985; Chapman 1997).

Because we were unable to find detailed data on the level of diffusion of each of these component innovations, we relied on two proxies as indicators of whether wind turbines were adopting component innovations: (1) specific yield which measures the power generated by a turbine per swept rotor area, and (2) decreases in the cost of wind generated electricity (CEC 1985-1994). Both measures indicate that turbine performance improved throughout the California "wind rush" of the

1980s, suggesting the diffusion of component innovation as there were no major breakthroughs in overall turbine design. This conclusion is augmented by interviews with companies that were producing turbines during the 1980s; those with longevity improved their turbine design over time by improving specific components.

Throughout the 1980s, wind generated electricity remained considerably more expensive than fossil generated electricity (average short-term buyback rates in California were about three cents per kW, while the cost of energy for the best turbines installed on good sites was estimated at five cents per kW). The wind turbine market grew in California not because it was the only state with a viable wind resource, but because of the state's implementation of PURPA, state tax incentives, and characterization of the wind resource. In the late 1970s, under the leadership of Governor Brown, California sponsored a mapping of its wind resource. This identified promising sites and reduced the cost for individual developers, critical for an emerging industry dominated by small investors (Davidson 1989, Divone 1994). Moving next to PURPA, this federal law required utilities to purchase at "avoided cost" electricity generated by some classes of small producers, including wind and gas-fired co-generators. States were left to set their own avoided costs. California's avoided cost calculations were generous, although they were not the highest in the country. More important were the long-term contracts required in California, set for 10 years with escalating prices based on the expectation that oil prices would continue to rise (Devine and Chartock 1987). These long-term contracts made it easier for developers to borrow capital for an emerging technology. The gap between California's avoided cost and the price of electricity generated from wind was filled by federal and state tax credits totaling 25 percent. The years 1984 and 1985 marked the heyday of wind turbine installation in California. In 1985 the federal tax credits expired and the California tax credits were reduced. In 1985, the long-term contracts were eliminated and in 1987 the California tax credits expired. The wind market diminished considerably at this point, as shown in Figure 5.

In summary, government activity in both supply and demand was important to the nascent commercialization of wind turbines. The big science efforts were not effective, but the efforts in small turbine components were. Because the component research was driven by the needs of the market, the government created market was important for both public and private sector innovation. The demand-pull policies were too inconsistent to create a lasting industry. They only acted in concert and strongly over a short period of time. The pattern of new turbine installations in California clearly shows a correlation to the presence of the tax credits and long-term contracts. Most manufactures did not survive the removal of these incentives, and many were not able to complete a second or third round of product design and refinement.

4   Gas Turbines

Gas Turbines were initially developed for jet engines during World War II. The technology was adopted in the power sector in the 1960s. The early power applications were not highly efficient, and could not compete with the cost of base-load coal or oil generation. However, due to their dispatch-ability, they were well-suited to provide peaking power. Considerable technological innovation over the last several decades has put gas turbines in their current position of being the most attractive technology for new power generation. Simple gas turbines have doubled their efficiency over this period, and the introduction of combined cycles triples the efficiency, as shown in Figure 7. In addition to having the lowest cost per kilowatt-hour at current fuel prices in the United States, gas turbines have the advantages of modularity, dispatchability, low capital costs, and low pollution compared to other fossil-fuel generating technologies. All these characteristics contribute to their attractiveness in the emerging competitive power generation market.

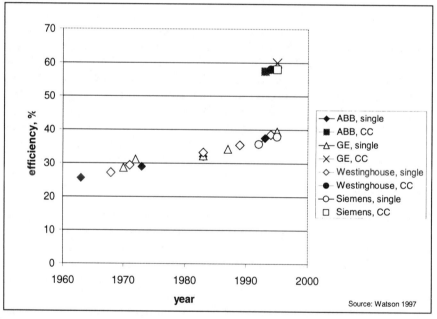

Source: Watson 1997

Figure 7:   Gas turbine efficiency 1960 - 1995

The analysis that follows is based largely on the research of W. James Watson 1997, and Darian Unger and Howard Herzog 1998. Figure 8 provides an overview of government policies that contributed to the development and diffusion of gas turbines from the 1960s to the present. Government played a critical but mostly indirect role in state of technology. Government policies, particularly regulation and deregulation of natural gas and electricity, also had a considerable effect on market demand and industry structure.

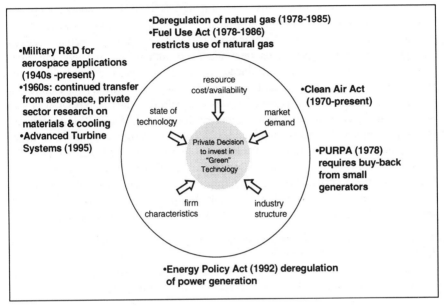

Figure 8:   Public policy for gas turbines

The sources of technological innovation for stationary gas turbines for power generation include: publicly sponsored military R&D for jet engine development, private sector R&D directed specifically to stationary gas turbines, and to a lesser extent government sponsored R&D directed specifically to stationary gas turbines. In addition, some technology has been transferred from steam turbines, oil and gas drilling, and the National Aeronautics and Space Agency research. Military R&D for jet engines was the basis of the first stationary gas turbines. In the US, the firms that developed the initial gas turbines for the power sector were all developers and manufactures of jet engines. By the early 1960s, these firms created separate divisions for their jet engine and power sector gas turbines, and started in-house R&D programs to improve gas turbine efficiency. In the early 1960s, efforts focused on compressor design and simplifying designs for package units. By the mid-1960s, firms began focusing their efforts on increasing efficiency to make gas turbines competitive for base-load electricity generation. This has been the main focus of the last three decades, and has been achieved through increases in firing temperatures, innovations in aerodynamics, and perfection of the combined cycle.

The technological developments that made higher temperatures possible occurred in two areas: materials and cooling systems. Unlike jet engines, stationary turbines did not need to operate in pristine environments or be lightweight; rather they needed to operate with more corrosive fuels and operating environments. In the 1960s and 1970s, many of the advances in materials were done independently by power generation engineering groups, such as those for improved heat tolerance and distribution for turbine inlet components. Others such as protective coatings on high temperature components stemmed from both power and aviation engineering groups. Private firms introduced cooling to stationary gas turbines in the mid-1960s. This technology was transferred initially from military jet engines. A later source of the cooling technology was the drilling industry. NASA was also an important source of analytical techniques for cooling design. Finite element analysis generated for space applications allowed for more complex and faster development of cooling designs. Building on these transferred technologies, the private sector invested in cooling research that led to design innovations. In the decade after the oil crisis, the U.S. government also invested directly in stationary gas turbine research through the US High Temperatures Technology Program, which contributed new technologies for both cooling and material coatings.

When the market for gas turbines picked up again in the mid-1980s, as will be discussed below, turbine firms renewed their efforts to increase the efficiency of gas turbines. By this time, there was a large untapped set of innovations in jet engine technology that had not been transferred to stationary gas turbines. Turbine manufactures drew on this knowledge to once again increase firing temperatures by improving materials and cooling systems, as well as increasing efficiency through improvements in turbine aerodynamics. Not surprisingly, GE, the U.S. manufacturer with an in-house jet engine division, was the first to market with the next generation of higher efficiency turbines. Other companies moved to match this by creating alliances with jet engine manufacturers. In the 1990s, the U.S. government invested directly in gas turbine technology through the Advanced Turbines Systems Program. The participants in this program include 6 US turbines manufactures, 83 universities, and DOE research centers. Further investigation into this program is necessary to understand its impacts. Watson concluded that this program may give U.S. manufactures an early competitive lead, but that it was not necessary for ongoing innovation in stationary gas turbines.

Turning now to the market for gas turbines, as mentioned above, gas turbines quick start-up and shut-down capabilities created their first market niche in the power sector. The great Northeast blackout of 1965 highlighted the need for peaking power, and although gas turbines were not yet competitive with base load oil and coal plants, sales to utilities grew to fill this need. During the first years of the 1970s, because efficiency had improved and capital costs were lower than the competing technologies, the gas turbine firms started reaching a new market, mid-size plants for the electric power industry.

This growing market for gas turbines was then stymied, due to the political responses to the oil crisis of 1973 and 1979, which included regulation of both gas and power sectors. During the 1970s, price controls on natural gas led to shortages. In 1977 deregulation of natural gas began, although it was not completed until 1985. During the process of deregulation (between 1977 and 1985), the price of natural gas continued to increase; upon completion of deregulation gas prices fell quickly and sharply, making gas a more competitive fuel. During nearly the same period, from 1978 through 1987, the Fuel Use Act restricted the use of natural gas for most new industrial facilities and all new power plants. This was based on the belief that supplies were limited and that natural gas should be saved for more critical applications such as residential and commercial heating. During this period, the U.S. market for gas turbines dried up, as shown in Figures 9a and 9b. Similar restrictions in the European Community limited the market there as well. The late 1970s and early 1980s were thus a time of great downturn in the market for stationary gas turbines. Firms strategies for surviving this crisis were to convert manufacturing facilities to other uses, reduce R&D, and scale-down their gas turbine business in favor of other power generation technologies. They also reached to markets in the developing world.

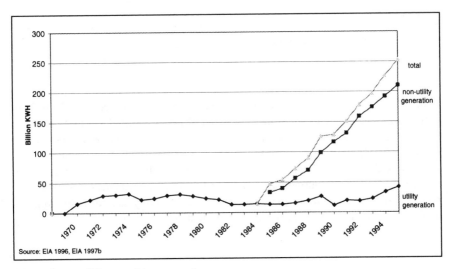

Figure 9a: US gas turbine generation

There were not specific environmental regulations that forced the use of natural gas. However, because it is the cleanest fossil fuel, it met the requirements of the Clean Air Act without need for additional pollution-control equipment. This contributed to its cost-competitiveness by keeping capital costs down, reducing operation and maintenance requirements associated with pollution-control, and reducing the need for permits and inspections required by coal power plants with scrubbers. Environmental regulations did force some technological innovation in systems for the control of NOx.

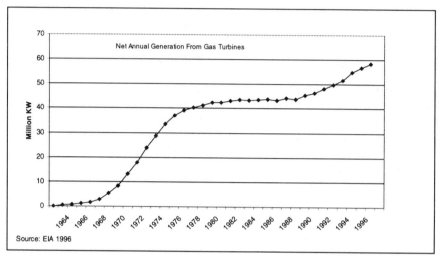

Figure 9b: US gas turbine capacity

In sum, as was the case with wind turbines, government played a role in both supply and demand. The government sponsored R&D, particularly military R&D for jet engines, created a technological storehouse that private firms drew on to increase the efficiency of gas turbines. On the demand side, government policy controlling the price and use of natural gas as well as the traditional regulation of utilities as a natural monopoly, created barriers to greater diffusion of this technology. With the removal of these barriers, the technology has been able to penetrate the marketplace without further government subsidies or standards.

5   Lessons for Future Energy and Environmental Policy

These two cases provide a stark contrast to each other. While both technologies improved dramatically in efficiency and reliability during the last three decades, and the cost of generating electricity from both fell significantly, gas turbines are a commercial success, while wind turbines still require subsidies to be attractive to private sector investors. This section takes two approaches to drawing lessons from these cases for future policy to promote energy technology innovation.[4] First, it examines three key differences between gas and wind turbines that have helped explain greater success of gas turbines. Second, drawing on the dilemmas in designing policy for technological change discussed in the first section, it takes a critical look at the achievements and failures of the government policies that influenced wind and gas turbine development.

Gas turbines for power sector applications were able to develop commercially with limited direct government intervention for three reasons: the ability to capture a private market niche, technology transfer from military applications, and an industry with complementary technological assets. Gas turbines were able to capture a private market niche prior to being fully cost competitive for base-load generation. This was due to their dispatchability, which made them perfect for peaking power. A region-wide blackout in the northeastern United States in 1965 highlighted the need for more peaking power, creating an initial opening for gas turbines in power generation. Later, gas turbines filled the market niche for mid-size power plants, and for cogeneration. Environmental regulation also added to the attractiveness of gas turbines, which are clean in comparison to other fossil fuels. In the new deregulated electricity marketplace, gas turbines are expected to be the technology of choice. They are attractive not only because they produce low-cost electricity, but also because of their dispatchability, modularity, and low capital cost. Second, gas turbines got a strong start from government investment in R&D for jet engines. Ongoing government R&D for jet engines, that has a $400 million annual budget, continues to be a key source of innovation for gas turbines. Third, the firms in the industry are large, produce multiple related products and have significant financial capability. This made it possible for them to invest in

---

[4]   An important concern to be addressed is the value of a comparison between the development of wind turbines and gas turbines. One might argue that gas turbines were simply a superior technology to wind turbines, and for this reason we would expect them to be developed with limited governmental stimulus. There is some merit to this argument, as gas turbines have some characteristics that are advantageous for electric power generation, including dispatchability, applicability for co-generation, modularity, and low capital cost. However, there is no reason to presume that further improvements of wind turbines will not lead to a cost-competitive technology. This discussion of cost-competitiveness ignores the issue of assigning the cost of externalities to fossil fuels. Repetto et al. (1992) estimated the cost of global warming at approximately $100 per ton of carbon. Using factors for the carbon content of fuels and thermal efficiency of electricity generation, this represents an external cost of 1.4 cents/kWh for natural gas and 2.5 cents/kWh for coal-fired generation. Drennen et al. (1996) estimated a similar cost for power-generation externalities other than climate change. The energy information administration (EIA 1996) estimated externalities for all emissions from fossil fuel plants at 0.8 to 5.4 cents/kWh, depending on generating technology. If internalized through taxes, these externalities would go far to closing the gap between the cost of wind generated electricity and gas generated electricity.

R&D specifically for the electric power gas turbine market. Private firms under-
took not only technology transfer, but also were responsible for key technological
breakthroughs. It also made it possible for firms to weather a near decade-long
regulatory-driven downturn in the market.

The situation for wind turbines is quite different. The advantage that wind turbines
have over their fossil-fuel competitors is based solely on environmental performance, i.e. on public good qualities.[5] In contrast to gas turbines' niche for peaking
power prior to being cost-competitive with base-load generation technologies,
wind turbines have not been able to find a private market willing to pay a premium for wind-generated electricity. Deregulation of the electric power sector is
providing the opportunity to market electricity to green consumers. As mentioned
previously, initial studies suggest that in the US there is not a large enough group
of green consumers willing to pay a large enough premium to bring wind turbines
through the commercialization stage (Wiser and Pickle 1997, Law Fund and Core
1997). Furthermore, wind turbines did not have a comparable source of on-going
R&D and were produced by single product firms without complementary assets or
deep pockets.

Given the fact that wind turbines are desired for their public good qualities alone,
and also the structure of the wind industry, policy must play a different role than it
did for gas turbines. The four incompatibilities between technology and policy
development – niche markets, dynamics of change, technological knowledge, and
timeframes – illuminate the reason for only partial success in the wind turbine
program, and suggests necessary strategies for future government efforts to support commercialization of wind and other renewable energy technologies. Looking
first at the development of a market niche, the commercial application of wind
turbines in the 1980s occurred because of government policies, including:
(1) PURPA, which required utilities to purchase power generated by small renewable sources; (2) California's implementation of PURPA, which required generous, long-term contracts, and (3) investment tax credits at both the state and national level. Each of these incentives alone were not large enough to create a
market, but for the few years in which they were simultaneously in place in California, a large amount of wind generation was brought online. During this period,
many of the turbines erected in California failed, but each year, better turbines
were brought online. Some companies had the opportunity to put up more than
one generation of turbine and demonstrated their ability for ongoing incremental
innovation. In other words, although short, during this period of adequate
government incentives to create a market for wind turbines, firms engaged in the
type of ongoing innovation necessary to bring a new technology through
commercialization. This contradicts the lesson many have taken from California's

---

5   This is true for wind turbines sized for connection to the electric grid. Smaller wind
     turbines have the potential of a niche in remote, low-density applications.

wind turbine experience – that overly generous subsidies encouraged the erection of lousy technologies.

Turning next to the issue of dynamics of change, not surprisingly, utilities demonstrated a preference for continued adoption of familiar technologies, in particular for large-scale fossil-fuel (and in some cases nuclear) generation plants. In the US, public mobilization against nuclear power and concern over air pollution and the rising cost of electricity put pressure on state public utility commissions and federal regulators to consider the emerging alternatives to large base-load plants. As one response, in 1978 PURPA opened the door for small renewable generators and co-generators. In the 1990s, further deregulation is bringing competition in power generation. Historically, deregulation of electricity and natural gas was adequate to open the market for gas turbines. For wind turbines, as discussed above, both deregulation and other market creation mechanisms have been necessary in the past and remain so today.

Switching now to the supply-push side of the equation, two issues related to technological knowledge are raised by these cases. The first is sources of technological knowledge. Gas turbines had a strong initial start due to publicly sponsored R&D for the development of jet engines. The emergence of a private market niche, first for peaking power and then for cogeneration created a strong enough market-pull for private investment in radical innovation. The firms in the gas turbine industry had both the technological and financial capability to respond by investing in both radical and incremental R&D. Even so, military R&D for the development of the next generation of jet engines has provided a continual source of new technologies applicable to stationary gas turbines. In contrast, wind turbine technology experienced only limited transfer from aerospace. The majority of the radical innovation for wind turbines came from government sponsored R&D directed solely toward wind turbine development. The firms in this industry lacked the financial capability, and had neither a comparable depth of technological capability nor a private market-pull to move forward without government support.

The second issue related to technological knowledge is the difficulties government has in directing research for commercial goods. This problem was demonstrated clearly through the two different approaches to development of wind turbine technology. The failure of the Mod program contrasts with the success of government-sponsored component innovation. The Mod program attempted a "big science" approach while the latter, more successful program took its direction from the experience with turbines operating in the field. An additional contrast between the programs is that the failed "big science" program contracted out to private firms but did not require cost-sharing, while the programs focusing on component innovation and the development of new turbines have been based on cost-sharing with the private sector.

The final dilemma outlined at the beginning of this paper was the problem of time frames, in other words, the fact that the development of power sector technology takes decades while government policy runs on a much shorter cycle. Short-term programs and fluctuating levels of investment hampered the ongoing development of wind turbine technology. The California "wind rush" of the 1980s was short-lived, but brought with it huge improvements in the technology. This was not because the technology reached a dead-end. We are now witnessing the next generation of wind turbines, again due to government programs in R&D and in market creation.

In conclusion, these cases highlight the interaction of supply-push and demand-pull in the commercialization process. In both cases, an initial market created incentives for private sector investment in R&D. For gas turbines, the initial market niche was based on advantages gas turbine technology had over the alternatives for peaking power. Ongoing innovation, carried out to large extent in the private sector, made this technology competitive for mid-size power generation and for cogeneration. Gas turbines are currently the preferred technology for base-load electricity generation, when gas is available. Although the private sector took the lead in innovation for commercial use of gas turbines, the dual-use nature of this technology was critical to its success. Government sponsorship of basic science and technological research for jet engines brought the technology through the innovation stage for military uses and subsequently continued to create break-throughs in materials cooling, and turbine design that had applicability for stationary turbines. In the case of wind turbines, the publicly-created market pulled some innovative activity, but government sponsorship of R&D specifically for wind turbine technology was necessary. The market pull was too short-lived and too insecure, and the firms were too shallow technologically and financially for the private sector to take over this function completely.

The lessons this provides as we look to bring renewable energy technologies into a competitive position are twofold. First a strong market pull will bring more private sector investment in R&D. We are witnessing this now for solar and wind turbine technology due to international activity on climate change and international financial transfers for these technologies. Further investigation is needed to see what types of innovative activity these new entrants are undertaking. Second, the gas case suggests there is a need for ongoing government support for R&D.

Acknowledgements

Jeff Loiter and Karlyn Cory's master thesis research contributed to the wind case. The research of Howard Herzog and Darian Unger at the MIT Energy Lab contributed to the Gas Turbine case. I received research support as well as the opportunity to present work in progress from the Center for Environmental Initiatives at MIT and the Environmental Technology Policy Program at MIT.

References

Abernathy, W.J. and J. Utterback (1978), Patterns of Industrial Innovation, *Technology Review* 80, 40-47.

Ashford, N.A. (1994), An Innovation-Based Strategy for the Environment, in: Finkel, A. and D. Golding (eds.), *Worst Things First: The Debate Over Risk-Based National Environmental Priorities*, Washington, D.C.

Ashford, N.A., C. Ayers, et al. (1985), Using Regulation to Change the Market for Innovation, *The Harvard Environmental Law Review* 9(2), 419-466.

Ashford, N.A. and G.R. Heaton (1983), Regulation and Technological Innovation in the Chemical Industry, *Law and Contemporary Problems* 46(3), 109-157.

Ausubel, J.H. (1989), Regularities in Technological Development: An Environmental View, in: Ausubel, J. and H. Sladovich (eds.), *Technology and Environment*, Washington, D.C., 70-91.

Becker, M. and N. Ashford (1995), Exploiting Opportunities for Pollution Prevention in EPA Enforcement Agreements, *Environmental Sciences and Technology* 29(5), 220A-226A.

Borrus, M. and J. Stowsky (1998) Technology Policy and Economic Growth, in: Branscomb, L. M. and J. H. Keller (eds.), *Investing in Innovation: Creating a Research and Innovation Policy the Works*, Cambridge, MA, 40-63.

Boyle, G. (1996), *Renewable Energy:Power for a Sustainable Future*, Oxford.

Branscomb, L. M. and J. H. Keller (eds.) (1998), *Investing in Innovation: Creating a Research and Innovation Policy the Works*, Cambridge, MA.

Brooks, L. and M. Freedman (1996), Section II: Federal Government R&D-Wind and Ocean Thermal, in: *Renewable Energy Sourcebook: A Primer for Action*, Washington, D.C.

Butraw, D. (1996), The SO_2 Emissions Trading Program: Cost Savings Without Allowance Trades, *Contemporary Economic Policy* XVI (April), 79-93.

Caldart, C., and N. Ashford (1999), Negotiation as a Means of Developing and Implementing Environmental and Occupational Health and Safety Policy, *The Harvard Environmental Law Review* 23(1), 142-202.

CEC (1985-1994), *Wind Performance Reporting System Annual Reports*, California Energy Commission.

Chapman, J. (1997), *OEM Development Corporation. Personal Communication*, March 25.

Dalpé, R. (1994), Effects of Government Procurement on Industrial Innovation, *Technology in Society* 16(1), 65-83.

Davidson, R. (1989), The California Covenant, *Windpower Monthly* 5(7), 18-20.

Davidson, R. (1991), Senate and House Agree to Double American Wind Budget, *Windpower Monthly* 7(8).

Devine, M.D., M.A. Chartock, et al.(1987), PURPA 210 Avoided Cost Rates: Economic and Implementation Issues, *Energy Systems and Policy* 11, 85-101.

Divone, L.V.(1994), Evolution of Modern Wind Turbines, in: Spera, D.A. (ed.), *Wind Turbine Technology*, New York.

DOE, U.S.(1995), *Wind Energy Program Overview*, United States Department of Energy, Washington, D.C., National Technical Information Service.

Drennen, T., J. Erickson, et al. (1996), Solar Power and Climate Change Policy in Developing Countries, *Energy Policy* 24(1), 9-16.

EIA (1996), *The Changing Structure of the Electric Power Industry: An Update*, DOE/EIA-0562. Washington, D.C.

EIA (1997a), *International Energy Outlook*, Washington, D.C.

EIA (1997b), *1996 Annual Energy Review*, Washington, D.C.

Eisele, J.(1996), Green Lights: Lighting the Path to Success, *Buildings: Construction & Management* March, 62-74.

EPA (1996), *Partnerships in Preventing Pollution: A Catalogue of the Agency's Partnership Programs*, Washington, D.C.

Freeman, J. (1997) Collaborative Governance in the Administrative State, *UCLA Law Review*, 45(1).

Galdwin, T.N. (1993), The Meaning of Greening: A Plea for Organizational Theory, in: K. Fischer and J. Schot (eds.), *Environmental Strategies for Industry*, Washington, D.C., 37-61.

Giovando, C.A. (1998), Wind Energy Catches Its ?Second Wind? in the US, *Power* May/June, 92-95.

Gipe, P. (1995), *Wind Energy Comes of Age*, New York.

Gottlieb, R. (ed.) (1995), *Reducing Toxics: A New Approach to Policy and Industrial Decisionmaking*, Washington, D.C.

Guey-Lee, L. (1998), *Wind Energy Developments: Incentives in Selected Countries*, Renewable Energy Annual, Washington, D.C.

Hart, S. (1997), Beyond Greening: Strategies for a Sustainable World, *Harvard Business Review,* January-February.

Holdren, J. (1998), Federal Energy Research and Development for the Challenges of the 21st Century, in: Branscomb, L. M. and J. H. Keller (eds.), *Investing in Innovation: Creating a Research and Innovation Policy the Works*, Cambridge, MA, 299-335.

Inform (1995) *Toxics Watch 1995*, New York.

Karnøe, P. (1993), *Approaches to Innovation in Modern Wind Energy Technology: Technology Policies, Science, Engineers and Craft Traditions*, Stanford, CA.

Keijers, G. (1999), *The Changing Ecological Arena: The Evolution of Dutch Environmental Policy from 1970 - 2000 (And Beyond)*, Environmental Technology Policy Project, working paper, Massachusetts Institute of Technology, Cambridge, MA.

Kemp, R., J. Schot, et al. (1998), Regime Shifts Through Processes of Niche Formation: The Approach of Strategic Niche Management, *Technology Analysis and Strategic Management* 10.

Kingdon, J. (1984), *Agendas, Alternatives, and Public Policies*, Boston.

Law and Water Fund of the Rockies and the Community Office for Resource Efficiency/ LAW Fund and CORE (1997), *Promoting Renewable Energy in a Market Environment: A Community-Based Approach for Aggregating Green Demand*, Boulder, CO.

Lifset, R. (1994), *Extending Producer Responsibility in North America: Progress, Pitfalls, and Prospects in the Mid-1990s*, Ch.4 of the Proceedings of the Symposium on Extended Producer Responsibility (14-15 November 1994), 37-55.

Loiter, J. and V. Norberg-Bohm (1997), *Technological Change and Public Policy: A Case Study of the Wind Energy Industry*, Cambridge, MA.

Loiter, J. and V. Norberg-Bohm (1999), Technology Policy and renewable Energy: Public Roles in the Development of New Energy Technologies, *Energy Policy* 27, 85-97.

Margolis, R.M. and D.M. Kammen (1999), Underinvestment: The Energy Technology and R&D Policy Challenge, *Science* July, 285.

Massachusetts Toxics Use Reduction Program (1997), *Evaluating Progress: A Report on the Findings of the Massachusetts Toxics Use Reduction Program Evaluation, Executive Summary*.

Maxwell, J., S. Rothenberg, F. Briscoe and A. Marcus (1997), Green Schemes: Comparing Environmental Strategies and Their Implementation, *California Management Review* Spring.

Mowery, D. and N. Rosenberg (1982), The Commercial Aircraft Industry, in: R.R. Nelson (ed.), *Government and Technical Progress: A Cross-Industry Analysis*, New York, 101-161.

Mowery, D. and N. Rosenberg (1979), The Influence of Market Demand Upon Innovation: A Critical Review of Some Recent Empirical Studies, *Research Policy* 12(2), 102-153.

Nelson, R.R. (1982), Government Stimulus of Technological Process: lessons from American History, in: R. R. Nelson (ed.), *Government and Technical Progress: A Cross-Industry Analysis*, New York.

Noll, R. and L. Cohen (1988), Economics, Politics, and Government Research and Development, in: Kraft, M. and N. Vig (eds.), *Technology and Politics*, Durham, NC.

Norberg-Bohm, V. and M. Rossi (1998), The Power of Incrementalism: Environmental Regulation and Technological Change in Pulp and Paper Bleaching in the US, *Technological Assessment and Strategic Management* 10(2).

Norberg-Bohm, V. (1999), Stimulating 'Green' Technological Innovation: An Analysis of Alternate Policy Mechanisms, Policy Sciences 32, 13-38.

Orts, E. (1995), Reflexive Environmental Law, *Northwest University Law Review* 89, 1227-90.

Parsons, B.(1998), *Grid-Connected Wind Energy Technology: Progress and Prospects*, paper presented at the North American Conference of the International Association of Energy Economists, Golden, Colorado, National Renewable Energy Laboratory, Albuquerque, NM, 18-21 October 1998.

PCAST (1997), *Federal Research and Development for the Challenges of the Twenty-First Century*, Washington, DC.

PCAST (1999), *Powerful Partnerships: The Federal Role in International Cooperation on Energy Innovation*, Washington, DC.

Pavitt, K. (1984), Sectoral Patterns of Technical Change: Towards a Taxonomy and a Theory, *Research Policy* 13.

Porter, M. and C. van der Linde (1995), Toward a New Conception of the Environment-Competitiveness Relationship, *Journal of Economic Perspectives* 9(4), 97-118.

Porter, M.E. and C. van der Linde (1995), Green and Competitive: Ending the Stalemate, *Harvard Business Review* September/October.

Repetto, R., R. Dower, et al. (1992), *Green Fees: How a tax shift can work for the environment and the economy*, Washington, D.C.

Righter, R.W. (1996), *Wind Energy in America: A History*, Norman, OK.

Rip, A. and R. Kemp (1998), Technological Change, in: Rayner, S. and E. Malone (eds.),, *Human Choices & Climate Change: Resources and Technology*, Columbus, OH, 327-400.

Rothwell, R. and W. Zegveld (1981), *Industrial Innovation and Public Policy: Preparing for the 1980s and 1990s*, Westport, CT.

Shepherd, D.G. (1994), Historical Development of the Windmill, in: Spera, D.A. (ed.), *Wind Turbine Technology*, New York.

Spera, D.A. (1994), Introduction to Modern Wind Turbines, in Spera, D.A. (ed.), *Wind Turbine Technology*, New York.

Stavins, R. and A. Jaffe (1995), Dynamic Incentives of Environmental Regulation: The Effects of Alternative Policy Instruments on Technology Diffusion, *Journal of Environmental Economics and Management* 29, S43-S63.

Stavins, R. N. (1997), What Can We Learn from the Grand Policy Experiment? Positive and Normative Lessons from the SO_2 Allowance Trading, *Journal of Economic Perspectives* July.

Stoughton, M. D. (1995), *An Evaluation of Voluntary Programs as Public Policies for Environmental Protection*, Master's thesis, Civil and Environmental Engineering, Massachusetts Institute of Technology.

Susskind, L., J. Secunda, et al., *The Risks and the Advantages of Agency Discretion: Evidence from EPA's Project XL*, working paper, Environmental Technology Policy, Massachusetts Institute of Technology, n.d.

Tangler, J. L. and D. M. Somers (1985), Advanced Airfoils for HAWTs, *Windpower '85*, San Fransisco, CA.

Tushman, M., P. Anderson, et al. (1997), Technology Cycles, Innovation Streams, and Ambidextrous Organizaitons: Organization Renewal Through Innovation Streams and Strategic Change, in: Tushman, M. and P. Anderson (eds.), *Managing Strategic Innovation and Change*, New York, 3-23.

Unger, D. and H. Herzog (1998), *Comparative Study on Energy R&D Performance: Gas Turbine Case Study*, working paper (EL 98-003), Energy Laboratory, Massachusetts Institute of Technology.

Wallace, D. (1995), *Environmental Policy and Industrial Innovation: Strategies in Europe, the US and Japan*, London, 1995).

Watson, James W. (1997), *Constucting Success in the Electric Power Industry: Combined Cycle Gas Turbines and Fluidised Beds*, Ph.D. diss., University of Sussex.

Wiser, R. and Pickle, S. (1997), Green Marketing, Renewables, and Free Riders: Increasing Customer Demand for a Public Good, Environmental Energy Technologies Division of the Lawrence Berkeley National laboratory, #LBNL-406+32/UC-1321.

The Example of the Thermal Insulation in Germany

Ulrike Lehr

Rhine Westphalia Institute for Economic Research (RWI)
Hohenzollernstr. 1-3, 45128 Essen
Germany

Keywords. *thermal insulation, residential energy use, environmental regulation, innovation.*

Abstract. Residential energy use is among the main sources for carbon dioxide in Germany. Although it has been subject to environmental regulation, a steady increase is observable. The author poses the question, whether the environmental standards in the building sector helped the development of new materials. The case of the windows and panes industry is analyzed in depth as an example. Field studies as well as econometric methods lead to the conclusion that environmental regulation lags behind the technological development.

Ecologically beneficial residencies as well as ecologically beneficial traffic does not exist; both activities of private households are by definition disturbances to the ecological system. The construction and maintenance of buildings come with significant uses of space, natural resources and large amounts of waste and waste water. The use of buildings affects the environment with the emission of carbon dioxide from fossil fuel burning – mostly for heating purposes.

The demand for energy of private households is a field that still shows a vast potential for energy savings. This is a rather surprising result, since the households' energy demand has been subject to regulation and taxation for several years. The main determinants of the households' energy demand are controlled by the Ordinance for Heating Systems, which sets a required minimum efficiency, and the Ordinance for Thermal Insulation. The latter used to solely affect newly constructed houses, but recently (1995) has been extended to maintenance work on existing buildings.

Although parts of the above mentioned potential could be realized by conventional means, one can raise the question, to which extent new products and materials are necessary and what fosters the development of such innovations. In the following we choose one specific trajectory from the large choice of possible innovative lines of production in the building sector, and ask how it has been affected by environmental regulation.

Facing the discrepancy between the intensive regulation on the one hand and the lack of energy efficiency on the other hand, we therefore ask, whether the policy mix has offered enough incentives for the invention and diffusion of new solutions and where the obstacles are. This problem is closely related to the question of innovative effects of environmental regulation. In other words, how should environmental regulation be designed to guarantee optimal benefits to the environment and incentives for innovation[1] and growth. At this point we may assume, that these incentives will differ for invention and deployment of innovations as well as for basic and incremental innovations.

This contribution relates to the framework of the FIU project (cf. Lehr/Löbbe in this volume). There, a positive influence of environmental regulation on innovation has been found in cases where regulation was dynamically tightened and flexible enough to allow for different new technologies. Here, we concentrate on the invention phase[2]. Taking the example of windows and panes we especially analyze the impact of the Ordinance on Thermal Insulation ("Wärmeschutzverordnung", WSchVO). We chose this example, because

- windows are a central determinant for the heat loss of a building,

- windows are used in all buildings in similar ways and thus allow for generalized results,

- panes show long term observable trajectories, which can be described by consistent parameters, therefore allowing for quantitative analysis and

- the WSchVO is tightened regularly and allows for the use of a wide range of materials to fulfill the standard (flexibility).

This paper is organized as follows. The first section lists the main technological development, the deployment potential and the market situation. The second section contains a survey of the relevant standards. The nature of the influence of regulation on the technological change is closely analyzed in the third section using an econometric causality test. The method is briefly presented. The paper closes with a summary and an outlook.

---

[1]   For a definition of environmental innovations and a discussion on the impact of environmental regulation see KLEMMER, LEHR, LÖBBE (1999)

[2]   For a discussion of the impact of environmental regulation on innovation in households see LEHR (1999a,b,c).

1 Technological Trajectories and Market Potential

1.1 Technological Development

The basic idea of a residential building – walls, roofs and windows – is not very flexible. The building materials, however, have changed significantly over time, as some spectacular projects show. The main development lines deal with the minimization of thermal transfers between different materials and through panes.

Windows are used for lighting purposes and protection from intrusion, noise and weather influences, the latter often go together, since a better thermal insulation often also decreases outside noise. The thermal insulation properties of materials are denoted by the thermal transmission coefficient (k-value). It describes the heat loss caused by transmission in Watt per square meter and degree (Kelvin) of the temperature difference between the inside and the outside surface of the material. Panes generally have a higher k-value and therefore worse insulating properties than the surrounding walls.

In the last thirty years of the technological development, however, significant efforts have been made, to improve the performance. In k-values the development can be described as in Table 1. Thus, the thermal characteristics of windows improved through various steps. Step one was the introduction of double panes, which had an air filled space at the beginning and later on the space between the panes was filled with different inert gases. The use of various gases leads to distinctive differences in the k-values, e.g. by using Krypton the k-value can be cut by half compared to an air filled space. The latest development is a transparent heat reflecting coating on the room side surface of the outer pane. This type of insulating window can decrease the thermal loss by 60 per cent and thus improve the heat balance of a building by up to 15 per cent. From the ecological point of view, windows were always considered as the weakest part of the building's outside. More recently, the aspect of heat gains through windows depending on the orientation of the building gained more and more attention. The latest version of the WSchVO includes these gains in the overall balance.

Window frames also have been the target of innovative work, because the combination of different materials, i.e. glass and metal, plastic or wood, leads to thermal flux. The characteristic indicator is again the k-value, that usually is much higher compared to the panes (typical values are between 2.2 and 1.7 W/m^2*K). Recently frames with k-values of less than 0.8 W/m^2*K have been developed for the use in so called "passive" houses.

From the above we note two basic innovations - the two pane technique and the reflecting coating - and some incremental innovations along these trajectories. The Ordinance on Thermal Insulation on the other side increased the standards for windows regularly. The motives that spurred the technological development may therefore be either found in the framework of the classical innovation theory, i.e. in pioneer positions and gains coming from it, or the change in regulatory framework triggered the innovation. To analyze the situation in deeper detail, we look at the market for windows and the demand for energy saving panes.

Table 1:   k-values of windows

year	k-value in W/m_2*K
1955	2,5
1974	2
1977	1,7
1985	1,2
1993	0,7
1998	0,7

Source: RWE-Energie Bauhandbuch 1998

1.2   Demand and Potentials

The market consists of two fields - construction and maintenance. Therefore, diffusion is determined by the activities in the construction sector and the life cycle of windows and panes. Additionally, windows are replaced during general maintenance work and refurbishing activities. Generally, the life span of panes is said to be between 13 and 17 years, the frames last much longer (30 to 50 years with wooden frames). However, one important determining factor for the diffusion is the activity in the construction sector.

While the activity concerning non-residential buildings has been relatively constant over time, residential construction shows large fluctuations. During the first half of the eighties, activities fell significantly and rose increasingly during the nineties partly enforced by unification. Especially the refurbishing sector in the eastern part of Germany contributed to this increase. From the middle of the nineties construction fell again (cf. Figure 1).

The data seem to contradict the assumption that window sales parallel construction activities, although typically the window areas per building vary very little. This deviation is mainly statistical, because the sales statistics registers a window when the order comes in usually long time before the building is finished. Additionally the official construction statistic only counts building activities that are connected with some paper work. It systematically underestimates refurbishing activities, which make for 60 per cent of window sales.

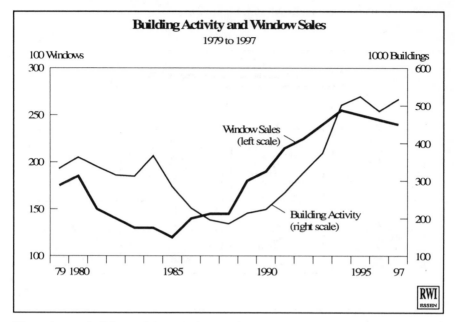

Figure 1:   Building activity and window sales

Innovations have to claim their market share against conventional products. They are in a quality and price competition with other products. Environmental innovations can be fostered by environmental regulation, which guarantees certain market shares and thus spurs innovative activities.

2   Environmental Regulation

Environmental policies are aimed at the protection of the environmental media (clean air, water, climate, soil etc.). For the residential problem this means the efficient use of energy for climate protection, the use of regenerative energies where it is possible, the prevention of an increasing soil sealing, among other goals. The main environmental protection laws in the field, however, were not passed for protective reasons, but as a reaction to the oil price shocks in the late seventies and early eighties. The Economy Act of Energy was passed 1976 and included the order to pass ordinances on thermal insulation, efficiency of heating systems (installation and maintenance) and the distribution of heating costs in rental buildings. The Ordinance of Thermal Insulation, the Ordinance on Heating

Systems, the Ordinance on the Distribution of Costs and the Ordinance on Small
Combustion plants were the result (c.f. Figure 2).

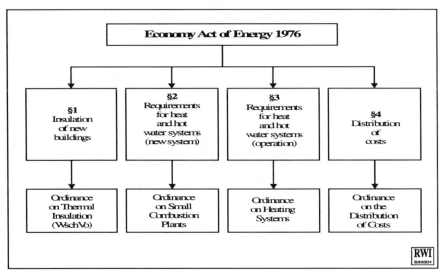

Figure 2:   Economy act of energy 1976

One important feature of the Economy Act of Energy is the operating efficiency
clause (§5). This clause includes that all measures according to the Economy Act
of Energy have to be economically reasonable. A measure is by definition economically reasonable, if amortization is reached within the life span of the measure. The Ordinances have been regularly adjusted to the state of the art.

The Ordinance on Thermal Insulation was passed 1977 (taking effect 1978) in
consequence of the DIN 4108. The first adjustment was passed 1982 (taking effect
1984). The Ordinance gives an upper limit for the heat transmission of different
parts of buildings and different materials for residential and non-residential buildings, with exemptions for buildings with lower room temperatures. Additionally it
includes calculation rules for the average heat transmission of all building parts
considering the building's shape and materials. The so called balancing technique,
where heat losses and gains may be weighed against each other, was included in
the latest adjustment of the ordinance, as well as some restrictions on refurbishing
activities. The next adjustment is planned for the year 2000, it will include the low
energy standard for new buildings and comprehensive standards for refurbishment.
Additionally, an integration of the Ordinance on Heating Systems is planned to
enhance the dialog between planners. However, a cautionary remark is necessary,
because the integration of the Ordinances may give way to new substitution poten-

tials between the different components, leading to less efficiency of the system as a whole.

The efficiency of standards is objectionable. Critiques often claim that standards are lacking dynamic behavior, adjust too slowly to the technological development and increase costs. The 1995 adjustment of the WSchVO tried to consider some of these points and implemented the dynamics - by announcing the further adjustments and the target corridor - and more flexibility by shifting to the heat balance view. The impact of this adjustment on innovation will be analyzed later in this paper.

3 Explanation of the Innovation Activity

The determinants of the innovation activities in the pane industry are analyzed by interviews with representatives of the industry with the help of a standardized questionnaire and via statistical causality tests.

3.1 Results from the Interviews

The assessment of the industry representatives is rather unequivocal. According to this assessment the main development has already taken place because modern panes are at the achievable limit between light transparency and heat impermeability. Technological development today concentrates on transparent insulation systems and is spurred by the desire to acquire new markets. The second line of development lies in protective glass for photovoltaic systems. In terms of incremental innovation the companies are improving fading resistance of colored glass, protective glass and the cost effectiveness of construction. High tech materials as the polymer coating for photovoltaic purposes, which have been discussed in the sciences years ago seem not to have entered the productive process.

From the interviews we seem to learn, that the reason for innovative strategies lies only in "classical incentives". The classical innovative company is driven by market shares, new markets and the competition in the market. Although the field shows a rather high regulation density, all interview partners denied their innovation activities being directly affected by it. Partly, the reason is that regulation does not focus on innovation. On the contrary, because the energy saving potential is very high and can be fulfilled with conventional means, the more degrees of freedom a regulation allows for, the more likely the use of conventional means is. Table 2 shows the relationship between the k-values of wall material, the shape of the building and the required k-values of windows.

Table 2:   k-values of wall material and required k-values of windows

k-value of the wall 1,2 W/m²*K Share of window in percent				k-value window	k-of the wall 1,5 W/m²*K Share of window in percent			
50	40	30	20		20	30	40	50
1,00	1,07	1,11	1,15	1,4	1,39	1,39	1,39	1,39
0,50	0,73	0,90	1,03	1,9	1,39	1,33	1,23	1,10
0,40	0,67	0,86	1,00	2,0	1,38	1,29	1,17	1,00
-	0,53	0,77	0,95	2,2	1,33	1,20	1,03	0,80
-	0,40	0,60	0,85	2,6	1,23	1,03	0,77	0,40
-	-	0,47	0,78	2,9	1,15	0,90	0,57	-
-	-	0,39	0,73	3,1	1,10	0,81	0,43	-

Source RWE-Bauhandbuch 1987/88

The last adjustment of the WSchVO, however, helped the *diffusion* of better win-dows. While before the share of highly insulating coated panes in all sales was 15 per cent, now it is up to 85 per cent. Sales started rising before the adjustment went into effect and led to a decrease in prices of the high grade panes. This confirms results predicted by the classical innovation theory that pioneer rents will decrease with a rising diffusion. While prices for the average panes stayed approximately constant during the eighties, prices for the higher grade panes fell sharply and stayed constant at a little higher level.

3.2   An Explorative Statistical Approach

In the following section we will try to empirically test the results gained from the interviews. Statistical methods cannot *explain* the innovation activities, but they can help to check the *causality* between technological progress and environmental regulation. What do we mean by causality in a statistical framework?

In econometrics we typically have explained (stochastic) and explanatory (sto-chastic) variables and use various techniques of analysis to find a meaningful rela-tionship between these. Plausible assumptions about the direction of precedence or causality enter the analysis mostly based on economic intuition. There is always the risk to deduct the direction of causality -even from a successful econometric regression -entirely wrong; the textbooks are full of examples.

In the following we will use a rather simple causality test that has been proposed by GRANGER (1969). The Granger test decides which out of two variables should preferably be the explanatory. Let x_t and y_t be two stochastic variables. The question we pose is whether the regression for y_t on $y_{t-1}...y_{t-n}$ can be significantly improved by including $x_t...x_{t-n}$ and vice versa. The test[3] involves estimating the following regressions:

$$y_t = \sum_{i=1}^{n} a_i * y_{t-i} + \sum_{i=1}^{n} b_i * x_{t-i} + u_{1t} \qquad \text{Eq. 1}$$

$$x_t = \sum_{i=1}^{n} a_i * x_{t-i} + \sum_{i=1}^{n} e_i * y_{t-i} + u_{2t} \qquad \text{Eq. 2}$$

where u_{1t} and u_{2t} are assumed to be uncorrelated. Equation 1 says that current values of y are dependent on lagged values of y and lagged values of x; equation 2 denotes the same for x. We may find four different possible relations between y and x:

1. Unidirectional causality from x to y; i.e. the coefficients bi are statistically different from zero and the coefficients ei are not statistically different from zero.

2. Unidirectional causality from y to x, with the above result reversed.

3. Feedback or bilateral causality with both sets of coefficients different from zero.

4. Independence when both sets of coefficients do not differ from zero.

The test is characterized by the following steps:

1. Regress current y on lagged y without lagged x. From this restricted regression obtain the restricted residual sum of squares RSS_E the restriction being that lagged x do not belong to the equation.

2. Regress current y on lagged y and lagged x and obtain the unrestricted residual sum of squares RSS_{UE}.

3. The null hypothesis is H_0: $\sum a_i = 0$, i.e. lagged values of x are not included in the regression. In other words the regression is not improved by including lagged values of x.

4. This hypothesis is tested by application of the F-Test.

$$F = (RSS_E - RSS_{UE})/m/RSS_{UE}/(n-k)$$

with

m: number of included lags of x

n: number of observations,

---

[3]   The description of the Granger test closely follows GUJARATI (1995).

k: number of parameters of the unrestricted regression.

5.   If the calculated F-statistics for a chosen level of significance exceed the optimal level, the null hypothesis has to be rejected.

6.   Repeat steps 1-5 vice versa.

The Granger test has been applied with an econometric program package that gives the level of significance and the F-statistics.

We apply the Granger test to find out, whether environmental regulation or innovation activity has been precedent in the above described development in the pane industry. We therefore have to develop time series, which characterize the technological development and the development of the environmental standards. The window and pane industry is a very good example for this test, because it shows a continuous development *and* has been subject to regulation over a long time period.

The development of panes has been described in detail in section 2. The resulting k-values lead to a time series given by Table 1. The Granger test is applicable to non-continuous, discrete time series, too. The time series for the development of regulation is harder to obtain, because the k-values of windows have not been subject to regulation from the beginning. Figure 3 shows the obtained time series. However, panes have earlier been subject to the DIN 4108, which required double panes for most parts of Germany[4].

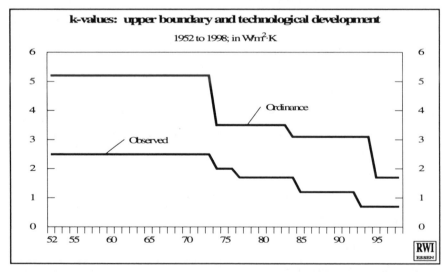

Figure 3:   k-values: upper boundary and technological development

---

[4]   The DIN 4108 distinguishes between three climatically different regions in Germany.

To obtain meaningful results the time series have to meet certain criteria. The distributions of the time series were tested for normality, skewness and deviation of a normal distribution. Whilst the data, which describe the innovation activity are not very sensitive towards a change in the number of observations, the k-values call for at least 24 observations (1975 to 1998) to be close enough to a normal distribution. Otherwise the Jarque-Bera test rejects the hypothesis of a normal distribution. Between 24 and 29 observations the distribution is slightly asymmetric to the right (positive values of the Jarque-Bera test) (Figure 4).

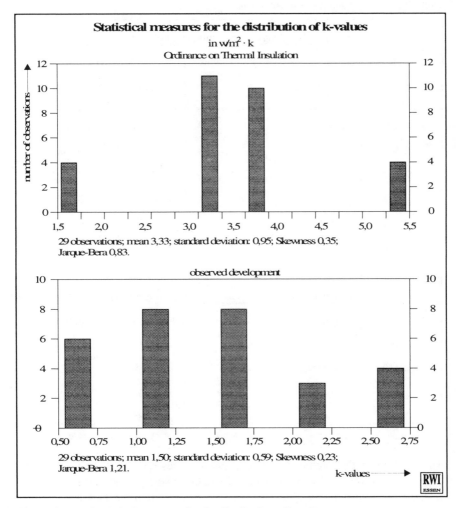

Figure 4:   Statistical measures for the distribution of k-values

The tested null hypothesis is: k-value$_{window}$ does not Granger cause k-value$_{regulation}$ and vice versa. This hypothesis has been tested for different numbers of lags and different numbers of observations. Table 3 gives the respective F-statistics and levels of significance. The null hypothesis "regulation does not Granger cause innovation" may not be rejected in any case. In other words the results in the right column of the table affirm the assumption that regulation does not influence the technological development.

Table 3: F-statistics and levels of significance

<table>
<tr><td colspan="6">Granger Test 2 lags, various number of observations</td></tr>
<tr><td colspan="2">Null hypothesis
k-value$_{window}$ does not Granger cause k-value$_{regulation}$</td><td>Observations</td><td colspan="2">Null hypothesis
k- value$_{regulation}$ does not Granger cause k- value$_{window}$</td></tr>
<tr><td>F-Statistic</td><td>Significance</td><td></td><td>F-Statistic</td><td>Significance</td></tr>
<tr><td>2,33362</td><td>0,11947</td><td>29</td><td>0,05331</td><td>0,94821</td></tr>
<tr><td>2,57832</td><td>0,09863</td><td>28</td><td>0,01999</td><td>0,98022</td></tr>
<tr><td>3,10848</td><td>0,06569</td><td>27</td><td>0,03557</td><td>0,96511</td></tr>
<tr><td>3,10848</td><td>0,06569</td><td>26</td><td>0,03557</td><td>0,96511</td></tr>
<tr><td>4,65322</td><td>0,02191</td><td>25</td><td>0,24457</td><td>0,78535</td></tr>
<tr><td>4,30358</td><td>0,02874</td><td>24</td><td>0,06852</td><td>0,93401</td></tr>
<tr><td colspan="6">Granger Test 29 observations, various number of lags</td></tr>
<tr><td>F-Statistic</td><td>Significance</td><td>Lags</td><td>F-Statistic</td><td>Significance</td></tr>
<tr><td>1,87761</td><td>0,16288</td><td>3</td><td>0,11919</td><td>0,94786</td></tr>
<tr><td>1,38412</td><td>0,27509</td><td>4</td><td>0,16669</td><td>0,95282</td></tr>
<tr><td>1,01613</td><td>0,43707</td><td>5</td><td>0,10430</td><td>0,98995</td></tr>
<tr><td>0,75355</td><td>0,61590</td><td>6</td><td>0,33085</td><td>0,91083</td></tr>
</table>

The assumption that technological progress precedes regulation may only be accepted on a lower level of significance. Including two lags, the null hypothesis is rejected on a sufficiently high level of significance. If more lags are included, technological progress loses influence on regulation, which makes sense in the light of the results from the interviews. Adjustments to regulation tries to include the most recent state of technological progress.

4   Summary and Results

In this paper we tried to elucidate the impact of regulation on innovative activities using the example of window in residential buildings. Our findings show that innovative activities of the firms are independent from or precede environmental regulation. These findings are supported by interviews with producers. Obviously we only tested existing regulation patterns and our results do not transfer do alternative policy strategies. However, the problem of lacking incentives originates mainly in the structure of the residential sector. The energy saving potential is rather high and it can be realized by conventional means. The barriers to investment in energy saving means in Germany are mainly institutional. Partly due to World War II Germany still has a comparably high share of rental homes. In combination with the German rent control system this leads to a rather low investment in the building stock. A regulation that gives incentives for innovative activities in the building materials and also in the furnace industry ought to be very specific. The alternative approach would be a very distinct subsidy for the diffusion of such technologies with all the perils that are caused by such programs

References

Granger, C.W.J. (1969), Investigating Causal Relations by Econometric Models and Cross Spectral Methods, *Econometrica*, 424-438.

Gujarati, D.N. (1994), *Basic Econometrics. Third Edition*, New York.

Klemmer, P., U. Lehr and K. Löbbe (1999), *Umweltinnovationen, Anreize und Hemmnisse*, Berlin. English version forthcoming.

Lehr, U. (1999a), *The Impact of Environmental Regulation on Innovation – the Example of Household Energy consumption*, Berlin.

Lehr, U. (1999b), Innovative Wirkungen umweltpolitischer Instrumente – das Beispiel des Energieverbrauchs der privaten Haushalte, in: Klemmer, P. (ed.), *Innovationen und Umwelt. Fallstudien zum Anpassungsverhalten in Wirtschaft und Gesellschaft*, Berlin, 305-328. English version forthcoming.

Lehr, U. (1999c), *Innovative Wirkungen umweltpolitischer Instrumente. Das Beispiel des Energieverbrauchs der Haushalte*, Berlin.

RWE (ed.), *RWE Bauhandbuch Essen 1989*.

Wärmeschutzverordnung (1994), *Bundesanzeiger* 46, 166a

Environmental Regulation and Innovation in the End-of-Life Vehicle Sector[*]

Roberto Zoboli

IDSE-CNR
via Ampère 56, I-20131 Milan
Italy

Keywords. end-of-life vehicles, car recycling, negotiated agreements, recyclable materials.

1 Introduction

During the last few years, the regulation of end-of-life vehicles (ELV) became a hot issue in the European environmental policy agenda. The recent developments of the EC Directive proposal on ELV highlight that most of the controversies are, in essence, about the appropriate policy approach to stimulate innovations in ELV management and about who should bear the costs of those innovations. ELV requires, in fact, a combination of different innovations involving different actors, and regulation can influence the choice of the innovative path. The systemic nature of the innovation process and the role of regulation instruments as a "selection device" – not necessarily pushing in the best direction – clearly emerge.

This paper is based on the preliminary results emerging from a research project on regulation and innovation in the case of ELV in Europe[1]. Compared to the wide

---

[*]   The paper is based on the project "Regulation and Innovation in the Area of End-of-Life Vehicle" being carried out by IDSE-CNR as a part of the IPTS-JRC framework-project "The Impact of Regulation on Innovation in European Industry". I am grateful to Karl Ludwig Brockmann for his helpful comments and suggestions on the first version of the paper. In preparing this paper, I received suggestions by Nicola De Liso, Riccardo Leoncini, Massimiliano Mazzanti and Sandro Montresor. Some of the ideas proposed here have been discussed with Gerhard Becher, Jens Hemmelskamp, René Kemp, Fabio Leone, Gérald Petit, Keith Smith and the other participants to the workshops of the IPTS-JRC "regulation-innovation" project. The usual disclaimer applies.

[1]   Starting from a preliminary analysis of innovation in ELV (Zoboli 1998), a series of interviews in Europe (more than 30) with representatives of the industries involved and the policy making institutions was carried out. The emerging links between

set of information arising from the project, the paper is very selective in the description of the ELV problem and policy developments, and it is instead focused on the main features of the regulation-innovation relationships emerging from the ELV case study.

The paper starts by introducing the main technical, environmental and economic aspects of the ELV problem, as well as the state of policy-making and industry-level initiatives in Europe (Section 2). In Section 3, after the description of some specific innovations in ELV, the paper addresses the nature of the innovative process, the interactions between policy-making and innovation, and the possible links between specific policy instruments and innovation. Some conclusions are presented in Section 4.

2   The ELV Problem, Policy Developments and Industrial Responses

2.1   The Problem

A systematic recording of facts related to ELV is still lacking and figures on ELV in Europe are rough estimates. Most of the information available has been elaborated as a part of the regulation-making process and the industry-level initiatives that took place during the 1990s (see in particular IPEE 1996)[2].

From deregistrations of passenger cars in EU countries, the number of ELV is estimated at around 8,8 million (1994) concentrated in the four largest countries (6.7 million in Germany, France, United Kingdom, Italy together). The average age of ELV is estimated at approximately 10-12 years. It must be stressed that the above figures are highly uncertain. Personal communications from car producers suggest that the total amount of ELV could be even half of the above figure. The reason is that the procedures for deregistration in the different countries are neither harmonised nor cross-checked, thus leaving rooms for a large "secondary market" for ELV (cars deregistered in some countries are sold and used in other EU as well as non-EU countries).

---

regulation and innovation were analysed. A research report (IDSE-CNR 1999) is being prepared together with some research papers (see Barbiroli 1999, Mazzanti and Zoboli 1999).

2   Additional information based on direct interviews are presented in IDSE-CNR (1999).

Few reliable figures are available on the number of abandoned ELV (i.e. not delivered to dismantlers) but the phenomenon is significant in various countries and regions.

The current rate of ELV recovery in the form of reuse or recycling is generally estimated at 75 per cent of car weight, which corresponds to the ferrous and non-ferrous metal content. At present, dismantlers receiving ELV recover spare parts, which has a value in the corresponding market, and deliver car wrecks to shredders, which extract the metals for recycling. The residue of the shredding activity, the Automobile Shredding Residue (ASR), which is estimated at around 1.8 million tons in the EU, is landfilled. A small amount of ASR is incinerated for energy recovery in some countries.

There is dispersion of pollutants in the dismantling and shredding phases if they are not performed according to environmental guidelines, and the lack of depollution activities in the dismantling industry depends on both the still weak regulatory framework and the weak economic motivations.

The landfilling of ASR is considered as the most significant environmental impact of ELV. Although ASR represents in general less than 0.3 per cent of total waste generated in many countries, it includes substances and hazardous waste (in particular PCB) which make it harmful. ASR is still classified in different ways in the EU countries and it is the subject of various ambiguities in international waste classifications that allow for its possible inclusion among hazardous waste (see Bontoux and Leone 1997, IPEE 1996).

There is an increasing amount of ASR relative to the recovered/reused/recycled fraction that is largely due to the changing material mix in car production. In 1965 a new European car contained on average 82 per cent of ferrous and non-ferrous metals (2 per cent aluminium) and 2 per cent of plastics. In the 1990s, the content of ferrous and non-ferrous metals averaged 72-75 per cent (with aluminium at 6 per cent) and plastics represented 10-13 per cent of total weight. Also the relative shares of glass, fibers and rubber were increasing in the last few decades.

The other trend making ASR problematic in the next future is the increasing average weight of European cars. The request of performance, comfort as well as passive/active safety caused an increase of weight that reached 20 per cent between 1987 and 1995 for some new car models (see IPTS-JRC 1996). In presence of decreasing share of easily recyclable materials, an increasing average car weight and an ever-increasing number of car circulating in Europe, the absolute amount of ASR is bounded to increase. The minimisation of ASR is thus the general objective of ELV policies.

The trade flows associated to ELV and ASR are not significant in relative terms, although the above-mentioned uncertainties about the "true" ELV number and the size of international "secondary market" should apply. During the 1990s, substantial export flows of ELV from Germany to Poland, France and the Netherlands were recorded. These flows created concerns in both Germany and the importing countries. The alleged causes of transboundary ELV flows include the high cost the last owners have to support in Germany for delivering ELV to dismantlers, the high costs of ASR landfilling, the relatively weak regulations on dismantling and waste disposal in Eastern European countries, and finally the above mentioned "second life" of ELV in importing countries.

2.2   Industrial Actors and Market Relationships

The industrial actors involved in the ELV problem are many and very heterogeneous. They are linked together by technical and economic relationships that are policy-sensitive and are significant for innovation. These links are also at the core of the initiatives for managing ELV developed in the various countries. A simplified scheme of the relationships is presented in Figure 1.

The European car industry has an oligopolistic structure with few producers operating with scale economies in differentiated products at the international or global level. During the 1980s and 1990s, the industry was subject to rapid industrial and strategic changes in which technological innovations, including those on materials, played a significant role (see, among others, Bianchi 1989, Calabrese 1997, Graves 1994, Wells and Rawlinson 1994).

The European dismantling industry, which has a pivotal role in the ELV problem, is characterised by an great number of operators most of which are small and technically backward – as labour intensive operations prevails – and with a limited geographical scope. A significant amount of illegal dismantling operations occurs in some countries. There is, however, a core of more efficient and well-organised dismantlers and the development of ELV management initiatives tends to enlarge this core.

The shredding industry performs the operations leading to metal/material recovery for recycling and the generation of ASR. In most European countries, the shredders are few large companies exploiting plant economies of scale, and some of them are also integrated with metal recyclers and producers. The strategic significance of ELV for shredders depends on the possibility to reduce the economic and environment-related costs of ASR disposal through its reduced amount or the development of additional economic uses.

The other main actors in ELV are the recycling industries and the material producers. The two industrial activities are vertically integrated in some sectors.

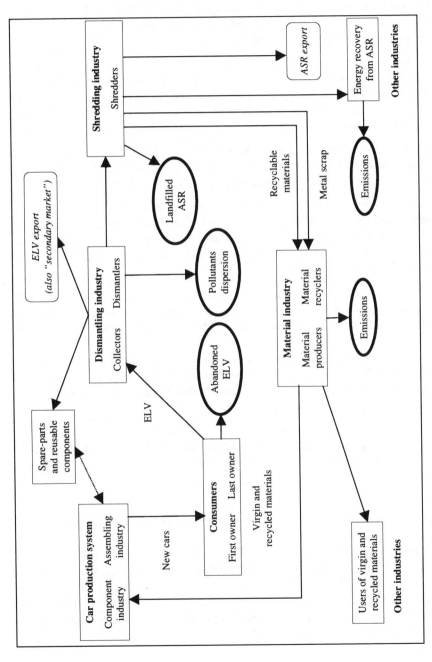

Figure 1:   The ELV system

Primary and recycled plastics producers are generally part of big companies of the chemical industry that have been subject to extensive restructuring during the 1980s and 1990s as a consequence of technological innovation, industrial reorganisation and globalisation. Given the importance of plastic recycling for solving ELV waste problem, plastics producers and recyclers consider ELV as a threat to their increasing control of key segments of the car material market as well as to their increasing role in the car components' industry.

The interest that metal producers/recyclers attach to ELV is twofold: (a) the possibility to stabilise supply of raw materials (scrap), given the importance of ELV for the well-developed secondary metal industry, and (b) an opportunity to contrast the ascent of plastics in car material market. These strategic attitudes are obviously differentiated between the different metal industries.

The other material industries involved in ELV (mainly glass, textile, rubber) seem to have a relatively passive attitude towards the problem, although some companies might have benefits from the increasing availability of recyclable materials.

Consumers are significant actors in ELV. They can decide about the timing of car renewal and, thus, the average age of ELV, and about the delivery to dismantlers (and to which dismantler) or the dispersion of ELV in the environment. Consumers have, however, a little role in influencing key factors as the material mix in car making and the forms of ASR disposal.

In the ELV relationships' chain, the car industry is a very important customer for many material industries and a very important supplier of scrap (through the final consumers) for downstream operations, i.e. dismantling, shredding, recycling, the latter being also the link between the two sides of the ELV chain. In both the upstream and the downstream part of the chain, competition is significant (e.g. between material suppliers) and the development of ELV policies and industrial experiences are stimulating economic interests that interact with innovation.

Most of the pollution flows focused by ELV policies occur at the level of consumers when they abandon ELV, in the storage/dismantling/shredding phases when they are performed in a non-environmentally sound way, at the level of ASR landfilling. Other policy-sensitive pollution flows are at the level of the ASR energy recovery and material recycling.

2.3 Developments of ELV Policies and Industrial Experiences

During the last decade, the ELV problem was tackled through many initiatives involving European car producers, the other industries of the ELV chain, the national-level and EU-level policy-makers. These developments belong to different categories: car-company experiences, national voluntary agreements between the industries involved, national-level legislation and, finally, the EU-level regulation based on the Directive proposal of 1997.

Most of these developments were in fact triggered by the long process of EU-level regulation making, starting from the inclusion of ELV among the "Priority Waste Streams" by the European Commission in 1989. Although there is some degrees of convergence between the different company-level, national-level and EU-level actions, the similarity is only apparent in many respects, and there are significant differences in the preferred approach and instruments. These differences can be significant for innovation. A simplified synopsis of the situation in the different countries is presented in Table 1. Without go into details, we shall describe in short the situation in some countries and the developments of EU regulation[3].

2.3.1   National-Level and Industry-Level Experiences

Germany

Between the late 1980s and the early 1990s, German car producers established various projects and study-groups that produced the "VDA concept" and a policy position based on "shared responsibility", no specific recycling targets, and the principle of self-regulation by industry for the technical and economic solutions. At the same time, the German Ministry of the Environment (BMU) developed policy proposals based on the principle stated in the WMA of 1986 and the new waste policies arising form the Toepfer Law of 1991. The proposals included "producer responsibility" and free-take back[4], various obligations for car producers and other ELV industries, new regulations on ASR (1992), emphasis on new car conception. The ELV policy debate in Germany evolved rapidly during the last few years. An ELV regulation finally entered into force in Germany in April 1998. It provides that the cars sold after April 1st, 1998 will be subject to free take-back when they will become ELV. Free take back will be applied only to ELV younger than 12 years, and then presumably to cars having still value for the dismantler. ARGE-Altauto, an organisation to which the industries involved participate, coordinates the industrial voluntary pledge on ELV. German car maker have taken various practical initiatives[5]. Two main patterns were followed. The first one can be referred to German shredders and metal producers. Large steel companies as Kloeckner, Preussang and Thyssen-Sonnenberg signed private contracts with car manufactures for organising the processing of ELV according to rigorous environmental standards. An example is the agreement between PRG (Preussang), Volkswagen-Audi and associated car dismantlers of 1994. The other pattern is based on the creation of an independent car dismantler network associated to car producers. This is the approach followed by BMW, Opel and Ford (see

---

3   See Zoboli 1998 and IDSE-CNR 1999 for more details.
4   In general, free take-back is the possibility for the last car-owner to receive a refund for the payment possibly requested the dismantler accepting the car.
5   See Den Hond (1996) and Schenk (1998).

BMW Recycling 1996). The car dismantlers in the network are bound by individual contracts specifying the technical and environmental profile of operations.

Table 1:   ELV initiatives and policies in EU countries (at July 1999)

Country	Agreement/ Legislation	Status	Cost/FTB*	Recovery targets**	
Austria	Industry + government + legislation	Signed 1992 - extended 1996 Effective 1995	Free^	from 80% up to 95%	
Belgium***	Industry + government	Signed Jun-99	Free^	85%>2005	95%>2015
Denmark	Legislation	Draft	Levy fund		
Finland	Industry + legislation	In discussion			
France	Industry + government	Effective 1993	No	85% >2002	95%>2015
Germany	Industry + legislation	Approved 1997 In force 1998	FTB	85% >2002	95%>2015
Greece	No specific initiatives				
Ireland	In preparation				
Italy	Industry + government + legislation	Started 1992 Protocol 1997 Effective 1997	No	85% >2002	95%>2010
Luxembourg	No specific initiatives				
Netherlands	Industry + government + legislation	Effective 1995	Recycling fee on new cars	86%>2000	
Portugal	Industry + government	Signed Jun-99	No	85% >2005	95%>2015
Spain	Industry + government	Effective 1996	No	85% >2002	95%>2015
Sweden	Industry + legislation	Effective 1975 Prod. Resp. 1998	FTB	85% >2002	95%>2015
UK	Industry + Government	Signed 1997	No	85% >2002	95%>2015

*   FTB: free take-back or cost reimbursement for last owner incurring costs in delivering to dismantler; Free^: free only for last-owner with new/old car sale.
**   Including reuse, recycling and incineration, in percent of car weight.
***   Project of law in Flanders, including FTB, similar to EU Directive proposal, with the same targets.
Source: based on information from Ford, Org-Consult and national sources.

France

In 1993, the French government and the industries involved in ELV agreed on the "Accord Cadre". The *Accord Cadre* includes specific objectives for reducing ELV disposal, the coordination among the participants based on free market principles, and free choice among different technologies and technical approaches, including energy recovery (see Aggeri and Hatchuel 1997, EEA 1997). The ELV industrial experiences in France was developed with different approaches by the two main car producers, i.e. Renault and PSA Peugeot Citroen (see Den Hond 1996, Renault 1998, personal communications). Renault developed a comprehensive approach to ELV based on the development of a logistic system, the development of recycling and energy recovery technologies, the improvement of recyclability. Great attention was devoted from the beginning to the research on plastic recyclability. The main partnership for developing ELV operations was with CFF-Compagnie General des Ferrailles. Currently, Currently, Renault has a network of approximately 200 dismantlers associated (see Renault 1998). The PSA Peugeot Citroen experience is mainly based on the project in Saint-Pierre-de-Chandieu. The main features of the project are the cooperation with CFF and with Vicat, a cement manufacturer, for the development of energy recovery from ASR.

The Netherlands

The Dutch policy on ELV was developed between late 1980s and early 1990s and resulted in the action programme of 1992. The target was to achieve an 86 per cent recycling rate by 2000 and the main policy instruments were different from those prevailing in the other national experiences. The system, in force from 1995, is based on a waste disposal fee paid by the first owner on new cars registered in the Netherlands (see ARN 1998, OECD 1996). The fees are delivered to a fund which reimburse the dismantlers and shredders for the extra costs incurred in draining and dismantling under the condition that their environmental performance is certified. An independent company, the ARN -Autorecycling Netherlands BV, representing industry's organisations, manages the system. The nation-wide network of dismantlers associated to ARN was composed by 266 companies in 1996. The system processed 210,000 ELV in 1996, corresponding to 80 per cent of total ELV in the country. 15,000 tons of 13 different materials (batteries, tyres, glass, rubber strips, PUR foam, etc.) and parts were dismantled. The possible competition impacts of the Dutch scheme have been questioned (see OECD 1996).

The United Kingdom

The ELV policy developments in the United Kingdom gave rise to the ACORD initiative (Automotive Consortium on Recycling and Disposal) which involved the car manufacturers and importers (SMMT), material and component suppliers, shredders, dismantlers, recycling industry and the Departments of Industry and of Environment. After a preliminary plan in 1992, ACORD launched the implementation plan in 1995 and was signed in 1997. The principles are those of shared responsibility and coordinated actions by the various industries. A research group (CARE) is supporting the agreement actions at the technical level. ASR energy recovery was included among the possible solutions. The targets are a recovery rate of 85 per cent by 2002 and a recovery rate of 95 per cent by 2015 (see IPEE 1996, ACORD 1998, personal communications).

Italy

ELV management in Italy is based on the initiative by FIAT through the FARE system (Fiat Auto Recycling). The system is operating since 1992 and was developed as an agreement between the car producer, a network of dismantling companies, one shredder and recycling companies in various sectors. The principles underlying the initiative are those of shared responsibility and free market. A national level agreement under the auspices of the Ministry of the Environment, which do not includes financial incentives, is under discussion. The FARE system is based on the integration of different activities with the main focus on dismantling and the creation of outlets for recyclates (including "cascade recycling") as well as ASR (energy recovery). Starting from few (six) dismantlers involved at the beginning, the participating dismantlers became 312 in all the Italian regions in 1997. The system includes the reciprocal agreement with Renault, BMW, and Rover. From the start of the FARE system to December 1997, more than 771,000 cars were treated and 21,290 tons of non-metallic materials were recycled (Di Carlo et al. 1998).

Other Countries

Excluding Finland, Greece and Luxembourg, most of the European countries have taken some initiatives on ELV that belongs to different categories: voluntary agreements between industries (similarly to Italy); VAs which include the government in the agreement (similarly to the UK); VAs together with formal national legislation on ELV (similarly to Germany and the Netherlands). Among the other experiences with specific legislation, a notable example is Sweden, where the car producers started in 1994 to develop projects and industrial agreement experiences (see ECRIS 1998) and a producer-responsibility system is in force from 1997. Among the experiences of VAs backed by governments (and some pieces of legislation) are Austria and Spain. The Austrian agreement came into force in 1996. In Spain, a framework agreement on ELV was signed in 1996 covering the period up to 2000. An agreement is being developed in Belgium (see Peelman 1999).

2.3.2   The EU Directive Proposal

After the inclusion of ELV among the "priority waste streams" in 1989, in the framework of the "Community Strategy for Waste Management", the European ELV Project Group was established in 1991 with the participation of European car producers, plastics producers, steel and glass producers, car dismantlers and shredders, member-states' representatives. The ELV Project Group produced a "strategy" in 1994 (ELV Project Group 1994). In addition to specific targets, the strategy also suggested a wide range of regulatory measure, including those at the Community level.

The EU-level regulation took the form of a Directive proposal, mainly representing the positions of DGXI, presented in 1997 (European Commission 1997). The Directive proposal explicitly departed from the background discussions by making specific regulation choices according to the view that ELV is mainly a waste management problem (see in particular Onida 1999). The Proposal caused various adverse reactions by the industrial actors (see in particular ACEA 1998), although with some notable differences among them. An extensive lobbying activity developed. At the Parliament debate in February 1999 the Proposal received more than 200 proposed amendments and some of them were accepted. In March 1999, the Council decided to postpone the approval until June 1999 upon request by the German delegation. In April 1999 the Commission produced an amended proposal.

The main provisions of the 1997 Directive proposal (European Commission 1997), some amendments by the Parliament (European Commission 1999a) and the amended proposal by the Commission (European Commission 1999b) are summarised below[6].

Collection. The collection of ELV up to 100 per cent should be achieved. The regulations on dismantling certificates and the free take-back should promote the achievement (see below).

Targets. By 2005 the recovery or reuse rate of *all* ELV will have to achieve 85 per cent in terms of weight and recycling or reuse 80 per cent; by 2015 the reuse or recovery rate of *all* ELV will have to be 95 per cent of the weight and reuse or recycling 85 per cent. The Parliament emended the targets by establishing that, for vehicles that received type-approval *before* 2005, the re-use/recovery shall be increased to a minimum of 85 per cent and, from 2015, to a minimum of 95 per cent (recycling not mentioned); for vehicles that received type approval *after* 2005 reuse/recovery shall increase to 95 per cent of weight by 2015, while reuse/recycling shall increase to 85 per cent.

Preference for mechanical recycling. Although energy recovery from ELV waste is implicitly allowed in the 1997 proposal up to 10 per cent of weight by 2015, material recovery is considered a priority "when environmentally viable". Further to the above reformulation of targets on re-use/recycling/recovery rates, the Parliament introduced the additional requirement that this preference is without

---

6   The Directive applies to vehicles and end-of-life vehicles of category M1 and N1 as defined in Annex II (A) to Directive 70/156/EEC and two or three wheel vehicles; the latter are excluded form the provisions of Articles 4 and 7 of the Directive.

prejudice to safety and environmental requirements of components, in particular those on exhaust gases and noise.

Authorised dismantling. The collection/storage/dismantling facilities must be authorised and registered. Last owners have to deliver ELV to authorised dismantling facilities, which have to fulfil various environmental requirements specified in the Directive. The last owners will receive a certificate of destruction which is a condition for the deregistration of the vehicle. The Parliament introduced the possibility to deliver ELV to the dealers/producers and made more detailed and precise requirements on storage-treatment for authorised dismantlers. The amended proposal substantially confirmed these provisions.

Heavy metals and PVC. Lead, mercury, chromium, cadmium shall be recycled or phased-out from new vehicles and prevented from being shredded, landfilled and incinerated. The environmental impacts of PVC will be faced by stimulating the progressive substitution by car producers; future horizontal initiatives, possibly leading to PVC phasing-out, will be considered by the Commission. The provisions on metals was modified by the Parliament by introducing a list of uses and limit-values for lead, mercury and hexavalent chromium in car components from 2005, while making more precise the exclusion of landfilling for lead, cadmium and hexavalent chromium from 2001 and shredding/landfilling/incineration for mercury.

Producer responsibility. The principle of producer responsibility is adopted. Free take-back of ELV is provided by allowing the last owner of a car with limited recoverability/recyclability (negative market value), to be entitled to receive reimbursement by the car producer of the costs incurred in delivering to the authorised dismantler. The provision was weakened by the Parliament by establishing that Member States shall ensure that "their respective collection systems do not give rise to any costs to the last holder and/or owner at delivery of the vehicle to an authorised treatment facility" when ELV possibly have a negative market value.

Recyclability. Specific measures, in the form of amendments on type approval regulations and the development of specific European standards, will be introduced to ensure that vehicles approved from 2005 will be reusable/recyclable to a minimum of 85 per cent and reusable/recoverable to a minimum of 95 per cent of weight through the development of "design for dismantling" and "design for recycling". Dismantling information and manuals should be provided to dismantling facilities. These provisions were integrated by Parliament amendments through the reference to producer responsibility and the need that car producers initiate these developments immediately.

Voluntary agreements. The Parliament introduced the possibility that Member States develop voluntary agreements with economic operators – a possibility not considered by the 1997 Proposal – to comply with article 5(1) on ELV collection. According to some interpretations (personal communications) this means also the implicit exclusion of national-level as well EU-level VAs for the other activities in the ELV chain.

In the Council session of June 1999, the difficulty of reaching a "common position" was still very clear. The possible solution emerging from the Council is to bring forward the date of entry into force of the free take-back obligation and the postponement of the date for vehicles already in the market.

3   The Regulation-Innovation Mechanism

If we accept a definition of innovation that includes organisational change as well as non-measurable adaptations of a qualitative nature (see Kemp 1997, Kemp et al. 1998), the developments in ELV management represent an extensive innovation process in which regulation has a significant role. We shall discuss the feature of the regulation-innovation mechanism at four levels.

The first level is the description of some specific innovations – still at uneven degree of development, from R&D to practical implementation – occurring in the car and other industries to address the ELV issue. The description is very selective and simplified (see IDSE-CNR 1999 for more details).

The second level is the systemic nature of the innovation process that involves combinations of interrelated changes by different actors, and a learning process that is differentiated among the different companies and the different national contexts.

The third level is the interpretation of the observed interactions between policy making and innovation (or between policy makers and industries) from the point of view of their reference principles and their use of technical knowledge.

The fourth level is the possibly critical role of specific policy instrument as a selection device even in the case they are part of complex policy packages as the EU Directive.

3.1   A Selection of Specific Innovations

Recycling departments and competencies. Between late-1980s and early-1990s, all the major European car producers (e.g. BMW, Daimler, FIAT, Ford, Peugeot, Renault, Rover, Volkswagen, Volvo) have created internal functions, generally inside the environmental departments, addressing ELV and recycling. In general, they have the features of a crossroads between heterogeneous tasks and competencies. They manage the relationships with other actors of ELV in the framework of covenants and VAs (if any), manage the R&D experiences and the pilot projects of the company (e.g. on dismantling), interact with the other functions and departments for the development of design for dismantling (DFD) and design for recycling (DFR), and interact with material and component suppliers. They are also the link with other car producers for information exchanges. The significance attributed to these departments is uneven in the different companies, but they represent the creation of functionally specialised competencies and skills not existing before in a structured form.

Design for dismantling. Most car producers have studied and adopted solutions for favouring efficient dismantling (reduce dismantling time and/or recover more and/or recover better). DFD sometimes consists of small changes in the part-assembling systems but, in other cases, it implies the change of some components and, thus, adaptations in other components and parts that can spill into more extensive design changes. These developments generally involve cooperative interactions inside and outside the company. Most car producers then introduced, during the last few years, dismantling manuals for each car model to be supplied to (associate) dismantlers and applied marking systems in order to identify the different polymers according to the available ISO and other standards.

Design for recycling. The developments of DFR are guided by still evolving criteria. DFR requires definitions and measures of recyclability. The common view by car producers is that, although from the technical point of view almost everything is recyclable, the problems for recyclability arise on economic grounds. Various materials from car do not have established secondary markets or can be so difficult to extract from alloys and combinations – mainly determined by the components' functions – that their recycling have to face lacking demand and economic losses. The problem, which is at the very core of the ELV issue, is selectively more significant for some materials, e.g. some polymers (see Mayne 1998, Ratcliffe 1994, Van den Berg et al. 1998). Recyclability is then a mixed technical and economic concept (see also Bontoux at al. 1996). Producers have tried to develop "recyclability coefficients" for the different models that include technical and economic variables and are usually not publicly available. In essence, we can speak of DFR as the prescription to use recyclable materials whenever possible, given the functions that materials, parts and components have to perform and given the relative costs of different materials. Recycling departments of various companies produce DFR manuals for internal designers that include the options and suggestions about recyclability choices, which are updated according to evolution of both internal knowledge and external variables.

DFR and LCA. The DFD and DFR manuals are part of a more general propensity to develop environment-related decision tools, and in particular LCA studies. Many car producers make LCA analysis but, in many cases, it is still limited to specific materials or single components because car is considered a too complex product to have complete LCAs (personal communications). Typically, LCA in car gives rise to a series of trade-offs even at the level of environmental impacts of different material/component choices. To solve trade-offs, additional technical or economic variables are used, including perceptions about the priorities of social actors (consumers, opinion makers) and policy making. This confirms that, at the practical level, the current state of LCA remains weak in many respects (see Ayres 1997, European Commission 1998).

DFR and material competition. The approach to DFR based on "use-recyclables-whenever-possible" criteria seems to push towards a simplified material regime somewhat biased in favour of traditional materials or "easily" (i.e. economically) recyclable materials. During the last two decades, the trend towards increasing intensity of polymers in car making assumed an extraordinary significance on many grounds, including the environmental one through lightness (see Amendola 1990, APME 1996, Cardani and De Liso 1991, Cohendet and Ledoux 1994). This trend seems to be slowing down despite the still very large potential of innovative polymer-based advanced materials, in particular composites (see APME 1998). The inter-polymer competition seems to be increasing and it favours those plastics with the best recycling possibilities. A relative decrease of thermosetting plastics and resins, which have difficulties in recycling, is observed while the thermoplastics share is relatively increasing. Among the thermoplastics, polypropylene is gaining share in Japanese and European car models. Composites materials are far from being favoured by recyclability requirements while they preserve a very important favourable position for energy and emission-saving requirements. These trends suggest the possibly ambiguous nature of the ELV-related innovation on environmental grounds (see below). In general, the changing environment for intra-material and inter-material competition is giving rise to an intensification of R&D efforts. The latter applies in particular to polymers but also to metals, rubber, and textiles (see Barbiroli 1999).

"Traditional" material competition. The ELV problem stimulates competition also between "traditional" materials, and in particular metals[7]. The position of steel in car production seems somewhat reinforced by ELV regulation given its well-developed secondary market. However, the Directive provisions for lead and other non-ferrous metals, which are intensively used in alloys, introduce a fundamental uncertainty, and the research process on substitutes and alternative solutions is already started. Other material substitution processes at work in car material regime have more ambiguous origins and implications. This is the case in particular with aluminium (AL). The trend bringing AL up to 10 per cent of total weight in some car models reflects its combination of favourable properties. It is fully recyclable and its lightness gives aluminium – especially recycled AL intensively used in car – very favourable LCA balances. However, AL is mainly a substitute for steel and other fully recycled metals and this reduces its contribution to

---

[7]   The inclusion of metals among "traditional" materials can be highly misleading and it is used here only for convenience of presentation. In facts, many metals, e.g. steel and its alloys, are subject to extensive innovation processes that change the properties of these materials up to the possibility of considering them as advanced materials (see, among others, Cohendet and Ledoux 1994).

overall recyclability. Given that AL reduces the weight and recycling targets are defined in percentage of total weight, the paradoxical result might be that the substitution of AL for steel can reduce – and not increase – the attainment of the non-disposal targets[8].

Energy recovery form ASR. Although the EU Directive seems to limit its possible development, the energy recovery of ASR and tyres (rubber) as well as other uses of ASR (e.g. cement industry) attracted significant innovative efforts. As mentioned above, the energy use of ASR has been a part of ELV pilot projects in France, Italy and Germany, while its use in the cement industry was tried in France. The increase of energy recovery of tyres is giving rise to experimental efforts in various countries also in combination with energy-from-waste developments. Plastic producers, given the advantages they can get from solutions based on energy recovery also support these experiences.

3.2   Systemic Features of the Innovation Process

Some of the above innovations – as DFD, DFR and material substitution – have a systemic nature at the micro-level because each specific change is usually accompanied by other technically-coherent changes aimed at preserving the function of the components involved. The systemic nature of ELV innovation, however, is much more general in that it requires common efforts and closer relationships between different industries. These features are revealed by both the development of VAs as heterogeneous inter-industry agreements and the EU Directive proposal that, differently from other waste regulations, covers the ELV treatment aspects together with some product-making aspects. The systemic relationships depend on at least two factors.

The first one is that some innovations occurring in a specific phase of the ELV chain require, for *technical and/or economic* reasons, other innovations in other parts of the ELV chain.

The second factor is that ELV-related innovation is a *finalised process* aiming at achieving specific objectives on decreasing ASR landfilled – be they self-imposed or imposed by policy. The "measurement" of the different innovations in terms of their contribution to the objectives reveals that none of them, if taken alone, seems to be able to achieve the targets.

---

8   Suppose that the initial weight of a car is 1000 kg with 750 kg of steel (75 per cent recyclable) and 250 kg of other materials (25 per cent non-recyclable). Suppose that 650 kg of aluminium can completely substitute for 750 kg steel giving rise to a weight decrease to 900 kg but still including 250 kg of non-recyclable materials. The recyclable share (aluminium) of total weight now amounts to around 72 per cent while the non-recyclable one is around 28 per cent.

The most important aspect of systemic relationships is that they define a dynamic process still far from equilibrium (if any). Different *innovation paths*, composed by interrelated specific innovations, are still open and their expected results are uncertain, given that some of the required innovations are still constrained by economic variables as well as policies.

Let us sketch, in a very simplified way, two alternative general innovation paths that can be defined as "market creation path" and "car conception path" (Figure 2).

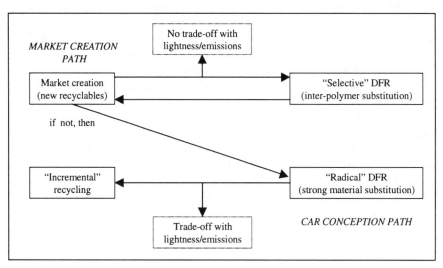

Figure 2:   Two general innovation paths

Market creation path. Taking as given the current material composition of a car, the sustainable achievement of a reduced amount of landfilled ASR is, in general, a problem of market creation for the parts, components and materials currently not recovered, reused and recycled (3RE). The "market creation path" is only partially a problem of incremental 3RE at the margin for materials that have already a market (e.g. steel). Take, for example, the creation of markets for recycled plastics. Some innovations are needed for the technical suitability of recycled plastics for existing or new uses, both outside and inside the car industry (i.e. closed-loop markets). This is not enough, however. In order to have the economic suitability of these innovative uses, appropriate (innovative) changes in the dismantling organisation are needed to have the materials at the appropriate quantities, qualities and costs. The latter achievements can be greatly helped by innovations in car making through the developments in DFD that, as described above, can have flexible boundaries with DFR. This can push in the direction of inter-polymer competition and selective polymer substitution. At the end, not only the process require interdependent changes but the increasing recycling of some polymers might have detrimental effects on other polymers in car material mix. In general, by preserving the role of polymers in car making, this path can be non-detrimental for the achievement of environmental goals on energy-emission to which the lightness of plastics greatly contributes. An alternative route of market creation is the development of energy recovery of ASR. It would create less complex feedbacks on the ELV chain, but it would involve the development of other (innovative) relationships with industries using ASR as energy source which are subject to other economic and technical constraints.

Car-conception path. The possible difficulties in pursuing the "market creation path", and thus in maintaining a stable material mix (in terms of material groups), can stimulate to pursue more radical adaptations in the upstream part of the ELV system, i.e. at the level of design and material choice. Let us define this innovation direction as "car conception path". Leaving aside for a moment the possible regulatory constraints to the use of specific materials (e.g. lead) and the associated innovation impulses, a radical design choice could be the substitution of those materials having weak markets for recycling. Suppose that they are some polymers and composites, and that substitution process favours some metals. The consequences could be extensive. A limitation on material choice, in particular on plastics, requires coherent adaptations, and the micro-technical compromises cannot eliminate the need for re-conception of various functions or performance aspects. Polymer-based materials, in fact, are at the core of the new material regime prevailing from the 1970s. Further to their contribution to production and assembling simplification, plastics and composite materials assumed an essential role for compensating the energy consumption and emission impact of the trend towards an increase in average car weight. Despite the significant role of engine technology and fuel enhancement, lightness remains an essential requirement for pursuing the trajectory of a low emission car, which is essential in the framework of post-Kyoto commitments by the car industry[9]. The possible trade-off between lower emission levels and more recyclability suggests that ELV innovation paths are open to other car innovation sub-systems, in particular that of energy-emission efficiency. Furthermore, it must be noted that the "car conception path", by involving radical choices on DFR and material mix, also changes the problem of markets for recycling. It reduces the need for developing "new" recycling market (e.g. some plastics) and creates, instead, a problem of marginally increasing quantities in well-established recycling markets (e.g. metals). Finally, the "car conception path" tends to reduce the need for innovations in ASR energy recovery.

The above paths are a very stylised picture and the real process has many other technical and economic degrees of freedom as well as technical and economic

---

[9]   The 1998 agreement between ACEA, the association of European car producers, and the European Commission includes the commitment by car producers to reduce CO2 emissions from new cars by 25 per cent in ten years up to 140g/CO2 per km in 2008.

constraints[10]. What is more, depending on many different variables, the two paths can be alternative, as sketched above, but can also be complementary through selective combinations, and then they can (or must) be pursued together. Various possibilities are still open because many specific innovations composing the two paths are not still well established or unevenly developed in the different company-level and national-level experiences.

The systemic relationships and the different innovation paths highlight some essential features of ELV innovation (see Zoboli 1998 for details).

First, although the car industry is the main actor and the "natural" leader/coordinator of the process, the other industries in the ELV chain have a specific innovative role to play that cannot be assumed by the car industry. The most natural way to tackle ELV is therefore to create inter-industry agreements based on integrated approaches, as the VAs illustrated in Section 2.3. Some of the relationships are completely new because the car industry traditionally had few operational links with the downstream (post-consumer) operations (dismantling, shredding, recycling, energy recovery). At the same time, the well-established links between car companies and the components and material industries receive new emphasis because of the common innovative effort to be done in both the "market creation" and "car conception" paths.

Second, the innovation process has the features of a knowledge process, marked by gradual achievements, uncertainty and learning from experience. It can be characterised as a capability creation process (see in particular Den Hond 1996) which is largely company-specific while entailing various externalities. The process is far from being completed as the car and the other industries are still exploring various possibilities and maintaining open as many options as possible. The flexibility asked by car makers in the adoption of different solutions also derives, therefore, from the still incomplete knowledge of the dynamic outcomes of various options from both the technical and economic point of view.

Third, given its capability dimension, the innovation process is differentiated between different companies and different national context. Although there are various similarities between the ELV initiatives by car makers, some car companies are more advanced along the "market creation path" and others along the "car conception path". The asymmetries depend on company-specific factors (e.g. different capabilities gained on DFD and DFR) but they also depend to a significant extent on the national features of the dismantling industry, material industries, recovery/recycling markets. The inter-industry dimension of the innovation process gives a great role to capabilities external to the car companies, and some capa-

---

[10]   For example, the creation of closed-loop markets for plastics in car making is bounded by the limited amount of demand for recycled plastics with specific properties in "cascade recycling" (see RECAP 1997).

bilities are localised in a defined geographical framework, especially in the "market creation path".

Fourth, given that both innovation paths involve a variety of actors and imply incremental and uncertain costs, economic variables assume a critical role for the features of the innovative process. Economic conflicts and competition on various grounds parallel technical co-operation. The incremental cost of "market creation", for example, creates distributional conflicts between dismantlers and other industries. Material substitution processes related to DFR induce the search for competitive responses that are based, however, on innovative solutions arising from technical cooperation with car makers.

Finally, the ELV innovation process is not closed in itself and is, instead, open to other areas of innovation in car making – especially environmental aspects as energy, emissions and climate – through technological variables (e.g. lightness) that can be influenced by the choice about different innovation paths. In this way, ELV is an open system even in terms of the relevant regulatory framework.

3.3   Interactions between Regulation Making and the Innovation Process

Innovation in ELV is apparently a case of impulse-response mechanism. In the absence of (expected) regulations and given the relatively high rate of recycling from car, the increase of non-disposal rate would have been the least concern by the car-related industries, except in the case that an upward trend in relative material and energy prices stimulated investments in recycling. Regulation can thus be considered the main cause of the innovation process. Furthermore, innovative response by industry seems to follow a standard model in which the short term adaptations based on organisational solutions are followed in the longer run by more radical changes (as DFR or innovations in plastics recycling). Finally, also compared to other environmental problems, innovation seems to be the main – or even the only – way for solving the ELV problem. The main involved actors are industries, no alternatives to reorganising and innovating do exist, and the making (up to the design) of a technologically complex product as the car is addressed.

The actual regulation-innovation relationship in ELV is much more complex, however, than suggested by the "linear model" of impulse-response. It is highly interactive and rich of feed-backs at each step, it is uncertain in terms of causation and it is endogenised to some extent. It requires a different representation in which the impulse is influenced by expected responses and the responses are influenced by expected impulses. Although these features might be neither new nor specific, as suggested by models highlighting the game-theoretical nature of environmental policy making, the case of ELV has some peculiarities.

First, the regulation-innovation relationship develops in a long time-frame – more than ten years – and different phases can be distinguished in which the interactions works in a different ways.

Second, it shows a specific attitude by regulation maker in taking into account the technical and economic knowledge arising from innovation experiences.

Third, it shows the possibly critical role of specific policy choices and instruments, even though they are part of complex policy packages, in giving the direction of the innovation process.

3.3.1 Interactions in Three Phases

Three different phases can be distinguished in the ELV regulation-innovation relations.

The first phase was that of problem identification, exploration and early experiences, and went approximately from the inclusion of ELV among Priority Waste Streams by the Commission (1989) to the conclusions of the ELV Project Group work (1994). This phase was marked by a collaborative discussion between the industries involved and policy makers in search for options' definition. During this phase, some innovative responses emerged, at least as a start-up, as in the cases of research investments and pilot experiences on plastic recycling, the car industry experiments on dismantling, the first cooperation schemes between car industry and associate dismantlers, the early definitions on DFD and DFR. The car-company specificity of these experiences, and then their asymmetries, did not allow significant actual achievements to occur. However, the early results of technical and organisational experiences created the reference for the technical contents of a regulation, and in particular the possibility of defining common recovery/recycling targets for ELV policy. In this phase, most of the national level policy scheme were designed (e.g. Germany, the Netherlands, the United Kingdom, Austria) or initiated (e.g. France, Sweden, Italy).

The second phase can be considered that from the conception of the EU Directive proposal (*circa* 1995) to the Directive approval (expected) in 1999. This phase was marked by a breakdown in the cooperative attitude between European environmental policy makers and most of economic actors involved in ELV. The Commission proposed a directive not indeed tailored on the positions of the car makers and other industries, although supported by some of the latter (i.e. dismantlers). The car and the other industries pursued various directions, most of them along the innovation lines defined in the first phase. At the same time, car producers went on with the development of organisational links with dismantlers and shredders, as well as plastic and other material producers. The plastic industry intensified the research on technological options for polymers in car making. Further steps on DFR were made in some companies. In the meantime, a significant lobbying activity by the different stakeholders occurred, also based on the accumulated knowledge and experience. During this phase, other national policy schemes or VAs, also backed by legislation, entered into force (the Netherlands, Austria, the United Kingdom) or where designed. In particular, the Dutch scheme created a new possible approach stimulating a strong opposition by car makers.

The third phase will start from the approval of the EU Directive and its transposition in the national legislations. Although the final version of the Directive might change in some important details and national-level transposition will surely take into account "national interests", the Directive will not create a favourable framework for national-level VAs. At the same time, many countries now have VAs with different features at different stage of development, including different instruments at work. Some of the Directive provisions (e.g. the possibility of free take-back) can create the potential for changing attitudes by some key actors of the national-level VAs, e.g. dismantlers and car makers. Furthermore, the regulation-innovation mechanism will shift towards the relationships between industry and standardisation bodies for defining recyclablity criteria in type-approval. In general, it can be expected that the Directive transposition process will reduce the variety of options and innovation possibilities currently open.

In the three-phases scheme, the most visible fact is that significant innovations occurred – or at least began – as early as the first phase and many developed during the second phase *before* the most important regulation impulse at EU level was completed and introduced in the system. This suggests that policy formation process itself had the nature of a complex impulse. This is mainly the result of a two-fold strategy by the car industry. On the one hand, industry tried to prevent a policy impulse in the form of detailed regulation and/or to influence its features through the result of VAs. On the other hand, car companies tried to not be the laggard and be prepared to operate in a regulated environment. This suggests the great role of *regulation expectations* in inducing innovation (see also Segerson and Miceli 1997).

The inability to avoid detailed regulation, although with the partial successes of some Parliament amendments, highlights the different attitudes of industry and policy makers on at least two grounds: the intra-EU harmonisation issue; the reference principles and the use of technological and economic knowledge in regulation making.

3.3.2 Harmonisation

The innovation outcomes of national-level and company-level VAs were asymmetric during both the first and the second phase, after ten years of problem story and experiences. The diversity can be considered "natural" in many respects, given the above-described features of the innovation process and the asymmetric importance of the car industry in the different countries. The ELV problem is unevenly distributed among European countries. Five countries account for over 80 per cent of European total "production", while "true" ELV trade (export) is estimated to be not significant. Other national asymmetries occurring in the dismantling-shredding-recycling capabilities have been mentioned above.

The obvious question is: does this "natural" asymmetry create the potential for internal markets distortions?

The answer by the car industry is that it does not. Voluntary agreements reflecting the national and companies' diversities and capabilities are considered as the best solution. Dismantling is the key phase to be harmonised because uneven dismantling rules and requirements can attract ELV flow across boundaries in search for the best conditions with distorting effects on competition. The possibility of reciprocal agreements between companies of different countries, as experienced by BMW, Renault, FIAT, can be another instrument to avoid distortions. Therefore, the main role of EU regulation should be to establish targets and regulate dismantling while leaving the countries choose their ways of attainment. In general, this position seems to fit the principles of recent international environmental agreements that allows even for differentiated targets among nations, given the excess costs induced by uniform targets for those countries with the lowest capabilities. Furthermore, it seems that in the case of ELV there is not the risk of the "race to the bottom" that justifies the centralisation of policies, even in derogation to subsidiarity principles, in other environmental areas (see Oates 1998 for a discussion). It can be noted, however, that the introduction of the Dutch scheme illustrates the possible implications of a complete freedom in choosing the instruments in national VAs because, according to some car-makers' view, the Dutch policy instruments create market distortions (personal communications).

The position of EU regulators is clearly different: uncoordinated national initiatives can create distorted competition. The argument applies specifically to dismantling but the Directive proposal takes this attitude at a more general level. The differences between the national schemes, both at work and being implemented, are considered to be too large for accepting national-level VAs as the main instrument for ELV management in Europe. What is needed is a common legislation background in all the countries. A Directive is considered as a sufficiently flexible instrument for allowing national-level variations around a common set of rules. However, the possibility of FTB in the Directive, while reflecting the great importance correctly attributed to the dismantling phase in the ELV problem, introduces the possibility that uneven *economic* conditions applies to dismantling in the different countries. FTB levels cannot be harmonised, and this might have the same effects of uneven environmental rules for dismantling in different countries (see Zoboli 1998).

The problem of harmonisation, therefore, is conditioned by fundamental uncertainties about *economic* behaviours in the system to be harmonised, and it leaves rooms for different positions that can be, to some extent, all flawed in some respects. In other words, harmonisation seems not to be the most critical issue in the design of ELV policy.

3.3.3 Economic and Technological Knowledge, and Policy Principles

While the policy position of industries seems to be dominated by technical knowledge and economic concerns, that of policy makers seems to be dominated by general principles and concerns about regulation coherence.

In the case of the industry, the relevant body of knowledge on ELV is that developed by industry itself during the late 1980s and the 1990s, and it has the systemic and dynamic features illustrated above. This knowledge body brings to some reference principles: (a) solutions cannot be forced from outside without creating technical trade-offs and excessive costs; (b) the flexibility of solutions' combination is very significant for targets achievement; (c) solutions have to be found by the car industry together with the other industries, and corresponding cost distribution mechanisms must be established (shared responsibility principle); (d) the development of more dismantling-recovery-recycling should be self-sustained in economic terms by making the opportunities to emerge (free market principle), although some incentives can be appropriate at the start-up.

Obviously, technological knowledge and the related principles have been used also in a strategic way by the industries involved, e.g. by emphasising some aspects in order to save (expected) costs and gain time. Furthermore, it is clear that in the VAs between industries with so different features as those involved in ELV, the problem of relative contractual power remains a moot point.

The position of regulators seems to be, instead, dominated by general principles now well established in European environmental policy. It is generally recognised that the ELV proposed Directive (1997) is in the spirit of the EU packaging directive (1994) and rooted in the same principles. The latter can be considered the producer responsibility principle (PRP) or the extended producer responsibility principle (EPRP), both representing legal-level evolutions of the Polluter-Pays-Principle (PPP). From the legal point of view, the Directive seems to be strongly backed by previous legislation on waste and generally coherent with the general framework supplied by the Treaty, while choosing specific directions when not constrained by the Treaty itself (see Onida 1999).

At the same time, environmental regulators took a specific attitude towards the technological and economic knowledge on ELV. The incompleteness, the variety and the remaining uncertainties of the knowledge produced so far on ELV has been taken as a limit of VAs and industrial initiatives. Furthermore, regulators did consider the knowledge proposed by industries as non-free from self-interest and strategic in nature. Finally, it can be claimed that there is not a truly alternative body of knowledge to that produced by industry, given the limited independent research effort developed by policy making in this specific area. In these conditions, the priority to EPRP can be clearly understood as a way for solving the problem of asymmetric information and assigning the car industry the role of the "best solver" (see Natale 1994) with a full social responsibility also in terms of costs.

The EU Directive, however, makes specific choices about instruments *as if* it is based on a specific (and alternative) knowledge on the technical options and the economic aspects of the ELV problem. This is the case with the limitation on ASR incineration, which implies the technical knowledge about the relative environmental merits of the alternative options in the *specific* case of the ELV. This is also the case with free take-back, which implies the knowledge of the technological – and then environmental – impacts of changing economic relationships in the ELV chain. The same applies to other specific provisions, e.g. DFD/DFR and recyclability, and to the implicit belief that car makers can easily solve the "more recyclability-less emissions" puzzle.

All in all, the EU Directive is rich of knowledge-dependent elements while grounded in the distrust about knowledge supplied by car-makers and in the absence of a truly alternative body of technical, economic, and environmental knowledge on ELV.

The use of knowledge in the Directive-making process deserves a further comment. There is a strong similarity between the targets established by the Directive and those adopted in the VAs. This depends partly on technical factors (similar rates of recovery/recycling and material composition of ELV in different countries). However, the proposition of these targets originated by the industry during the "first phase", when little experience and actual results in ELV management were available. At the same time, it seems that regulators did not elaborate about the socially optimal nature of this targets because such a calculation was considered extremely difficult and unreliable (see Onida 1999). Further to technical factors, the targets reflect, therefore, technological expectations and strategies. The definition of relatively ambitious targets by car makers suggests their self-confidence but, at the same time, the political message that a specific regulation is not needed. Policy makers seem to have taken these indications as the confirmation that the regulation-induced investments are not disruptive for the car and other industries, while taking the asymmetric distance from the targets by the national/company schemes as a demonstration of VAs ineffectiveness. The targets thus are becoming accepted as legally binding[11] while their time-frame specification remains an open issue[12]. This sort of "target game" can also explain why the

---

[11]   The free adoption of the same consensus targets in the national VAs initiated after the Directive presentation can be explained by the need to fit international expectations, even in spite of still lacking achievements.

[12]   The time specification of the targets is indeed of a great significance. The position of the car industry that the recycling targets must apply to car produced after regulation provisions are known and introduced (as reflected in the Parliament amendments) is the attempt to avoid "stranded costs", i.e. costs induced by an unforeseen change in regulation.

main conflicts on ELV rapidly moved on the ground of policy instruments and their relative merits.

3.4   Policy Instruments as a Selection Device

The EU Directive and national-level legislations are complex policy packages based on a combination of heterogeneous instruments. It is very difficult to define the role of specific instruments inside the package in terms of their possible "partial" impact, given their extensive cross-influences. This is a well-known problem with environmental policy, and in particular with the (generally lacking) empirical analysis of economic instruments (see also Hemmelskamp 1997, Zoboli 1994). Nonetheless, the specific features of ELV suggest the possibility to explore the role of specific instruments although it can be done in general terms and, given the lack of experience, mainly on the basis of the (diverging) views expressed by industries and policy makers. Let us consider two much-debated instruments: the limitations to ASR energy recovery and free take-back.

The limitations imposed to ASR energy recovery by the EU Directive tend to reduce the innovative efforts in this direction while giving impulse to innovation investments on "market creation" for recyclable materials, in particular on polymer recyclability. This preference stimulates the feedbacks along the ELV chain that, as described above, involve car makers, dismantlers and material producers. It is interesting to note that this impact brings in the direction of inter-industry relationships and agreements, as those promoted by the car industry but not supported by the EU Directive. Apart from this possible contradiction, this policy choice is selectively more favourable to some companies and countries, i.e. those with relatively more developed capabilities in mechanical recycling, while it is less favourable for those countries where energy recovery from waste is a well developed business. Furthermore, given the probabilistic nature of DFR developments, this policy choice might be selectively favourable to some polymers easier to recycle as well as other materials (e.g. some metals) that might substitute for non-easily recyclable polymers. All in all, the preference for mechanical recycling induces a selection mechanism inside the "market creation" path.

The introduction of free take-back (FTB) reflects the idea that the dismantling/recycling industries are the weakest ring in the ELV chain, and the cost of incremental dismantling/recycling should not be supported by those industries because the high cost is a consequence of car-making choices (design and material mix). In this way, FTB aims to stimulate favourable economic balances in dismantling/recycling and, *at the same time*, to stimulate car producers to make more recyclable cars through design adaptations (see European Commission 1997 and

1999b)[13]. FTB is then an incentive instrument based on expected economic behaviours, similar to the economic instruments for packaging adopted by many countries.

ELV, however, is not a packaging-type problem, and the *actual* impact of FTB can be an open issue because the expected technological and economic reactions cannot be taken for granted[14]. At the cost of some simplifications, the different possibilities can be sketched along the lines of the "innovation paths" described above.

If FTB reduces the costs and increases the economic quality of materials coming from incremental dismantling, it can help to develop recycling of additional materials along the "market creation path". The new recycling markets, however, would be incentive-based, and to see them evolving towards self-sustained markets, innovations in the recyclability of some material, e.g. some plastics, are required. If these recyclability innovations should occur, the value of FTB can be gradually absorbed: car makers can make limited adaptations in design/material mix while paying decreasing amounts of FTB. The need for cooperation inside the whole ELV chain, however, is very clear.

A less optimistic possibility is that innovations in recyclability are not enough to create self-sustained markets. FTB-based incentives might then become permanent subsidies to dismantling/recycling. In this case, car makers can make different choices according to the level of FTB and their technological capabilities. The first one is to preserve material mix and the associated advantages while accepting high FTB costs. The second choice is to make strong design/material adaptations in favour of easy-recyclable traditional materials thus reducing FTB costs. The latter choice would push in the direction that we have depicted as the "car conception path". The problem would become incremental recycling in well-established markets, e.g. metals, where incentives of the FTB-type are considered to be distorting by material producers (personal communications).

An additional uncertainty comes from the possibility that FTB is simply passed to the consumer through car prices. In this case, the innovation incentive of the policy instrument will be greatly reduced, and the main result would be the creation of new recycling markets steadily subsidised by consumers. Other undesired reactions are also possible. Car makers claims, for example, that FTB-type instruments create the incentives for their increasing economic involvement in downstream operations to control the levels of FTB. The result could be that the

---

13 *At the same time,* FTB should be an incentive for the last owner to deliver the car to the dismantler instead of abandoning it in the environment.

14 The differences with the packaging case are *at least* two: due to product differentiation strategies, there is an excess packaging in consumption goods that can be eliminated without substantially changing production processes; consumers can have a greater role in the packaging waste policies compared to the case of ELV.

"power" of car industry on dismantling/recycling industries becomes greater with FTB than with VAs.

In essence, according to a combination of technological and economic factors, FTB can have different innovation outcomes: (a) innovations in recyclability and new self-sustained recycling markets; (b) "backward-oriented" innovations, based on the return to "traditional" recyclable materials in car making[15]; (c) little innovation impacts on car making and new recycling markets subsidised by the consumers. To some extent, a combination of these outcomes is also possible. The limitations imposed on ASR energy recovery can be an additional constraint on the possible outcomes and the same applies to the commitments to reduce greenhouse gas emissions form car.

The innovation/adaptation paths possibly associated to VAs and disposal fees (i.e. the Dutch scheme) are different in that they can solve or, alternatively, amplify some of the uncertainties associated to FTB. The same applies to other instruments so far disregarded by ELV policy, as higher landfill taxes or virgin material taxes. Their possible impacts are different because they address different levels/industries of the ELV system thus putting into motion different reaction sequences (see Mazzanti and Zoboli 1999). These features suggest also the limitations of an approach based on the search of the "optimal" policy instruments (and their combination) when systemic innovation/adaptation do prevail.

The conclusion is that specific instruments can have *selective effects* on the *direction* of the induced innovation. In complex systems as ELV, these effects can be detected only in a probabilistic way, especially in the *ex ante* perspective. However, the awareness about the uncertain working of some policy instruments as *selection devices* should induce to base regulations on a greater amount of technological and economic knowledge. If the latter is not available, the less risky policy approach could be a combination of specific binding targets and flexible instruments, i.e. the possibility for countries and industries involved to use a variety of instruments under the only constraint that they have non-distorting impacts on the internal market.

4 Conclusion

The solution to ELV problem has the features of a finalised undertaking requiring a combination of innovative achievements. Various technical and economic factors contribute to the largely systemic nature of these achievements. The car industry and many other industrial actors, from dismantlers to material producers,

---

[15]   Even without referring to "traditional" materials (see footnote 7), the result can simply be the interruption of the trends favourable to composites and advanced materials.

are then pursuing together – in a combination of cooperation and conflicting interests – different innovation paths. The latter includes various specific innovations that can influence important aspects of car making, also for other environmental aspects (e.g. energy and emission savings). The process is still open. The available options, which are generally evolving, still present various constraints of economic or technological nature, as well as various uncertainties remain about the dynamic developments associated to the different innovation paths.

Starting from end 1980s, expectations about an EU-level regulation on ELV had a fundamental role in stimulating the innovation process. The relationships between regulation and induced innovation developed through different phases marked by various difficulties and changing degrees of cooperation. Many innovations in ELV began to develop during the long process of EU policy formation, and gave rise to a variety of experiences in the form of inter-industry VAs, also backed by legislation in some countries, that reflect the specificity of innovation capabilities of car companies and their national industrial context. EU regulation choices departed from the approach of VAs, thus revealing a different set of reference principles and different views about the role of technical and economic knowledge in policy making. EU regulation is then introducing a specific set of instruments, some of them debated by industry, than can have influence on the development of the innovation paths pursued by the car industry and the other industrial actors. Further to represent the fundamental stimulus to innovation by establishing targets that work as a "focusing device", regulation is therefore introducing, through its specific instrument choices, a "selection device" inside the innovation process, thus contributing to its dynamic uncertainty.

References

ACEA (1998), *Position Statement on the Commission's Proposal for a Directive on End-of-Life Vehicles*, Brussels.

ACORD (1998), *First Annual Report 1998*, SMMT, London.

Aggeri, F. and A. Hatchuel (1997), *A Dynamic Model of Environmental Policies. The Case of Innovation Oriented Voluntary Agreements*, Nota di Lavoro No 24.97, FEEM, Milan.

Amendola, G. (1990), The Diffusion of Synthetic Materials in the Automotive Industry: Towards a Major Breakthrough?, *Research Policy* 19, 485-500.

APME (1996), *A Material of Choice in the Automotive Industry 1995*, Brussels.

APME (1998), *Insight into Plastics Consumption and Recovery in Western Europe 1997*, Brussels.

ARN (1998), *Environmental Report 1997*, Amsterdam.

Ayres, R. (1995), Thermodynamics and Process Analysis for Future Economic Scenarios, *Environmental and Resource Economics* 6, 207-230.

Barbiroli, G. (1999), *Technical Options, Material Substitution and Recycling in ELV*, IDSE-CNR, Milan (in preparation).

Bianchi, P. (1989), *Industrial Reorganisation and Structural Change in the Automobile Industry*, CLUEB, Bologna.

BMW Recycling (1996), *Recyclingoptimierte Produktgestaltung*, BMW AG, Munich. (Italian translation).

Bontoux, L. and F. Leone (1997), *The Legal Definitions of Waste and their Impacts on Waste Management in Europe*, IPTS-JRC, October.

Bontoux, L., F. Leone, M. Nicolai and D. Papameletiou (1996), *The Recycling Industry in the European Union: Impediments and Prospects*, IPTS-JRC, EUR 17271, December.

Calabrese, G. (1997), *Buyer-Supplier Best Practices in Product Development: Evidence form the Car Industry*, CERIS-CNR, Working Paper No. 4/1997.

Cardani, M. and N. De Liso (1991), *The Economic Relevance of New Materials in an International Perspective*, Dynamis-Quaderni, No. 12/91, IDSE-CNR, Milan.

Cohendet, P. and M.-J. Ledoux (1994), European Strategies in New Materials, in: Quadrio Curzio A., M. Fortis and R. Zoboli (eds.), *Innovation, Resources and Economic Growth*, Heildelberg.

Den Hond, F. (1996), *In Search for a Useful Theory of Environmental Strategy: A Case Study on the Recycling of End-of-Life Vehicles from a Capabilities Perspective*, unpublished PhD thesis, Vrije Universiteit, Amsterdam.

Di Carlo, S., R. Serra and L. Giolitti (1998), *Nuove strategie per il riciclaggio delle vetture a fine vita*, paper presented at the Conference "Strategie per uno sviluppo più sostenibile. La riduzione dei rifiuti solidi non degradabili", Varese, March.

ECRIS (1998), *A Research Project in Environmental Car Recycling 1994-98*, Stockholm.

EEA (1997), *Environmental Agreements. Environmental Effectiveness, European Environment Agency*, Copenhagen.

ELV Project Group (1994), *Proposed Strategy of the ELV Project Group for the Treatment of End-of-Life Vehicles*, Paris.

European Commission (1997), *Proposal for a Council Directive on End-of-Life Vehicles*, COM(97)358 final, Brussels, 09.07.1997.

European Commission (1998), *Adoption by Industry of Life Cycle Approaches. Its Implications for Industry Competitiveness*, Kogan Page, Pentoville Road.

European Commission (1999a), *Proposal for a Council Directive on end of life vehicles*, COM(97)0358, Brussels.

European Commission (1999b), *Amended proposal for a Council Directive on end of life vehicles*, COM(1999)176 final, OJ C 156/5, 3.6.1999.

Graves, A. (1994), Innovation in a Globalising Industry: The Case of Automobiles, in: Dodgson M. and R. Rothwell (eds.), *The Handbook of Industrial Innovation*, Aldershot.

Hemmelskamp, J. (1997), Environmental Policy Instruments and their Effects on Innovation, *European Planning Studies* 5(2).

IPEE (1996), *End-of-Life Vehicles: Current Basic Data Reflecting the Overall Ecological and Economic Context of ELV Issue*, Report compiled for the DGXI, Paris, July.

IPTS-JRC (1996), The Car of the Future, the Future of the Car, EUR 17277, IPTS-JRC, Seville.

Kemp, R. (1997), *Environmental Policy and Technical Change*, Cheltenham.

Kemp, R., G. Becher and K. Smith (1999), *Environmental Regulation and Innovation: A Framework for Analysis and Research Guide*, Maastricht.

Mayne, N. (1998), *The Potential for Post-user Plastics Waste Recycling in Western Europe in the Period up to 2006*.

Mazzanti, M. and R. Zoboli (1999), *Environmental Policy Options and Instrument Choice in the Case of ELV*, IDSE-CNR, Milan (in preparation)

Natale, P. (1994), An Economic Analysis of the Toepfer Law, in: Quadrio Curzio A., L. Prosperetti and R. Zoboli (eds.), *The Management of Municipal Solid Waste in Europe, Elsevier Science Publishers*, Amsterdam.

Oates, W. (1998), Environmental Policy in the European Community: Harmonisation or National Standards, *Empirica* 25, 1-13.

OECD (1996), *Competition Policy and Environment*, OECD/GD(96)22, Paris.

Onida, M. (1999), *Challenges and Opportunities in EC Waste Management: The Case of End-of-Life Vehicles*, Brussels.

Peelman, M. (1999), *The Belgian Approach to Automotive Recycling*, paper presented at the Conference "Autorecycling in Europa. Quo Vadis?", Munich, March 10-11, 1999.

Ratcliffe, A. (1994), Mechanical Recycling of Plastics: Environmental Performance and Economics, *Industry and Environment* 17(3).

RECAP (1997), *Final Report*, Eureka Project "Recovery and Reuse of Plastic Materials Derived from Automobile Production and Scrapping", Milan, September.

Renault (1998), *Recycling Project Department*. Report on Activity 1996-97, Paris.

Schenk, M. (1998), *Altautomobilrecycling. Technisch-oekonomische Zusammenhaenge und wirtschaftspolitische Implikationen*, Wiesbaden (Italian translation).

Segerson, K. and T.J. Miceli (1997), *Voluntary Approaches to Environmental Protection: The Role of Legislative Threats*, Nota di Lavoro No. 21/97, FEEM, Milan.

Van den Berg, N., C. Van Halen and M. Goedkoop (1998), *Environmental Aspects of Plastics form ELVs*, Den Haag.

Wells, P. and M. Rawlinson (1994), *The New European Automobile Industry*, New York.

Zoboli, R. (1994), The Integrated Use of Economic Instruments in the Policy of Municipal Solid Waste, in: Quadrio Curzio A., L. Prosperetti and R. Zoboli (eds.), *The Management of Municipal Solid Waste in Europe*, Amsterdam.

Zoboli, R. (1998), *Implications of Environmental Regulation on Industrial Innovation: The Case of End-of-Life Vehicles*, IPTS-JRC, EUR 18688 EN, Seville, December.

PART III

ECONOMETRIC AND MODELLING STUDIES ON THE IMPACT OF REGULATION ON ENVIRONMENTAL INNOVATION

Environmental Technological Innovation and Diffusion: Model Analysis

Carlo Carraro

Department of Economics, University of Venice
S. Giobbe 873, 30121 Venezia
Italy

Keywords. *technological innovation, environmental policy, endogenous growth, environmental innovation.*

Abstract. This paper analyses the role of technological innovation and diffusion to control and reduce polluting emissions. First, the main effects of environmental innovation on growth and emissions are highlighted. Then, the incentives for firms to undertake R&D and carry out innovation are reviewed. Market imperfections and externalities imply that public innovation policies are necessary to supplement firms' investments in environmental innovation. Hence, the paper discusses how R&D and innovation are linked to environmental policies, analyses how optimal policy-mixes can be designed, and focuses on the impact of related externalities on technological diffusion, crowding-out and endogenous growth. Given the international dimension of many environmental problems, the paper also discusses the impact of environmental innovation on the geographic distribution of polluting industries and of environmental policies on the international dissemination of innovation. The first part of the paper is devoted to theoretical models, whereas the second part provides a survey of empirical attempts to model environmental technological innovation and diffusion.

1 Introduction

The difficulty of protecting the environment at a low economic cost and without harnessing economic growth, a task which is especially difficult in developing countries, has stimulated an increasing debate on the role of technical progress and on the prospective achievements of technological innovation in the field of emission abatement and low natural resource depletion.

The confidence that technical progress may provide important tools to lessen the trade-off between economic growth and environmental protection does not necessarily imply that investments in environment-friendly R&D and innovation will be undertaken by firms, nor that this R&D and innovation can be disseminated to give all world countries the opportunity to protect their environment at a low economic cost.

This paper addresses this issue by analysing the incentives for firms to undertake R&D and innovation, and by highlighting why market imperfections, externalities, international capital mobility, and other economic factors may lead to sub-optimal investments by firms in environmental R&D and innovation. This suggests that public innovation policies may become necessary to induce firms to modify their innovation strategies. Hence, the paper analyses different types of policy mixes and discusses the role of traditional environmental policies (taxes, permits and the like) but also the effects of other policies, e.g. trade or financial policies, that can affect firms' incentives to undertake environmental R&D and innovation.

The first seven sections of the paper are devoted to a synthesis of results that theoretical models have recently achieved on firms' innovation strategies, on the diffusion of innovation, on market imperfections and inefficiencies, and on the trade-off between environmental protection – which calls for a wide diffusion of environmental innovation – and firms profitability – which often induces firms to under-invest in R&D and to reduce the dissemination of environment-friendly innovation. In particular, Sections 5 and 7 attempt to identify combinations of environmental, trade, industrial – including market regulation – and financial policies that can achieve a socially optimal level of environmental innovation. Section 8 focuses on empirical models and on their attempt to capture and quantify the role of innovation in reducing polluting emissions (GHGs emissions above all). These models face the difficult task of providing a consistent and behavioural modelling of innovation, coupled with the need to achieve a proper statistical identification of the model and with the goal of capturing the interaction and feedbacks between innovation and the other main economic and environmental variables. A concluding section summarises the main achievements of this paper, and the consequent policy recommendations, and outlines a research agenda on environmental innovation and diffusion.

2 On the Role of Environmental Technological Innovation (Why Do We Need Environmental Innovation?)

The development and widespread adoption of new technologies is often proposed as the main option to lessen the trade-off between economic well-being and environmental quality. With current technologies, the reduction of air, water and solid waste streams poses a difficult trade-off between increasing environmental degradation if no action is taken, and the economic costs associated with emission abatements and reductions incurred through costly investments or through a process of economic contraction. This trade-off is especially difficult with regard to greenhouse gases (GHGs) where the magnitude of future environmental damages are unknown and where estimated abatement costs are likely to be significant and borne by current generations.

As said, improvements in technology can significantly alter this trade-off. There are indeed several aspects of technological innovation that affect the interactions and links between economic and environmental variables. In some cases the effect of innovation is straightforward. Innovation reduces emissions per unit of output, it lowers abatement costs, and facilitates the introduction of "greener" products. In other cases the effect of innovation may be indirect. Innovation and the resulting investment in new and improved processes of production is important for economic growth and the related use of natural resources. New products that result from innovation are crucial for improving living standards and thus the consumers' preference for environmental quality. Innovation is an important contributor to non-price competitiveness. Its effects on international competition are also relevant, as it modifies the pattern of geographical distribution of industrial activities and thus the incentive to locate plants in countries with lower environmental standards.

There is a recent body of empirical evidence which shows that a substantial reduction of important emissions, which are closely linked to economic activity, is likely to be achieved through technological innovation, rather than through the standard "textbook" substitutabilities in response to price changes. A good example is provided by cross-country studies, carried out by Holtz-Eakin and Selden (1995), Grossman (1995) and Baldwin (1995) on World Bank data and by Galeotti and Lanza (1998) on IEA/OECD data, that show that the relation between per capita CO_2 emissions (and also other pollutants) and per capita income depicts a "bell shaped" curve. Data from a great number of countries show that per capita pollution increases in the first phases of development, but subsequently decreases quite sharply, as development proceeds. This kind of "environmental Kuznets curves" are simple correlations, still in need of systematic explanation. The main determinants of the observed shape can be Engel's law, structural change of the economies, and accumulation of capital; in any case, the reduction of per capita emissions seems to have little relation to prices, which are basically the same across countries. According to preliminary investigations, the diffusion of innovation related to investment seems to play a crucial role, dominating price substitutions.[1]

---

[1]   Cf. Carraro and Siniscalco (1994). Chichilniski's (1994) stresses that differences in property rights across countries can also explain differences in the use of environmental resources.

It is also clear from recent theoretical work by Romer (1986, 1990) and Lucas (1988) that aggregate technological externalities within countries may help explain many of the observed patterns of growth across countries. The intuition is the usual one, but it is applied at the macro level. Technological ideas cannot be fully appropriated by investors (households or firms). These ideas spread, so increasing the productivity of many other households and firms. Diffusion can take place both within and across countries (in Romer's and Lucas' work, externalities are considered only within countries. Ciccone, 1996 extends their models to allow for cross-country externalities). These technological externalities are the crucial factors that lead to increased aggregate returns and endogenous growth.

If we link this latter result with those described above on the relationship between growth and pollution, the conclusion is straightforward: *technological innovation and diffusion are the engine of growth. Growth is correlated to increasing environmental efficiency. Hence, innovation and its diffusion are crucial to achieve substantial reductions of per capita emissions levels and of resource utilisation.* The question is therefore how to induce firms to undertake environmental innovation. This issue will be discussed in the next sections.

3   On the Incentives for Environmental Innovation (Why Do Firms Invest in R&D ?)

As said, technical change is an important component of the mechanism that leads to less-costly and timely emission control. However, it has been shown that, without adequate public policies, in many cases firms tend to underinvest and/or delay investment in environmental innovation (see Downing and White, 1986; Milliman and Prince, 1989; Echia and Mariotti, 1994; Carraro and Topa, 1995; Ulph, A. 1996; Ulph, D. 1997). Hence, public policies affecting the development and spread of new technologies may, over the long term, be one of the most important tools for environmental protection. As a first step towards designing such policies, it is therefore necessary to single out the factors driving the diffusion of new energy-saving technologies.

This is certainly an issue widely studied in the environmental literature, even if results are generally not environment-specific and are usually derived from the industrial organisation literature. The basic question is: why do firms invest in R&D? They do so not only to directly pursue new product and process innovation but also to develop and maintain their broader capacity to assimilate and exploit externally available innovation. Behind the "innovative" reason for R&D are two motivating forces: profitable investment and strategic advantage. Consider the former. Allocating resources to innovative R&D will, if successful, increase a firm's profits. One can usefully conceive of this as the incentive that a firm taking a decision in isolation would face. This is why Katz and Shapiro (1987) refer to it as the "stand-alone" incentive. The second incentive that makes firms engage in R&D is to give themselves a strategic advantage over their rivals. A better process or a better product can enhance a firm's market share. If a firm knows that its rivals are engaging in R&D then it will see its own competitive position as being under threat. This is why this force which stimulates innovation is sometimes called "competitive threat" (or "replacement effect").

These remarks lead to the following conclusion, that may seem trivial, but is sometimes neglected by policymakers. *Policies designed to stimulate innovation must provide an opportunity to increase firms' profits and competitiveness.* Let us consider an example. An increase in energy prices induced by an emission tax or by a system of tradable permits, may lead firms to innovate to reduce energy costs. At the same time, this innovation gives these firms the opportunity to reduce the competitiveness loss with respect to firms located in countries where energy prices were not raised. However, the cost increase induced by the tax reduces the firm's profit margins, thus reducing the financial resources for investment in R&D. It is therefore crucial to identify the appropriate policy-mix to achieve cost-effective R&D strategies.[2]

The economic literature has quite extensively analysed the mechanisms and incentives which lead to environmental R&D. Environmental innovation has been studied in a seminal paper by Downing and White (1986). These authors examine the effectiveness of different policies in inducing "environmentally-friendly" innovation by n identical firms. They consider a context of perfect competition and complete information for all agents: in particular, the government is assumed to know the production and abatement technology available to firms, and to be able to measure the amount of emissions discharged by each source. Moreover, in Downing and White (1986), the innovation process is modelled in a very simple manner: the authors assume that a new technology, providing firms with lower abatement cost functions, becomes exogenously and instantaneously available. Other papers on environmental innovation (e.g. Magat,1979; Malueg,1989; Milliman-Prince,1989) are subject to similar criticisms. Perfect competition and complete information are usually assumed; firms' innovation behaviour is modelled in a simple way; no strategic behaviour is introduced. In particular, the lack of any strategic incentives to carry out R&D is at odds with the answers to the question "why do firms invest in R&D?" provided above.

More recently, environmental innovation has been analysed in the context of imperfect markets where strategic incentives and interactions among firms can be accounted for. Hence, the work by Downing and White has been extended in sev-

---

2   Notice that recent research has highlighted the role of financial factors, rather than cost and price incentives, in stimulating environmental innovation. For example, Kopp, Harrington, Morgenstern, Pizer and Shih (1998), find that the financial health of parent firms is also strongly associated with the likelihood of technology adoption.

eral directions. The timing of innovation and the role of incomplete information is analysed in Carraro and Topa (1995), the interactions between production and innovation are studied in Ulph, D. (1994, 1996). Katsoulacos and Xepapadeas (1996) analyse a case where R&D spillovers exist between firms in the process of environmental innovation, thus introducing positive externalities in addition to the negative environmental externalities. Other models are surveyed in Ulph, D. (1997) who proposes a distinction between non-tournament and tournament models in order to organise the different approaches existing in the economic literature on environmental innovation.

In a *non-tournament model* there are potentially many firms that can obtain an equivalent improvement in the production process. This could arise for one of two reasons. The first is that there may be many different research paths that firms could follow, all of them leading to the same end. Thus, while any particular firm can obtain a patent that is completely effective in protecting the output of its own successful R&D, it cannot prevent other firms from getting equivalent improvements through spending equivalent amounts on R&D. Thus in this class of models, patents can protect firms against costless imitation by rivals, but not against costly innovation by rivals. The second might be that, while the new process is of an intrinsically unpatentable nature, its acquisition involves the sinking of costs. The models of environmental innovation mentioned above belong to the non-tournament group.

In a *tournament model*, the idea is that at any moment there can only be a limited number (possibly one) of successful innovators and the issue is whether and why a successful innovator at one time is more likely to be successful subsequently. One reason why there may be just a limited number of successful innovators at any moment would be if there were just a limited number of research paths leading to a new discovery, and whoever made the discovery first got an effective patent which prevented anyone else from using the discovery, even if they arrived at it independently and shortly after the successful firm. A model of this type is described in Ulph, D. (1997).

The economic literature has also paid a lot of attention to the links between *environmental innovation and international trade*. There has been much debate recently about the nature of environmental policy that will be set by governments concerned about the competitive advantage their industries might obtain in a world of fierce trade competition (Barrett, 1994, Ulph, A., 1997). Some authors claim that governments will set environmental policies that are too lax (Rauscher, 1995), while others claim that policies will be excessively tough (in order to spur firms to innovate).[3] Both these claims relate to the possibility that governments may distort

---

[3]   In particular, Michael Porter (1991) has argued that governments could provide a competitive advantage to their domestic producers by imposing environmental policies which are tougher than those faced by their rivals, since this will spur industries to introduce greener technologies ahead of their rivals, and enhance the

their environmental policies for strategic reasons, and testing them requires modelling environmental policy in a world of imperfect competition where there are strategic gains for governments which manipulate markets through their environmental policies, and for producers which manipulate markets through their R&D decisions. The next section will discuss this issue in more detail.

4 On the Geographical Diffusion of Environmental Innovation (Why Do We Need a Global Perspective?)

There are many reasons to believe that innovation may have relevant effects on the geographical distribution of economic activities. R&D activity carried out by multinationals is often geographically dispersed (Cantwell 1993; Kumar 1995). R&D is often carried out by networks of firms located in different countries, including developing countries (Contractor and Lorange, 1988; Vonortas, 1991; Pietrobelli, 1996). Aggregate evidence shows that international trade generates R&D spillovers: the larger the share of imports from countries rich in R&D capital, the larger the developing countries' foreign R&D capital and the larger their rate of growth (Coe, Helpman and Hoffmaister, 1995).

The above effects need to be considered when analysing the effects of environmental policies on innovation and its diffusion. There is however another more straightforward effect that has been stressed in the recent literature on environmental innovation. This effect is due more to capital than to knowledge mobility across countries. The idea is that countries which implement tougher environmental policies than others will suffer a loss in real income as production relocates both through trade and the physical re-location of plants to countries with more lax environmental policies. This prompts concern that, in the absence of international cooperation, the freeing up of trade will lead to environmental dumping – the uniform reduction by all countries in the toughness of their environmental policies. This raises two issues. The first is once more whether the potentially disruptive effects of environmental policies on resource re-allocation might be significantly mitigated through the encouragement these policies give to innovation. The second is whether environmental dumping will indeed take place when strategic innovation becomes a consideration. It has been suggested that countries might now have incentives to set excessively tough environmental poli-

---

long-run profitability of domestic industry. This view finds considerable support in the US administration, and is also commonly espoused in Germany and Japan. In its extreme form it suggests that environmental regulations are beneficial to both the environment and the economy.

cies, in order to spur the firms in their country to innovate ahead of rivals and so gain market advantage. This has become known as the "Porter hypothesis", following the article by Michael Porter (1991) which articulated this possibility.

The issue of whether environmental policies can really have an impact on the international allocation of capital is not only a theoretical question but also an empirical one. Theoretically, firms may shift their production when they face environmental regulations (either because they add new plants in foreign sites or because they shift existing capacity abroad). However, the question is "how significant is this phenomenon in practice?". That is, *is there considerable evidence that environmental regulations have really induced flows of capital towards pollution havens?*.

Wang and Winters (1994) review most of the literature on these issues. The literature analysed by the authors specifically focuses on the empirical evidence regarding potential capital flights from industrial (OECD) countries to developing ones (non-OECD). The authors conclude that in the studies surveyed there was little evidence of capital flight from industrial countries with stringent environmental legislation to pollution havens. Other factors, such as political and macroeconomic stability, market access, market size and growth, play a much higher role in firms' location decisions. Similar conclusions have also been reached by Rauscher (1994). The author reviews some other empirical literature on the subject and again concludes that the evidence does not give much support to the hypothesis that capital tends to fly towards countries with lax environmental regulation. However, he stresses that the empirical studies may be flawed because of measurement problems. Specifically, he underlines that a major problem in the empirical assessment of the impact of environmental legislation on firms' location choices, is the difficulty of measuring the strictness of environmental regulation itself (both because the proxies used may not be good enough and/or because it is extremely difficult to isolate, from aggregate data, the environmental component). These measurement problems should be kept in mind when analysing the empirical studies since they may seriously bias the results. The same doubts on the validity of some empirical studies have also been raised by Levinson (1996). The novelty of the study by Levinson (1996) is that the author examines firms' choices across most manufacturing industries employing a wide variety of measures of environmental stringency. Contrary to the use of aggregate data, Levinson studies location choices using establishment-level data (essentially plants' births). Again, this study confirms that there seems to be only weak evidence that environmental regulations deter new plant openings.

Despite the *little empirical evidence on the link between environmental policy and geographical distribution of economic activities*, the Porter hypothesis has attracted the attention of several theorists (Cf. Hoel, 1995, Rauscher, 1995; Ulph, A. 1997). In Carraro and Soubeyran (1998) a firm's decision to innovate is analysed jointly with its decision to relocate its plants abroad whenever environmental policy in the foreign country is less stringent. The main conclusion of their paper is as follows. In general, three stable groups of firms emerge. Even if firms are symmetric, their equilibrium choice in response to the introduction of an environmental policy is different. Some of them re-locate their plants abroad, others invest in R&D and develop new, environment-friendly technologies, and others introduce the environmental innovation by buying the licences. The size of the three groups is influenced by the technological and institutional parameters prevailing in the industry. For example, the government can affect the number of firms which decide to cooperate by changing the R&D incentives and/or its trade policy.

It is therefore interesting to analyse whether innovation has significant effects when a firm is allowed to move its plants abroad in response to the introduction of an environmental policy. And if there are other policies that can increase these effects. In a recent paper, Boetti, Botteon, Carraro and Soubeyran (1998) run some simulation experiments in order to evaluate (i) the number and size of the groups of firms which are likely to emerge in the presence of an environmental tax and when R&D and innovation is accounted for; (ii) how the size of the three groups of firms is likely to change when other policy measures are adopted, e.g. an industrial policy aimed at stimulating R&D and innovation, or a trade policy. They show that:

- a higher marginal tax rate does not seem to have a significant impact on firms' relocation choices (consistent with empirical findings);

- a higher R&D incentive policy increases the number of both co-operating and imitating firms, thereby decreasing the number of relocating firms;

- a more stringent tariff policy that prevents imports from countries where environmental regulation is less stringent may be counterproductive.

These results clarify how important public innovation policies can be both in protecting the environment and in stimulating domestic economic growth, thus preventing re-location effects. They also suggest the importance of finding an *adequate policy mix between industrial (R&D), environmental and trade policies* in order to achieve the above policy goals. Hence, it is important to carefully discuss the issue of policy design, as is done in the next section.

5   On Policies to Stimulate Environmental Innovation (Why Do We Need Public Environmental Innovation Strategies?)

There are three types of market failure at work when we consider the question of innovation and the environment. The first is the conventional market failure associated with externalities. If innovation results developed by one firm spill-over other firms, there is an incentive for firms to distort their innovation effort. The second is the conventional *static* market failure associated with imperfect competition – typically output is too low, prices too high, and there is excessive entry. The third aspect of this market failure has only recently received serious attention. This is the *dynamic* market failure surrounding R&D and innovation. It arises fundamentally from the nature of knowledge as a public good, which is expensive to produce, but cheap to reproduce. It is particularly important for basic research, but it also holds for applied research.

This dynamic market failure gives rise to a complex set of questions which involve both innovation and its diffusion: (i) How many firms should engage in R&D? (ii) What information should they share (a) with each other; (b) with other non-innovating firms? (iii) How much R&D should each of the innovating firms carry out? (iv) What degree of protection of environmental innovation should firms be guaranteed; (v) How can public policy intervene to reduce the negative effects of market failures on innovation?

A partial solution to some of the market failures associated with R&D is the creation of a system of property rights, the most obvious one being patent protection. The problem with this is that it typically provides too much protection and so prevents socially beneficial sharing of information. In particular, it prevents a socially efficient diffusion of environmental innovation and hence reduces the environmental benefit that innovation provides. This distortion of the information-sharing aspects of R&D generates further distortions on the decisions about the amount of R&D being done. Thus we know that in non-tournament models, where many firms can achieve the same innovation, each firm typically does too little R&D, but there is excessive duplication of R&D. However, in tournament models, where there is a race to be the unique innovator, each firm undertakes too much R&D (see Ulph, D. 1997 for a survey of these models). For these reasons a lot of *the focus of technology policy is now on arrangements like research joint ventures (RJVs) which correct the distortions of the patent system by promoting more in-formation-sharing.* The difficulty now is that we have only a very limited understanding of how well these perform, mainly because, with the exception of the recent paper by Katsoulacos and Ulph (1996), the literature on RJVs treats the amount of information-sharing as exogenous.

Therefore, even without the complications introduced by accounting for environmental market failures, we are far from having a complete understanding of R&D policy design. What we can conclude, however, is that *efficient innovation patterns in terms of R&D and investments cannot be achieved by a market system alone. Public policies are necessary to set guidelines, provide incentives, and regulate strategic behaviour.*

Let us now include specific environmental concerns in the analysis. There are two effects of environmental policy, taxes or standards, on innovation. The *direct effect* is to alter the effectiveness of R&D in lowering costs. However the *indirect effect* of the policy is to change the value to the firm of lowering costs. These effects go in opposite directions, though the sign depends on the nature of the policy instrument. An environmental tax or a system of tradable permits has a positive direct effect and negative indirect effect, whereas standards have a negative direct effect and positive indirect effect. These conclusions are very general and do not depend greatly on the nature of either product market competition or R&D competition (Cf. Ulph, D. 1997). However the balance between the two effects does depend on the nature of R&D competition. Hence, in non-tournament models it will typically be the case that higher environmental taxes will stimulate R&D, whereas in tournament models the balance between the effects depends sensitively on the competitiveness of the product market (Cf. Jaffee and Stavins, 1995; Jung, Krutilla and Boyd, 1996).

Let us consider some specific results on optimal environmental innovation policies. Katsoulacos and Xepapadeas (1996) propose an optimal scheme of simultaneous application of taxes on emissions and subsidies on environmental R&D. The government can use receipts from taxing pollution to subsidise the firms' R&D efforts, thus implementing a recycling policy which differs from the one often proposed in the "double dividend theory" – where tax revenues are recycled in the labour market – and coincides with the one analysed through an econometric model in Carraro and Galeotti (1997). Furthermore, because of the R&D spillovers, the government subsidy corrects the appropriability problem that firms face when investing in R&D, while the tax corrects the pollution externality. Katsoulacos and Xepapadeas (1996) show that the optimal emission tax is less than the marginal damage, while the subsidy depends on three factors: (i) the deviation between emission taxes and marginal pollution damages; (ii) the deviation between the private and the social marginal product of R&D; (iii) firms' strategic incentives to invest in R&D.[4]

A similar framework is used in Requate (1995), where the goal is a comparison of the effects of emission taxes and tradable permits on environmental innovation in the context of a n-firms oligopoly. Requate shows that only a subset of firms would adopt the new environment-friendly technology. Moreover, both policy instruments may lead to too much or too little adoption with respect to the socially optimal rate. Taxes may cause too much adoption when little adoption is optimal and vice versa, whereas the effects of permits are the opposite of those of taxes. The incentives to environmental innovation as a tool to bypass the cost of buying permits are also analysed in Laffont and Tirole (1996). This paper shows again that firms invest excessively in new technologies as a reaction to environmental policy. This excess adoption can be mitigated by the introduction of future markets for emission permits along with the usual spot market.

---

[4]   A paradoxical result is that when spillovers are sufficiently small the optimal subsidy may be negative; that is, it may be optimal to tax environmental R&D. This is to avoid over-investment in R&D, a problem also emphasised in Laffont and Tirole (1996).

The inefficiency of using a single policy instrument is stressed again in Carraro and Topa (1995), where a dynamic model of firms' environmental innovation is proposed. Here the issue is not excess adoption but rather excess timing of adoption, i.e. firms tend to delay the introduction of new environment-friendly technologies. Carraro and Topa show that an environmental tax can indeed induce firms to adopt cleaner technologies, but that, without appropriate incentives, the timing of the adoption is socially sub-optimal (because firms do not fully account for the environmental benefit of their innovation even when pollution is taxed). Hence, to prevent firms from delaying innovation, the government should subsidise R&D costs.

Ulph and Ulph (1996) provide a general treatment of the optimal design of environmental policy when trade effects are accounted for. They allow both governments and producers to act strategically, and producers' R&D to reduce both costs of production and emissions, but without imposing special functional forms. Their conclusions depend crucially on whether an increase in a country's environmental tax causes the costs of firms located in that country to rise or fall. In Ulph, D. (1994) it is shown that this depends on whether the increase in environmental R&D induced by the tax is more or less than the level needed to offset the direct effect of the tax increase on costs, and this in turn depends on the precise form of the relationship between emissions and R&D. Adding in process R&D does nothing to alter this.[5] If, ignoring process R&D, costs rise as a result of the tax, this will cause firms to lose market share. But this will lower the incentive to undertake process R&D and so merely exacerbate the effect of the tax on firms' costs. Conversely, if ignoring process R&D, firms' costs fall as the tax rises, this will increase their market share. In turn, this will increase the incentive for process R&D, which will simply reinforce the effects produced by the analysis in which there is only environmental R&D.

It has recently been suggested that traditional environmental policies that affects firms' costs and correct distortions through R&D subsidies may not be the most effective means of inducing environmental innovation. Recent empirical analyses emphasise the role of firms' plant size and their financial health. Kopp et al. (1998) find that technology adoption is positively related to the size of the plant. Past trends in energy prices and use are important control variables, but it is unclear whether "adoption-prone" plants are more likely to have had higher energy costs in the past, encouraging them to adopt energy saving technologies, or alternatively, that adopters are more likely to have had lower energy costs in the past, reflecting a long-term tendency to seek greater energy efficiency. The econometric analysis performed by Kopp et al. (1998) which looks at the adoption of new energy-saving technologies, suggests that financial health is an important determinant of technology adoption. The effect of energy prices in this model is positive but

---

[5]   Environmental R&D is aimed at reducing the emission-output ratio, whereas process R&D aims at lowering production costs.

neither statistically nor economically significant, generating only a 3 per cent swing in the likelihood of adoption (versus more than 10 per cent for both working capital and profit margin). However, looking at individual technologies instead of pooling across all technologies yields inconclusive results. The research carried out by Kopp *et al.* has therefore revealed important patterns in the adoption of new energy-efficient technologies, but also leaves unresolved some competing hypotheses. The association of financial health with technology adoption indicates that investment incentives may be an important avenue for speeding technology diffusion. It may, however, simply reflect that better-managed companies – proxied by financial health – are the ones that invest in energy-saving technologies. If that were the case, a variety of low cost policies, e.g., those which disseminate information to firms about new technologies, might also prove to be an effective means of disseminating new technologies.

The role of optimal policy mixes directed to stimulate and support environment-friendly innovation is also crucial when a dynamic perspective is accounted for. As already said, aggregate technological externalities within countries may help explain many of the observed patterns of growth across countries (Romer, 1986, 1990; Lucas, 1988). Product innovation is at least as important as process innovation in producing external effects and endogenous growth. Following the seminal work by Grossman and Helpman (1991), both Hung, Chang and Blackburn (1994) and Verdier (1995) introduce environmental variables in an endogenous growth model with product variety. Each product is characterised by a particular emission-output ratio. In the R&D stage, firms can chose the emission-output ratio of the new product introduced in the market. Designing cleaner products requires more resources to be spent in R&D. This feature naturally introduces a trade-off between the growth of product variety and the "cleanness" of the products developed.

In this setting it is possible to show that small emission taxes need not reduce growth and may, on the contrary, boost the number of products developed in the economy. The intuitive reason is that an emission tax increases the relative price of manufactured goods, and decreases the demand and the quantity produced for these goods. This in turn releases resources to be used in the R&D sector and consequently promotes growth. Note that the issue of crowding-out emerges right away, because even in an endogenous growth model it is crucial to design a policy which stimulates environmental R&D without reducing the amount of resources devoted to other economic activities or other forms of R&D. Again a problem of optimal policy-mix arises.

In Verdier (1995) there is also a comparison of the growth performance of an emission tax and a technological standard which implement the same pollution target. As expected, technological standards have a greater negative effect on economic growth than emission taxes. However, in terms of welfare the comparison is more difficult and does not lead to clear conclusions because there are potentially many market failures (outside pollution) in the economy: imperfect competition,

R&D market failures, spillover effects. In a second-best world where the regulator cannot use all the necessary instruments to correct for the various distortions, it is not clear whether emission taxes dominate technological standards. For example, for severe pollution targets, technological standards may be more efficient, in terms of welfare, than emission taxes. The reason for this result is simply that when pollution targets are severely binding, an emission tax induces industrial growth below the socially optimal rate. In other words, too many resources are devoted to environmental protection, thus crowding-out resources for other economic activities.

The crowding-out issue is also raised by Goulder and Schneider (1996) whose theoretical model explicitly accounts for the possibility that increased investment in R&D by one sector (the alternative fuels sector), by demanding scarce knowledge-generating resources, might "crowd-out" investment in R&D by other sectors. To the extent that such crowding-out occurs, rapid technological change in one sector will be accompanied by less rapid change in other sectors. The model by Goulder and Schneider (1996) reveals analytically the connections between induced technical change and the costs of abatement policies and thus can explore how public policies oriented toward one industry affect R&D incentives in other industries and the economy-wide level of output and rate of technological progress. The crucial variable is the degree of inefficiency of R&D markets. If there are no such inefficiencies, the probability of R&D crowding-out is large, with consequent reduced effect on growth and pollution abatement of the proposed environmental R&D policy.

6   On Diffusion Processes[6]

The discussion of the previous sections mainly focused on analyses devoted to define an optimal policy mix which can provide adequate incentives to environmental innovation. Even if diffusion processes were explicitly considered in the previous sections, particularly when analysing the role of spillovers and the impact of innovations on growth, little attention was devoted to the sluggishness and inertia of diffusion processes. These may be important problems to be faced when designing an innovation policy whose goal is to achieve environmental benefits.

There is a large body of economic research on the subject of technology diffusion. The single most important conclusion of this literature, well summarised in Jaffe and Stavins (1994), is that diffusion of new, economically superior technologies is

---

[6]   Part of this section is based on the report "Climate Change and the Challenge for Research and Technological Development Policy" prepared for the EU Commission by Carlo Carraro, Reinhard Coenen, Ken Guy, Jean-Charles Hourcade, René Kemp, Jim Skea, Walter R. Stahel, Uno Svedin and Ferenc Toth.

a gradual rather than instantaneous process (Griliches, 1957; Mansfield, 1968; Davies, 1979; Oster, 1982; Levin et al., 1987). Specifically, diffusion is often portrayed as a *sigmoid* curve over time. That is, the rate of adoption begins slowly, speeds up, then eventually slows down again as market saturation approaches. One justification for the sigmoid curve is based on an *epidemic* model of diffusion. Due to a lack of knowledge or confidence, the rate of adoption of a new technology increases with the growing popularity of the technology. From this intuition, it makes sense that the rate of adoption will be slow in the beginning (when there is little popularity) and in the end (when there are few non-users). In this model, the probability of adopting the technology depends entirely on the number of other firms in the industry who have already adopted it.

The pioneering work of Griliches (1957) extends this model by establishing that the diffusion of new technology can be understood in an economic framework by allowing the rate of diffusion to be partly determined by the (expected) economic return to adoption. Mansfield (1968) then demonstrates that the rate of diffusion can depend on the size of adopting firms, the perceived riskiness of the new technology, and the size of the required investment. In subsequent work, firm size has been argued to have both positive and negative effects on adoption (Davies 1979; Oster 1982; Boyd and Karlson 1993). Arguments for the former are based on the resources (financial, experience, expertise) associated with large firms, while arguments for the latter hinge on potentially oligopolistic market structure which may reduce the competitive pressures to innovate. The possibility of varying diffusion rates for different technologies has been qualitatively described as the difference between different types of innovations. Minor innovations presumably diffuse quickly, innovations which are considerably more invasive diffuse more slowly (Cohen and Levin 1989; Davies 1979).

According to this line of thinking, economic factors (beyond firm size) influence the overall rate of diffusion based on idiosyncratic characteristics of the *technology*. Such factors do not, however, distinguish the rate of adoption by different firms. Similarly sized firms are considered to be homogeneous with respect to their rate of adoption. A natural alternative is to focus on inherent differences or heterogeneity among firms (David, 1969). This model is sometimes known as the *probit* approach, after the commonly employed statistical technique for limited dependent variables, which shares a conceptual foundation with the diffusion model (Stoneman, 1983). In this model the crucial factor for explaining the gradual diffusion process is that potential adopters are significantly different from one another in some aspect that affects the value of the innovation to them. Such aspects might include the cost of equipment, cost of learning about a new technology, cost of adapting existing processes, or future benefits of the technology. One can imagine a threshold above which it pays to adopt the new technology and below which it does not. The threshold differs across firms and, over time, the cost of the innovation may fall and/or the quality may improve, thereby lowering the threshold.

Beside idiosyncratic, firm-specific effects, diffusion process also depends on systemic variables, i.e. on the dynamics of R&D and innovation within complex social, economic and technical systems. Indeed, technological change occurs incrementally within existing technological trajectories, and only occasionally does innovation lead to the establishment of entirely new trajectories. In turn, all these trajectories are embedded within extremely complex and intricate social and technical systems in which the dynamics of change are themselves complicated, with institutional inertia and technical lock-in often inhibiting rates of change (Cf. Rip and Kemp, 1998; Kemp, Schot and Hoogma,1998).

Many sources of inertia govern the rate at which techno-economic systems change. These include low capital stock turnover rates in some sectors; the time needed for innovations to incubate; institutional barriers to diffusion; weak mechanisms incapable of translating political or societal imperatives into effective economic signals; and self-reinforcing loops between particular technical options and consumption patterns, which create technological 'lock-in' and discourage radical innovation.

Problems of lock-in and inertia are particularly keen in 'complex technology systems' characterised by massive investment in 'long-life' capital stock and extensive associated infrastructure, e.g. transport systems and energy production and distribution systems. They are of less concern in sectors where capital stock turnover rates are comparatively low. Rates range from five years for electrical appliances, one to four decades for industrial production facilities, three to four decades for power plants, and four to ten decades for transport and urban infrastructure developments. However, even though turnover rates are low in some sectors of the economy, the inertia of overall socio-technical systems is exacerbated when the options for change within one sector or area are linked or modified by the options for change in other areas. The architecture of a building, for example, determines air conditioning requirements; and urban planning structures determine not only transportation needs but also the relative share of journeys made on foot, on a bicycle, by rail or by private car. The net result is that the inertia of an inter-related system as a whole is governed by the most inert component of the system, just as the strength of a chain depends upon its weakest link. Lock-in then stifles the opportunities for change.

Remedying structural inertia is difficult. Decision-making within complex socio-technical systems takes place at many levels (households, industry, public authorities etc.), all governed by different priorities, and diverting complete systems onto less environmentally harmful technological trajectories is a daunting task. Price signals like the ones discussed in the previous section will undoubtedly have some effect on the technological paths taken by the various actors involved in complex systems, but there are genuine fears that these prices will reflect short-term expediency rather than longer-term societal and environmental needs, and that they will be too low to overcome structural inertia as far as innovation is concerned. There is also the added complication that many parts of complex socio-technical systems are comparatively insensitive to price variations, with decisions on future behaviour driven primarily by other factors, e.g. cost/speed ratios in the transportation sector; aesthetics in architecture; the price of land in urban planning.

In such situations, the important task is to make sure that future technological options are attractive to even the 'weakest link' sectors, i.e. those with high structural inertia and low price sensitivity. In fact, since 'chains' are dependent on their 'weakest links', targeting these sectors (transport, buildings, urban forms) becomes a high priority. There is therefore the need for socio-economic and policy research into the complementary economic and regulatory policy mechanisms which will be needed to ensure that these new technological options are adopted and diffused.

In addition, apart from research, there is also a great need for public policies supporting experimentation with new technologies, especially radical technologies for which a market is not defined. This would help suppliers to get a better idea of user requirements and the performance of technologies in real life situations. It would also help users to develop a better understanding of new technologies and how they might benefit from them. It would also help to build a constituency for products and guide private and public actors in their policies. User experiments offer a way of breaking the gridlock of structural inertia by facilitating assessments of the claims for and against new technologies.

7   Blue-Prints for Environmental Innovation Policies

It is clear from the above analysis that innovation policies need to be carefully designed according to a multi-faceted approach. On the one hand, they must promote *knowledge diffusion*, by disseminating information to firms about new technologies. They must also promote *basic learning* by stimulating interactions between academic research and applied innovation. This is one of the most effective ways of stimulating technological spillovers, which increase growth and emission abatement at the same time (Cf. Lucas, 1988). Finally, they should support technology diffusion, reduce inertia, and increase the amount of spillovers induced by the adoption of environment-friendly technologies.

On the other hand, policies must follow a carrot-and-stick policy. The threat of coercive regulation (Cf. Cadot and Sinclair-Desgagne, 1996) and the higher costs introduced by a tradable permit system can act as *stimuli for energy-efficient R&D*, but must be coupled with measures to *protect firms' financial intertemporal health*, particularly for small and medium size firms which are more likely to suffer as a result of financial swings.

Market failures must also be offset, on the one hand by protecting energy-efficient innovation through adequate patent rules, and on the other by supporting *innova-*

tions obtained through research joint ventures in order to promote knowledge sharing.

It is also necessary that policies be explicitly aimed at creative *alternative paths of development*. Some ways to do this are: support for new ideas offering long-term benefits through science and technology programmes, the creation of niches for promising technologies through government procurement policies, subsidies, regulation, experimentation, and the formulation of policy goals and targets for the medium term (Kemp, Schot and Hoogma,1998).

Policies should also take international R&D, trade and location effects into account. Hence a high degree of *international coordination and cooperation* should characterise environmental innovation policies.

8 Empirical Models and Results

In many models used to assess the effects of policies designed to control polluting emissions, technical change has an exogenous representation which is quite unsatisfactory. Hence the need for a "new generation" of environmental-economic models which endogenise the linkages between economic variables (policy variables, in particular) and technical progress. Here we provide a brief description of some preliminary attempts to model induced technical change.

8.1 Innovation and R&D

The approaches just described do not introduce an explicit link between environmental variables and policies, technical change and economic growth. There are some recent efforts in this direction. The first one was probably proposed by Jorgenson and Wilcoxen (1990). They assume a translog unit cost function containing terms in which the input prices interact with the time trend – a proxy of technical progress. Therefore, the firms' costs depend on input prices and on the time trend. Finally, technical progress influences input demands, without interacting with any other variable. The authors show that the time trend, in addition to prices, affects the rate of total factor productivity. Thus environmental policy decisions affecting relative prices determine an endogenous change in total factor productivity. In this way, the proposal by Jorgenson and Wilcoxen partially endogenises technical progress.

A more satisfactory treatment of technical progress in recent AGE/CGE models relying on the concept of vintage capital can be found in Conrad and Henseler-Unger (1986) and Conrad and Ehrlich (1993). Here substitution possibilities are more feasible with the most recent capital vintages. Thus, adjusting to relative price shocks does not only depend on the elasticity of substitution but also on the capital replacement rate. This is a novelty with respect to previous CGE modelling approaches because technical change shows its effects on the firms' cost structure through a parametrization of each vintage's cost functions. Another vintage model has been proposed in Carlevaro et al. (1992).

Models using the idea of capital vintages have some drawbacks too, because they do not provide a precise evaluation of the mechanisms through which markets and agents can modify existing technologies toward energy saving and environmental potentials. As an example, the model by Carlevaro et al. (1992) uses technical coefficients defining, say, the energy/capital ratio, which are endogenous but depend only on the future trend of energy prices. In a similar way to the technical-economic models, this approach does not explicitly take into account the economic profitability of the new technologies: the existence of a new, less polluting, technology does not imply that it will be adopted by firms.

The main difficulty faced by modellers when they try to endogenise technical change is the non-observability of this variable. This is why old-fashioned models use a deterministic trend as a proxy of technical change. And this is why this is the starting point of some *ad hoc* attempts to model technical change. For example, in Boone et al. (1992), Carraro and Galeotti (1996) and Dowlatabadi and Oravetz (1996), technical progress is still represented by a variable which is added to the main equations of the model. However, this variable is no longer a deterministic function of time. It is rather a stochastic function of time, in which other economic effects are also accounted for.

In Boone et al. (1992) (see also Hall et al., 1994) the dynamics of technical change can be inferred by looking at the dynamics of factor demand (a similar approached was proposed by Gao, 1994 and Slade, 1989). In Carraro and Galeotti (1996) the basic idea is also that technical progress cannot be observed and that it must be inferred by observing the dynamics of other variables. However, the focus is on the capital stock. It is assumed that the capital stock can be broken down into two parts: the energy-saving/environment-friendly capital stock and the energy-consuming one. Each year a new vintage of the capital stock becomes operational. In this way new capital is added to the two components. The characteristics of this new capital depend on a number of economic variables which affect a firm's decision to install energy-saving capital. Among the variables which explain the dynamics of the two components there is the amount of R&D carried out by firms. An increase in R&D expenditure can indeed increase the technological potential of the economic system and is therefore likely to produce investment in environment-friendly capital (of course, relative prices, market demand and other variables also intervene in the decision process). The amount of R&D carried out by firms depends on policy variables such as environmental taxation and innovation subsidies, and on relative prices, sales, and other endogenous economic variables. The model equations which capture the dynamics of the aggregate capital stock and its components are estimated using the Kalman filter. An indicator of environmental technical progress, which can be interpreted as an indicator of the environmental quality of the capital stock, can then be given by the ratio between the environment-friendly and the polluting capital stocks.

With this approach, the role of technical progress is completely endogenised. Let us assume, as an example, that firms are asked to pay a carbon tax. This raises the relative price of energy. This increase has two effects: it induces firms to substitute energy with other production factors (if technology is not of the Leontief-type); and it raises firms' R&D expenditure, as suggested in Carraro and Topa (1994), thus accelerating technical progress, and increasing the environmental quality of the capital stock. This reduces energy demand without excessively penalising output, but reducing energy prices. These two variables feed-back into the equations determining the dynamics of technical progress.

The problem with this approach is its *ad hoc* nature. There is no explicit solution of the firms' optimisation problem that determines the optimal amount of R&D and investments in the two types of capital. Therefore, links between these variables are mainly statistical, but lack a clear economic interpretation. A similar remark concerns the work by Dowlatabadi and Oravetz (1996). In this paper, there is a direct econometric link between price variables (which depend on environmental policies) and technical change. Aside from their *ad hoc* nature, these models share another common feature. The efficacy of abatement policies is greater and the cost of curbing emissions are lower than in the case in which technical change is modelled through an exogenous trend.

The same difficulties with the observability and measurement of technical change affect the proposal by Newell, Jaffee and Stavins (1996). Here the model is more sophisticated and represents the economic structure of innovation decisions. However, the problem lies in the necessity of defining a statistical *ad hoc* model to construct the time series to be used in estimating the structural model of technological innovation. Hence, the model is still somehow ad hoc, even if the problem is confined to the estimation procedure.

Of course, this problem does not exist in those models in which parameters are calibrated rather than estimated. In this case, it is possible to construct and simulate a structural model of R&D and innovation even if the price to be paid is a set of values for the model parameters that cannot easily be tested. Some preliminary but very interesting examples of this approach are contained in Goulder and Mathai (1996).

8.2 Spillovers, Diffusion, Learning-by-Doing and Crowding-out

As previously said, new technologies are typically developed by the most innovative firms and not immediately available to all. Factors that influence the rate and timing of diffusion are of fundamental importance in assessing the ultimate effectiveness of the innovation. Modelling this factor is obstructed by certain characteristics of empirical environmental models. Usually, top-down models do not provide the degree of sector disaggregation that would be required for analysis at the level of the firm, while bottom-up studies do not consider strategic market behaviour that may delay the diffusion of innovation. There are however some attempts to model spillovers and diffusion.

One idea comes directly from the empirical literature on endogenous growth (Cf. Mankiw, Romer and Weil, 1992; Ciccone, 1996). Here, the production function is specified in order to account for positive R&D externalities. These externalities, which may also depend on the volume of trade, as in the model by Helpman and Grossman, are the mechanism through which endogenous growth takes place. This mechanism is empirically very relevant. For example, the Solow growth model, with physical capital only and with a share of physical capital in national income of about 1/3, requires an exogenous annual growth rate of total factor productivity of 1.4 per cent to explain an annual growth rate of labour productivity of 2 per cent. The Solow model extended for human capital (see Mankiw, Romer and Weil, 1992) requires an exogenous annual growth rate of total factor productivity of 0.7 per cent to explain a 2 per cent annual growth rate of labour productivity. If we allow for externalities and technological interdependence, the exogenous annual growth rate of total factor productivity necessary to explain a 2 per cent annual growth rate of labour productivity is only 0.2 per cent (see Ciccone, 1996). It is clear therefore that the modelling of externalities plays a crucial rule and greatly influences both the dynamics of the relevant variables in the "business as usual" scenario and the effects of simulated environmental policies.

The issue of crowding-out has also received some attention in the empirical literature. Goulder and Schneider (1996) quantify the costs of carbon taxes in the presence of induced technical change and crowding-out. If there are no prior inefficiencies in R&D markets, policies that stimulate environmental R&D crowd-out other forms of R&D, which implies that the gross costs (before accounting for environment-related benefits) of carbon taxes are higher than they would be if there were no induced technical change. The result may be reversed in the presence of inefficiencies in R&D markets. More importantly, the environmental benefits are likely to be larger when induced technical change is taken into account (because there is more abatement) and the benefits from the additional abatement more than compensate for the higher gross costs (whenever this is actually the case).

Another recent interesting development of the literature on induced technical change is constituted by the attempt to represent technological progress as a learning-by-doing process. The model by Grubler and Messner (1996) is based on the concept of learning curves and describes future costs and performance improvements of new technologies as a function of accumulated R&D, and learning and experience gained in diffusion of new technologies. Thus, technological learning depends on previous, accumulated investments in R&D, demonstration plants and gradually expanding niche markets.

8.3 Implementation of Already Commercially Available Technologies

This is an issue which is better captured by existing models. The bottom-up approach considers the possibility of substitution among different techniques through absolute shifts. Therefore, it risks underestimating transaction costs and being too optimistic about the potential for market penetration. At the level of the firm, elements that deserve more consideration are all those factors which impose a degree of inertia on the energy system, thereby reducing the scope for immediate adoption of available technologies. At the consumer level, market failures such as information costs and high discount rates can result in limited exploitation of the available options. In top-down studies, the possibility of substituting the existing technologies is no longer absolute as in the previous case, but relative to variation in the prices of the techniques, i.e. they are typically expressed through the concept of elasticity. Most models assign constant values to the parameters representing the elasticities. Price substitution along a given production isoquant is likely to underestimate the real impact of technology on the emission/output ratio; in particular, it does not account for changes in factor demands (i.e. energy) which take place through shifts of the production isoquant. The possibility of non-price induced energy intensity reduction is assumed to be extremely limited in the majority of cases.

Note that most of the models described above in Section 6.1 do not distinguish clearly between R&D of new technologies and the adoption/diffusion of existing best-available technologies (BATs). Being *ad hoc* reduced form models, they tend to combine all types of technological change and therefore capture the dynamic effects of both R&D and the diffusion of BATs.

9   Conclusion and Research Agenda

Both theoretical analysis and empirical evidence agree on the following basic conclusion: technological innovation and diffusion are the main engine of growth. Growth is correlated with increasing environmental efficiency. Hence, innovation accomplishes a twofold task: it stimulates growth and competitiveness and reduces pollution levels

However, several market failures characterise existing innovation systems. Spillover effects, inefficiency in the banking sector and financial markets, risk aversion, the nature of knowledge as a public good, lack of coordination, are all elements that reduce private incentives to undertake R&D and innovation and call for public intervention.[7]

The global dimension of many environmental problems and the increasing mobility of capital and goods call for action in both developed and developing countries. It is therefore crucial to increase:

(i) *knowledge diffusion*, by disseminating information about new environment-friendly technologies;

(ii) *basic learning and innovation*, by stimulating interactions between academic research and applied environmental innovation;

(iii) *technology diffusion*, by improving the quality of the role of multinationals in the global economy and by implementing technological cooperation agreements.

The long-term dimension calls for action on R&D and innovation that enhances *long-run competitiveness* in environmentally sensitive sectors, that increases financial resources provided by the banking sector, e.g. by partly involving banks in the liability process, that guarantees *protection* for energy efficient innovation, and supports *cooperation and RJVs* designed to undertake environmental R&D.

In this framework, environmental innovation policies are structurally linked and interact with competition, industrial and trade policies. These should support R&D cooperation, increase the competitiveness of the banking system, protect innovation and introduce lender liability schemes, and support trade rules that favour technology transfers.

The above conclusions are based on a large body of economic literature which is only partly environment-specific. Most analyses of the role of innovation, the problems with its diffusion, the effects of different public policies, have indeed been developed independently of environmental concerns. These analyses have proved to be useful to understand the complexity of environmental innovation, even if new elements had to be added, particularly because the main benefits provided by environmental R&D and innovation are mostly public goods. There are several research issues that deserve further attention. From a theoretical viewpoint, it would be useful to achieve a better understanding of the links between environmental, trade, industrial and financial policies. Current research is carried out in a partial equilibrium framework where each issue is analysed separately. A general equilibrium analysis of the optimal policy mix needs to be undertaken. In the previous section, we argued that environmental innovation and its diffusion are strictly intertwined. This is also an issue that needs further theoretical research (possibly using dynamic models in which inertia and lock in effects can be ex-

---

[7]   These market failures are even stronger in the case of international and global environmental problems, e.g. climate change. Climate change is a global, long-term, uncertain phenomenon. These features crucially reduce firms' incentives to undertake R&D and innovation.

plored). Similarly, there is a need for socio-economic and policy research into the complementary economic and regulatory policy mechanisms which can be necessary to ensure that new technological options are adopted and diffused.

The largest gap to fill in order to achieve reliable information for policy design concerns applied research. Existing applied analyses of environmental innovations are very preliminary and limited by lack of good data. As previously said, no empirical study is able to distinguish environmental innovation from other forms of innovation, or to distinguish between innovation and diffusion. An assessment of the incentives necessary for firms to undertake and adopt environment-friendly technologies would also be valuable in order to provide policymakers with a rough order of magnitude of the policies to be implemented. Empirical research is also necessary to evaluate innovation spillovers and their impact on aggregate growth and to quantify the constraints imposed by inertia on environmental and industrial policies. Finally, an empirical assessment of the long-term value of basic research on environmental issues (particularly on climate issues) would help defining the optimal timing of environmental policies.[8]

Acknowledgements

The Author is grateful to David Ulph, Yannis Katsoulacos and Antoine Soubeyran for useful discussions. The Author is nonetheless the sole responsible for possible misrepresentations and errors.

References

Baldwin, R. (1995), Does Sustainability Require Growth, in: Goldin, I. and A. Winters (eds.), *The Economics of Sustainable Development*, Cambridge.

Barrett, S. (1994), Strategic Environmental Policy and International Trade, *Journal of Public Economics* 54, 325-338.

Boetti, M., M. Botteon, C. Carraro and A. Soubeyran (1996) On the Effects of Industrial, Trade and Environmental Policies on the Location Choices of Firms, *Revue d'Economie Industrielle* 83, 63-80.

Boone, L., S. Hall and D. Kemball-Cook (1992), Endogenous Technical Progress in Fossil Fuel Demand, Center for Economic Forecasting, London Business School.

---

[8]   On this topic, see the special issue of Energy Economics edited by Carlo Carraro and Jean-Charles Hourcade at the end of 1998.

Cadot, O. and B. Sinclair-Desgagne (1996), Innovation under the threat of stricter environmental standards, in: Carraro C., Y. Katsoulacos and A. Xepapadeas (eds.), *Environmental Policy and Market Structure*, Dordrecht, 131-141.

Cantwell, J. (1993), *Multinational Corporations and Innovatory Activities: Towards a New Evolutionary Approach*, University of Reading, Department of Economics, Discussion Papers in International Investment and Business Studies, N.172 Series B vol V.

Carlevaro, F., M. Garbely and T. Müller (1992), *Vers une modélisation en équilibre général des mesures de politique énergétique en Suisse*, Serie de Publications du CUEPE No. 49, Université de Genève.

Carraro, C. and M. Galeotti (1996), WARM: A European Model for Energy and Environmental Analysis, *Environmental Modelling and Assessment* 2, 171-189.

Carraro, C. and M. Galeotti (1997), Economic Growth, International Competitiveness and Environmental Protection: R&D and Innovation Strategies with the WARM Model, *Energy Economics* 19, 2-29

Carraro, C. and J.C. Hourcade (eds.) (1998), Optimal Timing of Climate Change Policies, special issue of *Energy Economics*, Amsterdam.

Carraro, C. and D. Siniscalco (1994), Environmental Policy Reconsidered: The Role of Technological Innovation, *European Economic Review* 38, 545-555.

Carraro, C. and A. Soubeyran (1998), R&D Cooperation, Innovation Spillovers and Firm Location in a Model of Environmental Policy, in Petrakis, E., E. Sartzetakis and A Xepapadeas (eds.), *Environmental Regulation and Market Structure*, Cheltenham.

Carraro, C. and G. Topa (1994), Should Environmental Innovation Policy be Internationally Coordinated?, in C. Carraro (ed.), *Trade, Innovation, Environment*, Dordrecht.

Carraro, C. and G. Topa (1995), Taxation and Environmental Innovation, in: Carraro, C. and J. Filar (eds.), *Game-Theoretic Models of the Environment*, Boston.

Chichilniski, G. (1994), Property Rights and the Dynamics of Renewable Resources in North-South Trade, in: Carraro, C. (ed.) (1994), *Trade, Innovation, Environment*, Dordrecht.

Ciccone, A. (1996), *Externalities and Interdependent Growth: Theory and Evidence*, University of California at Berkeley.

Coe, D.T., E. Helpman and A. W. Hoffmaister (1995), *North South R&D Spillovers*, Centre for Economic Policy Research Discussion Paper Series, N.1133, London.

Cohen, W. and R. Levin (1989), Empirical Studies of Innovation and Market Structure, *Handbook of Industrial Organization* 2 chapter 18.

Conrad, K. and I. Henseler-Unger (1986), Applied General Equilibrium Modelling for Long-Term Energy Policy in Germany, *Journal of Policy Modelling* 8, 531-549.

Conrad, K. and M. Ehrlich (1993), The Impact of Embodied and Disembodies Technical Progress on Productivity Gaps – An Applied General Equilibrium Analysis for Germany and Spain, *Journal of Productivity Analysis* 4, 317-335.

Contractor, F.J. and P. Lorange (1988), *Cooperative Strategies in International Business*, New York.

Davies, S. W. (1979), Inter-firm Diffusion of Process Innovations, *European Economic Review* 12, 299-317.

Dowlatabadi, H. and M. Oravetz (1996), *Modelling U.S. Long Term Energy Intensity: an Exploration of Endogenous Technical Change*, presented at the CEC-DGXII Symposium on Prospects for Integrated Environmental Assessment, Toulouse, 24-26.10.96.

Downing, P.B. and L.J. White (1986), Innovation in Pollution Control, *Journal of Environmental Economics and Management* 13, 18-29

Echia. G. and M. Mariotti (1994), *A Survey on Environmental Policy: Technological Innovation and Strategic Issues*, FEEM Working Paper, Milan.

Galeotti, M. and A. Lanza (1998), *Desperately Seeking Environmental Kuznets*, FEEM Working Paper, Milan.

Gao, X.M. (1994), Measuring Technological Change Using a Latent Variable Approach, *European Review of Agricultural Economics* 21, 113-129.

Goulder, L. and K. Mathai (1996), *Optimal CO_2 abatement in the Presence of Induced Technical Change*, University of Stanford.

Goulder, L. and S. Schneider (1996), *Induced Technical Change, Crowding Out and the Attractiveness of CO_2 Emission Abatement*, University of Stanford.

Griliches, Z. (1957), Hybrid Corn: An Exploration in the Economics of Technological Change, *Econometrica* 25, 501-522.

Grossman, G. (1995), Pollution and Growth: What Do We Know?, in Goldin, I. and A. Winters (eds.), *The Economics of Sustainable Development*, Cambridge.

Grossman, G. and E. Helpman (1991), Quality Ladders in the Theory of Growth, *Review of Economic Studies* 58, 43-61.

Grubler, A. and S. Messner (1996), *Technological Change and the Timing of Abatement Measures*, IIASA, Vienna.

Hall, S., N. Mabey and C. Smith (1994), *Macroeconomic Modelling of International Carbon Tax Regimes*, Department of Economics Discussion Paper n.94-08, University of Birmingham.

Hoel, M. (1995), *Environmental Policy as a Game between Governments when Plant Locations are Endogenous*, paper presented at the 21st EARIE Conference, Crete, 4-6.9, 1994.

Holtz-Eakin, D. and T.M. Selden (1995), Stoking the Fires? CO_2 Emissions and Economic Growth, *Journal of Public Economics* 61, 428-437.

Hung, V., P. Chang and K. Blackburn (1994), Endogenous Growth, Environment and R&D, in: Carraro C. (ed.), *Trade Innovation, Environment*, Dordrecht.

Katsoulacos, Y. and A. Xepapadeas (1996), Environmental innovation, spillovers and optimal policy rules, in: Carraro, C., Y. Katsoulacos and A. Xepapadeas (eds.), *Environmental Policy and Market Structure*, Dordrecht, 143-150.

Katsoulacos, Y. and D. Ulph (1996), *Endogenous Information Sharing and Technology Policy*, CEPR Discussion Paper No 1407, London.

Katz, M.L. and C. Shapiro (1987), R&D Rivalry with Licensing and Imitation, *American Economic Review* 77, 402-420.

Kemp, R., J. Schot and R. Hoogma (1998), Regime Shifts to Sustainability through Processes of Niche Formation. The Approach of Strategic Niche Management, *Technology Analysis and Strategic Management*, 10(2), 175-95

Kopp, R.J., W. Harrington, R.D. Morgenstern, W.A. Pizer, and J. S. Shih (1998), *Diffusion of New Technologies: A Microeconomic Analysis of Firm Decision Making at the Plant Level, Resources for the Future*, Washington.

Kumar, N. (1995), *Intellectual Property Protection, Foreign Direct Investments and Location of Overseas R&D Activities by Multinational Enterprises*, United Nation University, Institute for New Technologies, Maastricht.

Jaffe, A. B. and R. N. Stavins (1994), The Energy Paradox and the Diffusion of Conservation Technology, *Resource and Energy Economics* 16, 91-122.

Jaffee, A and R.N. Stavins (1995), Dynamic Incentives and Environmental Regulation: The Effects of Alternative Policy Instruments on Technology Diffusion, *Journal of Environmental Economics and Management* 29, 43-63.

Jorgenson, D.W. and P.J. Wilcoxen (1990), Intertemporal General Equilibrium Modelling of U.S. Environmental Regulation, *Journal of Policy Modelling* 12, 715-744.

Jung, C., K. Krutilla and R. Boyd (1996), Incentives for Advanced Pollution Abatement Technology at the Industry Level: An Evaluation of Policy Alternatives, *Journal of Environmental Economics and Management* 30, 95-111.

Laffont, J.J. and J. Tirole (1996), A Note on Environmental Innovation, *Journal of Public Economics* 62, 138-147.

Levin, S. G., S. L. Levin, and J. B. Meisel (1987), A Dynamic Analysis of the Adoption of a New Technology: The Case of Optical Scanners, *Review of Economics and Statistics* 69, 12-17.

Levinson, J. (1996), Environmental Policy and Plant Location, *Journal of Public Economics* 62, 1-18.

Lucas, R.E. (1988), On the Mechanics of Economic Development, *Journal of Monetary Economics* 100, 223-251.

Magat, W. (1979), The effects of environmental regulation on innovation, *Law and Contemporary Problems* 43, 4-25.

Malueg, D.A. (1989), Emission Credit Trading and the Incentive to adopt New Pollution Abatement Technology, *Journal of Environmental Economics and Management* 18, 297-300

Mankiw, N.G., D. Romer and D.N. Weil (1992), A Contribution to the Empirics of Economic Growth, *Quarterly Journal of Economics*, 407-437.

Mansfield, E. (1968), *Industrial Research and Technological Innovation*, New York.

Milliman, S. R. and R. Prince (1989), Firm Incentives to Promote Technological Change in Pollution Control, *Journal of Environmental Economics and Management* 17, 247-265.

Newell, R.G., A. Jaffee and R. Stavins (1996), *Energy-Saving Technological Innovation: the Effect of Economic Incentives and Direct Regulation*, presented at the NBER Workshop on Public Policy and the Environment, Cambridge, 29-30.7.96.

Oster, S. (1982), The Diffusion of Innovation Among Steel Firms: The Basic Oxygen Furnace, *The Bell Journal of Economics* 13, 45-56.

Pietrobelli, C. (1996), *Emerging Forms of Technological Cooperation: the Case for Technology Partnership*, Unctad, Division for Science and Technology,

Porter, M. (1991), America's Green Strategy, *Scientific American,* 168.

Rauscher, M. (1994), On Ecological Dumping, *Oxford Economic Papers* 46, 822-840.

Rauscher, M. (1995), *Environmental Regulation and the Location of Polluting Industries*, paper presented at the 50th IIPF Conference, Cambridge, MA, 22-25.8, 1994.

Requate, T. (1995), Incentives to Adopt New Technologies under Different Pollution-Control Policies, *International Tax and Public Finance* 2, 295-317.

Rip, A. and R. Kemp (1998), Technological Change, in: Rayner, S. and L. Malone (eds.), *Human Choice and Climate Change*, Vol 2 (chapter 6), Columbus, Ohio.

Romer, P. (1986), Increasing Returns and Long-Run Growth, *Journal of Political Economy* 98, 71-102.

Romer, P. (1990), Endogenous Technological Change, *Journal of Political Economy* 94, 1002-1037.

Slade, M.E. (1989), Modelling Stochastic and Cyclical Components of Technical Change: An Application of the Kalman Filter, *Journal of Econometrics* 41, 363-383.

Ulph, A. (1996), Strategic Environmental Policy, in: Carraro, C., Y. Katsoulacos and A. Xepapadeas (eds.), *Environmental Policy and Market Structure*, Dordrecht, 99-127.

Ulph, A. (1997), Environmental Policy and International Trade – A Survey of Recent Economic Analysis, in: Carraro, C. and D. Siniscalco (ed.), *New Directions in the Economic Theory of the Environment*, Cambridge.

Ulph, A. and Ulph. D. (1996), Trade, strategic innovation and strategic environmental policy – a general analysis, in: Carraro, C., Y. Katsoulacos and A. Xepapadeas (eds.), *Environmental Policy and Market Structure*, Dordrecht, 181-208.

Ulph, D. (1994), Strategic Innovation and Strategic Environmental Policy, in: Carraro, C. (ed.), Trade Innovation, Environment, Dordrecht.

Ulph, D. (1997), Environmental Policy and Technological Innovation, in: Carraro, C. and D. Siniscalco (ed.), *New Directions in the Economic Theory of the Environment*, Cambridge.

Verdier, T. (1995), Environmental Pollution and Endogenous Growth, in: Carraro, C. and J. Filar (eds.), Control and Game – Theoretic Models of the Environment, Boston.

Vonortas, N.S. (1991), *Research Cooperation in R&D Intensive Industries*, Aldershot.

Wilson, D. and J. Swisher (1993), Exploring the Gap: Top-down Versus Bottom-up Analyses of the Cost of Mitigating Global Warming, *Energy Policy* March, 249-263.

Reducing Pressures on the Environment: Forward-Looking Solutions and the Role of Formal Models

Faye Duchin

Dean, School of Humanities and Social Sciences
Rensselaer Polytechnic Institute, Troy, NY,
USA

Keywords. demonstration projects, lifestyle decisions, households, structual models.

1. Environmental problems result in substantial part as by-products of industrial production. These problems are sufficiently severe as to require independent analysis to determine where the public interest lies, and governmental intervention to assure that it is taken into account, because the profit-seeking orientation of industrial decision-makers is often at odds with avoiding environmental problems. The interventions may be direct, taking the form of regulations that require or prohibit certain actions, or indirect, in that they change the perceived attractiveness (e.g., the relative costs) of different courses of action.

Since regulations are necessarily based on current understandings of environmental problems and technological practices, they will inevitably become obsolete. While they may be useful initially, their existence hinders the development of better practices. To avoid this bind, government decision-makers need approaches to environmental policy that promote exploration and innovation. These can take the form of prototypes, test beds, incubators – in short the public equivalent of the development and testing concept of the corporate R&D lab. For convenience, I will refer to this set of items as demonstration projects.

2. The insights and experience of researchers can help decision-makers by providing relevant theory, systematic data and illustrative case studies, and results of model-based analysis. By taking its distance from short-term problems, theory can offer a broader or longer-term perspective on the systemic nature of the challenges and on possible solution concepts, or scenarios. Case studies can reveal strengths and weaknesses of specific hypothetical or actual demonstration projects or other

kinds of scenarios. Models can be used with databases to quantify the implications of alternative scenarios for the wider system.

I would like to make 3 main points today. First, I propose a conceptual framework that expands the domain of relevant decision-makers beyond those mentioned above to explicitly include lifestyle decisions made by households. Second, I propose demonstration projects, especially ones involving not only production but also household lifestyles, as a forward-looking complement to regulation or other policy approaches, and the case study as the methodological basis for building scenarios about such projects. Finally, I consider some characteristics formal models need to possess to be useful for analyzing scenarios describing forward-looking solutions and end with a few examples of applications.

3. Environmental problems are associated with all human activities, not only production of goods and services. In addition to industry and government decision-makers, there are also household decision-makers. Like industrial producers, the last are capable of innovative behavior with respect to the environment especially in terms of their consumption and discard practices. Substantial changes in these behaviors, however, require changes in underlying lifestyles. It is a new idea, but one that is gathering an increasing following among social scientists and the public more generally, that effective environmental policy requires understanding not only technological but also lifestyle dynamics.

The challenges that affluent lifestyles pose for the environment have naturally been realized first in the rich, industrialized countries. Fortunately, while people often operate in their self-interest, they also have a demonstrable concern about environmental degradation, interest in the public good, and openness to improving the quality of personal and social life. From the point of view of environmental damage, the potential payoff for achieving certain kinds of changes in lifestyle patterns is strong, since imitation of consumption patterns of the middle classes of affluent countries is as important in developing countries as is the transfer of technology. Almost all population growth and most of the increase in wealth in the decades ahead can be expected in today's developing countries.

Structural economics is a conceptual and methodological framework mainly concerned with the structure of production in different industries, based on their technological choices, and the structure of consumption in different categories of households, based on their lifestyle choices. The social accounting matrix, which is part of the System of National Accounts, provides descriptive data for the past and present not only about production but also about different kinds of households. This modeling framework has been exploited for policy analysis thus far mainly for the limited purpose of examining changes in the distribution of income in developing countries. It is a powerful basis for the formal analysis of scenarios about changes in technology and lifestyles.

4. When it comes to the question of the content of policy, there is a tension between the appealing simplicity of general principles (e.g., get the prices right) and the concreteness of detailed, situation-specific actions (e.g., ban lead in gasoline or elemental chlorine in pulping). There is another kind of strategy that requires rounds of decisions for its realization, such as the widespread switch from petroleum to hydrogen-based or biomass-based liquid fuels or the adoption of living patterns that entail substantially reduced reliance on automobiles. Case studies would develop specialized scenarios about the future and translate them into the language of the model. An example case is the examination of daily activities and mobility in communities with varying intensity of use of the automobile to identify and quantify key variables for achieving changes in potentially generalizable ways. It is not obvious whether or not such scenarios are materially feasible, environmentally benign, economically interesting, or socially desirable. The public interest is served by the energetic investigation of these kinds of ideas through demonstration projects, subjected to formal analysis. Such activities may yield commercially useful results while opening up new lines of exploration for technological and institutional change.

5. The strength of economic models and databases is that they represent the interdependence of various parts of a national or regional economy. The analyst develops a scenario and, on the basis of a computation with the model, examines the implications of the scenario for the various parts of the economy. The model is used to quantify the various ways in which the scenario makes a difference. There are two strong restrictions on the usefulness of a particular kind of model for analyzing a particular kind of scenario. First, the model needs to be capable of capturing the important aspects of the scenario in terms of its variables and parameters. To be specific, a model with highly aggregative production functions is too blunt an instrument for distinguishing the effects of alternative technologies. Likewise, one with a highly aggregated representation of consumption is not useful for exploring the effects of lifestyle changes. Second, the assumptions underlying the model need to be an explicit criterion for its suitability, since they limit the kinds of results that can be obtained. In a model that assumes that the lowest-cost option is chosen in each time period, for example, one cannot expect a strategy with only longer-term economic payoffs – let alone one that is economically costly but may still be socially desirable – to emerge as a viable choice.

My own experience is with structural models. I believe that on both counts structural models are well suited to examining the implications of detailed scenarios about changes in technologies and in lifestyles. I offer two examples. First is the analysis of a scenario based on the Brundtland Report's assumptions about the adoption of environmentally desirable production and household technologies (Duchin and Lange 1994). Using a model and database representing the world economy over the period from 1970 to 2020, we found that the scenario envisaged by the Brundtland Report was not nearly adequate to offset the undesirable effects on the environment of increasing populations and rising standards of living.

Second is an analysis for the Indonesian economy of alternative scenarios about self-sufficiency in food against a back-drop of modernization of industry. My colleagues and I found that food would need to be imported in any case, but that different scenarios had vastly different implications for water availability and land use. For example, modest investment in improving the efficiency of rice irrigation could more than solve the water problems. We also found that all scenarios about modernization would result in dramatic changes in the lifestyles (in particular in employment and consumption) of almost all Indonesian households (Duchin 1998).

These examples are intended to illustrate the potential of the approach. Truly bold scenarios can readily be analyzed within such a framework. However, it will require a team of individuals rich in social commitment and imagination as well as technological or social science expertise to develop the kinds of scenarios that can stimulate new thinking about solutions, especially about prospects for lifestyle changes.

References

Duchin, F. (1998), *Structural Economics: Measuring Change in Technology, Lifestyles, and the Environment*, Washington, D.C.

Duchin, F. and G. Lange (1994). *The Future of the Environment*, Oxford.

Environmental Taxes and Standards: An Empirical Analysis of the Impact on Innovation*

by Jens Hemmelskamp

European Commision, Joint Research Centre,
Institute for Prospective Technological Studies (IPTS)
W.T.C. Isla de la Cartuja, E-41092 Sevilla
Spain

Keywords. innovation panel, industry survey, econometric models, environmental innovation.

1 Introduction

By shaping the external framework conditions for companies, the state is an essential determinant of the extent and direction of company innovation. Since the beginning of the 1970s, environmental policy instruments have been implemented in many countries, thereby exerting a considerable influence on the behaviour of companies with respect to the environment.

With the increasing importance of environmental policy intervention in the economy, it is becoming ever more important to be able to determine the interaction between the application of environmental policy instruments and innovative behaviour. While it is generally recognised that it has been possible to decouple pollutant emission trends from economic growth (Walz et al. 1992) through the influence of state environmental policy, its effects on innovative behaviour and the competitiveness of businesses is nonetheless a controversial topic in the debate on national competitiveness. One side argues that the burdens placed on business by environmental policy, where environmental standards have been dominant up to now, limit the readiness to innovate and could therefore harm international competitiveness. The other side puts the case that environmental policy measures pro-

---

* I should like to thank Dr. Norbert Janz (Centre for European Economic Research Mannheim) and Prof. D. Hitchens (European Commission JRC-IPTS and Queens University Belfast) particularly for their valuable suggestions and comments on this paper.

vide stimuli to innovate and drive technological change forward (Porter and van der Linde 1995).

This paper aims to study the operation and effects of environmental policy instruments on the environmentally innovative behaviour of companies in an empirical analysis, narrowing to some extent the research gap here.

2   The Theoretical Framework and the Data

The paper takes a relatively broad, microeconomic definition of innovation, which makes it easier to distinguish innovation, which can prove difficult in practice. In addition, the innovations at company level, which are especially important for the environment, can be adequately registered. Environmental innovation is defined as innovation which serves to prevent or reduce anthropogenic burdens on the environment, clean up damage already caused or diagnose and monitor environmental problems.

In the debate on factors influencing innovation, innovation economists are now agreed that both supply-push and demand-pull factors have an effect (Pavitt 1984, Becher et al. 1993). However, the special qualities of environmental innovation and the specific importance of environmental policy instruments as regulatory-push and regulatory-pull factors has until now been more or less ignored. The majority of available studies on the relationship between environmental policy and innovation have come from environmental economics. As a result, economic instruments such as taxes or permits are shown to have advantages in this respect (Milliman/Prince 1989). However, the fault in an environmental economics approach is its failure to note the complexity of existing structures influencing environmental innovation. For example, the existing emitter structure or different technical options, like a distinction between clean, integrated and end-of-pipe technologies, are mainly not considered.

Looking at the influence of environmental policy from the perspective of innovation research, it becomes clear that the use of environmental policy instruments must be considered as a part of a system of economic, political or social determinant factors influencing innovative behaviour. Factors include, for example, the influence of further regulatory instruments, the characteristics of companies affected by environmental regulations, or the structure of the market affected by environmental regulations (Kemp 1998; Ashford 1993; Rothwell 1992). Attention must then be focused on whether linear, mechanically reproducible cause-and-effect relationships exist between the use of environmental policy instruments and the generation of innovations, or whether the influence of environmental policy instruments is being disguised or intensified by other factors and their interactions.

For an analysis, a linkage is therefore necessary between the results of environmental economics and innovation research as described for example by Kemp, Smith and Becher in this volume (see also Kemp 1998). The use of environmental policy instruments then represents an additional factor within a package of important framework conditions, through which the room for manoeuvre in environmentally oriented innovation decisions by companies is greatly restricted. It is also important to distinguish between factors influencing the development and the application of environmental technologies, as users are not necessarily also the developers of such technologies, so that environmental innovation can also be observed in companies not directly affected by environmental policy measures.

Thus, the basic hypothesis of the paper is that an environmental policy instrument is simply one more decision-taking parameter for companies' innovation-related decisions. The impacts of a environmental policy instrument is not linear but strongly depends on a multitude of further factors and consequently can be positive in one case and negative in an other case.

The paper evaluates data collected in 1993 for the Mannheim Innovation Panel (MIP) from German companies.[1] These data entail variables information necessary to analyse the complex relationships between environmental policies, other framework conditions and the innovation behaviour of companies in an econometric study. The 1993 MIP innovation survey was part of the Community Innovation Survey (CIS), initiated by the EU Commission and EUROSTAT and conducted in every member state (Felder et al. 1994). The gross sample of the Mannheim Innovation Panel is based on the company data base of the "Verband der Vereine Creditreform (VVC)" – the largest credit rating agency in Germany – which early in 1993 contained data on some 1.5 million companies from the Old Federal States and some 200,000 companies from the New Federal States. In 1993, companies were asked about innovation objectives which also included environmental targets. This included questions about the importance of environmental innovation in products and processes and of reducing consumption of energy and raw materials. Thus cross-sectoral data at the company level are available, making it possible to highlight differences between their attitudes to environmental innovation and to identify microeconomic categories of environmentally innovative behaviour.

In 1993, questionnaires were sent to a total of 13,317 companies, of which 2,954 participated in the survey. The response rate corresponds to the normal rate in written company surveys, around 25 per cent. Microeconometric methods are used to correct response biases so that weighted data are only affected to a small extend (see Harhoff/Licht et al. 1996 for this method).[2] But not environmental issues leaded to these biases but, for example, an overrepresentation of companies un-

---

[1]   For a description of the Mannheim Innovation Panels see Harhoff, D./ Licht, G. (1994: 255ff.).

[2]   Large companies and companies undertaken R&D are over-represented in the sample

dertaking R&D. For the present study, 2,481 companies were selected from the sample. The selection considered only companies in manufacturing industry, ignoring the service sector. Of the 2,481, 67 per cent are located in the Old Federal States, 33 per cent in the New Federal States. The NACE industry categories have been grouped into 13 industries for the purposes of this survey. Tables 1 and 2 show the distribution of the chosen companies among these industries and according to the five company sizes.

Table 1:   Share of industries in the sample
                 [unweighted and weighted data in % of the companies]

Industries	unweighted	weighted
mining	4,9	1,2
food	4,7	9,3
textiles	4,9	8,2
wood	6,0	14,0
chemicals	14,3	12,2
ceramics	4,3	5,6
basic metal	3,6	2,6
metal working	10,0	15,5
machinery	21,5	10,9
office equipment	8,7	6,4
control eng.	7,1	5,9
transport	6,2	2,5
other	3,9	6,0
total	100	100

Source: MIP 1993

In addition to the information derived from the MIP, a quantitative indicator was needed which is able to measure regulation density. Information on the pressure to act brought to bear on companies by environmental policy instruments is not available. Many studies therefore create auxiliary indicators which depict the influence of instruments. In a panel study, for example, Jaffe/Palmer (1996) use the rate of environmental investment expenditure for the industry as an indicator of the pressure exerted on companies by environmental regulations.[3] However, its appropriateness for this study is limited, i.e. because, data on company environmental investment considers principally end-of-pipe technologies, as investment in

---

[3]   see also Lanjou/ Mody (1996), Green et al. (1994), Malaman (1996), Cottica (1994).

integrated technologies is hard to identify statistically. An indicator based on these data would therefore show too low a regulatory intensity in precisely those industries where environmental successes have been achieved to a great extent with integrated technologies. Another measure of regulatory intensity is the size and number of environmental laws and regulations passed. This indicator is, however, also unsuitable for the present study, as conclusions can only be drawn from analyses over a number of years. A sector-specific study cannot be carried out, and one can scarcely assume that there is a correlation between the length of legal texts and the pressure for action which they exert. Finally, this indicator also fails to permit differentiation between different environmental policy instruments.

Table 2:   Share of companies in the size classes
[unweighted and weighted data in % of the companies]

Size	unweighted	weighted
< 50	34,0	74,4
50 – 199	27,0	21,1
200 – 499	16,4	3,0
500 – 999	9,9	0,8
> 1000	12,7	0,7
Summe	100	100

Source: MIP 1993

As indirect indicators seem to have several disadvantages, a survey to derive a direct indicator was conducted. As it was not possible to carry out an additional company survey, a limited written survey of the German chambers of commerce (IHKs) was conducted for the purposes of this study. The environment officers at the IHKs were asked to estimate the extent to which companies were affected by environmental policy instruments at industry level, something which the IHKs, with their intersectoral functions and information, are in a good position to estimate. In contrast, industrial associations, such as for the chemicals industry (VDC) or engineering (VDMA), are less suitable because of their sector-specific perspectives.

The disadvantage of this industry indicator is that the variation in regulatory intensity within the industry cannot be determined. For example, operators of old plant are more heavily affected by environmental regulations on exhaust gases than those operating new plant. The assessments reached by the IHKs must also be seen in the context of the different economic structure of their respective regions, which strongly determined their judgement.

The IHKs were asked in three questions to estimate the extent to which the 13 industries defined for the study were affected by environmental policy in general and environmental taxes or standards in particular. Answers were given on a 9-point scale from "not affected" to "heavily affected". 80 questionnaires were sent to the IHKs, 19 of which responded. 18 responses could be evaluated, corresponding to a more or less standard response rate of 22 per cent for written surveys. The results of the survey are summarised in Figure 1 which shows the median for each industry. The burden for the chemical industry is assessed as the highest followed by the mining and energy sector. A differentiation between the environmental policy instruments is given in half of the industries. In interpreting these results, it should nevertheless be noted that environmental taxes are used only in isolated cases in Germany. As Oates et al. (1994:22) point out: "Finding the appropriate data (...) to test for differential effects of command and control versus incentive-based environmental regulation could be difficult given the dearth experience with regulations other than command and control". It can therefore be assumed that that judgements on the extent of the impact of taxes are characterised less by experiences with this instrument, and rather more by the heated debate on the introduction of eco-taxes.

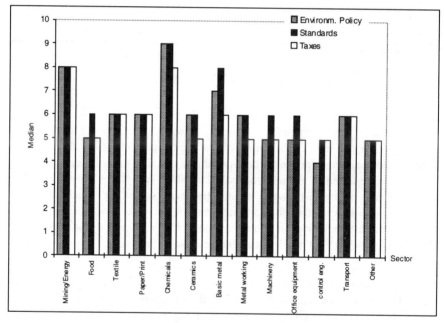

Figure 1:   Impact on German industries caused by environmental policy [median]

3 Descriptive Analysis

Based on the interdependent correlations of the various economic, legal or technological factors relevant to innovative behaviour, significant parameters of environment-oriented innovative behaviour were identified using the data of the MIP. This data is presented in the following descriptive analyses.

3.1 Environmental Innovation Objectives

In the MIP companies were asked about their innovation objectives (see Table 3). Those surveyed were requested to give a subjective assessment of the significance of suggested innovation objectives using a scale ranging from 1 to 5 ("unimportant" to "extremely important").

Table 3:   Innovation objectives

Innovation objectives	median
Defend or enlarge market share	5
Improve product quality	5
Reduce wages	4
Reduce rejects in production	4
Expand main activities	4
Increase flexibility of production process	4
New markets in the "Old Laender"	4
Replace old products	4
Reduce set-up time of production	4
Cut down on raw materials used	4
Improve working conditions	4
Develop environmentally-friendly products	4
Cut down on energy used	3
Reduce environmental impact of production	3
New markets in the "New Laender"	3
New markets within the European Union	3
Expand other activities	2
New markets in Eastern Europe	1
New markets in other countries	1
New markets in the United States	1
New markets in Japan	1

Source: MIP 1993

One possibility for distilling the relevant environmental innovation objectives from the given innovation objectives is a factor analysis. Here structures can be drawn out between the individual innovation objectives, thereby giving an indication as to which innovation objectives can be assigned to a particular innovation strategy.

Using factor analysis, five factors were drawn from the mass of variables made up by the innovation objectives. These can be interpreted as innovation strategies for reducing costs, expanding global markets, expanding local markets, environmental protection and securing markets. An overview of the results of the factor analysis is given in Table 4. The higher the absolute values that have been determined, the closer the correlation between the latent structure of objectives and the importance of the innovation objective in question according to the companies in the survey. Some innovation objectives are closely related, not only to one, but also to several business strategies. An interpretation must take account of the relationships between these goals and the corresponding strategies. The closest relationships between the individual objectives have been highlighted.

The innovation strategy "environmental protection", which is of interest to the main question of this study, encompasses five innovation objectives. Companies look at developing environmentally-friendly products, cutting back on the energy used and reducing the environmental impact of production as well as at the improvement of product quality and of working conditions against the background of improved environmental protection. Objective complementarities are evident, too.

It is unsurprising that developing environmentally friendly products and reducing energy consumption or pollution belong to the environmental protection strategy. The environmental aspect in reducing environmental stress during production and developing environmentally friendly products is obvious. The contribution from reducing energy consumption is also understandable, with the possible reductions in emissions from energy production. Alongside these three objectives, improving product quality and improving working conditions can also be assigned to environmental protection, although improving product quality has relatively low factor values both for environmental protection and for reducing costs and securing markets, and so this objective is not used in interpreting the environmental protection strategy.

The high factor value for improving working conditions can be explained by the close relationship between safety at work and environmental protection. Environmentally harmful production processes, for example pollutant emissions in automobile paint shops, can affect the health of those working there, or accidents at the workplace, such as when working with poisonous substances, can lead to considerable environmental pollution. On the other hand, it is surprising that environmental protection receives such a low value from reducing materials consumption, even though reducing the consumption of resources is an essential component in measures to realise sustainable development (cf. Pearce/Turner 1990:43). Reducing materials consumption has a high factor value only with the reducing costs strategy, form which it can be concluded that reducing materials intensity is seen by companies primarily in terms of efficiency, as a measure for saving costs.

Table 4:   Factor analysis: Structure of the innovation objectives

	reducing costs	expanding global markets	expanding local markets	environ-mental protection	securing markets
Replace old products	0,091	0,273	0,132	-0,013	0,404
Defend or enlarge market share	0,123	0,100	0,209	0,043	0,406
Expand main activities	0,087	0,092	0,213	0,055	0,360
Expand other activities	0,085	0,094	0,112	0,050	0,216
New markets in the Old Laender	0,106	0,099	0,626	0,045	0,092
New markets in the New Laender	0,114	-0,005	0,633	0,123	0,046
New markets in Eastern Europe	0,049	0,343	0,447	0,066	0,053
New markets within the European Union	0,095	0,519	0,467	-0,003	0,091
New markets in Japan	0,012	0,737	-0,004	0,079	0,041
New markets in the United States	0,031	0,822	-0,013	-0,006	0,039
New markets in other countries	0,046	0,688	0,187	0,017	-0,007
Improve product quality	0,286	0,034	0,131	0,293	0,301
Develop environmentally-friendly products	0,074	0,124	0,134	0,518	0,194
Increase flexibility of production process	0,405	0,006	0,162	0,277	0,246
Reduce wages	0,592	0,039	0,054	-0,010	0,072
Cut down on raw material used	0,628	0,076	0,085	0,125	0,025
Cut down on energy used	0,554	-0,033	0,087	0,427	-0,104
Reduce set-up time of production	0,643	0,080	0,093	0,208	0,073
Reduce rejects in production process	0,557	0,068	0,045	0,314	0,124
Improve working conditions	0,385	-0,004	0,091	0,563	0,031
Reduce environmental impact	0,241	0,037	0,010	0,679	-0,025

Note: unweighted data; Cronbachs α =0,818; The highlighted figures indicate the most important relationships in each row
Source: MIP 1993

As well as identifying the objectives of environmental innovation, the factor analysis also allows further conclusions as to company innovation activities. Innovation objectives with a high factor value for several innovation strategies imply complementary goals, i.e. that other intentions are simultaneously associated with an innovation goal. Cottica (1994:32) shows that environmental innovation in the Italian packaging industry cannot be separated from innovation to reduce costs. For German manufacturing industry, such a link between efficiency and environmental protection can only be found for reduction of energy consumption.

This innovation objective has high values both for environmental protection and for reducing costs. The higher factor value for reducing costs nevertheless implies its somewhat greater significance as motivation for reducing energy consumption than that of environmental protection.

Furthermore, the factor analysis reveals that environmental-related aspects still only play a minor part in innovation strategies of German companies, e.g. with regard to tapping new markets and market potentials.

In the following analyses, the four innovation objectives of reducing environmental stress during production, developing environmentally friendly products, reducing energy consumption and improving working conditions are defined as environmental innovation goals. However, because of its importance to the idea of sustainable development, the innovation goal of reducing materials consumption is also included in the analyses.

3.2 Environmental Innovative Versus Non-Environmental-Innovative Companies

The descriptive analysis refers to selected factors that can influence environmental innovation. These factors are the size class, the sector industry, technological opportunities, location, market structure, market demand, appropriability conditions, sources of information and state influence (Kemp 1996, Hemmelskamp 1997).

The environmental innovation objectives (reducing environmental impact of production" and "developing environmentally friendly products" are used to subdivide the sample into two sub-samples. Companies regarding these environmentally-relevant objectives as significant or highly significant innovation objectives are called "environmentally-innovative companies" and companies attaching no or only little significance make up the sub-sample of "non-environmentally-innovative companies" (see Figure 2).

The main results of the descriptive analysis are as follows. We can see that environmental innovations can be more important to large companies than to small and medium-sized ones (see Table 5). The distribution among the size classes shows that some 65 per cent of the small and medium-sized companies with a workforce of up to 500 belong to the environmentally-innovative companies. On the other hand, more than 75 per cent of the larger companies with over 500 workers are found in the group of environmentally-innovative companies.

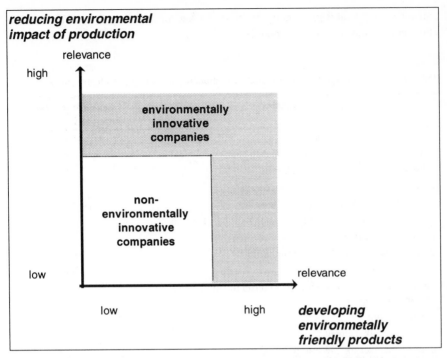

Figure 2:   Environmentally- and non-environmentally-innovative companies

Table 5:   Share of environmentally-innovative companies according to size [in %]

size	environmentally innovative companies
< 50	65,4
50 - 199	66,2
200 - 499	64,3
500 - 999	75,5
> 1,000	78,6

Source: MIP 1993

Depending on the direction of production and its scope, the share of environmentally-innovative companies differs in the various industries. Compared with other
industries, the relative share of environmentally-innovative companies is highest in
the primary industries and consumption related such as industries "food, beverages

and tobacco", "wood-processing, pulp, paper and printing" or "refineries, chemicals, rubber, plastics", for example (see Table 6).

Table 6:   Environmentally-innovative companies according to industry [in %]

Industry	environmentally-innovative companies
food, beverages and tobacco	84,2
woodprocessing, paper, printing, publishing	83,1
refineries, chemicals, rubber, plastics	82,3
transport (cars, trains, vessels, spacecraft)	78,8
furniture, toys, sports equipment, jewellery	74,2
office equipment, computers, communications, electronics	63,5
metal, iron and steel	62,1
mining, gas and petroleum, public utilities	60,4
textiles, garments	59,5
mechanical engineering, electrical household applicances, arms and ammunition	59,5
metal-working	54,8
ceramics, chalk, cement	47,3
control engineering, metrology	47,2

Source: MIP 1993

More than 46 per cent of all companies are continuously engaged in research and development activities. The percentage for non-environmentally-innovative companies is about 50 per cent and for environmentally-innovative ones it is around 45 per cent. At just under 4.4 per cent environmentally-oriented companies have on average a lower R&D intensity than non-environmentally-oriented companies (5.5 per cent).

There are also significant differences between environmentally-innovative and non-environmentally-innovative companies in their assessment of the innovation-impeding effects of overly long administrative procedures. This discrepancy in the assessment of state influence could reflect the effects of environmental policy measures.

The appropriability conditions (i.e. patents or secrecy) that limit the extent of spill-over effects and thus may protect the competitive advantages of new or improved products and processes are more important to environmentally innovative companies than to environmentally non-innovative ones (see Table 7). This is true for product as well as for process innovations.

Environmental-innovative companies also expect a greater sales potential then non-environmental-innovative companies. They view the development of demand between 1993 and 1995 more positively (see Table 8).

Table 7:   Relevance of appropriability conditions [median]

Mechanisms	Product-innovation		Process-innovation	
	Environ-mentally-innovative companies	non-environmentally-innovative companies	Environ-mentally-innovative companies	non-environmentally-innovative companies
Patents	3	1	2	1
Copyright	3	2	2	1
Secrecy	4	3	4	3
Complexity of product design	4	3	4	3
First mover	5	4	4	4
Long-term employee relations	5	4	4	4

Quelle: MIP 1993

Finally, the information requirement of environmentally innovative companies is higher. It can be seen that the marketing and sales departments in particular are important internal sources of information and customers an important external source for environmentally innovative companies.

Table 8:   Expected market demand [in % of the companies]

Expected demand for 1993 – 1995	(– –)	(–)	(0)	(+)	(++)	Σ
Environmentally-innovative companies	5,86	18,31	34,02	29,84	11,97	100
non-environmentally-innovative companies	7,66	24,40	37,98	24,89	5,06	100

Quelle: MIP 1993

To sum-up, according to the results of the descriptive analysis, the environmentally innovative and non-environmentally innovative companies are distinguishable as follows:

- The larger the company, the more environmentally innovative it is.

- Share of environmental innovative companies is higher in environmental intensive and consumption related industries

- Environmentally innovative companies have low R&D intensity.

- Environmentally innovative companies are heavily involved in R&D cooperation.

- Environmental innovation is strongly dependent on positive expectations about demand.

- Protecting ·returns on innovation is especially important for environmental innovation.

- Environmental innovation demands that companies possess a great amount of internal and external information.

- The greater the obstruction by lengthy administrative procedures, the greater the importance of environmental innovation.

4   Econometric Analysis of the Factors Influencing Environmental Innovation

4.1   The Models

Five multivariate models in all are estimated. The endogenous variables in the German analysis are five innovation objectives investigated in the MIP Panel:

- reducing the environmental impact of production,

- development of environmentally friendly products,

- reduction of energy consumption

- reduction of material consumption and

- improving working conditions.

These variables are given an ordinal value on a scale of 1 (no importance) to 5 (very great importance). On the basis of these categories of endogenous variable – and assuming a normal distribution – ordered probit models are estimated. If the coefficient in the model is positive, the factor has a positive effect on the importance of an innovation goal. The model coefficient estimates and t-statistics are presented in Table 9.

Table 9:   Results of model estimations

Innovation objective / Exogenous variable	Environmental friendly products Coeff. (t-statistic)	Environmental impact production Coeff. (t-statistic)	Material consumption Coeff. (t-statistic)	Energy consumption Coeff. (t-statistic)	Improving Working conditions Coeff. (t-statistic)
Environmental policy					
Standards	-0,108 (-1,744)	0,028 (0,453)	0,905 (1,555)	0,177 (2,882)	0,075 (1,212)
Taxes	0,309 (4,438)	0,118 (1,724)	-0,101 (-1,489)	-0,124 (-1,811)	-0,089 (-1,280)
Market structure					
company size in employees (log)	-0,281 (-3,213)	-0,349 (-3,893)	0,092 (1,130)	-0,017 (-2,073)	-0,391 (-4,521)
company size in employees (log^2)	0,027 (3,564)	0,034 (4,446)	-0,001 (-0,190)	0,018 (2,486)	0,031 (4,192)
Technological Opport.					
R&D-co-operation				-0,171 (-2,489)	-0,176 (-2,540)
R&D-intensity	-1,477 (-3,034)	-1,736 (-3,524)	-1,302 (-2,762)	-2,789 (-5,617)	-1,744 (-3,478)
Approbriability cond.					
First mover	0,164 (5,035)	0,057 (2,204)		0,064 (2,416)	
Complexity of process					
Long-term employee relation			0,088 (3,068)		
Copyright	0,066 (2,518)				
other		0,091 (3,351)	0,074 (2,795)		0,074 (2,754)
State influence, costs, risks					
Innovation risk too high	-0,071 (-2,496)				
Administrative procedures too long	0,106 (4,897)	0,095 (4,379)		0,078 (3,593)	0,085 (3,893)
Lack of capital		-0,051 (-2,196)			

Table 9: continued

Innovation objective	Environmental friendly products	Environmental impact production	Material consumption	Energy consumption	Improving Working conditions
Exogenous variable	Coeff. (t-statistic)	Coeff. (t-statistic)	Coeff. (t-statistic)	Coeff. (t-statistic)	Coeff. (t-statistic)
Sources of information					
Company internal	0,125 (3,324)	0,137 (3,739)		0,216 (5,762)	0,116 (3,130)
Suppliers: materials, components	0,166 (5,617)		0,140 (4,926)	- 0,079 (-2,415)	
Universities	0,126 (4,684)	0,098 (3,731)		0,073 (2,524)	0,053 (1,782)
Immediate competitors			0,107 (3,857)		
Customers					0,105 (2,955)
Consultants, market researchers	0,066 (2,172)				0,103 (3,217)
Industry-financed research institutes				0,073 (2,275)	0,084 (2,477)
Supplier of equipment		0,140 (4,979)		0,229 (7,315)	0,147 (5,169)
Region					
New Federal States			0,235 (3,170)	0,559 (7,257)	0,133 (1,740)
Statistics					
Number of observations	1195	1161	1206	1171	1148
Likelihood-ratio-test Chi²:	292,56 (13)	230,33 (12)	104,11 (10)	252,93 (14)	207,53 (15)
Log Likelihood	- 1703,56	-1726,53	-1702,17	- 1714,19	- 1574,21
Pseudo R²	0,079	0,063	0,03	0,069	0,062

Note: Wald-test of joint significance of variables for appropriability conditions, market structure, sources of information, and environmental policy. The goodness of fit of the ordered probit models is within the bounds of comparable econometric cross-sectoral studies.

The factors which were observed to affect the importance of environmental innovation objectives in the descriptive analyses are accounted for as exogenous variables in the models. Alongside the two variables for regulatory intensity also the majority of the exogenous variables are given an ordinal value (see Annex 1). The hypothesis that environmentally innovative companies show a comparatively low R&D intensity is tested in the model by considering the share of R&D expenditure in total turnover for 1992. The influence of protection mechanisms is registered in variables for the importance of a first mover or copyright, for example. The importance of various source of information is measured through variables for the importance of internal and external information exchange. The significance of R&D cooperation and the company's location are measured as binary variables. Company size is given in terms of employees, using both the logarithm of the employees (in full-time equivalencies) and the log squared, in order to discover any non-linear relations between levels of employment and the importance of environmentally oriented product innovation. On a logarithmic scale, the differences in company size are no longer weighted linearly.

4.2 Results from the Econometric Models

The econometric models (see Table 9) confirm that environmentally oriented innovation is determined by a complex interaction between various factors. However, the hypotheses formulated above in the descriptive analysis about the factors influencing environmentally innovative behaviour are only partially confirmed by the multivariate analysis.

In the descriptive analysis, lengthy administrative procedures were seen to obstruct environmentally innovative companies more than others. It was therefore assumed that the importance of environmental innovation would increase as the companies faced more obstacles from drawn-out administrative procedures. One explanation for such a relationship between administrative procedures and environmental innovation might be the considerable red tape brought by environmental policy measures. If this relation proved to be the case, the administrative burden placed on companies could be used as a proxy variable for regulatory intensity. However, the econometric models show that the significant influence of administrative procedures on environmental innovation objectives remains even when regulatory indicators are taken into account. This means that the variable for administrative burden reflects the effects of other state actions, for example in case of product innovations the structure of public administration and the influence of bans, permissions and registration procedures, regulations for use or obligatory informational instruments decreed for health and safety reasons. The correlation might also indicate the importance of the time-lapse between planning and realising process innovation, which can be drawn out by public protest or objections on the grounds of environmental risk. In this case it can be assumed that public resistance which lengthens procedures increases the willingness of companies to defuse existing environmental disputes with the public or representatives of environmental interests by developing and introducing environmentally sound production processes, thereby speeding up the realisation of investment processes.

The regulatory indicators used are meaningful variables for estimating the correlation between environmental policy instruments and the innovative behaviour of companies. Above all, they permit a comparative evaluation of the influence of an instrument to be made in the models, and thereby enable the hypothesis that a stronger incentive to innovate is produced by taxes than by standards to be tested.

It becomes clear that nothing can be said about the general advantages of one type of instrument over another. Innovation to reduce the environmental impact of production and to develop environmentally friendly products, for example, can be stimulated through the use of environmental taxes whereas standards would either have no or a negative innovation impact. In particular, the coefficients for taxes are different in these two models which, with some statistical reservation, suggests that environmental taxes have a stronger positive impact on environmental product innovation then on process innovation. On the contrary, the introduction or tightening up of standards would hinder the development of environmentally friendly products and would have no impact on the importance of innovations to reduce the environmental impact of production.

One advantage of standards over taxes can be found in case of the stimulation of innovation to reduce energy consumption. A significant positive correlation at 1 per cent exists between environmental standards and the innovation objective, while the correlation between taxes and the goal is significant and negative at 10 per cent. The result is surprising in the context of the debate in environmental economics. As described above environmental taxes are held to be more efficient than regulation, partly because of their more powerful effect on innovation. The result from the model estimation should therefore be interpreted in the light of the heated debate in Germany over introducing energy taxes which took place in the early 1990s. The dominant view in German companies was that the introduction of energy taxes would bring about a considerable worsening of their international competitiveness, especially in the energy-intensive sectors (Voss 1995). Because of the great uncertainty about the operation and effects of these taxes, it can be assumed that standards are preferred by companies as, after many years of experience with them, they can better estimate the effects of these familiar instruments.

Environmental policy has no effect on the importance of innovation to reduce consumption of materials or improve conditions at the company workplace. The likelihood of more innovation to reduce consumption by companies does not rise with the introduction or tightening up of existing standards. Nor can a greater importance be expected for innovative efforts to save materials from the introduction of environmental taxes. This is surprising, in view of the financial incentives provided by taxes, which would lead one to assume that cost reduction and environmental objectives would complement one another. The result should be interpreted above all in the light of inadequate incentives for innovation in current output-oriented environmental policy and the scant experience companies have had with environmental taxes.

Thus the results show that a economic instruments seems to have advantages in case of environmental product innovations but that there are no general advantages of one type of instrument over another related to environmental process innovations. The hypothesis that economic instruments should be generally preferred over standards must be rejected. The results prove instead the importance for innovation of a case-by-case choice of instruments, taking account of the respective framework conditions for innovation. The necessity of such a policy approach can also be seen in the example of water conservation described by Jänicke (1997). Under the influence of a variety of factors, taxes proved an effective instrument in the Netherlands, which success was achieved in Sweden through the use of subsidies.

However, the model analysis also confirm that besides environmental policy a number of further interrelated factors also effects the relevance of environmental innovation behaviour of companies. The factors with a potential to influence environmental innovation include the size of the company. Opinion in the innovation literature is divided as to the impact of large or small companies on the development of new technologies (Kleinknecht 1989). In the descriptive analyses it was observed that the status of environmental innovation objectives was higher in larger companies than in smaller ones. This leads to the hypothesis, greater company size means a rise in the importance of environmentally oriented innovation objectives, one which is reinforced by results from the research of Georg et al. (1992), which points to the restrictive effects on innovation from insufficient experience operating integrated technology in small and medium-sized companies. Rothwell (1992:455) also emphasises the disadvantages of smaller companies and points to the heavier burden from environmental policy measures which they bear, in comparison to larger ones. However, this research hypothesis is borne out only to a limited extent by the econometric analyses. While company size has no noticeable effect on innovation to save materials, the other models show a non-linear correlation between company size and the importance of innovation objectives. Thus environmental innovation enjoys a high status above all in very small or very large companies, and is least important in medium-sized ones. Any distortion due to different R&D intensities can be excluded by including it as a variable. For example, up to around 171 employees, the importance of the innovation objective to reduce the environmental impact of production falls as employment levels rise. However, its importance then rises as the number of employees' increases. The accumulated upward trend nonetheless fails to reach the levels found with very low employment until the number of employees rises to about 28,500. In case of the development of environmental-friendly products the structure of small and medium-sized companies among suppliers of environmentally friendly products makes itself felt. Adler et al. (1994.), for example, showed in a written survey that over 58 per cent of companies in the environmental technology industry in Germany had under 100 employees (see also Halstrick-Schwenk et al. 1994). For small innovative companies, this result indicates, among other things, advantages in flexibility through less complex production processes and a greater willingness to exploit niche markets. The importance to very large companies can be explained both by reasons of image, as the development and launch of environmentally friendly products enables well-known companies to present themselves in a positive light to what is a critical public, and by the stricter monitoring carried out by state environmental bodies (Brännlund et al.1995:33).

The hypothesis that the importance of environmental innovation objectives falls as R&D intensity rises is confirmed for all environmental innovation in the models. The result contradicts Jaffe and Palmer (1996), who noted a significant positive correlation between the level of environmental investment and R&D expenditure in a regulated sector. To interpret this result, as distinction must be drawn between product innovation and process innovation. In the case of environmental process innovation, the environmental technology industry is presumably very important as a technology supplier, and process innovators therefore require no intensive R&D. But environmental product innovators, who also include suppliers of environmental technology, ascribe little importance to R&D. One explanation may be the current dominance of end-of-pipe technologies, which are essentially merely incremental improvements to existing technological solutions, so that R&D is only required to a limited extent. This is supported by the significant negative relationship between the innovation risk and the importance of the development of environmental friendly products as an innovation objective. It can be assumed that innovation is heavily concentrated on low-risk incremental change in parts or components of products already on the market, and therefore builds predominantly on existing technological discoveries.

Environmental innovations involves economic risks that originate from the fact that companies find it hard to gain an overview of the available environmental technologies and to obtain full information on their effect and their applicability. As might be expected, exploiting the existing external technological structure is an important source of information for environmental innovation. For example, suppliers of equipment have an important function in providing information for innovation to reduce production-related environmental pollution. The result reinforces the idea that process innovators obtain their environmental technologies predominantly from specialised technology suppliers. Suppliers of primary products, materials and components provide important information for developing environmentally friendly products and reducing consumption of materials. This appears sensible in both cases, as the environmental soundness of a product is heavily dependent on the materials used, and reducing materials consumption depends upon, among other things, information about possibilities for substitution. However, while Georg et al. (1992), for example, ascribe great importance to the customer as a source of information for environmental product innovation, the models reveal no influence on the importance of environmental innovation. Instead the public research infrastructure, i.e. the availability of information from universities and technical colleges exerts strong influence on the development of environmentally friendly products.

Concerning the influence of demand on the importance attached to environmental innovation, the hypothesis was formulated that environmentally innovative companies see demand trends more positively than others. However, this hypothesis must be rejected, as no impact of market demand development could be found for environmental objectives. Surprisingly, neither past nor expected market demand up to 1996 has particular importance for the status of environmentally friendly product innovation. It might have been supposed that, contrary to this result, market forces – i.e. demand for environmental technologies – from companies facing regulation or environmentally aware consumers would provide a decisive stimulus for generating environmentally oriented product innovation. In the paper industry, for example, it has been shown that demand from end users had a strong influence of the development and introduction of clean process innovations as well as the launch of recycled paper products (Wong et al. 1995, see also Blazejczak/Edler in this volume). However, this result could be partly due to qualitative changes in market demand, without any quantitative effects.

Furthermore, the econometric analyses also make clear that appropriating returns on individual examples of environmental innovation takes place with a variety of instruments. Although an increase in the number of environmental patent applications has been observed in Germany in recent years, the models show that patent protection, as a classic means of legal protection for creating temporary barriers to market entry, has no influence on the perceived value of environmental innovation. This could indicate that environmental process and product innovation is less easy to patent, and that environmental innovation is therefore predominantly incremental in nature. In its place, a first mover behaviour is seen as valuable in protecting environmental product innovation. Companies can exploit this advantage to bind customers to a product and benefit from learning effects. On the other hand, a complicated process which competitors find hard to imitate influences innovation to reduce environmental stress caused by production. However, further differences emerge between specific innovations in production processes. For example, maintaining long-term working relationships with qualified personnel is significant in the case of process innovation to reduce material consumption in production and achieving to be a first mover with energy-saving process innovation.

Innovation to reduce energy consumption as well as materials consumption is more important to companies in the New Federal States than in the Old Federal States. There is a significant positive correlation between location in the New Federal States and the importance of these innovation objectives. This might be related to the inefficient use of energy and materials in industrial production in the New Federal States at the start of the 1990s.

5   Conclusion

This paper examines the influence of environmental policy instruments on innovative behaviour by companies using quantitative and qualitative analysis in the context of interdependent structures of influence. Because of the complexity of the factors and the difficulty in isolating the effects of environmental policy instruments, the study is explorative in terms of methodology and as an empirical investigation.

The criticism about the lack of innovation effects of standards can only partly be supported. The analysis confirmed that environmental taxes and standards could have an impact on innovation both positive and negative as well. However, in the context of current experience the use of environmental policy instruments may have a smaller impact on environmental innovation than has been assumed in the environmental economics debate, as other factors exert an equally powerful influence on innovative behaviour and thereby on the effects of the instruments. Environmental policy cannot therefore in itself promote environmental innovation, but policy measures must be implemented to take account of the respective technical and economic framework conditions in the situation to be regulated and of changes over time. These are, for example, other governmental measures, the company size, the information flow between companies, universities, and customers or the risk behaviour of companies decision makes.

As a consequence neither levies nor regulations prove to be clearly superior instruments. Regulators must consider a broader framework that stresses policy coherence, the integration of various policies and inter-linkages within innovation systems. Evidently the ideal environmental policy is based on a policy-mix in which the comparative advantages of individual instruments can be utilised and their individual disadvantages can be mitigated in the careful structuring and co-ordination of the various instruments.

However, an innovation-oriented environmental policy should keep in mind that once a certain direction has been taken in development of environmentally benign technologies and products it is very difficult to change the direction. The alleviation of acute hazards must always be based on environmental policy instruments that work quickly, like standards. For the long-range challenge of sustainable development long-term perspectives should nevertheless be defined in a way that companies can incorporate them early on in their innovation planning. Therefore, these measures could support fundamental ecological structural change in a long-range context. The goal should be to integrate environmental protection considerations more fully into innovation processes in order to integrate environmental protection into the research and development phase.[4]

---

[4]   In this context is worth to mention that the European Commission JRC-IPTS has developed a tool (Integrated Appraisal Methdology – IA [Plus]) that enables the

Further studies need to develop this approach further with a combination of environmental economics and innovation economics approaches. In particular, use should be made of policy evaluation approaches, as it is not only the use of an instrument, but also the political process of formulating demands and implementing policies which is important for the effectiveness of an environmental policy instrument. The effects of various instruments could be studied in more detail in microeconomic examinations, whereby the effects of instruments on different technology alternatives should be estimated. Here it is important to develop meaningful indicators for the effects of instruments and possibilities for depicting the characteristics of different technologies. The specific qualities of individual phases in the innovation process should receive more attention, because of the market failure, there is not only a lack of motivation for their use, but also above all of an incentive to develop new environmental technologies. Finally, time-series analyses seem necessary for studying the development of technologies over time. The basic data which is lacking here could be provided by a regular environmental innovation survey of companies in manufacturing industry and the service sector.

References

Adler, U., E.-M. Bauer, N. Heller and J. Wackerbauer (1994), *Additiver und integrierter Umweltschutz und dessen Bedeutung im internationalen Wettbewerb*. Munich.

Ashford, N. (1993), Understanding Technological Responses of Industrial Firms to Environmental Problems: Implications for Government Policy, in: Fischer, K. and J. Schot (eds.), *Environmental Strategies for Industry*, Washington, 277-307.

Blazejczak, J. and D. Edler (1999), Innovationsfreundlicher Politikmuster – ein internationaler Vergleich am Beispiel der Papierindustrie, in: Klemmer, P. (ed.), *Innovationen und Umwelt*, Berlin.

Becher, G., J. Hemmelskamp, W. Weibert and H. Wolff (1993), *Ansatzpunkte fuer eine Verbesserung der Standortbedingungen fuer Forschung, Entwicklung und Technologie in der Bundesrepublik*. Basel.

Brännlund, R., R. Färe and S. Grosskopf (1995), Environmental Regulation and Profitability: An Application to Swedish Pulp and Paper Mills, *Environmental and Resource Economics* 6, 23-36.

Cottica, A. (1994), *The microeconomics of environmental innovation in the European packaging industry*. Paper at the 5th Conference of the European Association of Environmental and Resource Economists. Dublin.

---

assessment of initiatives and policies in terms of environmental innovation and competitiveness issues (cf. Leone et al. 1999).

Felder, J., D. Harhoff, G. Licht, E. Nerlinger and H. Stahl (1994), *Innovationsverhalten der deutschen Wirtschaft. Ergebnisse der Innovationserhebung 1993*, Dokumentation 94-01, Centre for European Economic Research (ZEW), Mannheim.

Georg, S., I. Ropke and U. Jorgensen (1992), Clean Technology – Innovation and Environmental Regulation, *Environmental and Resource Economics* 2, 533-550.

Green, K., A. McMeekin and A. Irwin (1994), Technological Trajectories and R&D for Environmental Innovation in UK Firms, *Futures* 26(10), 1047-1059.

Halstrick-Schwenk, M., L. Horbach, K. Löbbe and J. Walter (1994*), Die Umwelttechnische Industrie in der Bundesrepublik Deutschland*, Periodical No. 12, Rhine-Westphalia Institute for Economic Research (RWI), Essen

Harhoff, D., and G. Licht (1994), Das Mannheimer Innovationspanel, in: Hochmuth, U. and J. Wagner (eds.), *Firmenpanelstudien in Deutschland*, Tübingen, 255-284.

Harhoff, D., G. Licht, et al. (1996), *Innovationsaktivitäten kleiner und mittlerer Unternehmen. Ergebnisse des Mannheimer Innovationspanels*. Publication Series of the Centre for European Economic Research (ZEW), No. 8. Baden-Baden.

Hemmelskamp, J. (1997), Environmental Policy Instruments and their Effects on Innovation, *European Planning Studies* 2, 177-194.

Hemmelskamp, J. (1999), *Umweltpolitik und technischer Fortschritt*, Heidelberg.

Jänicke, M. (1997), *Umweltinnovationen aus der Sicht der Policy-Analyse: vom instrumentellen zum strategischen Ansatz der Umweltpolitik*. FFU-rep 97-3. Berlin.

Jaffe, A.B. and K. Palmer (1996), *Environmental Regulation and Innovation: A Panel Data Study*, Working Paper 5545, National Bureau of Economic Research, Cambridge (MA).

Kemp, R. (1996), *Environmental Policy and Technical Change: A Comparison of the Technological Impact of Policy Instruments*, Cheltenham.

Kemp, R. (1998), Environmental Regulation and Innovation Key Issues and Questions for Research, in Hemmelskamp, J. and F. Leone (eds.), *The Impact of EU-Regulation on Innovation of European Industry*, Technical Report EUR 18111 EN. Seville.

Kleinknecht, A. (1989), Firm Size and Innovation. Observations in Dutch Manufacturing Industries. *Small Business Economics* 1, 215-222.

Lanjouw, J.O. and A. Mody (1995), Innovation and the international diffusion of environmentally responsive technology, *Research Policy* 25, 549-571.

Leone, F., J. Hemmelskamp, C. Pompa, D. Bradford, A. Zanfei, H. Valve and B. Elling (1999), *Integrated Appraisal Methodology – Guidline for Environmental Integration of DG Entreprise Projects and Policies*, Project Report. European Commission, JRC-Institute for Prospective Technological Studies. Sevilla.

MIP (1993), *Mannheimer Innovationspanel. Daten der ersten Welle aus dem Jahre 1993*, Mannheim.

Milliman, S.R. and R. Prince (1989), Firm Incentives to promote Technological Change in Pollution Control, *Journal of Environmental Economics and Management* 17, 247-265.

Pavitt, K. (1984), Sectoral Patterns of technical change: Towards a taxonomy and a theory, *Research Policy* 13, 343-373.

Porter, M. E. and Claas van der Linde (1995), Towards a new Conception of the Environment-Competitiveness Relationship, *Journal of Economic Perspectives* 9, 97-118.

Rothwell, R. (1992), Industrial innovation and government environmental regulation: Some lessons from the past, *Technovation* 12 (7), 447-458.

Voss, G. (1995), Folgen ökologisch motivierter Energiesteuern, in Hohmeyer, O. (ed.), *Ökologische Steuerreform*, Wirtschaftsanalysen, No. 1, Baden-Baden.

Walz, R., E. Gruber, H. Hiessl and T. Reiß (1992*), Neue Technologien und Ressourcenschonung*, Abschlußbericht des FhG-ISI an das BMFT, Karlsruhe.

Wong, V., W. Turner, and P. Stoneman (1995), *Marketing Strategies and Market Prospects for Environmentally Friendly Consumer Products*. Coventry: Warwick Business School.

Annex 1:   Complexes of questions contained in the MIP

Complex	Information
company profile	associated companies, turnover, exports, workforce, investments, input in terms of material, medium-term expectations and development in recent years concerning demand, intensity of competition and employment
R&D activities	regular R&D, R&D department, people employed in R&D, R&D expenditure, purpose of R&D expenditure, regional origin of R&D co-operation partners, fields of technology
expenditure on innovation	amount and breakdown
indicators of successful innovation	product life cycle, turnover for innovative products at home and abroad, share of innovation in the strict sense of the word
transfer and acquisition of technological know-how	ways of transferring and acquiring technology, mechanisms for the protection of technological know-how
sources of information for innovations	company-, external and state-funded R&D facilities etc.
innovation objectives	e.g. new markets, market share, diversification, reduction in costs, environment, more efficient use of energy
innovation impediments	general economic factors, company-specific factors, factors such as legislation, administrative procedures
regional aspects	the name of the corresponding Land

Annex 2:   Overview of the exogenous variables in the models

Variable	*Values*
Market structure and growth	
Development of demand in the next three years	ordinal (-2 - +2)
Company size in employees (log)	Number of employees, logarithm
Company size in employees (log^2)	Number of employees, logarithm, squared
Technological opportunities	
R&D intensity	R&D expenditure / turnover
R&D cooperation	(0/1)
Technical possibilities exhausted	ordinal (1 – 5)
Lack of information on external knowledge	ordinal (1 – 5)
Appropriability conditions	
Patents	ordinal (1 - 5)
Copyright	ordinal (1 - 5)
Secrecy	ordinal (1 - 5)
First mover	ordinal (1 - 5)
Complexity of product	ordinal (1 - 5)
Long-term employee relations with qualified personnel	ordinal (1 - 5)
Sources of information	
Internal	ordinal (1 - 5)
Suppliers of primary products, materials, components	ordinal (1 - 5)
Suppliers of equipment	ordinal (1 - 5)
Customers	ordinal (1 - 5)
Immediate competitors	ordinal (1 - 5)
Consultants, market researchers	ordinal (1 - 5)
Industry-financed research institutes	ordinal (1 - 5)
Universities and technical colleges	ordinal (1 - 5)
Large research institutes	ordinal (1 - 5)
State influence, costs, risks	
Innovation risk too high	ordinal (1 - 5)
Lack of capital	ordinal (1 - 5)
Administrative procedures too long	ordinal (1 - 5)
Region	
Old /New-Federal States	(0/1)
Environmental policy	
Environmental standards	ordinal (1 - 9)
Environmental taxes	ordinal (1 - 9)

Determinants of Environmental Product and Process Innovation – Evidence from the Mannheim Innovation Panel and a Follow-Up Telephone Survey[1]

Thomas Cleff, Klaus Rennings

Centre for European Economic Research (ZEW)
P.O. Box 103443, D-68034 Mannheim
Germany

Keywords. integrated product policy, product innovation, process innovation, innovation survey.

Abstract. While Integrated Product Policy (IPP) receives increasing attention, it is still not well understood which factors and policy instruments influence the environmental performance of products. Thus this paper investigates the determinants of innovative behaviour in companies with regard to various areas of end-of-pipe and integrated environmental protection, including integrated product innovation. It pays particular attention to the influence of environmental policy instruments on product and process innovation. Its approach could be placed somewhere between environmental and industrial economics: in contrast to the up to now dominant approach of environmental economics, it integrates discoveries from the field of innovation research. The paper takes its data from the Mannheim Innovation Panel (1996), complemented by a subsequent telephone survey of environmental innovators. In a multivariate analysis, significant influence from strategic market goals on environment-related product innovation becomes evident. This differs from environment-related process innovation which is mainly determined by regulation. With respect to individual environmental policy instruments, a significant influence of so-called "soft" regulation (e.g. labels, eco-audits) on product integrated environmental innovation can be discerned.

---

[1]   Reprint from: European Environment, Special issue on Integrated Product Policy, edited by H. Karl and C. Orwat, Vol. 9., No. 5., pp. 191-201.

1   Introduction

The paper of the European Commission (1998) on Integrated Product Policy (IPP) has shown increasing interest of policy makers in managing the environmental performance of products. Following this new approach, it seems to be crucial to get a better understanding which factors determine and which policy instruments affect product related environmental innovations in firms. Against this background, this paper analyses the determinants of such activities in comparison to other environmental innovations (e.g. process integrated measures, end-of-pipe measures). The aim of this paper is mainly to identify peculiarities and characteristics of integrated product innovation, compared to other kinds of environmental innovation.

Thus it is structured as follows: Section 2 describes the theoretical approach. In section 3 the general database and underlying innovation survey is explained. More specific information on different kinds of environmental innovation (including product innovation) has been drawn from an additional telephone survey which is described in section 4. In section 5, a first attempt is made to specify a model explaining the determinants of different kinds of eco-innovation. Finally, section 6 draws some conclusions concerning determinants and especially the role of environmental policy.

2   Theoretical Approaches

2.1   Environmental Economics

In the environmental economics literature, the basic research question for analysing cleaner products and processes has been the identification of optimal policy instruments to stimulate environmental innovation. Market-based instruments like taxes and tradable permits have been identified as the environmental policy instruments with the highest dynamic efficiency (innovation efficiency). Their advantage is that they give permanent incentives for further, cost-efficient emissions reductions. By contrast, regulatory regimes driven by technical standards (either in a command-and-control system or in a regime of voluntary agreements in which standards are negotiated between government and industry) are not cost-efficient and the incentives for progress in emission reduction vanish after the standards are met.

Thus the superiority of market-based instruments has been the basic lesson from environmental economics concerning innovation. However, several exceptions and modifications to the rule have been made recently (see for details Rennings 1998 and Kemp 1997). Especially in models where technological innovation is endogeneous, no clear-cut case for preferring any one policy instrument on the grounds of dynamic efficiency can be detected (Fischer, Parry and Pizer 1998).

Furthermore, approaches based on the theory of environmental economics follow a very simple, mechanistic stimulus-response-approach of environmental regulation. Other relevant factors influencing innovation, like market demand and technology push effects, are ignored. But what is most important concerning IPP is the missing distinction between product and process innovation which is not addressed at all in the environmental economics literature. Thus it is necessary for the scope of this paper to consider elements of innovation economics as they are introduced in the next section.

2.2   Innovation Economics

Environmental friendly innovations are confronted with the problem of two kinds of external effects. Firstly, the innovation process induces spillover effects to other firms. Secondly, the new product or process itself produces less environmental externalities. This double externality problem (see for details Rennings 1998) results in a sub-optimal investment and thus induces a peculiarity of environmental innovations: the importance of the regulatory framework as a key determinant for eco-innovative behavior in firms, households and other institutions.

The main discussion in innovation economics has been whether technological innovation has been driven by technological development (technology push) or by demand factors (market pull). Empirical evidence has shown that both are relevant (Pavitt 1984). With regard to environmental innovation, new eco-efficient technologies can be subsumed under technology push factors, while preferences for environmentally friendly products or image can be subsumed under market pull factors. Due to the externality problem of eco-innovations, the traditional discussion of innovation economists has to be extended to the influence of the regulatory framework (regulatory push/pull). Figure 1 illustrates the determinants of eco-innovation. As empirical evidence shows (Green et al. 1994; Porter and van der Linde 1995; Kemp 1997), the regulatory framework and especially environmental policy have a strong impact on eco-innovation. Eco-innovations are, in contrast to such technologies as microelectronics and telecommunications, normally not self-enforcing. Since factors of technology push and market pull alone do not seem to be strong enough, eco-innovations need specific regulatory support.

With regard to IPP, it is very important to mention that a distinction is made between product and process innovations in the literature on innovation economics. However, in innovation economics the regulatory push/pull effect is ignored. Thus, we follow a hybrid approach combining elements of the theoretical streams from environmental and innovation economics.

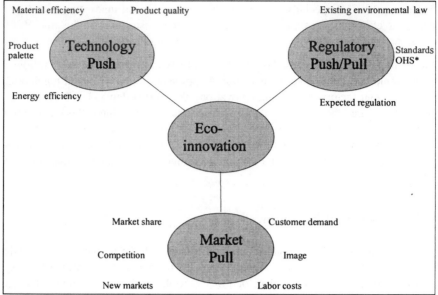

Material efficiency   Product quality   Existing environmental law

*OSH = Occupational Health and Safety
Source: ZEW

Figure 1:   Determinants of Environmental Innovation

3   Database and Design of the Telephone Survey

Data is drawn from two surveys, whose aim was to identify peculiarities and determinants of environmental innovations. The surveys were

- The Mannheim Innovation Panel (MIP) 1996, into which additional questions
  on environmental innovation were integrated, in order to identify environmental innovators and the determinants of environmental innovation, and

- An additional telephone survey, conducted in 1997, following up on the 1996
  wave of the Panel. The telephone survey was intended to glean more specific
  information on the goals of environmental innovation (e.g. product vs. process
  innovation, integrated vs. end-of-pipe technologies) and the influence of environmental policy instruments.

3.1   The Mannheim Innovation Panel

The MIP company survey has been conducted annually by the Centre for European Economic Research (ZEW) and the Institute for Applied Social Science (infas) for the German Ministry for Education, Science, Research and Technology (BMBF) since 1993. Companies in manufacturing and those offering services to business across Germany are surveyed. In the MIP, alongside some general questions on the structure and size of the companies, the questioning focuses on their innovation activities (see for details Licht/Stahl 1997). Innovation is understood according to the European standard developed in the Oslo Manual (1992). The survey concentrates on the goals of innovation, obstacles and measuring its success. In addition, information is gathered on use of resources, export activities, technological cooperation and transfer, as well as trends in employment levels. The written questionnaire was answered by a total of 2,264 companies in 1996.

3.2   Identifying Environmental Innovators

A company is considered innovative if, in the three years up to the survey, i.e. between 1993 and 1995, it has been innovative with respect to its products or processes. This applies to 56.6 per cent of the companies questioned.

To identify environmentally innovative companies, the questionnaire named potential areas for environmental protection (product integration, process integration, process external recycling, process internal recycling, end-of-pipe measures) under which the companies could classify their innovative activities. Companies are described as environmentally innovative if they mark at least one of these potential areas as important or very important.

In what follows, companies are considered environmentally innovative if at least one of the above criteria is met, which nonetheless produces 72 per cent (929 companies in total) environmental innovators among the innovators as a whole. This is highly plausible, as virtually every large company today makes use of or innovates in environmental technology or organisational environmental protection in one form or another.

3.3   Relevant Topics of the Telephone Questionnaire

The 929 companies classed as environmentally innovative according to the characteristic assessment were contacted by telephone and asked additional questions about innovation in environmental technologies. The definition of the specific characteristics of environmental innovation in the innovation panel were slightly modified (see Table 1) for compatibility with the federal government's newly completed environmental research programme (BMBF 1997). The 419 actual interviews correspond to a response rate of 45 per cent.

The relevant topics for this paper which have been covered by the questionnaire of the telephone survey are:

- Goals of environmental innovations (environmental policy, market strategy, cost reduction, public relation) and

- Importance of policy instruments for environmental innovations (command and control, duties, informational measures, voluntary measures, support programmes).

Table 1:   Proportion of Companies Practising Additive and Integrated Environmental Protection

	Additive/Integrated			Additive			Integrated		
	All	West	East	All	West	East	All	West	East
Additive environmental protection	90.9	92.8	84.0	---	---	---	87.6	89.3	87.6
Waste recovery	76.3	78.7	67.9	84.0	84.8	80.9	76.1	78.2	67.6
Waste disposal	27.2	30.6	14.8	29.9	33.0	17.6	27.3	30.2	16.2
Soil decontamination	18.5	17.2	23.5	20.4	18.5	27.9	19.1	18.7	20.6
Emissions control	57.3	60.1	46.9	63.0	64.8	55.9	59.7	62.6	48.5
Integrated environmental protection	88.7	90.0	84.0	89.7	92.0	80.9	---	---	---
Eco-friendly products	52.2	55.0	42.0	53.0	55.9	41.2	58.8	61.1	50.0
Process integration	77.4	79.0	71.6	77.2	79.6	67.6	87.3	87.8	85.3

Source: ZEW

4   Peculiarities of Specific Kinds of Environmental Innovation

4.1   Additive and Integrated Innovation in Environmental Protection

As can be seen from Table 1, a total of 90.9 per cent of companies claimed to be engaged in innovation with additive environmental protection. This is given by the high proportion of companies taking action to recover waste (76.3 per cent) and using end-of-pipe emissions control (57.3 per cent). Only a small proportion of companies were innovating with waste disposal (27.2 per cent) or land decontamination (27.2 per cent). Integrated environmental protection measures are being conducted by an equally large share of the sample (88.7 per cent). This implies a similarly strong association between additive and integrated environmental measures, as 87.6 per cent of companies using additive measures also apply integrated measures, and 89.7 per cent of those applying integrated measures also use additive measures. Of the integrated measures, process integration dominates with 87.3 per cent, ahead of environmentally sound products (58.8 per cent). Longevity and repairability of products as well as substitution of harmful substances were explicitly mentioned as examples of product integrated innovations by the interviewers.

If the results for the old and new Länder are considered separately, a consistently lower proportion of individual environmental protection measures in the new Länder is apparent. While 92.8 per cent of companies in the old Länder engage in additive, and 90 per cent in integrated environmental protection, the figures for the new Länder are 84 per cent. Only in the case of land decontamination, with 23.5 per cent do companies in the new Länder overtake those in the rest of Germany. As a multivariate analysis of the data has shown, the lower level of environmental innovation in the East German regions can be explained by their lower labour productivity.

4.2   Goals of Environmental Innovation

The importance of specific goals for environmental innovation exhibits a slight spread. Nonetheless, single goals can certainly emerge as important for single companies. As can be seen in Table 2, "complying with existing legislation" is at the top of the list of goals for environmental innovation. In both old (80.4 per cent) and new (82.7 per cent) Länder, most companies ascribe great or very great importance to this goal. In contrast, environmental innovations which are to be applied solely "in expectation of future (more stringent) legislation" are only moderately important. Only the goals of "entering new markets" and "maintaining/increasing market share" are associated less with environmental innovation. Environmental awareness, both internal – e.g. among staff – and external, in the associated improvements in public image, are seen by companies as particularly important strategic goals in relation to environmental innovation. Further innovation goals are reductions in energy, disposal and material costs. Well over 60 per cent of companies consider these goals important. Only to a limited extent can such a strong association with innovation in environmental protection be found for reductions in labour costs, with just one half of companies recognising a significant connection in this respect.

Thus environmental innovation gains particular importance when legislation forces companies to carry out environmental protection measures or when companies can gain an improved image or cost savings with environmentally friendly products (e.g. savings of energy, material or waste). Company action to protect the environment is therefore only a partial goal in the struggle for competitive advantage.

Close examination of the statistical results suggests that the importance levels for individual innovation goals correlate with one another. The results of the factor analysis (major component analysis) confirm this proposition. The package of goal variables can be reduced to a simple structure of four factors that are cost reductions, maintaining/increasing market share, environmental awareness and complying with legislation (see Table 3).

Table 2: The Importance of Environmental Innovation Goals

	Importance in the old Länder			Importance in the new Länder		
	great/ very great	medium	low/none at all	great/ very great	medium	low/none at all
Complying with legislation	80.4	11.0	8.6	82.7	9.9	7.4
Expected future legislation	49.1	26.5	24.4	49.4	24.7	25.9
Maintaining/increasing market share	53.6	14.5	31.8	45.7	17.3	37.0
Entering new markets	44.6	16.0	39.4	45.7	16.0	38.3
Reducing energy costs	66.3	19.6	14.1	66.7	9.9	23.5
Reducing material costs	63.2	16.2	20.6	66.7	14.8	18.5
Reducing disposal costs	73.5	14.1	12.4	60.5	22.2	17.3
Reducing labour costs	52.6	18.0	29.4	53.1	18.5	28.4
Improving public image	62.5	21.3	16.2	72.8	11.1	16.0
Company environmental awareness	70.8	21.0	8.2	75.3	16.0	8.6

Source: ZEW

4.3   Importance of Environmental Policy Instruments for the Implementation of Environmental Innovation

The great importance ascribed to the goal of "complying with legal regulations" already implies strong influence on environmentally innovative behaviour from the regulatory framework. The following looks at this in more detail, differentiating between various environmental policy instruments. As is shown in Table 4 , the instruments range from sanctions such as acts of parliament at one end to direct subsidies for environmental protection in research funding programmes at the other end. Since the individual instruments are more or less important to the companies, their specific importance for environmentally innovative behaviour can be determined.

Table 3:   Factor Structure (VARIMAX) of Innovation Goals

	Factors (importance)			
	Cost reduction	Market share	Environmental awareness	Complying with Legislation
Complying with legislation	.14	.06	.06	.81
Expected future legislation	.04	.02	.17	.78
Maintaining/increasing market share	.13	.89	.07	.08
Entering new markets	.17	.88	.14	.02
Reducing energy costs	.68	.19	.19	.03
Reducing material costs	.77	.26	.08	.03
Reducing disposal costs	.78	.08	.09	.08
Reducing labour costs	.57	.49	.06	-.01
Improving public image	.14	.41	.70	.08
Company environmental awareness	.15	.06	.86	.11

Source: ZEW

Table 4 :   The Importance of Environmental Policy Instruments

	Importance in the old Länder			Importance in the new Länder		
	great/ very great	medium	low/ none at all	great/ very great	medium	low/ none at all
State regulations and prohibitions	71.1	17.9	11.0	63.0	21.0	16.0
Environmental Impact Assessment	42.3	25.1	32.6	39.5	25.9	34.6
Sewage, waste, hazardous waste charges	51.2	22.7	26.1	45.7	21.0	33.3
Energy charges, taxes	47.1	24.1	28.9	57.5	11.3	31.3
Liability for environmental risk	57.4	17.2	25.4	46.9	17.3	35.8
Eco-audits	43.6	21.0	35.4	35.8	27.2	37.0
Green Dot	19.9	21.3	58.8	34.6	13.6	51.9
Eco-labels (e.g. Blue Angel, European Flower)	12.1	14.5	73.4	16.0	12.3	71.6
Sectoral voluntary commitments	45.2	23.1	31.7	51.3	15.4	33.3
Subsidy/state assistance programmes	24.4	15.8	59.8	32.1	17.3	50.6

Source: ZEW

Factor analysis groups the instruments into the five dimensions shown in Table 5. Interestingly, the structure of environmental policy instruments which emerges runs according to their "degree of hardness", as defined by Zimmermann (1996: 43 ff.):

- "Hard" instruments: these cover civil law and charges, listed separately in the factor analysis.

- "Medium hard" instruments, i.e. subsidies, user benefits and the environmental impact assessment.

- "Soft" instruments: covers voluntary and informational instruments. The factor analysis differentiates between eco-labels and other "soft" instruments (audits, voluntary commitments, liability law).

The factor values have a simple structure, although the substantive content of some of the items could be assigned to various factors. For example, "liability for environmental risk" would be assigned clearly to the "soft" environmental policy instruments. However, a high factor value of 0.49 indicates that liability regulations are interpreted by companies as a "charge" or "cost". This makes sense, as liability law can be understood as an instrument for "soft" behavioural modification, but certainly also as an internalising economic instrument.

Table 5:   Factor Structure (VARIMAX) of Environmental Policy Instruments

	Factors (importance)				
	"soft" instruments	eco-labels	"medium" instruments	charges	civil law
Liability for environmental risk	0.57	-0.06	0.12	0.49	0.12
Eco-audits	0.87	0.07	0.10	0.02	0.02
Sectoral voluntary commitments	0.57	0.22	0.19	0.22	0.04
Green Dot	-0.06	0.89	0.07	0.07	0.03
Other eco-labels	0.33	0.77	0.08	-0.04	-0.02
Environmental Impact Assessment	0.34	0.06	0.63	0.08	0.41
Subsidy/state assistance programmes	0.11	0.12	0.86	0.14	-0.20
Sewage, waste, hazardous waste charges	0.05	0.11	0.03	0.85	0.15
Energy charges, taxes	0.18	-0.05	0.14	0.80	-0.07
State regulations and prohibitions	0.04	0.01	-0.05	0.08	0.93

Source: ZEW

5   Towards an Econometric Model

A decision for or against a specific environmental technology is related to variables whose influence can be determined with the help of econometric models. The models used in the following are an attempt to identify the essential factors influencing certain forms of environmental innovation

Environmental innovation, divided into the six areas given in the telephone survey (waste recovery and disposal, land decontamination, end-of-pipe emissions control, integrated environmental protection for products and processes), is given a multivariate examination as a dependent vector in the following, looking for significant influences from other variables.

The variables from the telephone interviews which are considered are those which, on the basis of the descriptive analysis in the previous section, can be assumed to contribute towards explaining company's decisions on environmental protection. These include structural influences such as the company's size, the geographical origin of the company (old or new Länder), as well as the question of whether the company manufactures consumer goods or belongs to the basic materials or investment goods sectors. The international dimension of a company is included in terms of the share of exports in total turnover. Alongside these variables, strategic influences are investigated. These include the (factor values of the) strategic goals associated with innovation in the company and the (factor values of the) importance of the environmental policy instruments.

The properties of the multinomial Logit models, measured according to D. Mc Fadden, are within an acceptable area for all estimates. The approximations are listed in Table 6. Variables with significant coefficients are highlighted in grey. If the estimate's coefficient is positive, the factor has a positive influence on the likelihood that certain environmental innovation will be implemented.

5.1   Influence of Environmental Innovation Goals

As Table 6 shows, innovation in the various areas of additive environmental protection cannot be significantly explained by differing environmental innovation goals. This leads one to suppose that strategic considerations have a subordinate importance in deciding whether a company innovates in one of these areas.

On the other hand, a significant influence from environmental innovation goals on integrated environmental protection can be found in the multivariate analysis. Innovators in integrated environmental protection at the product level pursue the goal of maintaining or increasing their market shares more frequently. In contrast, it is compliance with existing legislation and anticipation of future laws which has especial importance for innovators in process integrated environmental measures.

Table 6: Determinants for Specific Areas of Environmental Protection: (Logit Models)

	Waste recovery		Waste disposal		Soil decontamination		Product integration		Emissions control		Process integration	
	Coef.	Sig.	Coef.	Sig.	Coef.	Sig.	Coef.	Sig.	Coef.	Sig.	Coef.	Sig.
Goal: cost reduction	0.213	0.1370	0.156	0.3000	-0.090	0.6040	-0.159	0.2140	-0.128	0.3210	0.221	0.1340
Goal: market share	0.133	0.3400	0.187	0.1930	0.221	0.1790	0.258	0.0340	-0.094	0.4400	-0.026	0.8590
Goal: environmental protection	-0.148	0.2920	-0.087	0.5640	-0.237	0.1590	0.049	0.6900	0.007	0.9520	-0.028	0.8440
Goal: complying with legislation	0.094	0.4850	0.074	0.6000	-0.060	0.7170	-0.031	0.7980	0.107	0.3790	0.280	0.0410
Instrument: charges	0.191	0.1780	-0.042	0.7750	0.078	0.6510	0.189	0.1290	0.399	0.0020	0.228	0.1210
Instrument: "soft"	-0.088	0.5530	0.322	0.0380	0.675	0.0000	0.264	0.0430	0.354	0.0070	0.375	0.0160
Instrument: eco-labels	0.307	0.0280	0.351	0.0070	0.145	0.3370	0.212	0.0660	0.134	0.2510	0.148	0.3010
Instrument: "medium"	0.073	0.6170	0.432	0.0030	-0.045	0.7840	0.129	0.3040	0.251	0.0510	-0.025	0.8710
Instrument: civil law	-0.057	0.6800	-0.283	0.0380	-0.032	0.8400	0.196	0.1020	0.008	0.9470	0.020	0.8900
Company size	0.739	0.2870	-0.598	0.1760	2.004	0.0010	0.927	0.0920	-0.243	0.4190	0.751	0.3580
New Länder	-0.671	0.0260	-1.204	0.0010	0.916	0.0080	-0.365	0.1880	-0.726	0.0090	-0.319	0.3330
Consumer goods	0.334	0.2370	0.175	0.5190	-0.718	0.0380	0.276	0.2430	-0.195	0.4160	0.261	0.3770
Constants	1.203	0.0000	-0.904	0.0000	-1.867	0.0000	0.009	0.9570	0.570	0.0000	1.347	0.0000
Likelihood Ratio Test (Sig.)	-184.8	0.014	-184.3	0.000	-145.9	0.000	-231.1	0.001	-227.5	0.001	-170.2	0.001
Observations	358		358		358		358		358		358	
Mc Fadden Pseudo R²	0.064		0.115		0.154		0.067		0.069		0.087	

Source: ZEW

This can be explained by the fact that integrated environmental protection at the level of the process generally confers little or no additional benefit on the customer and therefore receives comparatively little reward from the market, while integrated environmental protection at the product level (e.g. organically grown baby food, solvent-free paints) brings added benefit to the customer, explaining the strategic interest in this for innovation.

What is surprising in the comparison between determinants of additive and integrated process innovation is the fact that the goal of complying with legislation exerts a significant influence only on process innovations in integrated, and not in additive environmental protection. One reason could lie in the structure of the models, as the influence of compliance with legislation could possibly be overlaid by that of the individual instruments. As a control, the environmental policy instruments as explanatory variable were removed from the model (not shown in Table 6). It emerges that in this case, compliance also shows a significant influence on emissions control. This influence can apparently be better explained by the combined influence of various environmental policy instruments for end-of-pipe than for integrated environmental protection, as the latter has up to now been subject to less regulation and is more strongly determined by anticipation of future developments.

5.2   Influence of Environmental Policy Instruments

Environmental policy instruments exert a significant influence on innovative activities in the various fields of integrated and additive environmental protection, with the influence of different instruments manifesting itself differently in the various forms of environmental innovation.

As the significance of eco-labels (including here in particular the "Green Dot") rises, so does the likelihood of implementing waste recovery measures. "Soft" environmental policy instruments (eco-audits, voluntary commitments, liability law) increase innovative integrated measures at the process level. They also have an influence on land decontamination – which can be traced back in particular to the role played by liability law in this area – and integrated environmental protection at the product level, which fits into the overall picture of a these companies' following a market-oriented strategy.

The profile of environmental policy influence on end-of-pipe emissions control is less clear: here, both "soft" instruments such as charges and "medium" instruments (EIAs, subsidies) play a significant role. Environmental innovation in waste disposal is also influenced by a package of instruments: as the importance of "soft" instruments like eco-labels and "medium" instruments rises, so does the likelihood that innovations will be implemented in this area; on the other hand, civil law is relatively unimportant.

Overall, it emerges that the environmentally innovative behaviour of companies can be explained in five areas by "soft" ·instruments, but there is a (negative) relationship with "hard" civil regulations in only one area. The effects of civil law are apparently long-term and diffuse (Kuntze 1997). From the perspective of innovators it belongs amongst the most important components of the general framework conditions for innovation, but can only be ascribed to concrete innovation with comparative difficulty and after considerable delays. In other words, civil regulations are seen as important, but they are not decisive. Moreover, an explanation for the negative relationship between innovation and command-and-control instruments can be

- that innovative, proactive firms go in their environmental performance already ahead of the existing environmental law,

- while passive, non-innovative firms are more affected by the actual state regulation.

The ability of charges, which can be considered among the "hard" environmental policy instruments, to explain innovation is also relatively slight. Eco-labels are rated significant above all in respect of waste (what can be explained by the importance of the "Green Dot" in this area) and in integrated environmental protection at the level of products (what can be explained by the importance of eco-labels like the "Blue Angel").

In interpreting these results, it should not be forgotten that environmental policy instruments have been applied to varying extents up to now, as is reflected in the answers given by the companies. Thus the trend away from civil regulation towards a "soft" regulatory framework, which can be observed during the period under study, clearly also has an effect on the innovative behaviour of the companies. Furthermore, economic incentives/disincentives such as charges have still been little used up to now. Because the companies had no experience with emissions trading regimes, the telephone survey had to do without estimating the role of tradable emissions rights. Although, especially in the wake of the Kyoto conference, it is not unrealistic to suppose that tradable permits will be used increasingly in future global environmental and climate policy and that these will provide a stimulus to innovation. In this respect it is important to interpret the survey results according to the actual experience of the companies questioned.

5.3   Other Factors

The size of the companies correlates significantly with innovation in respect of land decontamination and product integration. Eastern German companies innovate significantly more often in land conservation, less often in end-of-pipe environmental protection. Significant influence from the sector of the company can only be shown in the case of land clean-up, which is conducted above all by companies in the basic materials and investment goods industries. It can be assumed that there are further sectoral effects, but that these cannot be demonstrated by this simple model.

6   Concluding Remarks and Policy Recommendations

Theoretical considerations and the preceding descriptive analyses have demonstrated the complexity of the framework conditions affecting environmental innovation and the internal company factors which can only be approximated with the current state of knowledge. It can be concluded that the simplified, mechanistic stimulus-response-approach of environmental policy followed in the environmental economics literature is not appropriate for explaining the determinants of environmental innovations. On the other hand, innovation economics has ignored the innovation effects of environmental regulation up to now. Thus we used a hybrid approach based on innovation theory but introducing what we call the "regulatory push/pull effect" of environmental regulation.

The telephone survey conducted within our study permits a differentiated examination of various areas of end-of-pipe and integrated environmental protection, as well as an explicit look at the role of individual environmental policy instruments. Thus six preliminary statements can be made from the analysis of environmentally innovative behaviour presented here which are relevant for the IPP approach of the European Commission:

1. Although the percentage of other areas (process integration, end-of-pipe measures) is higher, a broad basis of existing activities being relevant for IPP has been identified. More than 50 percent of innovators in German industry are innovators in product integrated measures.

2. The study has shown a strong influence of regulation on eco-innovation. Thus, also product integrated measures in firms can be substantially improved by adequate additional IPP measures.

3. Concerning the distinction between environmental product and process innovation, it has been shown that strategic market goals are a significant influence especially on innovation in integrated environmental protection at the product level, while environmental process innovation is determined more by environmental regulations. Market benefits of environmental product innovation are recognised by firms and may increase the acceptance of IPP compared to a regulation of processes.

4. The results indicate that especially firms being innovative in environmental-friendly products see improved environmental performance frequently as a component in a comprehensive company efficiency strategy. Porter's thesis

that environmental efficiency is an increasingly important competitive factor in global markets (Porter and van der Linde 1995: 133) may be especially true for product innovations. Thus IPP has the chance to create win-win-options. Such options are harder to realise by using process regulation. Firms earn money by selling products, not processes.

5. As for the influence of individual policy instruments on environmental product innovation, influence from "soft" regulatory instruments (environmental liability, eco-audits, voluntary commitments) and from eco-labels can be found. These instruments are important tools for environmental product innovators. They enable firms to use their environmental performance in their marketing strategies or in negotiations with the state. Eco-labels like the "Blue Angel", which certify a certain environmental product quality, stimulate product innovations, while the "Green Dot" has innovative effects for recycling activities.

6. Environmentally innovative firms seem to be less dependent on "hard" state regulation than other, more passive firms. Thus "soft" and voluntary environmental policy measures may be sufficient for pioneers. However, "hard" measures (command and control instruments, duties) seem to be still necessary for a diffusion of IPP to non-innovative firms.

Acknowledgements:

We would especially like to thank Carsten Orwat, Helmut Karl, Ernst Mohr, Doris Blechinger, Jens Hemmelskamp, Georg Licht, Friedhelm Pfeiffer and anonymous referees for their help, useful comments and suggestions.

References

Bundesministerium für Bildung, Wissenschaft, Forschung und Technologie (BMBF) (1997), *Forschung fuer die Umwelt – Programm der Bundesregierung*, Bonn.

European Commission, DG XI (1998), *Integrated Product Policy*, Brussels.

Green, K., A. McMeekin, A. Irwin (1994), Technological trajectories and R&D for Environmental Innovation in UK Firms, *Futures* 26, 1047-1059.

Fischer, C., I.W. Parry and W.A. Pizer (1998), *Instrument Choice for Environmental Protection when Technological Innovation is Endogeneous*, Resources for the Future, Discussion Paper, Washington.

Kemp, R.(1997), *Environmental Policy and Technical Change*, Cheltenham.

Kuntze, U. (1997), *Analyse der innovativen Wirkungen des Ordnungsrechts*, Teilprojekt 7 des Forschungsverbundes Innovative Wirkungen umweltpolitischer Instrumente (FIU), Zusammenfassung der Ergebnisse. Fraunhofer-Institut für Systemtechnik und Innovationsforschung (ISI), Karlsruhe.

Licht, G. and H. Stahl (1997), *Ergebnisse der Innovationserhebung 1996*, ZEW-Dokumentation Nr. 97-07, Mannheim.

Pavitt, K. (1984), Sectoral Patterns of Technical Change: Towards an Taxonomy and a Theory, *Research Policy* 13, 343-373.

Porter, M.E. and C. van der Linde (1995), Green and Competitive: Ending the Stalemate, *Harvard Business Review* September - October, 120-134.

Rennings, K. (1998), *Towards a Theory and Policy of Eco Innovation – Neoclassical and (Co-)Evolutionary Perspectives*, Centre for European Economic Research, Discussion Paper 98-24, Mannheim.

Zimmermann, H. (1996), *Nicht-marktbezogene Umweltinnovationen und ihr Bezug zu umweltpolitischen Instrumenten*, Bericht zum Teilprojekt des Forschungsverbundes "Innovative Wirkungen umweltpolitischer Instrumente". Universität Marburg, Abteilung für Finanzwissenschaft.